CW00555505

HEALTH, MEDICINE AND MIGRATION

HEALTH, MEDICINE AND MIGRATION

The Formation of Indentured Labour

*c.*1834–1920

MADHWI

PRIMUS
BOOKS

PRIMUS BOOKS
An imprint of Ratna Sagar P. Ltd.
Virat Bhavan
Mukherjee Nagar Commercial Complex
Delhi 110 009

Offices at CHENNAI LUCKNOW AGRA AHMEDABAD BENGALURU
COIMBATORE DEHRADUN GUWAHATI HYDERABAD JAIPUR
JALANDHAR KANPUR KOCHI KOLKATA MADURAI MUMBAI
PATNA RANCHI VARANASI

© *Madhwi, 2020*

First published 2020

ISBN: 978-93-90232-68-0 (Hardback)
ISBN: 978-93-90232-69-7 (POD)

Published by Primus Books

Lasertypeset by Sai Graphic Design
Arakashan Road, Paharganj, New Delhi 110 055

Contents

Abbreviations

BL	British Library
CDA	Contagious Diseases Act
LSHTM	London School of Hygiene and Tropical Medicine
NAI	National Archives of India
NMML	Nehru Memorial Museum & Library
TNA	The National Archives of UK
VD	Venereal Disease
WTL	Wellcome Trust Library

Maps, Illustrations, and Tables

Maps

Illustrations

Tables

Acknowledgements

This book envisions to revisiting the lives of the indentured in two British colonies in the Indian Ocean—Mauritius and Natal, through the lens of medicine, sanitation, and hygiene. I have tried to reconstruct what the medical regime meant for the indentured and non-indentured communities in overseas colonies. I have also tried to unearth the relationship between exploitation and disease, and include them in the colonial discourse on migration. The pre-assumptions on miasma, tropics, and Asiatic diseases helped in the development of the colonial medical regime in the overseas plantations.

In the course of writing this book, I have obtained enormous help and support from many people and institutions. I am grateful to them for their valuable and selfless support, without which it would not have been possible for me to complete this work. Dr Prabhu Mohapatra supervised my research from which this book has emerged. His profound knowledge, deep interest, and innovative approach towards the subject continually inspired and guided me. The idea of publishing this work was primarily nurtured by late Dr. Biswamoy Pati, whose untimely demise left it at its nascent stage. I cannot thank him enough for his encouragement. Special thanks is also due to Prof. Amar Farooqui for all the help, support, and suggestions that he has provided. The inspiring teachings of Dilip Menon, Shahid Amin, and Chitra Joshi has been a source of motivation for inculcating my interest in colonial study. Shalini Shah not only encouraged me to publish my work but almost convinced me about the importance of its publication; I thank her for the kind help which she offered.

Besides his encouragement, a few sessions of discussion with Raj Shekhar Basu has also introduced me to some different sources of migration. Deepak Kumar has also been a proven source of motivation for this book. I appreciate the interest shown by Jane Buckingham in my work. I also acknowledge the support and help I received from a number of people—Riyad Koya, for sending me a number of useful articles; Spencer Leonard, for his priceless records from his personal collection that he has lent me; and Sarath Pillai, for providing useful material—to name a few.

I owe my thanks to the staff of various libraries and institutions, in particular the National Archives of India at New Delhi, the Central Secretariat Library, the Nehru Memorial Museum & Library, the Centre for Studies of Developing Societies, the National Library of Kolkata, the West Bengal State Archives, the Asiatic Society Library at Kolkata, the A.N. Sinha Institute of Social Studies Library at Patna, The National Archives of UK at Kew, The British Library at London, the Wellcome Trust Library, the Senate House Library, University of London, and the libraries of various other universities.

Special thanks is due to Mrs Sheila Ludden for providing me the homely environment of her residence during my stay at London. I am indebted to Dr Anjali Bhardwaj for opening up her home to me during my stay in Cambridge. I also wish to acknowledge the help and support I received from Ms Victoria, the librarian at the Centre of South Asian Studies, Cambridge University, and the archivist of the London School of Hygiene and Tropical Medicine.

I am grateful to the ICSSR-CSDS agency for providing a doctoral fellowship for my research. I acknowledge the financial support I received from the Society for the Social History of Medicine Travel Grant, the Charles Wallace India Trust, and the Indian Council of Historical Research. I am also thankful to a number of institutions which have provided me with platforms for discussing my work, namely, the Indian National Science Academy, Delhi (which organized the National Seminar on Historiographic Science in India); the University of Sheffield, England; the Tata Institute of Social Science, Patna; the University of Delhi; the Friedrich-Meinecke-Institut, Freie Universitat, Berlin (which arranged the Global History Conference); the Mediterranean Institute, University of Malta (which hosted the conference of the International Network for the History of Hospitals); and the Humboldt University, Berlin.

On a more personal note, I am indebted to my friends Madhuri, Bornali, Deepak, Shilpi, Suparna, Neelu, and Manish. I am also thankful to Sudhansu for his constant help and unwavering support while reworking on this book. Besides my friends, I am grateful to my parents and family members for their support.

Health, Medicine and Indentured Labour in Plantation Economy
An Introduction

'If the wages earned by a healthy labourer be the measures of the value of that labourer's health and life to the state, it is evident that [the state] is benefited in the same measures whenever a labourer, through the instrumentality of its hospitals, is saved from death or chronic disease.'

—*Royal Gazette*, 1 September 1840

Indenture and Health Measures

The professional and curative aspirations of plantation economy show a close identification of a colony's (here, Mauritius and Natal's) economic well-being with the bodily strength of the labourers. Treating immigrant labourers in the plantations was neither an end in itself, nor a gesture of medical generosity, or charity. It was emerging only as part of an elaborate social system, whereby the sick were forced to return to work. The commercial health of the colony and the health of the labourers were, therefore, bound by institutional practices of the colonial or public hospitals. The history of medicine in India can be placed in the wider historiography of colonial expansion. There are various versions of the arguments among scholars about the cause of expansion of the British Empire and its rule over one-third of the world. One group of historians has focused on cultural and ideological control, while another group has focused on technological control, along with other political and economic factors of new imperialism. Historians have also emphasized the pivotal role of technology in making expeditions and colonial expansion possible for the British. It has been argued that both the 'tools of empire'—such as the steamers, quinine, and the quick-firing guns—and the confident ideology of progress and political rationality, assisted and sustained the Europeans abroad and provided the foundation for British rule in the colonies.[1] The regime of medicine comprised of both the technical as well as the cultural and ideological control of the Raj.

Apart from the practical benefits, it provided for the ruling class (Europeans, and particularly the British) comforting bloodlettings, purgatives, and an array of therapeutics, as well as guidance on food habits, inhabitation, and dressing. Thus, medicine was a powerful representation of a wider social and political force.[2] In the nineteenth century, Western medicine emerged as a superior mode of treatment to its practitioners as compared to 'native' practices. David Arnold characterized the nature of 'Western medicine' in the colonies as— 'Western medicine…was never content to be confined to the white ghetto: it was too restlessly ambitious merely to minister to sick civil servants and ailing generals, even had it been deemed practical to draw a neat dividing line between European and "native" health.'[3]

The belief in the superiority of Western medicines therefore provided another angle to investigate the rhetorical weave of superiority and progress which upheld the British Raj. Medicine was considered to be more than just a liberator from diseases; it was also viewed as a means by which Indians could be liberated from ignorance and superstitions. Diseases affecting the Indian society were also seen as a moral and cultural problem. As David Aickin mentions, '…it not only had the power to explain, define and catalogue, but could thereby help broker a relationship with non-Europeans, bolster political institutions, give force to administrative decisions and, last but not the least, provide a measure of self-justification for the British presence in foreign lands.'[4] Through the measure of providing medical facilities, the British government tried to lay claim over the legitimacy of indentured trade in the plantation economy, which was thought of by critics, and later historians, as another form of slavery.[5]

This book is intended towards exploring the link between colonial health policy, development of medical knowledge and practices, and the experiences of indentured labourers. It focuses on the ways in which medical knowledge, its practices, and policies circulated between colonial India (source of the indentured labourers) and the colonies of Mauritius and Natal.

Mauritius and Natal, both British colonies located in the Indian Ocean, received nearly half a million indentured labourers from India (Mauritius received 453,063 and Natal received 152,184) between 1834 and 1920. The present work aims to fill a glaring lacuna in the historiography of medicine in the colonial period (which has totally neglected the Indian migrants) and indentured labour history (which has neglected the public health aspects); by examining the sanitary laws and health policies of the colonial governments of Natal and Mauritius. It also tries to explore their impact on the social status of the Indian migrant labourers. The plantation economy of these colonies worked on the basis of 'racial superiority' and the so-called 'scientific knowledge' which acted as an imperative instrument of social and cultural control over the migrants. It was during this period that colonial science and knowledge about the physiognomy and propensity to disease of the Indian population was being acquired, both in India and other colonies. In this context, Indian migrants became a target population to be studied and managed under the tight scrutiny of the colonial regime. This knowledge then became the basis for the formulation of appropriate sanitary and healthcare policies, whose effects necessarily spilled over to affect the wider populations of the colonies. There was thus a dialectic at work: acquisition of knowledge about disease propagation and sanitary behaviour of the Indian population, and its practical application that led to changes in health and sanitary policies. Further, the sanitary laws that were enacted aimed to 'civilize' and subjugate the uncivilized 'other'. The indentured migrant had to remain healthy and disease-free like the army, in order to strengthen and maintain British rule in the colonies. A reliable and continuous supply of cheap labour was thus a vital necessity for the plantations. In this context, in order to minimize their expenditure on the sick and non-able-bodied labourers, both the planters and the government began to emphasize on the health of the indentured labourers while recruiting them in India, on the depot, on voyages, and in plantations. These reasons, in turn, reinforced the racial superiority and consolidated the hold of the white planters over the emigrants.

In formal historiography, very few references are available on the indentured health issues. The social history of medicine emerged as a new point of focus among the historians in the 1980s. The available references briefly discuss how and why Western medicine entered the realm of colonial societies. It can be said that the indentured migrant's historiography has evolved through various stages, and each stage raises new questions and issues, and historians have different kinds of approaches towards them. The existing historiography provides us with insights related to the economic, political, and social history of these people.[6] Historians have also focused on the cultural history of the migrants.[7] Some others like Brij V. Lal, Marina Carter, and Prabhu P. Mohapatra, have provided us with new dimensions of the indentured system when it comes to the life of the indentured women migrants.[8]

The very few existing evidences in historiography of the health issues of the indentured can be divided into two trends. The first trend, which is very much indebted to the work of Philip D. Curtin on the Trans-Atlantic slave trade, focuses on the mortality of Indian labourers on voyage.[9] In the second trend, one can include those writings which focus on the indentured health issues in the overseas colonies irrespective of whether the Government of Indian or the overseas governments made any effort to provide public health facilities. Nevertheless, we find that issues related to the health of the indentured migrants have been largely ignored.

Various official writings are available on aspects of public health in Mauritius since its existence as a British colony. Baron Marrier d'Unienville was a British colonial archivist who produced a detailed document on the historical, commercial, and agricultural aspects of Mauritius and its dependencies, in three volumes. There are several works and memoirs of travellers, officers, and missionaries such as those of Charles Darwin (1836), James Backhouse (1844, Quaker missionary who wrote about his visit to a military hospital[10]), and Dr F.J. Mouat (1851, British medical officer). These writers did not forget to mention the physical condition of Mauritius and the indentured Indians as well. They found the former as a healthy place and the latter as the carriers of diseases from India to that place.

Hugh Tinker studies the whole process of emigration from India across the seas to more than a dozen countries.[11] He states, as the title of his book suggests, that there was little change in the labour system of the plantations when the colonies changed from 'slavery' to 'free labour'. Tinker presents a humanist, anti-colonial approach towards the issues of indentured emigration. His work deals with questions about the origin of the indentured in the 1830s as a product of slave emancipation, to its abolition in 1920. Tinker gives a detailed description of the structure of the Indian indentured system. He argues that the plantations differed very little from the former slave colonies. This was because, the indentured were paid very low wages, allotted appalling living quarters, and subjected to brutal punishment. Incidences of sexual immorality were also rampant because of the shortage of emigrant women. While raising the question why the Government of British India allowed such a system to develop and continue, he mentions at the same time that it probably happened because the officers were anxious to preserve the economic well-being of the plantations. In his writing, he attacks the government policies and regulations that failed to provide protection to these migrants. Tinker also stresses on the role of kidnapping and fraudulent practices in overseas labour mobilization and concludes that indentured and other forms of servitude did indeed approximate to the actual condition of slavery. He describes the indentured women as a 'sorry sisterhood' of those who were from low castes, were alone, and often were the outcasts of their society. According to Tinker, women were sexual victims of the plantation economy, and the scarcity of women was the main cause for all kinds of violence and crime against them. Few women led the competition among men for suitable partners, and in case of failure, the men killed the women or attempted suicide out of 'sexual jealousy'. Thus, in a very moralist tone, Tinker criticizes the indentured system at large. In this context, it might be mentioned that some historians have also emphasized on the non-economic pressures for women migrants (caused by family quarrels, desire for adventure, desire to escape responsibility and burdensome social restrictions, death of parents or husband, and undertaking of pilgrimages), which diminished their 'labour value'.[12]

Tinker's work has also been mindful of the significance of mortality suffered at sea, while telling the story of the labour migration. He states:

…the killing diseases—cholera, typhoid, dysentery, and a dozen others—were a constant feature of depot and shipboard existence. The Indian Ocean, the Atlantic, and the South Pacific—oceans of menace and mighty force—had to be tackled by sailing ships and their crews…it was only in the twentieth century, in the dying years of the system, that science and technology acquired some sort of mastery over the hazards of Indian emigration.[13]

He further compares these voyages with the 'Middle Passage' of slavery. Tinker states that the transfer of diseases took place by means of ships that carried goods and people from one port to another in the Indian Ocean. In this context, Arnold also states that the arrival of the Indians brought a radical change in the occurrence of diseases in Mauritius. He declares that regulations for healthcare were 'a mere facade', as they were generally not implemented. He compares the estate hospitals to the 'hot houses' of the slavery period, where the sick were admitted with the aim of controlling them, rather than curing them. However, Tinker does not highlight the health policies adopted by colonial authorities and their relationship with the changing mortality rates. He adopts the 'no change' approach towards the indentured labour regime and indentured health policies. This approach, however, might not be applied to the whole of the nineteenth century. Therefore, an in-depth study is required on a number of themes such as healthcare, diseases and their treatment, settlement, and sanitation; to find out the evolutionary change that took place in the late nineteenth and early twentieth centuries.

P.C. Emmer has rewritten the emigration experience for the indentured, particularly the women, and has described migration as an opportunity to escape from an 'illiberal, inhibiting and very hierarchical social system', calling it a 'great escape'.[14] He has further argued that it was their rational decision to emigrate, to escape from hunger, starvation, low earning wages, and certain personal problems such as widowhood, abandonment by husband or family, prostitution, etc. They enjoyed a great deal of personal freedom in the plantation colonies than they did in India.[15] According to him, indentured emigration from India to overseas colonies was a deliberate choice of the migrants, prompted by the hope of bettering their future prospects. But Emmer fails to see the miserable and despondent condition of the migrant women in the plantations. Apart from this, he also ignores the brutality, violence, and coercion which the labourers had to face in these colonies. Again, P. Mohapatra[16] and Gail Omvedt argue that the indentured system was mainly based on coercion, since the employers used varied social and economic tactics to control the labour force. It was a system based on manipulation and exploitation, and absence of freedom was the main characteristic of the indentured.

In this context, Brij V. Lal's work has provided a new dimension in the historiography on indentured migrants. Lal, in his various works, presented a social and cultural history of *girmitiyas* (indentured Indian migrants) in Fiji. He focused on the culture of *jahaji bhai*[17] on ship and their experience, which he compared with *narak* (hell). He also emphasized on the abuses and loopholes of the indentured system.

The work of Marina Carter becomes an important turning point in the historiography of Indian immigrants in Mauritius. This writer moves away from some of the established views held by the previous historians, for example, arguments which linked the indentured system to slavery or such views that upheld that Indians were mostly 'lured' and forced to join indenturedship. She argues that the Indians 'lured' by the prospects of a better life as an indentured were disillusioned in the early years of emigration, and in the later period, when more and more Indians were travelling to Mauritius, they were well aware of the existing conditions in the island. Carter provides an analytical account of the indentured system: from the recruitment process to the depots and Indian ports, the voyages and life at the sea, to their landing in Mauritius, and finally their life and condition on the sugar estates. She is able to take her discussions outside the colonial discourse to include the perspectives of the migrants. She further argues that Indians were able to establish a 'semi-autonomous social and cultural life' and to assert their religious traditions, languages, and dress.[18] Carter addresses another serious lacuna in indentured historiography by focusing on the women immigrants. She redefines their role in the system, and instead of presenting them as 'followers, dependents and unproductive labour', she finds that they played diverse positive roles, such as those of wives and mothers, and also certain important economic roles as hawkers, recruiters, and even entrepreneurs.

Some feminist historians, on the other hand, have argued that 'emigration provided women an opportunity to exercise a degree of control over their social and sexual lives which they never had before… now they could leave their husband for another or have a parallel relationship with more than one.'[19] However, these historians at times underplay the violence and exploitation that women had to face in these colonies because they were considered physically weak.

The work of Carter also provides insights on the planters' concern for the recruitment of healthy-bodied labourers. She states that there was a demand for the 'quality' recruits, labourers who were fit for work—strong and healthy. She describes the depot settlements where the recruits were examined and vaccinated against small pox, before they were sent on the voyage. In the limited period during which she made her study (1834–74), she found that the sick among the newly arrived were quite large in number. She describes the high mortality rate during cholera epidemics in the 1850s, and a higher death rate among the new recruits because of dysentery, diarrhoea, fever, and also general debility. She talks about the establishment of quarantine system in Mauritius to avoid the introduction of diseases from the newly arrived Indians to those who had landed there earlier. She argues that though regulations were passed, their implementation was difficult. Similar to what Arnold has stated, Carter also mentions that hospitals became a place of detention, rather than organized establishments where medical treatment was provided to the sick. Further, she refers to women's health problems, their adherence to traditional practices, their reluctance to visit hospitals, and their avoidance of Western medicine.

The healthcare measures which were adopted by the Government of Mauritius after 1878 still need to be studied. Saloni Deerpalsingh and Carter's *Selected Documents on Indian Immigrants in Mauritius*

1834-1926 contains documents on Indian immigration, drawn from the archival collections in Mauritius, England, and India. They have been very useful for the researchers in their studies.[20]

In this regard, Ralph Shlomowitz and John McDonald's pioneering work on the indentured migrants' health, focuses on the quantitative aspects of the migrants' mortality during the voyage.[21] Shlomowitz tries to analyse the higher mortality rate and its causes on the ships carrying indentured labours to the plantation colonies such as West Indies, Natal, Mauritius, Reunion, and Fiji. In their work, they have tried to make a comparative study of the European immigrants' voyage with the Indian indentured voyage and the voyage of the African slaves. They argue that the average death rate on the Indian indentured voyage was higher than that on the European immigrants' voyage, because India had a much more epidemiologically hostile environment than Europe. This was primarily because diseases like cholera and malaria were endemic in India, but not in Europe. Secondly, India was much less nutritionally secure than Europe, and much of India's internal and external migration appeared to have been induced by famine conditions.[22] Africa too suffered mainly from these two problems and on these grounds, it was to be expected that the average death rate in the African vessels carrying slaves would have been higher than on the European immigrants' voyages. Shlomowitz and McDonald state that the nineteenth century medical officials, despite being informed by an incorrect theory of diseases (miasma)—were able to reduce mortality rate in emigrants and on the ocean voyages through a series of administrative reforms in healthcare.[23] According to them:

...these reforms were the result of a learning process as medical officials responded, on a trial and error basis, to periodic epidemics and included the more effective screening out of sick prospective emigrants, refusing their admission on depot or passage overseas; the provision of a more nutritious diet with clean water and uncontaminated food; the provision of facilities which made possible the isolation of the sick from the healthy; a reduction in crowding; and enforcing adequate sanitary standards, relating to keeping the steerage quarters clean, the disposal of human waste and personal hygiene.[24]

Shlomowitz and McDonald state that preventing the embarkation of sick passengers probably did not result in a reduction in the overall death rate; it merely shifted the place of death from the sea to the land. But they too just provide the statistical (demographic structure) analyses of the mortality or death rate of the migrants in colonies or on the ships.

These writings somehow neglect the qualitative analyses of health with respect to the indentured migrants. They fail to provide any insight into the impact of these reforms on the life of the indentured, except their death rate. The issues of health and sanitation in the plantations are not a part of their work. In this context, a work by Anil Persaud can be cited, which explores the health policies of the British government on the ships carrying the indentured migrants.[25] Persaud very effectively describes the condition of the indentured migrants on voyages, mentioning the impact of colonial science and medicine on there life of the indentured. In his opinion, the ship served as a laboratory in which an experiment to find minimums was conducted—minimum space, minimum diet, minimum light, minimum air, etc. Most of the indentured migrants entered the 'medical zone' for the first time and encountered allopathic medicine. In this regime, the indentured were required not only to know their body, but also to describe it in a way that science understood. He states:

…coolies could actually feel the political economy of space in the air they breathed. The conflicting impulses that moved them from shore to shore—for example the desire on the part of the ship captains for higher profits, the planters' demand for more bodies to be delivered and the concern of the planters and colonial officials that the bodies delivered, be alive and healthy—often made their lives rougher than the seas they sailed upon.[26]

However, Persaud does not focus on the reaction of the indentured labourers against this process of medicalization of their bodies. His work makes it appear as if the indentured became passive followers of these experiments.[27]

Writings of historians like Hilda Kuper,[28] Mabel Palmer, Surendra Bhana,[29] C.G. Henning,[30] and the work of Goolam Vahed and Ashwin Desai have helped to shape our understanding of the indentured system in Natal. These historians have focused on the economic and working conditions of Indians in Natal.[31] Vahed and Desai have adopted a subaltern's approach in their writings, and thus their work is a significant addition to the history of indentured Indians in Natal.[32] Their work is an essential read for anyone studying this field. It critiques the colonial state policy and the indentured system. They stated that the medical facilities on the estates remained inefficient and Indians were accused of having 'dirty habits', which was mostly due to the lack of sanitary facilities in the labourers' quarters. Vahed and Desai's work is also important because they explore the subaltern voices and have used vernacular sources, such as songs, for drawing out information. Thus, it can be said that this work has been influenced by an anti-elitist approach to writing history.

An interesting comparative study of the political economies of Mauritius and Natal has been done by M.D. North-Coombes.[33] The author analyses the issue of racism in the plantation economy and the role of the colonial state in the victimization of the Indians. He states that the condition of labourers in the sectors of healthcare and education could have been better, had the colonial state taken firm measures to counteract the reluctance of planters to improve the situation of Indians. J.B. Brain and P. Brain, in an article, have tried to provide a very brief account of governmental health policies related to the indentured migrants in the recruitment process, on the voyages, and in the plantation economy.[34] Although it provides valuable information about the government policies, the article does not deal with the consequences of these policies on the life-style of the indentured in the plantations.

The pioneering work of Soma Hewa deals with the deteriorating health condition of labourers in Sri Lanka.[35] According to him, in the nineteenth century in Sri Lanka, the health needs of the labouring masses received little attention from the government or the plantation owners.[36] The Government of Sri Lanka refused to provide any medical facilities by arguing that it was not responsible for the welfare of the estate workers. There were no medical facilities that were provided by the coolie laws to the indentured labourers who were working on the tea, coffee, and rubber plantations. The hospitals', 'Friends-in-need' appealed to the planters on humanitarian grounds to provide proper medical facilities to the sick labourers. But they received very few responses from the planters. In 1843, the recorded death rate (annual) in the colony was sixty per cent.[37] He suggests that it was illegal to recruit Indian labourers for Sri Lanka. Indian labourers could be recruited in the other overseas plantation economies such as Mauritius, British Guiana, Jamaica, and Trinidad.[38] The absence of labour laws in Sri Lanka was chiefly responsible for the higher number of sick and the high mortality rate among the indentured. In Sri Lanka, the policy of the government was a clear case of laissez-faire, and the government adopted the policy of complete non-interference.

It was the general perception of the British colonial rule that the development of the colonies was a gradual, 'evolutionary process, and that the impetus for such development should come from the Europeans, not from the indigenous people. The medical and sanitary requirements of Europeans living in the colonies were thus the prime motives for the development of 'tropical medicine'; every attempt was made to meet their needs in order to protect the empire. Therefore, medical developments were, first and foremost, used to provide a safer environment for the Europeans residing in the colonies. In Britain, the political establishment began to assume greater responsibility for public health, and the first public health insurance act, the National Insurance Act, was passed in 1911. Hewa mentions that in the colonies, state intervention in health was limited only to specific services, such as lunatic asylums and leprosariums. Public welfare in general was left to missionaries and other charitable organizations.[39]

An unpublished doctoral thesis by Aickin, submitted in 2001, also proves to be an important addition into the present historiography.[40] In this work, he deals with the transformation of the colonial attitude towards 'native' health. Health facilities changed in the colony of British Guiana because of the concern about the health of migrant labourers. Aickin looks at the questions of fertility, population, and the problem of infant mortality in the colony. According to him, the widening focus on medical provisions was not simply the outcome of local political concern, but was shaped by wider considerations, including ideas of race, civilization, gender, and; the influence of metropolitan (British) and larger imperial political interests. In his work, Aickin shows that the use of Western medicine did not just spread in the colony, but was a part of the complex process of knowledge dissemination that involved contestation and negotiation. Though Aickin poses various questions about the indentured health policy, he saw 'construction of motherhood' as the only core area of public health policy in the colony.

Raj Boodhoo's work extensively covers the aspects of medicine and sanitation in Mauritius.[41] His work examines the interplay between the colonial authorities' attempts to regulate health conditions on the island, the planters' perceptions and reactions towards the labourers, and the habits and customs of the Indian migrants. He asserts that till 1875, there was no change in the medical facilities available to the indentured. It was only after the Royal Commission of 1875 and the new labour law of 1878, that a change became obvious. He further states that it was after this that the Government of Mauritius set up a proper structure for better supervision of health conditions prevailing in the estates. This, and a few other positive changes were noted only during the last quarter of the nineteenth century. The diverse and interesting nature of the material used by the author provides extremely valuable information for future research. The closing line of the conclusion is quite revealing— 'Mauritius is only a few hours away by air from the countries round the

Indian Ocean…the Island is vulnerable now as it was in the past. There is a need to understand how disease is transmitted from one country to another, and what measures can be taken to control them.'[42] This shows that the author, to some extent, believed in the earlier portrayal of Mauritius as a healthy island and that the Indians and their ships were the carriers of diseases to the country. Boodhoo, however, overlooked colonial interference as a cause of the spreading of diseases and epidemics, while solely focusing on better medical facilities and scientific research in the early twentieth century. Even today, in the era of globalization, health issues can hardly be considered a local problem.

It can be seen that existing historiography raises new questions related to indentured health issues in the political economy of overseas colonies. What was the perception of Indian coolies and 'Western medical' regime towards the diseases that existed in the colonies? Who was responsible for the spread of diseases or epidemics, the Indians or miserable working conditions in the plantations? In order to explore the complexity of indentured lives, some historians have critically analysed 'state policy' regarding health policies and sanitary laws. Thus, they have opened up new areas of research in this process. The writing of history in the context of health and sanitary issues in plantation economy is still in its infancy. Nonetheless, issues related to health of the indentured migrants remains a less explored area of research. The present book tries to show how medicine helped in the integration and utilization of the indentured labourers in a colonial plantation economy, even though these medical interventions were marked by deep-seated contradictions.

'Western Medicine' and the Empire

For a long time, the history of health, diseases, and medicines had been written by the medical practitioners for their own fraternity. Over time, with the incorporation of the cultural, political, and economic lives of the common people in these writings, the interest of non-practitioners in medical history writing was enhanced. Arnold argues that when interest in the history of medicine started to grow in the 1980s, there was still no consensus on the central issues that needed to be developed; and the existing literature concentrating on Europe and North America had only been explanatory in character.[43] In recent times, scholars have gradually turned their attention towards the former European colonies such as India and Africa.

In this context, Arnold, Biswamoy Pati, Mark Harrison, Anil Kumar, Deepak Kumar, and Seema Alavi, to name a few, have brought forth pioneering works that have attempted to unravel the purpose and aim of medicine and health policies within the empire.[44] The historians working on the social history of medicine have produced a number of works, in which they have dealt with several themes concerning health and medicine in colonial India, such as the impact of Western medicine on the Indian population or on indigenous medicine on Europeans, and the emergence of medical institutions in India, such as dispensaries, hospitals, lock hospitals, and also lunatic and leprosy asylums.

The lower life expectancy of the British in India, as compared to that in Europe, and the difficulties of living in a tropical climate, forced the Europeans to enhance their knowledge about the diseases in this region and their treatment. The higher rate of disease and death rate among the Europeans forced them to look up the aspects of medicine and sanitation of the colony and that remained confined only to the Europeans. The British came across many diseases in India which existed in Europe as well, but they associated Indians with outbreaks of smallpox, plague, cholera, and malaria. The fear of contracting 'native' diseases, in the early phase, forced them to withdraw from making any social contact with the 'natives'. Therefore, they adopted the 'isolation', 'prohibition', and 'repression' policy, as per which they built their residences away from the 'native' areas. The main causes of death among the Europeans in India were dysentery, diarrhoea, fever, cholera, liver diseases, and venereal diseases.[45] Cholera caused a large number of deaths and led to much suffering among the European troops in India. Medical practitioners and scientists, who were with colonial officials, pointed out that India was the breeding ground for diseases, and from India it spread out to other parts of the globe. Little was, however, known about the causes of the diseases. Before the 1800s, the British consulted Indian doctors, vaids, and pundits. This was because of the non-availability of European doctors then, due to high transportation costs. The medicine which was supplied from England was not only expensive but also available only in small amounts. Therefore, it was largely restricted to the British settlements and places like barracks, jails, and hospitals. However, Western medicine gradually tried to extend its boundary to the rest of the 'native' population.

Initially, Western medicine could not provide treatment for all the diseases or provided only precautionary measures for the prevention of diseases that prevailed in India. It was around the early nineteenth century that scientific research was carried out about the causes, treatment, and prevention of tropical diseases. Many theories attribute factors such as the warm climate, the landscape, and the soil, to the genesis of these diseases. A number of institutions were set up in India and England to study tropical medicine.

Samiksha Sehrawat pointed out that 'the development of medical care in India took a peculiar trajectory which was shaped by its colonial context'.[46] Western medical care policy changed its role according to the political, economic, social, and cultural needs of the Raj. In order to fulfil the state's 'biopolitics'[47] purpose, Western medicine had to struggle for a long time to establish itself in India.[48] Rural India remained out of the reach of Western medicine, where traditional and indigenous forms of treatment persisted. In course of time, the government came up with various laws against the native healers and practitioners who carried out these indigenous modes of treatment. This also seemed to have happened in Mauritius and Natal. However, the government remained unsuccessful in these attempts both in India as well as overseas. In the cities, especially in the presidencies, medical colleges were set up by the colonial (Indian) government to train Europeans and Indian subordinate staff in the different fields of medicine. In the view of the colonial government, Western medicine was held not only as the justification of the colonial rule, but was described as one of the harbingers of progress towards a more 'civilized' social and environmental order.[49] North-Coombes has argued that the 'civilising mission' was an aspect of racist ideology, a pseudo-scientific doctrine of social Darwinism. Quoting Curtin, he adds that this concept provided the rationale, 'for imperialism, which allowed the rape of the African and Asian continents to be portrayed as a "civilising mission".'[50] Historians have criticized the role of Western medicine in the colonies over time; they have argued that imperialism had turned India into an immense laboratory, a prized colony for Western science, a vehicle of imperial ideas and their application.[51]

During the same period, in England, Edwin Chadwick's work[52] revealed the atrocious conditions of health and sanitation, low life expectancy, and mortality of the inhabitants of the industrial towns such as Leeds, Manchester, Liverpool, Glasgow, and Bradford. Chadwick's report shocked the higher classes of the society, as it revealed for the first time the realities of the living conditions of the poor people in England:

...a poor family consisting of man and wife with seven children, each require 600 cubic feet of breathing room...shut up in a chamber not containing more than 1000 feet for the whole. …both parents and children rising at five o'clock in the morning, and labouring in other unhealthy atmospheres…in London workers had to drink untreated water from the Thames.[53]

The unregulated employment of women and children for excessive hours and bad working conditions exposed the growing class of industrial workers not only to insanitary living conditions and hardships, but also to tuberculosis and epidemics of diseases like cholera.[54] During 1831–2 and 1847–8, cholera killed hundreds of people in several parts of England, raising an alarm among the people. Most of the European countries adopted a vigorous quarantine policy to stop diseases like cholera from entering their territories. However, Britain ended its quarantine policy because of its commercial interest and laissez-faire policy in trade. Instead, it adopted the policy of port inspection and isolation of affected people. Even so, Chadwick's report of 1842 forced the government to pass the first Public Health Act of 1848 in England. This act extended the power of the local authorities to construct drains, supply clean water, and carry out sanitary works. Though this report played an important role in emphasizing the impact of industrial economy on the life of the labouring poor, it took a long time to apply the welfare measures for the 'natives' in the colonies.

The existing historiography on the social history of medicine has focused on three major roles of 'Western medicine'[55] in the colonies: as a tool of the empire, as a part of constructive imperialism, and as an instrument of social control. D.R. Headrick, in two of his books,[56] argues that among the technologies (which may include medicine) which helped to open up Africa to European penetration and conquest during the nineteenth century: one of the most significant was the use of quinine as a prophylactic against malaria.[57] The book 'Tools of Empire' raises questions on the nature and significance of Western medicine. Headrick tries to locate Western medicine as a 'system' in the context of British imperialism, and its consequences. He lists medicine as one among several technologies which proved crucial to the success of European expansion and domination over large parts of the world. Curtin, in his works,[58] shows the impact of colonialism on the health of the European soldiers in Africa. He argues that the improvement in sanitation and medical facilities in the military camps helped lower the mortality rate among the Europeans.

Theories regarding the pivotal role of medicine as a tool of colonization have been challenged by historians. Arnold argues that Headrick's reading of the evidence (in the form of medicine in general and quinine in particular) is rather selective, and that he has overestimated the effectiveness of quinine as a weapon in the armoury of the nineteenth century Empire.[59] Unlike Headrick, he asserts that it was the imperial expansion which provided the stimulus to technological innovation, rather than the reverse. Historians like Arnold and Harrison state that the absence of effective medical intervention did not prevent the progress of colonial rule in other parts of the world. According to Harrison, it was not only in the military sphere that medicine came to be viewed as a 'tool of empire'. 'In the early eighteenth century, medicine entered the discourse of economic efficiency, with inoculation against smallpox introduced on slaving vessels, and limited medical provisions being made for slaves in plantations in the West Indies and the Americas.'[60] He further adds that medicine did not become prominent in the rhetoric of the empire until in the late nineteenth century.

The 'constructive imperialism' theory of the role of medicine focuses more on the economic utility of medical intervention. Arnold and Harrison argue that medical intervention improved labour efficiency, thus opening up impenetrable areas of the tropics. The foundation of the London School of Tropical Medicine in 1899 and the Liverpool School of Tropical Medicine in 1898; was promoted mainly by mercantile interests. By the end of the nineteenth century, the British boasted that they had brought 'civilization' to India, and had implanted among Indians, the desire for further reform. Ronald Ross[61] was convinced that British rule was essential to India's development, and he believed that the British were 'superior' to subject peoples in natural ability, integrity and science. They had introduced honesty, law, justice, order, roads, posts, railway, irrigation, hospitals…and what was necessary for civilization, a final superior authority.'[62]

Arnold explains 'certain themes like tropical diseases, their causes and their cure or their ways of propagation that are emerging now are concerned mainly with diseases and medicine as a subject of contact, convergence and conflict between colonial powers and the "natives".'[63] Cholera, malaria, and smallpox had existed in Europe in the nineteenth century, but these diseases have been described as tropical diseases in the scientific and medical circle of Europe. Among the Europeans, Asia and Africa were known as reservoirs of fatal diseases. Arnold further mentions that the doctors functioned, in effect, as one of the agencies by which the colonial system tried to maintain the image of physical and moral superiority of the ruling race, while medicine helped to define the spatial and social distance between the European officials and the Indians with whom they came into contact, and to determine the conditions of the soldiers' work and recreation. According to him, medicine was to serve, from time to time, the broader material interests of the British in India. Medical measures were often impelled by this narrowly materialistic view of the state's interest in checking diseases. He showed that the European planters, traders, and industrialists forced the Government of India to adopt a protective approach towards the labouring communities and the indigenous population. Arnold claims that from the 1850s in India, dispensaries were a notable feature of the medical landscape and could be seen as part of the 'improving' presence of the British in India.[64] But this was not a uniform response for the whole colony; local factors were important in shaping colonial policies as well. For example, urban trade centres, cities, military camps, port cities, markets, and pilgrimage centres attracted government attention, and dispensaries and hospitals were opened at these places in the hope of fixing the 'native' health conditions. However, these measures remained selective and unsatisfactory.

Arnold's views were further strengthened by D. Kumar, who also claims that colonial science and medicine played a very important role in colonizing India. He asserts—'...it functioned in several ways: as an instrument of control which would swing between coercion and persuasion as the exigencies demanded, and as a site for interaction and often resistance.'[65] Thus, it served the state and helped it to ensure complete domination over the people. He further argues that medicine was mediated not only by considerations of political economy but also by several other factors like the polity and biology. The circumstances of material life and new knowledge interacted and produced this discourse.

On the other hand, Pati and Harrison question the importance of 'colonial medicine' and science as a 'tool of empire' in their work.[66] They also show the limitation of the government on this issue. It is suggested by them that the government was responsible only for the legislation, thus compelling or enabling local authorities to take action in sanitary matters. They are of the opinion that the colonial government had neglected the indigenous people's health and had developed a distinct 'colonial' mode of healthcare, characterized by residential segregation of Indians from Europeans and negligence of the indigenous population. These historians also argue that the colonial government did not allot necessary funds for the people's health and medicine. Harrison, however, mentions that the government neglected the health of the indigenous people because of their resistance against these reforms.

Harrison argues that the relationship between colonial priorities and medical policies was much less straightforward than has generally been suggested.[67] He suggests that the formulation of public health policy is perhaps best understood as a contest between two different conceptions of the empire—one, authoritarian and paternalistic, emphasizing Europe's 'civilizing' mission in the tropics; the other, liberal and decentralist, stressing on the constraints imposed upon government action by shortage of revenue, indigenous resistance, and competing claims on the resources of local and central governments. He states that civil unrest against colonial sanitary reforms changed the official approach towards public health, which was now sought to be based on co-operation, rather than confrontation.[68] He also mentions that the public healthcare measures in colonial India in the early phase were usually taken care of by the East India Company servants and some Indians acting in a private capacity; with only occasional support from municipal bodies and the Company.[69]

The healthcare measures for non-Europeans during the nineteenth century changed over time and varied across regions; and political and economic dynamics at the local level were crucial in shaping government attitudes and motivations towards providing it. In the colonies of Mauritius and Natal, though medicine did not directly help in the conquest of the colonies, it helped in the consolidation of the empire. Medicine was also presented as a 'constructive work' of the empire for the well-being of the colonies and the 'native' people of the colonies, along with Indian labourers.

Reflections

The present study focuses on colonial Mauritius and Natal, both of which were British colonies, and covers the period from 1834 to 1920, also providing a brief history of indentured migrants in these two regions. The recruitment of indentured labour started in 1834, and ended in 1920, which is the cut-off period for my study. Mauritius was a plantation economy, while Natal had a diversified economy. In the 1860s, when Natal started the recruitment of indentured labourers from India for the first time, it adopted the Mauritian immigration law and promised to treat the indentured labour as stipulated in these laws. Though there are similarities between the two colonies, I intend to enquire how the diversified economic needs, and the political and racial discriminations along with the local politics, shaped the healthcare provisions in these two colonies.

This work intends to examine the interactions between the colonial authorities, estate owners, and the Indian immigrants, set in a context of diseases, epidemics, and healthcare in colonial Mauritius and Natal, through a number of questions. What role did the health policies play in colonial plantation economy? How and when did policies related to the maintenance of the indentured labour emerge? What was the nature of these health policies in the two colonies? How were the labourers treated and diagnosed in the estate hospitals and dispensaries? What role did law play in the shaping of health policies in the colonies? Did these laws prove to be beneficial for the colonial government and planters in getting a stable labour force for the plantation economy (by weeding out the 'frail', 'idle', and the 'redundant' people from the workforce)? To what extent did the laws become a tool for 'civilizing' and subjugating the uncivilized 'other', and can they be regarded as the basis of ideological legitimacy for the colonial government in the plantations? To what extent were these health measures different from slavery?

Further, the book also explores the response of the Indians towards these reform measures and laws. It tries to contextualize the conflict between the indentured labourers and the colonial government and planters, and the impact of this conflict on the health policies in the colonies. To what extent were the governments successful in fulfilling their purpose? Was there any Indian mode of medical treatment that was adopted to contest colonial science and medicine? The gender angle, when it came to medical practices and health policies related to women migrants, and the role it played in further strengthening the control over women's sexuality and body, and in the subordination of women in the plantation society (for example, the Contagious Diseases Act in Natal and the establishment of the 'Lock Hospital'), will also be discussed in this work.

The health of the migrants was a significant area of concern for the colonial government, right from the inception of indentured migration. The history of medicine in both colonies (Mauritius and Natal) is documented in official records. The report of immigration officers and surgeon generals, the journals of the both the colonies' medical profession, and the correspondence between the plantation colonies and India provide valuable insight into the workings of the minds of the authorities and the place of medicine in the colonies. High mortality and its causes were investigated regularly and the proneness of certain groups of migrants to diseases and epidemics were minutely examined in commissions and committees. Similarly, the voyages and the ships were objects of special attention by colonial officials and medical personnel. Valuable information and data about sickness on board ships were regularly collected and treatment regimens were prescribed accordingly in manuals and laws. After their arrival at the destination, the indentured labourers were quarantined, and plantation estates were made sites of disease investigations. Detailed records of sicknesses of the labourers and their causes were kept and circulated among the emerging medical fraternity and the colonial officialdom. Thus, during the phase their recruitment in India, on board ships, and at the destinations (plantations), the labourers were subjects of specialized medical study and changing medical practices. These reports, if read 'against the grain', can also, on occasions, reveal the non-European perspective on Western health provisions, although the voice of the non-Europeans were usually inaudible to officials and rarely entered the official records. This work focuses on all of these three sites to explore the links between medical knowledge, its practice, and public health policy.

The reconstruction of the history of healthcare in plantations in the nineteenth century colonial context, has been based on the documents which are dispersed in various archival collections. This study is based on a number of primary sources at the National Archives of India, the West Bengal State Archives, Patna State Archives, The National Archives of UK, and the British Library. The files of various government departments and the correspondence between the colonies and British administrators provide significant information on the policies and decisions taken in the colonies. The annual reports of the protectors of Indian immigrants and medical officers of Mauritius and Natal have also provided facts and figures on the recruitment and condition of labourers, and the various aspects of the indentured medical realm.

Until 1905, there were fifteen and twenty-five central hospitals, that were established for the Indians in Natal and Mauritius, respectively. It was the duty of every surgeon in these hospitals to submit an annual report of his circle to the protector of immigrants. In this report, the surgeon mentioned all the details of his circle regarding the health and sanitary issues of Indians, the prominent diseases of the circle, the number of patients admitted and discharged during the year, the number and causes of deaths, etc. Apart from these, the reports also provided information regarding the development in medical facilities available at the hospitals. Thus, they proved to be an important and rich source of information. Certain subaltern writings are also valuable sources of information in this context. For example, the autobiographies of the indentured labourers like Baba Ram Chandra, Totaram Sandhya, Munshi Rahman Khan, and that of Dr Kesaveloo Goonaruthnum Naidoo (Dr Goonam), etc., give us a vivid description of their lives and times.[70]

The first chapter of this book explores the geographical and political history of Mauritius and Natal. It is followed up with a brief account of the establishment of colonies by the British. An attempt has been made in the chapter to delineate the economic development of sugar and other industries, and show how it led to the demand for indentured labourers from India, to the colonies. The chapter tries to provide a summary of the colonial government's emigration policy from 1834 to 1910 and analyse how it was developed and revised during the course of time. An assessment of the related settlement policies has also been made. The chapter deals with the condition of indentured migrants in the colonies and the governmental policies for their settlement in the plantations; at the same time, discussing briefly the political and economic conditions of the emigrants in these places. It is suggested that the overseas colonies' government and the Government of India (under British rule) introduced a number of laws for both the employer and the employees. These laws, designed to protect the Indian emigrants in the colonies, were neither strictly executed nor enforced. In case of the overseas colonies, the employers usually interpreted the law to suit their own interests. It was difficult for the illiterate indentured labourer to understand the jargon of law. Consequently, they were subjected to great hardships by their employers. Their lives were plagued by the actions of the authorities, which included dehumanisation, petty prosecution, constant injustice, and treatment with appalling cruelty— all of which contributed to a high rate of suicide among the labourers.

The second chapter looks closely at the process of making the indentured labourers 'suitable' for the colonies. The long-term experiences of indentured trade (in general with weak, poor and sick, coolies and particular with hill coolies; those who were not able to survive in Mauritius), and demands of the plantation economy enforced the concerned authorities to adopt some measures in the selection of indentured labourers, on the basis of medical grounds and the physical condition of their bodies. The recruiters were directed to recruit only muscular, healthy, and able-bodied labourers; and the 'unfit', the aged, and those with 'non-able' bodies were rejected. In order to reduce costs during recruitment, the recruits became subjects of medical checkups at the sub-depots, main depots, and before boarding the ships, at the Calcutta and Madras ports, by the European doctors. The documentation of the recruits' bodily aspects in medical certificates became indispensable for their departure overseas. This further increased the hurdle of Indians who were looking for employment overseas. Depots became the places where medical officers tested the population and tried to physically prepare the selected individuals for the long and arduous voyages. The emphasis on isolation of the depots from local people was added to the duty of the medical staff; they needed to ensure that only the medically 'fit' could enter the premises and be admitted thereafter. Official reports show that there were some restrictions, but not complete prohibition, on the movement of coolies outside the depots. At least in theory, depots were maintained to provide good quality food, water, proper medical facilities, and sanitation measures. In order to fulfil the required number of coolies for transportation, recruits had to wait on the depots from the statutory seven day minimum to several months, or in the case of prolonged illnesses, even more than a year. However, the annual medical reports always raised questions about the quantity and quality of food, accommodation, water supply, maintenance of hospitals, and sanitation. These took several years to reach a satisfactory level. This suggests that the depots were established in order to make the 'fit' indentured body further 'suitable' for sea voyages, by giving them proper food, medicines, and treatment as required. However, the resistance of intending emigrants towards these medicines, treatments, and the 'process of making them suitable'; forced the government to make some changes in their policies.

The third chapter moves further from the existing historiography on indentured voyages and excavates the medical and sanitation conditions on the voyages. It also deals with the effects of technological developments on the voyages of the indentured. The higher death rate on these voyages and accidents at sea due to storms, fires, or navigational problems demanded new measures to be taken and structural changes to be made on the ships. The enquiry commission to examine the high mortality rates during voyages recognized that the causes of this were mainly overcrowding, dampness in the ships, ill-defined amount of space for the travellers on the ships, and also the long duration of journey. Newer technologies and large, fast steamers were thus introduced to overcome these problems. However, the introduction of newer technologies and large steamers with a fixed amount of space for individuals could not bring down the sickness and deaths rates. This was because the officials were inclined to carry more people than the usual capacity of the ships. This chapter also enquires into the diseases that prevailed on the ships, the method of their treatment, and the efforts to reform the medical and other aspects of the (transportation) trade. Attempts have been made to examine the impact of new diet, sanitation laws, medical facilities, and seasickness on the health and daily routine of the indentured.

The third chapter also argues that the voyages played a crucial role in altering the lifestyle of the indentured to suit the plantation colonies. They became sources and objects of experiments. The European notions of civilization, morality, chastity, and purity became a part of the medical science, which they (the colonizers) imposed on the indentured body. Emigration rules and regulations made several provisions for the comfort and benefit of the indentured over the voyages, but most of the time these remained only an unfulfilled promise.

The fourth chapter tries to explore the role of medical facilities in the forging of relationships between the indentured labour and the planters. Indians were regarded as the 'carriers of diseases', who caused 'chaos'. This chapter focuses on quarantine as a preventive measure (based on the theory of contagion of diseases) adopted by the two colonies, understanding how it affected the indentured trade and the health of the labourers. However, in spite of adopting a strict quarantine law, the colonies failed to stop the spread of epidemics. This chapter looks thoroughly into the laws that were passed in Mauritius and Natal to provide medical benefits to the indentured labourers. These laws were amended multiple times before they became capable of benefitting the labourers. The medical legislations of both colonies slowly opened up the private sphere of plantation to government interference, though it was quite limited. The planters, naturally, considered these laws as a curtailment of their rights, and more importantly, profits.

It has been highlighted in this chapter that the regulations to improve medical provisions on the plantation estates provided the bureaucratic system with instruments to harmonize indentured trade principles and mass transport of labourers in the colonies. The ultimate aim of these medical interventions was the survival and more efficient working of the plantation system. The lack of government control on the estate doctors provided the planters an opportunity for negotiation with the labourers. Medical benefits remained in the hands of the planters, which forced the labourers to be obedient, hardworking, and morally upright. On the other hand, the labourers recorded their resistance against Western medical treatments and the confinement of hospitals, which was often against their caste, and religious and cultural norms.

The fifth chapter enquires into the major epidemics in the colonies and to what extent these affected the management of the colonial government and labour power. It explores in detail the sanitation measures adopted by the two colonies to cope with diseases like malaria, plague, hookworm, and venereal diseases among the indentured labourers. This chapter also looks into the conditions of accommodation, ration, and water supply for the emigrants. The widespread outbreak of epidemics in the colonies forced the governments to extend their health policies to the 'native' Africans and free-indentured population. The history of the epidemics and their effect on the labour population and the colonies' economy have been recovered from diverse sources, which include monographs written by the medical superintendents of the colonies, enquiry commission records, and annual reports of the medical inspectors of the colonies and estates.

After the failure of quarantine laws in the prevention of epidemics, the colonies took up strict sanitation measures. During this period, medical science proved that freedom from diseases depended, amongst other things, upon proper sanitation, clean water, nutritious food, and fresh air, as well as on eliminating disorder/indiscipline, ignorance, and immorality amongst the colony's poor. Drawing together municipal and government policies, and moving individuals into following desirable civic practices became the prime task for the medical practitioners in the colonies. The governments reified the medical regimen in order to achieve medical, moral, and even sexual control over the poor and the labourers. The chapter suggests that the colonial government regularized the sanitation measures in the colony through policing, terror, fines, physical punishment, and imprisonment, though their efforts remained unfruitful.

Notes

1. Thomas R. Metcalf, *Ideologies of the Raj*, The New Cambridge History of India, part III, vol. 4, New Delhi: Cambridge University Press, 1998, pp. 29–43; D.R. Headrick, *The Tentacles of Progress: Technology Transfer in the Age of Imperialism, 1850-1940*, New York: Oxford University Press, 1988, pp. 4–10. Also see D.R. Headrick, *Tools of Empire: Technology and*

European Imperialism in the Nineteenth Century, New York: Oxford University Press, 1981.

2. David Aickin, 'From Plantation Medicine to Public Health: The State and Medicine in British Guiana 1838-1914', unpublished PhD thesis, University College London, 2001, p. 14.

3. David Arnold, *Colonizing the Body: State Medicine and Epidemic Disease in Nineteenth-Century India*, London: University of California Press, 1993, p. 291.

4. Aickin, 'Plantation Medicine to Public Health', p. 14.

5. For details, see Hugh Tinker, *A New System of Slavery: The Export of Indian Labour Overseas, 1830-1920*, London: Oxford University Press, 1974.

6. Panchanan Saha, *Emigration of Indian Labour, 1834-1900*, New Delhi: People's Publishing House, 1970; I. M. Cumpston, *Indians Overseas in British Territories, 1834-1854*, London: Dawsons of Pall Mall, 1969; Tinker, *A New System of Slavery*; Basdeo Mangru, *Benevolent Neutrality: Indian Government Policy and Labour Migration to British Guiana 1854-1884*, London: Hansib Publishing Limited, 1987; Mabel Palmer, *History of the Indians in Natal*, Westport, Connecticut: Greenwood Press, 1957; Hilda Kuper, *Indian People in Natal*, Natal: University of Natal Press, 1960; Surendra Bhana, *Indentured Indian Emigrants to Natal, 1860-1902: A Study based on Ships' Lists*, New Delhi: Promilla & Co., 1991; C.G. Henning, *The Indentured Indian in Natal, 1860-1917*, New Delhi: Promilla & Co., 1993.

7. Goolam Vahed and Ashwin Desai, *Inside Indenture: A South African Story, 1860-1914*, Durban: Madiba Publishers, 2007.

8. Brij V. Lal, *Chalo Jahaji: Journey through Indenture in Fiji*, Suva: Prashant Pacific, 2000; Marina Carter, *Servants, Sirdars and Settlers: Indians in Mauritius, 1834-1874*, Delhi: Oxford University Press, 1995; Prabhu P. Mohapatra, '"Restoring the Family": Wife Murders and the Making of a Sexual Contract for Indian Immigrant Labour in the British Caribbean Colonies, 1860-1920', *Studies in History*, vol. XI, no. 2, 1995, pp. 227–60; P.C. Emmer, 'The Great Escape: The Migration of Female Indentured Servants from British India to Surinam, 1873-1916', in *Abolition and its Aftermath: The Historical Context, 1790-1916*, ed. D. Richardson, London: Frank Cass, 1985, pp. 245–66; John D. Kelly, *A Politics of Virtue: Hinduism, Sexuality, and Countercolonial Discourse in Fiji*, Chicago: University of Chicago Press, 1991; Shobita Jain and Rhoda E. Reddock, eds., *Women Plantation Workers: International Experiences*, New York: Oxford University Press, 1998.

9. Philip D. Curtin, 'Epidemiology and the Slave Trade', *Political Science Quarterly*, vol. 83, no. 2, 1968, pp. 190–216; Philip D. Curtin, *Death by Migration: Europe's Encounter with the Tropical World in the Nineteenth Century*, New York: Cambridge University Press, 1989.

10. James Backhouse, *A Narrative of a Visit to the Mauritius and South Africa*, London: Hamilton, Adams, New York: J. L. Linney, 1844.

11. Tinker, *A New System of Slavery*.
12. See K.L. Gillion, 'The Sources of Indian Emigration to Fiji', *Population Studies*, vol. X, no. 2, 1956, p. 150; Also see K.L. Gillion, 'A History of Indian Immigration and Settlement in Fiji', unpublished PhD diss., Australian National University, Australia, 1958, p. 94.
13. Tinker, *A New System of Slavery*, p. 117.
14. Emmer, 'The Great Escape', p. 248; P.C. Emmer, 'The Meek Hindu: The Recruitment of Indian Indentured Labourers for Service Overseas, 1870-1916', in *Colonialism and Migration; Indentured Labour Before and After Slavery*, ed., P.C. Emmer, Dordrecht: Martinus Nijhoff Publishers, 1986, pp. 187–207.
15. Emmer, 'The Great Escape', p. 247.
16. Prabhu P. Mohapatra, 'Eurocentrism, Forced Labour, and Global Migration: A Critical Assessment', *International Review of Social History*, vol. 52, no. 1, 2007, pp. 110–15.
17. Lal argued that the ship became the site of a 'massive social disruption'. All the travellers ate together in a *pangat* (community feast), sat together, drank water from the same container, and shared and cleaned same toilet. These activities bonded them and created a feeling of commonness, referred to as *jahaji bhai* (ship brother). See Lal, *Chalo Jahaji*.
18. Carter, *Servants, Sirdars and Settlers*, p. 295.
19. Rhoda E. Reddock, 'Indian Women and Indentureship in Trinidad and Tobago, 1845-1917', *Economic and Political Weekly*, vol. XX, no. 43, 1985, pp. 84–5.
20. Saloni Deerpalsingh and Marina Carter, *Selected Documents on Indian Immigrants in Mauritius 1834-1926*, 3 vols., Moka: Mahatma Gandhi Institute Press, 1994–6.
21. Ralph Shlomowitz and John McDonald, 'Mortality of Indian Labour on Ocean Voyages, 1843-1917', *Studies in History*, vol. 6, no. 1, 1990, pp. 35–65.
22. Shlomowitz and McDonald, 'Mortality of Indian Labour', p. 50.
23. Shlomowitz and McDonald are of the opinion that the adherence of contemporary government officials to the miasma theory also explains their continuing debate over whether deaths during the voyages were due to germs carried on board the ships at the time of embarkation, or due to germs 'spontaneously generated' from the overcrowded and unsanitary conditions in the vessels. We now know, of course, that germs causing a disease cannot be spontaneously generated, but have to be brought aboard a vessel, either through contaminated water and food, or by infected passengers and the accompanying animals. Conditions on board the vessels, such as a crowded and unsanitary environment, could then promote the spread of disease, and poor nutrition on the voyage could lower the resistance of the infected passengers.
24. Shlomowitz and McDonald, 'Mortality of Indian Labour', pp. 62–3.

25. Anil Persaud, 'Transformed Over Seas: Medical Comforts aboard Nineteenth Century Emigrant Ships', in *Labour Matter: Towards Global Histories*, ed. Prabhu P. Mohapatra and Marcel van der Linden, New Delhi: Tulika Books, 2009, pp. 22–56.
26. Ibid., p. 50.
27. Amit Kumar Mishra, *Mauritius*, New Delhi: National Book Trust, 2009; P.S. Vivek, *From Indentured Labour to Liberated Nation: Public Policy and Small Planters in Mauritius*, Bangalore: Focus Press Publication, 2007; Richard B. Allen, *Slaves, Freedmen, and Indentured Laborers in Colonial Mauritius*, Cambridge: Cambridge University Press, 1999. These works have focused on the social and economic transformations seen in the context of the reorganization of the sugar industry and the rise of big and small Indian planters. Particularly, the works of Vivek and Allen on the land acquisition process is important to understand the establishment of villages outside the sugar estates. It also explains the transformation of the Indian community from indentured labourers to independent proprietors, cultivators, and shopkeepers.
28. Kuper, *Indian People in Natal*, p. 118. She studied the family, community, caste, and religio-cultural norms of Indian settlers in the colony of Natal. She has focused on the caste, religion, and traditional derivation of Gujaratis in India and the descendants of indentured Indians (who were from Gujarat). She demonstrated that the Gujarati traders followed their endogamous marriage customs and their caste practices, while among the descendants of the indentured labourers, these practices were not so strong. She put emphasis on the condition of Hindu orthodox wives, who were expected to be pure and chaste. A man was allowed by custom to beat his wife if she had committed a misdemeanor, while the woman should not raise her hand against him, even in self-protection.
29. Surendra Bhana offers an interesting study using a new source material—the statistical information tabulated in 384 ship lists, which he himself compiled. His work provides very useful information about the indentured labourers, such as their socio-religious background, caste identities, names and places of origin, gender, physical markings, rate of mortality, etc., which is useful for a researcher who may not have the opportunity to look at the ship lists. Apart from a sketchy and brief history of the indentured system, working conditions in the plantations, employer and employee relations, etc., the book does not provide any in-depth information about the life of the indentured people in colonial Natal and nor does it adopt a critical stance towards colonial state policy.
30. Henning, *Indentured Indian in Natal*, p. 20. Here, Henning gives detailed information about the indentured system, process of recruitment of the labourers, and their living and working conditions in Natal. In the last two chapters, he deals with the political, social, and cultural lives of the Indians. Henning also describes the role of law and legislation in the life of the

indentured. He explains the loopholes in legislation that failed to provide proper facilities for the health, sanitation, and working and living conditions of these migrants. He mentions that the Indian Immigration Act of 1883 was important because it provided for proper medical facilities of the indentured labourers on board vessels and in the colony (Natal). He asserts that the system of indentured labour was inhuman and demoralizing, and that it had dehumanizing effect on the workers. He also points to the fact that the colonial government was more powerful and organized, which made the Indians in the colony helpless, and therefore they could not protest against the injustice of the state. This book is thus silent on the political protests and struggles of the immigrant labourers.

31. Palmer, *History of Indians in Natal*, p. 43.
32. Vahed and Desai, *Inside Indenture*.
33. M.D. North-Coombes, *Studies in the Political Economy of Mauritius*, Moka: Mahatma Gandhi Institute, 2000, cited in Raj Boodhoo, *Health, Disease and Indian Immigrants in Nineteenth Century Mauritius*, Port Louis: Aapravasi Ghat Trust Fund, 2010, p. 26.
34. J.B. Brain and P. Brain, 'The Health of Indentured Indian Migrants to Natal, 1860-1911', *South Africa Medical Journal*, vol. 62, no. 20, 1982, pp. 739–42.
35. Soma Hewa, *Colonialism, Tropical Disease and Imperial Medicine: Rockefeller Philanthropy in Sri Lanka*, Lanham, MD: University Press of America, 1995.
36. Ibid., p. 44.
37. Ibid., p. 41.
38. Ibid., p. 43.
39. Ibid., p. 63.
40. Aickin, 'Plantation Medicine to Public Health'.
41. Boodhoo, *Health, Disease and Indian Immigrants*.
42. Ibid., p. 333.
43. David Arnold, *Imperial Medicine and Indigenous Societies*, Delhi: Oxford University Press, 1989.
44. Ibid.; Also see Arnold, *Colonizing the Body*; Anil Kumar, *Medicine and the Raj: British Medical Policy in India, 1835-1911*, New Delhi: Sage, 1998; Deepak Kumar, ed., *Science and the Empire: Essays in the Indian Context, 1700-1947*, New Delhi: Oxford University Press, 1991.
45. Arnold, *Colonizing the Body*.
46. Samiksha Sehrawat, *Colonial Medical Care in North India: Gender, State, and Society, c.1840-1920*, New Delhi: Oxford University Press, 2013, p. xx.
47. Government regulation of the population has been characterized as 'biopolitics' by Michel Foucault. According to him, 'biopolitics' involved both the discipline of individual bodies as a machine but also the regula-tion of the health of the state's population by focusing on 'the preservation, upkeep, and conservation of the "labourforce"'. For details,

see Michel Foucault, 'The Politics of Health in the Eighteenth Century', *Power*, vol. 3 of *Essential Works of Foucault, 1954-84*, ed. James D. Faubion, tr. Robert Hurley, New York: The New Press, 1994, p. 95.

48. Arnold, *Colonizing the Body*, pp. 25–7.

49. Ibid., p. 51.

50. North-Coombes, *Studies in Political Economy of Mauritius*, cited in Boodhoo, *Health, Disease and Indian Immigrants*, p. 35.

51. Kumar, *Medicine and the Raj*, p. 10.

52. Edwin Chadwick, *Report on the Sanitary Condition of the Labouring Population of Great Britain*, London: W. Clowes and Sons, 1843, see https://babel.hathitrust.org/cgi/pt, accessed 26 July 2014.

53. Ibid.

54. David Thomson, *Europe since Napoleon*, Delhi: Surjeet Publications, 2007, pp. 158–9; Also see Eric Hobsbawm, *The Age of Revolution: 1789-1848*, England: Clays Ltd., 2008, pp. 42–72.

55. Scholars have raised questions on the term 'Western medicine' or 'colonial medicine', on the basis of the fact that it was not purely 'Western', and remained unchanged in the colonies. This monograph has used the term 'Western medicine' or 'colonial medicine' to refer to the Western (modern) medical tradition. D. Kumar and Rajshekhar Basu, in their work, have depicted the ways through which it ('Western medicine') interacted and borrowed from the indigenous medical practices. They mention that 'indigenous practitioners stoutly defended their knowledge system and did not believe that their tradition was confined in the veils of unscientific or irrational thoughts.' See Deepak Kumar and Raj Shekhar Basu, eds., *Medical Encounters in British India*, New Delhi: Oxford University Press, 2013. Also see Samiksha Sehrawat, *Colonial Medical Care in North India Gender, State, and Society c.1840-1920*, New Delhi: Oxford University Press, 2013.

56. Headrick, *Tentacles of Progress*; Headrick, *Tools of Empire*.

57. Cited in David Arnold, 'Medical Priorities and Practice in Nineteenth-Century British India', *South Asia Research*, vol. V, no. 2, 1985, p. 167.

58. Philip D. Curtin, '"The White Man's Grave": Image and Reality, 1780-1850', *Journal of British Studies*, vol. I, no. 1, 1961, pp. 94–110; Curtin, *Death by Migration*.

59. Arnold, *Imperial Medicine and Indigenous Societies*, pp. 10–11. Arnold criticized Headrick for his focus on means rather than motives.

60. Mark Harrison, *Public Health in British India: Anglo-Indian Preventive Medicine, 1859-1914*, New Delhi: Cambridge University Press, 1994, p. 2.

61. Sir Ronald Ross won the Nobel Prize for his discovery of the vector that transmitted malaria.

62. Quoted in Harrison, *Public Health in British India*, p. 151.

63. Cited in Arnold, 'Medical Priorities and Practice', p. 169.

64. Arnold, *Colonizing the Body*, p. 248.

65. Deepak Kumar, ed., *Disease and Medicine in India: A Historical Overview*, New Delhi: Tulika Books, 2001, p. xvii.
66. Biswamoy Pati and Mark Harrison, eds., *Health, Medicine and Empire: Perspectives on Colonial India*, Hyderabad: Orient Longman Limited, 2001; Also see Biswamoy Pati and Mark Harrison, eds., *The Social History of Health and Medicine in Colonial India*, London and New York: Routledge, 2009.
67. Harrison, *Public Health in British India*, p. 4.
68. Ibid., p. 5.
69. Mark Harrison, 'Public Health and Medicine in British India: An Assessment of the British Contribution', based on a paper delivered to the Liverpool Medical Society on 5 March 1988, see http://www.evolve360. co.uk/Data/10/Docs/10/10Harrison.pdf, accessed on 22 July 2014.
70. Baba Ramchandra Private Papers, file 2A, notebook 2, NMML, Delhi; Totaram Sanadhya, *Fiji Dwip Mein Mere Ikkis Varsh* (My Twenty-One Years in the Fiji Islands), Agra: Rajput Anglo-Oriental Press, 1914; 4th edn., Varanasi: Pandit Banarasidas Chaturvedi, 1973, also see Totaram Sanadhya, 'Mere Fiji Dwip Mein Ikkis Varsh and the Second Abolition', lecture at the University of Maryland, Baltimore, 4 April 2012; see www. youtube.com/watch?v=fMDS6iM8oWE, accessed December 2014; Kathinka Kerkhoff-Sinha et al., trs., *Autobiography of an Indian Indentured Labourer: Munshi Rahman Khan, 1874-1972*, Delhi: Jeevan Prakash Shipra Publications, 2005; Goonam, *Coolie Doctor: An Autobiography*, Hyderabad: Orient Longman Limited, 1998.

CHAPTER ONE

Regulating the Indentured System
Mauritius and Natal, 1834–1920

> I am happy to state that I consider their [indentured labour] introduction is an immense benefit to the proprietors in Mauritius, as well as an advantage to the Indians, but I also humbly conceive that it would be well to protect them from every chance of injustice, in a colony where there has always been such a tendency to take advantage of the labouring population.
>
> —A MAGISTRATE OF THE ROYAL COMMISSION,
> *Report of the Royal Commissioners Appointed to Enquire
> into the Treatment of Immigrants in Mauritius*

Historians have opined that the emergence of the overseas indentured labour trade in the nineteenth century was the result of two separate but overlapping factors. One of them was the shortage of labourers due to the 'emancipation' of slaves in the British plantation colonies. The second was the development of a new phase of imperialism in the nineteenth century, in which Western capital, settlers, and technology penetrated a world opened up to their overwhelming power and skill, which led to an expansion in the demand for labourers in the overseas colonies.[1]

The first section of this chapter will look at the geographical location of Mauritius and Natal, and the next section will look at the development of these two during the colonial period, which led to an increased demand for cheap and 'reliable' labour. The discussion will be followed up by a brief description of indentured migration and government policies regarding emigration. An attempt will also be made to unravel what went into the 'making' of the indentured labourers. Further, this chapter will deal briefly with the condition of the emigrants in these places.

Location of Mauritius and Natal

'If you travel in Mauritius you gather the idea that Mauritius was made first and then heaven; and that heaven was copied after Mauritius.'[2]

In one of the most strategic positions in the Indian Ocean, at a latitude of 20 °S and longitude of 57 °E, lies the famed island of Mauritius. Ranbir Singh described Mauritius on the world map as a tiny dot because of its very small geographical spread. It's about 1,400 mi. from the east coast of Africa and 500 mi. to the east of Madagascar. It has an area of just 720 sq. mi. By geological standards, the island is very young. It is considered to be a late starter in terms of having human inhabitants,[3] though now it attracts thousands of tourists every year. About 13 million years ago, volcanic activity started far below the surface of the sea and masses of molten lava swelled and rose up to the surface of the water, cooled down, and solidified; with further volcanic activity, the solidified lava rose higher than any of the peaks that exist today.[4] Mauritius was formed during three periods of eruption, from the early Tertiary to the mid-Pleistocene. The earliest period gave rise to a great cone, but erosion and subsequent intrusion from later periods of volcanism have reduced the original cone to fragments.[5] Jagged, tooth-like mountains are all that remain of the original caldera. Lava from twenty well-preserved craters, which flowed in all directions, whose remains are found across the upland plateau, helped in the creation of the fertile soil.[6]

Among Indians, Mauritius was known as 'Mareech-Desh'. In Indian mythology, its existence has a different story:

Kahani bahut purani hai us samay ki jab Ram ko apane pita ke vachanon ki laaj rakhane ke liye apani patni Sita aur Bhai ke saath vanvaas jaana pada tha. Panchvati me Laxaman ke dwara Raavan ki bahin ki naak kat liye jaane ke baad, Lanka ke raja Raavan ne badala lene ke liye ek jaal failaya, usane Mareech ko sone ke hiran ka roop dekar panchvati bheja jahan Ram ke haathon vo mara gaya. Ram ka teer jab use laga to vo apane asali roop me aa gaya. Mareech ne karahate hue Ram se kaha ki 'aapane mujh par bahut badi kripa ki hai ki mujhe aapake haathon yeh shareer chodane ka sobhagya mila. Ab meri ek hi ichchha baanki hai ki aap mujhe aisa vardan den ki meri aatma hamesha aapaka naam sunti rahe.' Bhagwan ka haath use laga to vah moti me badal gaya jise unhone saagar me phenk diya, door se jab ise naavik dekhate the to yahi samajhate the ki yah ek dweep hai…jab kaliyug me British kaal me bharat se khaskar bihar se bhartiy majdoor aaye to ve apane saath ramayan bhi lekar aaye…dinbhar ki majdoori ke baad raat ko ve ramayan ka path karate the, tabhi jaakar Mareech ki ichchha puri ho paai.[7]

[The story is very old and goes back to the time when lord Rama had to go into exile along with his wife Sita and brother in order to keep his father's word. In the Panchvati forest, Laxman had a tussle with Raavan's sister and struck her nose off; and so Raavan conspired to take revenge. He sent Mareech in the guise of a golden deer to Panchvati forest where Mareech was killed by Ram. Mareech, before dying, prayed to Ram, 'Lord, you have done a big favour as I am freed from this body by your hand. My only wish now is that my soul always gets reminded of your name.' When Ram touched him, Mareech was magically converted into a pearl; and Ram threw the pearl into the ocean. When the sailors saw it from a distance, they conceived it to be an island…During the time of the British, Indians, particularly from Bihar, who came to Mauritius as indentured, carried Ramayana along with them…they used to read it every evening after their day-long work. It was then that the wish of Mareech came to be fulfilled.] (Translation mine)

Mauritius has a typical subtropical maritime climate, which has hot, humid (frequently above 80 per cent) summers (November to April), and mild winters (May to October).[8] The hills of Mauritius, its rivers, valleys, waterfalls, plateaus, plains, and coral reefs constitute its landscape; mountains cover about 18 per cent of the landscape of the island. There are three main ranges—Marklong Range in the north-west region; Riviere Noire and Savanne Ranges in the south-west region; and Grand Port Range in the south-east region of the island. Apart from these ranges, some isolated mountains also dot the landscape. Some of these mountains have distinct physical appearances, and they are named accordingly. For example, the Pieter Both Mountain has a rock on the top; in popular idiom of Indian diaspora in Mauritius, it is called '*Mudia Pahar*' or mountain with a head, and is associated with a mythical story of a fairy and Indian immigrant labourer. Again, the Le Pouce Mountain is in the shape of a thumb; the Lion Mountain in the Grand Port Range appears like a sitting lion; and the Trois Mamelles has three protruding peaks.[9] Outside the ring of mountain ranges are the low coastal plains, which also include undulated slopes, and cover about 46 per cent of the land mass of Mauritius. The largest plain here is the Northern Plains. The plains are used for cultivation of sugar cane and vegetables. Rivers and streams, along with lakes (both natural and man-made), are the source of water for domestic use, for irrigation, and for the production of hydroelectricity. In addition to many man-made reservoirs, there are two natural lakes (crater lakes) in Mauritius; one of those, the Grand Bassin, is an important place of worship for the Hindu population of Mauritius. It is called the 'Ganga Talab' and worshippers of lord Shiva from all cross the island, during the Shivratri festival, come to this pond and collect water to pour on the idol of Shiva in the nearby temple complex.[10]

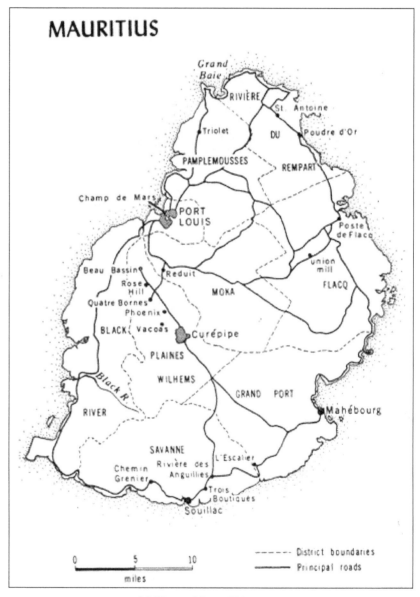

MAP 1.1: Map of Mauritius

Source: Adele Smith Simmons, *Modern Mauritius: The Politics of Decolonization*, Bloomington: Indiana University Press, 1982, p. 2.

The Republic of Mauritius includes the island of Mauritius and three dependencies—the islands of Rodrigues, Agalega, and Cargados Carajos Shoals (also known as Saint Brandon island). The national capital is Port Louis, which is situated in the north-west part of Mauritius. Port Louis is also the main harbour and port for commercial purposes. The island of Mauritius (see Map 1.1) is divided into nine districts (district capitals are given in parentheses): Riviere du Rempart (Mapou), Pamplemousses (Triolet), Port Louis (Port Louis), Moka (Moka), Flacq (Centre de Flacq), Plaines Wilhems (Curepipe and Rose-Hill), Grand Port (Rose-Belle), Riviere Noire or Black River (Bambous), and Savanne (Souillac).

Natal (see Map 1.3), now called KwaZulu-Natal, on the other hand, is situated in South Africa (see Map 1.2); it was named by Vasco da Gama in the fifteenth century.[11] Natal is a fertile strip of land lying between the Drakensberg and the south-east coast of Africa, and is around 35,500 sq. mi. in area.[12] The province has three different

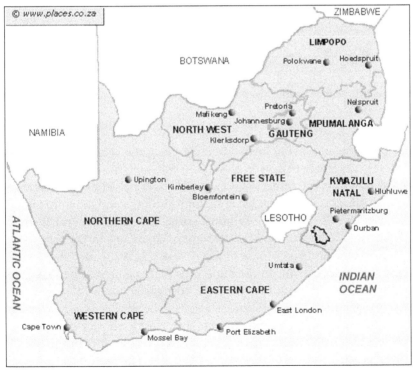

MAP 1.2: Map of South Africa

Source: https://www.places.co.za/html/visualfind.html, accessed 6 March 2015.

MAP 1.3: Map of Natal

Source: http://www.south-africa-info.com/kwazulu-natal/main.htm, accessed 6 March 2015.

geographical areas—the lowland region along the Indian Ocean coast, which is extremely narrow in the south, widening in the northern part of the province; the central region, called the Natal Midlands, which is an undulating hilly plateau rising towards the west; and the third region consists of the two mountainous areas, namely the Drakensberg Mountains in the west and the Lebombo Mountains in the north.

The Drakensberg Mountains experience heavy winter snow, with light snow occasionally on the highest peaks in summer. The Zululand north coast has the warmest climate and highest humidity, supporting many sugar cane farms around Pongola. The midlands areas have a more temperate climate, and are suitable for cattle rearing and growing maize and other cereals. There are also several coal mines in this area.[13] Silver, copper, and iron are also found in this province. Natal receives sufficient rainfall and thus has never suffered from droughts. After the defeat of the Boers, the British acquired complete control over the useful and profitable harbours of Natal, but in those days the lack of an efficient transportation system was a major disadvantage in this area. Although there were many rivers, they could not be used as a means of transport.

Discovery and Early Inhabitants of Mauritius and Natal

The discovery of Mauritius is one of the most contentious issues in the historiography of the country. The earliest human settlement in Mauritius is about 300 years old. The island had no permanent population, but only visitors in earlier days. The existing historiography claims that the Phoenicians arrived there about 2,500 years ago, and who may have been the first people to visit Mauritius. The Arabs arrived in the tenth century or earlier. They were probably the first to record Mauritius on their sea charts. But they did not make any attempt to settle there.

During the end of the fifteenth century, the Portuguese wanted to challenge the Arab trading hegemony and captured the entire Indian Ocean trade network. They explored Mauritius in the first decade of the sixteenth century and named it 'Ilha do Cirne', or Island of Swans.[14] The Portuguese did not live permanently in Mauritius either, but they introduced pigs, goats and cattle, and (unintentionally) rats to the island. They were followed by the Dutch, under the leadership of a merchant from Amsterdam, in 1598. Unlike the previous visitors, however, the Dutch occupied Mauritius and remained there from 1598 to 1710. They named it 'Mauritius' after Prince Maurice of Orange. Cornelins Simonsz Gooyer was appointed as the first Dutch Governor of Mauritius. He was sent with a contingent of twenty-five men to commence human settlement in Mauritius and develop it for Dutch commercial interests.

However, the Dutch could not succeed in settling there because of several reasons. It is often said that the Dutch failed because of the rats that they had brought over (which destroyed their agriculture products), and the adverse conditions of climate (cyclones, droughts, and floods were common in Mauritius). Another reason for their failure was their small number. At any time, the number of inhabitants was not more than 400, which was neither sufficient for clearing the land to make it cultivable nor to begin community life.[15] Although they planted oranges, bananas, and coconuts and other fruit trees, the Dutch did not have any great plans for the development of the island, and thus it gradually turned into a burden for them. Mauritius remained unoccupied and uninhabited for only five years after the withdrawal of the Dutch in 1710, after which the French appeared on the scene. A French ship under Guillaume Dufresne d'Arsel, sailing home from the Indies, encountered rough weather and reached Mauritius in 1715. Captain d'Arsel thereupon hoisted the French flag and took possession of the island in the name of His most 'Christian Majesty' (the King of France, Louis XV) and Mauritius was renamed 'Isle de France'.[16] The French colony grew steadily and Mauritius remained under French occupation for nearly a century.

The great French colonial administrator and famous naval officer, Bertrand-Francois Mahe de La Bourdonnais, ruled over the island with great energy and sagacity for 18 years. He promoted the cultivation of sugar cane on a large scale, built roads, and established the capital of Mauritius at Port Louis.[17] The island thus prospered under French occupation. The Dutch had brought slaves from Africa to the island, and the French followed in their path, bringing in more slaves. By 1797, there were about 4,500 whites and more or less 60,000 blacks in Mauritius.[18] During this period, France and Britain were in conflict with each other in India. In this conflict with the British, France realized that Mauritius would be an important post for them, and therefore they paid careful attention to the fortification of the island. The name of Port Louis was also changed to Port Napoleon in 1804. The island's territorial boundaries were defined and the fortifications of the port and town were strengthened. Many new constructions were undertaken to build roads, buildings, etc. However all this was short-lived. Soon, Mauritius was attacked by the British naval force, after their recapturing of the Cape in 1806.[19]

Mauritius was captured by the East India Company in 1810. Under the terms of capitulation, the French colonists were allowed to keep all their laws and customs; and the civil code of Napoleon, though modified, is still in force in Mauritius. French civilians were given the option of leaving the island within two years. Thus, the island with its 75,000 inhabitants consisting of whites, blacks, and coloured people passed to the British Crown. The Treaty of Paris in 1814 finally ceded Isle de France to the English, who restored the Dutch name (Mauritius) of the island.[20] The history of British rule in Mauritius was marked by three distinctive features. The first was the abolition of slavery in 1810, the second feature was the evolution of Mauritius as a sugar colony, and the third was the immigration of indentured labourers from India.

In Natal, on the other hand, the British came as traders and missionaries who wanted to propagate religion to 'civilize' the warlike Africans. They had been in the province since 1824, by when a small, unofficial British settlement on the coast had grown around the harbour of Port Natal. Gradually, the British started exercising control over the local people, such as the Zulus and the Boers, and their economic resources. However, they soon had to face tough resistance from these people.

The Boers, or Afrikaners, were mainly descendants of the early Dutch colonists, with 'Boer' being the Dutch word for 'farmer'. Many Boers were also descended from French Huguenots or German settlers. They formed the majority of the white population of South Africa. Afrikaans, one of the official languages of the Republic of South Africa, developed from seventeenth century Dutch. The Zulus were the largest ethnic group in South Africa. They believed that they were descendants of a chief from the Congo area and in the sixteenth century they migrated south, picking up many of the traditions and customs of the San, who also inhabited this area of South Africa. During the seventeenth and eighteenth centuries, many of the powerful local chiefs made treaties and gave control of the Zulu villages to the British. The conversation between Chief Dingaan, the successor of Chaka (chief of the country), and Captain Gardiner would be helpful in understanding the nature of the conflict that the British faced in their purpose of expansion. As Dingaan said to Gardiner:

…You are come to establish teachers of your religion among us. I cannot allow that here, but I give up all claim to the country between the Tutugal and Umzimcoolu Rivers and the Quathlamba Mountains. There you may teach. I wish to be friendly with the white King, but some of your people at Natal are unruly; they have enticed away my people, taken Zoolah women, and traded where I said I did not want them. My councillors asked me to kill them, but I did not do it. They must have a chief to whom I can speak.[21]

The British expansion caused much conflict because the Zulus had strong village government systems which fought against the British; but the Zulus could not win because their strength was not enough to counter the British. After the war, much of the Zulu area was given to the British. There was a war between the British and the Zulu again in 1879, in which the Zulu were initially victorious, but were conquered by the British in the subsequent six months, and the Zulu kings were sent into exile. The Zulu kingdom was consequently divided. In 1906, another Zulu uprising occurred, and they tried to gain back what they considered to be their ancient kingdom. However, the British achieved an easy victory over them, and gained complete control over the region.

During 1835–7, some 10,000 Boer herdsmen, farmers, and their families, who came to be known as Voortrekkers, left the Cape in the 'Great Trek', seeking new lands and freedom from British authority. The Boers, who were forced to leave Natal, migrated north and east and settled in different parts of South Africa, mainly in Transvaal and Orange River areas, founding the Orange Free State, and Transvaal as their territory. They had a very strong feeling of patriotism and soon founded their own republic in these areas. But the discovery of gold and diamond near the Orange River and in Kimberly forced the British to bring these areas under their direct control. Since these areas were under the command of the Boer Republics and the African tribes, therefore, for a short while after the discovery of diamonds, it was uncertain where the political control of this valuable new asset would lie. The diamond and gold treks were largely responsible for reuniting South Africa; for eliminating independent African tribes; and for extending British control not only to the northern borders of the Transvaal, but far beyond into Rhodesia and Central Africa.

In 1877, the British government interfered in the affairs of Transvaal on the grounds of bankruptcy and collapse of the internal administration. Soon, in 1877 itself, the British succeeded in hoisting their flag there, without any overt opposition. However, this annexation was short-lived, because in 1880, the Boers resisted and declared their independence. In 1881, they defeated the British at Majuba and consequently, the British government signed the Pretoria Convention, granting independence to Transvaal, but the foreign and native policies were still subject to the British control. Thus, the British adopted an expansionist policy for economic growth and development. Minor clashes between the two took place in the 1890s, but in 1899, a full scale war broke out. This war is known as the second Boer war. Initially, the Boers had an advantage over the British, because of their guerilla warfare method. But the British adopted harsh counter-measures to bring them to terms. Lord Roberts, who replaced General Redvers Buller, formally annexed Transvaal on 31 May 1902 and a peace treaty was signed between the Boers and the British. Thus, the two republics—Transvaal and Cape Town—came under the British flag, making the unification of South Africa possible. The British expanded their power and established their control over Cape Town, Orange Free State, and Transvaal in the later periods and finally, on 31 May 1910, the Union of South Africa came into existence. This union had a great impact on the economic development of South Africa. Economically speaking, a closer union that would abolish custom barriers and have a common railway policy had become highly desirable. Also, though there were still many differences, the four colonies (Cape Town, Orange Free State, Transvaal, and Natal) had much in common in terms of law, religion, social customs, and pastimes.[22]

Emergence of Mauritius and Natal as Plantation Colonies

The Dutch were the first to introduce sugarcane cultivation in Mauritius, though it did not start off in full force till the arrival of the French Governor La Bourdonnais, who took keen interest in growing sugarcane on a large scale. Sugarcane is well-suited to Mauritius, as it is one of the few crops that can withstand the cyclonic weather conditions of the island.[23] Two sugar estates were established in 1740, and by 1789, there were ten sugar factories in Mauritius, with only 1,000 arpents of land under cultivation. In the beginning of the nineteenth century, with the increasing price of sugar after the Haitian revolution and the Napoleonic wars, there was a change in the attitude of the colonizers. Now they started to take interest in sugarcane cultivation. During 1806–10, the total area under cultivation reached about 9,000–10,000 arpents and the sugar production increased to between 3,000 and 4,000 tons a year.[24] By the beginning of the twentieth century, the Mauritius sugar industry dominated the sugar market of the world, and in the period of 1930–9, it had produced an yearly average of 251,792 metric tons (see Table 1.1).

Earlier, the Caribbean colonies exported sugar to the British, and a higher export duty was imposed on Mauritian sugar. Eventually, in 1825, due to the Mauritian planters' and the British sugar merchants' persuasion, the preferential duty for Caribbean sugar export was abolished and Mauritius was allowed to export sugar to Britain at the same tariff rates.[25] On account of this encouragement, sugar production in Mauritius doubled from 10,869 tons in 1825 to 21,244 tons in 1826. In course of time, Mauritian economy emerged as a monocrop cultivation culture, in which people devoted all their energy to sugarcane cultivation; they wanted to uproot everything else and plant sugarcane.[26] From 1806

TABLE 1.1: Mauritius Sugar and the World Market, 1820–1939

Period	Average yearly production (in metric tons)	% of world sugar cane production	% of world sugar production
1820–9	15,559	–	–
1830–9	33,443	–	–
1840–9	45,388	4.8	4.5
1850–9	97,407	7.8	6.5
1860–9	115,778	7.8	5.6
1870–9	112,184	6.2	3.7
1880–9	116,016	5.3	2.5
1890–9	132,663	4.3	1.8
1900–9	182,848	3.1	1.4
1910–19	225,775	2.2	1.3
1920–9	225,808	1.5	1.0
1930–9	251,792	1.5	0.9

Source: Larry W. Bowman, *Mauritius: Democracy and Development in the Indian Ocean*, London: Westview Press, 1991, p. 20.

to 1830, the percentage of cultivable land for food crops dropped from 65 to 30.4 per cent, while land allocated for cash or export crops jumped from 35 to 69.6 per cent.[27]

The first British governor of the island, Sir Robert Farquhar, encouraged sugar cane cultivation by obtaining equalization of duty in 1825, and London merchants helped in the development of the industry by providing loans to planters amounting to 1.5 million pounds between 1826 and 1848. This transfer of funds brought in its wake a group of English traders who settled in the island as intermediaries between the London financiers and the local planters; they subsequently moved into the sugar industry after acquiring landed properties.[28] The sugar industry of Mauritius was in its infancy, when the great enthusiasm that had swept over Mauritian planters in 1843 gave way in 1846 to gloomy anticipation of the future when an unknown cane disease, the blight, ruined the crops and absorbed the indemnity that the slave owners had received at the time of liberation. The money advanced by London financiers in support of an industry established on the strength of the 1825 protective duties; was also absorbed.[29]

Sugar production in Mauritius grew steadily right into the twentieth century. The heyday for the Mauritian economy, however, was in the

1850s, when the island had clearly emerged as the principal British sugar producing colony. From 1855 to 1859, Mauritius produced 9.4 per cent of the world's sugar cane and 7.4 per cent of the world's sugar. The values and institution of the colonial slave society deeply influenced the emerging plantation society. In his work on the indentured labour system, Hugh Tinker argued 'a monoculture creates a particular kind of slavery and sugar created an authoritarian system…there is a symbiosis which links sugar and servitude together.'[30] It was in this setting of industrial agriculture, where the challenge to the system would be 'to produce a larger volume of sugar at cheaper prices that indentured labour was drawn.'[31] As stated by Larry W. Bowman, the demand for sugar in the market was 'one of the massive demographic forces in the world history'.[32] Bowman stated, 'this was certainly true for Mauritius, where the surge of immigrants during the middle of the nineteenth century totally changed the demographic character of the island.'[33]

The rapidly expanding sugar economy necessitated that the planters look for alternative supplies of labour, as they could gauge that the existing slave population would not be enough to meet the increasing demand for planters. Consequently, they explored every possible source for bringing in Indian labourers under the indentured system. With the introduction of Indian indentured labourers, the Mauritian sugar industry reached its zenith in the late 1850s. In 1860, there were 258 sugar mills running in Mauritius. Sir James Higginson, Governor of Mauritius (1851 to 1857), focused his attention on the importance of Indian workers in the Mauritian sugar industry and pointed out—'The prosperity of the colony is to be attributed, first and foremost, to the unique expansion of sugar cultivation made possible by Indian labour.'[34]

In the beginning of the 1860s, the island's sugar industry declined because of varied pressures. First, as sugar beet production and sugarcane production in other countries increased, world prices declined. Second, the opening of the Suez Canal in 1869 shifted trade routes away from the Indian Ocean. And, in addition to regularly occurring droughts and cyclones, a deadly malaria epidemic killed more than 40,000 people here between 1867 and 1869. As a result, the Franco-Mauritian plantation owners responded in several ways. They cut costs by centralizing sugar production in fewer factories.[35] Further, these circumstances also affected the Indian labourers in the colony and the recruitment of new indentured labourers from India. J.F. Trotter (Protector of Immigrants in Mauritius) mentioned in his letter to the acting colonial secretary that:

…There certainly has been depression in the sugar industry, which has had a serious effect upon the Indian labourers in this island…able body labourers find work easily enough at the present moment, but at rates lower than was paid before the depression. Indian labourers who have large families find it difficult now to make both ends meet, especially if their children are too small to work….

…it is principally from this class that application are received for free return passage to India, and in no case is such an application refused to pay their embarkation…it is probable that the recent rise in the prices of our staple product, sugar, may renew confidence in capitalists and thus make the money market easier. If this happens as I hope it will, the planters will be able to spend more money in the cultivation of their land and the Indians will soon find more remunerative employment than can be had at present.[36]

In order to solve the problem of the small sugar estates' inability to finance modern improvements, the planters had resorted to the establishment of factories equipped with modern machinery, which would process the canes from several estates surrounding the factory. The process of centralization began in 1860, and fifty-five factories closed down during the following decades.[37] It was the beginning of a new era in Mauritius. Among other developments, it saw the beginning of the separation of the processing of sugarcane from the cultivation of the crop in the sugar industry, and the establishment of Indian labourers as small planters. With the establishment of centralized factories, the process of manufacturing sugar was carried out with all the advantages of an improved system under the direction of competent technicians.[38]

Furthermore, to increase the profitability of their operations, from the 1870s to about the 1920s, the planters sold the less productive portions of their landholdings. This process was known as grand 'morcellement'. The idea behind this was to sell off barren and rocky lands on the hills to the 'old immigrants'[39] on the condition that they cultivated sugarcane on them.[40] In spite of the meager wages and the adverse conditions prevailing during the early years, the immigrants saved some money, which enabled them to buy these lands. This process permitted many Indians, who could put together enough capital, to become small landowners. This meant that for the first time, sugarcane was produced on small plots with free labour. By the year 1900, 30 per cent of the total land under cane cultivation was held by Indians or peasant proprietors, and it contributed to almost 20 per cent of the national cane production.[41] Also, at the expiration of their estate residence, the indentured labourers were induced to accept land for establishment of Indian villages, instead of providing them with return passage. Thus, the Indian labourers established permanent ties with the colony.

After Mauritius went into decline, Natal became the most attractive destination in the Indian Ocean for Indians, because of the expanding employment opportunities in South Africa.[42] From 1850 to 1870, there was a tremendous growth in the economy of Natal. The commercialization of crops and establishment of banks by the British settlers played an important role in the process of diversification of the economy of Natal. Natal's economy was not based only on sugarcane plantations like Mauritius. By 1863, there were already five banks in Natal, with the first one—Natal Bank—being established in 1854.[43] These banks provided Natal with capital essential for the economic growth of this colony.

In the earlier period, the British experimented with a varied number of agricultural products in order to commercialize agriculture. Initially, they got little success, but soon sugarcane cultivation was started in the coastal area of Natal. The wide coastal belt, with its sub-tropical maritime climate and rich soil proved to be ideal conditions for the cultivation of sugarcane.[44] By the middle of 1850s, there was an increase in the number of sugarcane crushing/processing factories, which helped in the commercialization of agriculture, based on the plantation model of farming.

In 1847, the colonist Edmund Morewood, father of the sugar industry in Natal, established the first plantation there. He arrived in Natal for the first time in 1833, and after having spent a considerable time in Australia, New Zealand, and Mauritius. He returned to Natal in 1838 after the Battle of Blood River, when British military forces had been temporarily withdrawn and the flag of the Voortrekker Republic of Natalia had been hoisted at the port. Morewood was on good terms with the Voortrekkers, and was one of the men chosen to visit the Zulu King Mpande, in the hopes of making a peace treaty. In 1840, Morewood was appointed Harbour Master and Commissioner of Customs under the Republican government, and it was in this capacity that he became involved in the events of 1842, when the vessels *Conch* and *Southampton* brought reinforcements to assist in raising the siege of a British force at what is now the Old Fort, Durban. Morewood remained in Natal and though the British authorities retained some understandable suspicions as to his allegiance, he quickly adjusted to the new British regime and began to pursue his interest in sugarcane cultivation. In November 1847, the first plant was brought to Natal from Mauritius on the *Sarah Bell*, by the Milner Brothers.

According to John Robinson:[45]

...before 1850 agriculture in this colony was confined to the growth of a little wheat by the Boers, and of a fair quantity of maize by the natives. Cotton culture had been attempted at New Germany (by the Bergtheil Settlers), a few coffee bushes were bearing berries in the garden of a private householder of Durban, and a small patch of sugarcane was being planted by Mr Morewood at Compensation. Arrowroot (to a value of £31) was the first agricultural product to be exported from Natal, in 1853. But the following year the export record showed a new export: 'Sugar, £2'. It was a small beginning, but one of great significance. After that date, sugar was exported every year in increasing quantities. As Morewood wrote to his brother in 1848, 'I still think that sugar will be a staple article of Natal.'[46]

George Lamond, who arrived in Durban in June 1850, also noted: '... We had six acres under cane...When I left in 1854 we had more than 100 acres of cane ready for crushing.'[47]

In January 1852, *The Natal Times* reported that E. Morewood Esq. had succeeded in perfecting the process of production of sugar on his estate, and that the sample shown was of quality to prove incontestably the necessity for adaption of the coastal lands of the colony for the successful production of this valuable article.[48] By 1854, sugarcane was being grown at Umhlali, Tongaat, Umgeni, Umbilo, Isipingo, and Umkomaas, and there were six sugar mills at work.[49] Ephraim Frederick Rathbone, Caractacus Reliance Rathbone, Archibald Sinclair, Charles Povall, John Leyland Feilden, William Joyner, Michael Jeffls, and Richard ('Dick') King, were the main sugarcane planters in Natal.[50]

By 1860, about 4,953 ha. in Natal, mostly on the north coast, were planted with cane and twenty-three sugar mills were in operation. After 1860, the industry changed in character due to the investment of capital in the introduction of indentured workers from India as a reliable labour force, and the use of new strains of sugarcane plants.[51] Apart from that, the Natal colonial government's tariff policy also proved favourable for the growth of the sugar industry, and consequently, the planters. In 1864, there were sixty mills, of which fifty-six were steam-driven.[52] The government was able and willing to intervene to protect the planters against foreign competition, without making any great financial sacrifices to executive commitments extended.[53] As a result, Natal was able to operate a tariff policy that was more or less consistently favorable to sugar. In 1856, 1867, 1876, and 1886, important alterations were made to the sugar duties in the colony, in order to protect the interests of the planters.[54] As Peter Richardson mentioned:

Positive discrimination in favor of the sugar planters was further extended through 'free import schedules' which operated from 1856 onwards. Similarly, rum (an important and lucrative by-product of sugar) was subject to increasingly favorable protection. Between 1846 and 1867, the protective duty on proof spirits was raised, from two shillings per gallon to over eight shillings.[55]

Thus, these government policies helped the sugar industry to grow to a considerable extent. The growth of the sugar industry, in turn, led to economic growth in the colony, which increased the demand for labour force.

Sugar production, with a strict schedule of planting, weeding, and harvesting (the cane has to be cut as soon as it ripens, otherwise it rapidly loses its sucrose content), was a labour-intensive work then. Consequently, the planters faced difficulties in maintaining a constant labour force, as the local population was not willing to sell their labour to the white planters. The colonizers portrayed Africans as 'uncivilized' and 'barbarous', and their 'civilizing mission' was often driven by the need to turn Africans into labourers for the colonists. The colonial state thus made several efforts to win over the local people, but those were all in vain.

In such circumstances, the Natal planters pressurized their government to import Indians as indentured labourers. Most of the indentured workers and non-indentured African labourers did unskilled work; and some Indians were hired to do skilled work. However, most of the skilled work was done by the whites, many of whom came from Mauritius with some experience in the sugar industry. The work assignment on the plantations was a racially differentiated hierarchy of skill and control.[56] Indentured labour was indispensable to a successful sugar industry and growth in output went hand in hand with the increase in the number of Indian labourers. In 1880, some 7,328 ha. were under cane cultivation and seventy mills were in operation.[57] By the mid-1880s, with a resident indentured population of some 10,000 Indians, sugar production doubled to 20,000 tons and sugar export was worth £215,000.[58]

Natal's sugar had three main outlets: the Cape, which took 50 per cent of the sugar between 1852 and 1900; Witwatersrand, in the South African Republic, after the 1880s; and the domestic market. The percentage of exported sugar increased from 32 per cent to 65 per cent by the year 1900.[59]

During 1865–9, there was a short-term depression in the sugar industry of Natal. This was due to intensive monoculture and the consequent sapping of the coastal soil's natural fertility. The lack of capital and natural disasters that hit the industry from time to time were some of the factors that adversely affected the sugar industry. In the case of the Umzinto Sugar Company, a more profound reason for the failure to develop central milling was found in the infrastructural obstacles. These obstacles for the planters became strikingly evident in the depression of 1865–9. Another consequence of the crisis of the late 1860s was an almost permanent hostility towards the sugar industry on part of the banks, since it had failed 'through too much to do with sugar'.[60] The aim was to drive many planters into the hands of merchant brokers in search of credit, and encumber their estates with debts through the high rates of interests and commissions that such consignees extracted.[61] Apart from these, the market for Natal sugar posed serious problems for planters. Crop disposal was a constant difficulty, and getting cane to the mill in the age of the ox wagon limited both the extent of cane acreages and the economic capacity of the mills. During this time, railway networks were not developed in Natal. It was only after the 1870s, and because of the development of diamond fields, that the prospects of a rich interior trade encouraged the plans for the development of railways, from which the sugar industry stood to gain a lot.[62]

During the later decades of the nineteenth century, there was a decline in sugar production. This difficult economic condition forced small planters to leave the individual production process. Although small plantations remained a feature of the Natal sugar industry for another twenty years, their importance declined significantly after the 1880s. By contrast, there began to emerge a highly capitalized and extensive system of large milling and planting concerns. This was the beginning of the productive unit known today in the South African sugar industry as the: 'miller-cum-planter'.[63] From the 1880s, domestically owned plantations were replaced by centralized factories owned by large corporations such as Tongaat Hulett and Reynolds Brother. The numbers of mills declined from seventy-five in 1877 to thirty-seven in 1898.[64] By 1910, the industry had been reorganized thoroughly and only twenty-five mills remained in use, although 23,658 ha. of land were under cane plantation.[65]

The emergence of miller-cum-planter estates was not the only result of centralization of sugar production at the end of the nineteenth century in Natal. There was also a perceptible growth in sugar cultivation and demand for new areas of land to increase the actual and potential production.[66] For example, in the 1880s there was a demand to break up the African reserve lands on the coastal belt to increase white settlements, for sugar production. Also, in the 1890s, Britishers put pressure on the Africans to open Zululand to white settlement, again largely to promote the cultivation of sugarcane.[67] The annexation of Zululand by Natal (British government) in 1897 provided the expansionists with a major opportunity for the establishment of a central factory system. This paved the way for the beginning of a new era in the history of the sugar industry.

Natal had a diversified economy in which other industrial sectors also played a very important role. The other leader in the agricultural sector of Natal's economy was tea plantations that gained much prominence in the 1890s. The Natal tea planters imported tea seeds from Assam and other significant tea growing areas. By 1891, there were twenty-five tea estates in the Tugela divisions. In 1890–1 Hulett's and Kearsney's estates produced over 300,000 pounds of tea, with an estimated value of 15,000 pound sterlings. Apart from these two (tea and sugar), there were also other commercial crops like coffee, tobacco, beans, maize, and myriad of fruits and vegetables that added a good portion of income to the economy of Natal. These agricultural produce also contributed to the growth of the industrial sector.

The discovery of diamond and gold in the Orange River region and around Kimberley in 1871 had an significant impact on the economic development of Natal. These discoveries brought Natal closer to other parts of South Africa. This also gave birth to the industrial revolution in South Africa.

During the 1870s and the 1880s, other emerging sectors like the railways and the coal mines also depended on the continuous and cheap supply of indentured labourers. In 1870, the advent of railways proved instrumental in the development of the country by solving the problem of transportation. Initially, the construction of the railways was under the control of a private company, but it was taken over by the Natal government, and consequently the Natal Government Railway (NGR) was formed. From 1874 to 1895, 309 mi. of track had been laid to reach the Transvaal border.[68] The coal mines also developed at a great pace. In 1909, there were more than 60 mines in the colony.[69] Thus, the growth of the mining industry, the spread of railways, and the quickened pace of urbanization in South Africa resulted in the development of new markets and a steady demand for Natal's agricultural products.[70]

The indentured Indians in Natal, besides working in the plantations, also worked in hospitals, hotels, restaurants, private clubs, dockyards, and as domestic and 'special' servants; they were at times also employed as policemen, clerks, and interpreters as well.[71] It should be noted that this stratum of Indians was more conscious about their position and condition than the labourers working in the plantations and other industries.

Different sectors of Natal's economy were all thus heavily dependent on the indentured labourers. Sometimes this demand was so high that it was very difficult to fulfill it. In 1903, the emigration agent received applications from 15,000 indentured labours, while only 8,000 labourers were supplied. Apart from this, the increasing white population also resulted in an increase in the demand for indentured labourers as domestic servants, who received higher wages in comparison to the plantation labourers.[72] The distribution of indentured labourers in Natal is given in Table 1.2.

The importance of indentured labour in the diversified economy of colonial Natal, even in the year when the migration of indentured labourers was stopped, is shown in Table 1.2. Further, it is important to note that the number of indentured labourers in the sugar plantations (in spite of being the largest employer) was less than one-third of the total indentured population. The Protector J.A. Polkinghorne once remarked '...without Indians, Natal employers can do absolutely

TABLE 1.2: Distribution of Indentured Labour in Natal, 1909

Sector	Number of labourers
Farming	6,146
Sugar estates	7,008
Coal mines	3,239
Tea estates	1,722
Natal Government Railway	2,371
Domestic servants	1,949
Corporations	1,062
Brick yards, etc.	740
Wattle plantations	606
Landing and shipping agents	432
Miscellaneous	313
Total	25,569
Number of employers	2,429

Source: C.G. Henning, *The Indentured Indian in Natal, 1860-1917*, Delhi: Promila & Co., 1993, p. 123.

nothing'.[73] They (colonial authorities) also accepted that 'employment of indentured labour has provided opportunities for whites that would otherwise have not existed'.[74] Natal's political economy was not based only on the agricultural sector, but also on diversified industrial and service sectors. The different sectors of economy made Natal different from the other colonial plantations. This economic diversity also forced the Natal government to change its policies, from time to time, towards the indentured migrants.

Indian Migration to Mauritius and Natal

The British and French colonies that were importing Indian labourers were in the tropical belt; the only exception was Natal, which is in the sub-tropical region. The original natives of these countries (the colonies), living for generations by practicing subsistence agriculture, were usually unfit for farming on a large scale. The European enterprises attacked these countries with the hope of carrying off the agricultural produce which were usually not available or were of inferior quality in their own countries, but found the indigenous natives unsuited for aiding them in work. Therefore, coolie labour had to be introduced, and the only places where suitable labour was found to be available were India and China. When slavery was abolished by the British Parliament in 1834, the slaves were allowed to refuse to work on the fields. In such circumstances, the plantation colonies were forced to look towards India and China, since the inhabitants of these countries were considered to be able-bodied labourers with considerable agricultural skill and a wonderful capacity for continuous hard work.

Indians, however, were not altogether unknown in pre-British Mauritius. There is mention of a man named Calcuty, who accompanied the Dutch when they finally withdrew from Mauritius in 1710,— Calcuty is the inflected form of 'kalkatyia', i.e. a person (or thing) from Calcutta.[75] Mauritius had quite a sizeable Indian population during the French period; and forty Indian labourers from Pondicherry were brought to Mauritius in the year 1736. They worked as artisans in the construction of Port Louis harbour.[76] Some Indian traders also settled down in Mauritius during the French period. They formed a large section of the Indian population. Convicts from Bengal worked as domestic servants in Mauritius. Indian labourers also worked in the construction of roads and buildings, and the demand for these labourers was quite high. The Hindu settlers in Mauritius were called 'Malabars' and the Muslims, 'Lascars'. They were gradually converted to Christianity, married to Mauritian (Negro) women, and were merged with the local population. Mauritius was the first British colony to import free labour (non-slave labourers; in this case, the indentured were considered as free labour) in a large number from another part of the British Empire. In 1834, C.G. Arbuthnot, on behalf of Hunter Arbuthnot and Co. of Mauritius, recruited 36 'hill coolies' of the Dhangar class to work in a sugar estate, the property of Hunter Arbuthnot and Co., for a term of five years. The permission to land these 36 hill coolies was given on 3 November 1834. They were to be paid Rs.5 per month, according to clause 4 of the agreement of recruitment. The house of Hunter Arbuthnot was the responsibility of the government, with the condition that on the expiry of their term, the coolies would not be the burden of the (colonial) Government of Mauritius. The return passage of the indentured was assured by the government. In addition to the pay, clause 5 of the agreement provided that each labourer would be supplied a fixed quantity of food—2 lb. of rice and ½ lb. of *dholl*, 2 oz. of salt, and some oil and tamarind daily. Accommodation would also be provided to them, along with an annual supply of clothing as follows: 4 dhotis, 1 bedsheet, 2 blankets, 1 jacket, and 2 caps.[77] In less than a year and a half from 1 August 1834 to the end of 1835, as many as fourteen ships transported Indian labourers to Port Louis.[78] The white population was not employed as labourers in these plantations because of the notions of racial superiority, and also because they were not suited for hard physical labour in the tropical climate. The view of the colonizers that Indians were physically most suitable for hard labour in the tropical climate was expressed by a writer in the staunchly pro-planter newspaper, *The Royal Gazette*, in 1834: 'NO OTHER race of mankind can be found capable of doing a reasonable day's field labour in the burning sun of the Tropics.'[79] Apart from the climatic suitability of these hill coolies, other advantages soon emerged. As Gillanders Arbuthnot persuasively observed, the Indian labourers were 'perfectly ignorant of the place they agreed to go to, or the length of the voyages they are undertaking.' Even more pertinently, given the post-emancipation weakening of planter control over the labour process, Indian labourers were 'docile and easily managed'.[80] It was within these people that merchants identified the most desirable qualities of labour—inexpensive, manageable, and hardworking. As stated by British Guiana Governor Arbuthnot, the Dhangars '...have no religion, no education, and in their present state, no wants beyond eating, drinking, and sleeping; and to procure which they are willing to work.'[81] Applications were made from different sectors (mainly plantations) for permission to introduce Indian labourers in the island.

Thus, the high demand of labourers forced the government to issue a notice which impressed upon the employers (of labourers) the necessity of observing utmost care in the selection of recruits. The notice, issued on 5 March 1836, stated:

...His Excellency cannot too strongly recommend that special care be now taken to ensure that the persons who may be engaged shall have been known as really agricultural labourers in their own country (of the class called Hill Coolies, when coming from Calcutta) and that they and the chief or *sirdar* who accompanies them hither shall have been mutually known to each other before being engaged.[82]

Lieutenant-General Sir W. Nicolay, Governor of Mauritius, exhorted the Mauritian agents to be careful in the selection of recruits. He also advised the importers of labourers to seek the permission of the Government of India to include a certain number of women in every batch of labourers, because the paucity of women was responsible for grave disorder on some estates where Indians were mixed with 'apprentices' (now free slave women).[83] However, Indian labourers were found to be worth the money spent on them, and continued to be imported in fairly large numbers, so much so that by August 1838, there were about 24,000 Indian labourers in Mauritius. They replaced the creoles (freed slaves), who would no longer work in the fields.

However, the immigrants had to face miserable living conditions and there were high mortality rates during the voyages. The Government of India was alarmed at this and refused to allow any more Indian labourers to be taken to Mauritius until better shipping arrangements were made for the migrants. On the other hand, in the colony, the planters had been long accustomed to a mentality of coercive control over slaves' labour power. They tended to overlook the fundamental difference between the indentured and the slave. However, the Government of India was not ignorant about this ill treatment. Therefore, the Government of Bengal enquired about the condition of Indians living in Mauritius. Sir Nicolay, wrote in reply that the general laws of the colony were as much applicable to the Indians as to the rest of the population.[84] In his reply, he suggested that vaccination and medical inspection should be made compulsory for the labourers. Messrs J.P. Woodstock and J.C. Scott of the Bengal Civil Service had, in the meanwhile, paid visits to Mauritius. Woodstock had reported to Governor-General Lord Auckland (1836–42) that conditions during voyages to Mauritius were unsatisfactory and left much scope for improvement.[85] Agitation in the press and the report of Indian officers forced the Government of India to pass Act V of 1837. It was initially applicable only to the port of Calcutta, but through the Act XXXII of 1837, it was extended to the ports of Madras and Bombay as well. Through this Act, the government tried to control and keep a check on the recruitment of Indians and their condition during the voyage and in the plantation colonies. Lord Glenelg, the Secretary of State for colonies, thought that the Act would give complete protection to the Indian migrants in Mauritius.

Act V of 1837 spawned the system under which a labourer had to work for five years whomever he might be allotted to. Change of work or employer during the period of indenture was not permitted. The labourers got fix wages. The number of women was relatively small as compared to the number of men. All employers of indentured labourers were under the legal obligation to provide 'fixed wages, free housing, medical attendance and other amenities to their labourers'.[86] The coolie traffic from India was temporarily suspended on Sir Nicolay's initiative in December 1837. However, the trade was resumed soon after and there was a steady flow of the indentured to Mauritius. A number of cases of abuse were noticed soon after the resumption of the indenture trade. The malpractices that came hand in hand with the export of labour from India were bitterly attacked in the British Parliament in 1837–8. Some English missionaries in Calcutta took a serious interest in the examination of coolies before they sailed for Mauritius. In this process, they delved into the conditions that the coolies had to face during their export from Calcutta and the ill treatment of Indians in Mauritius.[87] The Court of Directors of East India Company ruled the total prohibition of emigration from India. Emigration from India was suspended from July 1838.

The Government of Mauritius, at the request of the Government of India, had appointed a committee on 15 October 1838, to conduct enquiries in the island simultaneously with an investigation in India.[88] A member of the committee, Special Justice Anderson, submitted a report in which he emphasized on the miserable condition of Indian labourers in Mauritius. He mentioned 'the accommodation provided to them was "too confined and disgustfully filthy", the employers were indifferent to their sick labourers, medical advice and attendance were not provided, eight or nine per cent of the workers had been persuaded to leave for India by gross fraud.'[89] Governor Nicolay also pointed out that most of the abuses complained of had their roots in India, and argued that these evils could be remedied only in India, not in Mauritius. Under such circumstances, the Government of India suspended emigration from India in 1838, and it was finally prohibited in 1840. During this period, Mauritian planters tried to employ Negro 'apprentices', who were nearly 17,000 in number.[90] But this recruitment drive could not fulfill the demand of the Mauritian plantation economy. Governor Nicolay requested the Government of India in February 1841 to permit emigration from India again. He argued, '...even the most ill-disposed and unsympathetic planters could be restrained from the exercise of arbitrary or unjust power.'[91] The planters, traders, and merchants also requested, at the same time, that the ban on emigration from India be lifted. Lord Ellenborough, who succeeded Governor-General Lord Auckland, agreed with him that the migration of coolies to Mauritius might be carried on smoothly, and drafted a memorandum on 28 October 1841. Colonial Secretary E. Stanley further suggested that the Governor-General (Ellenborough) should not be authorized to insist on the inclusion of more than 33 per cent women in each batch of emigrants, which he suggested in the drafted memorandum. In 1868, the colonial authorities decided the norm to be forty women for one hundred men.[92] Colonial Secretary Stanley also thought that Ellenborough's proposal of permitting the 'coolies' to take their families with them to Mauritius free of charge would be useless for all practical purposes as the 'better class women' would not agree to go to Mauritius with their menfolk, nor would most men like to take their womenfolk.[93]

On 2 December 1842, the Emigration Act was passed to regulate migration from India to Mauritius. Emigration was permitted from the ports of Calcutta, Madras, and Bombay. An agent of the Government of Mauritius was to be posted at each port of embarkation. Each emigrant's agent had to submit monthly reports to the government. A protector of immigrants was to look after the well-being of the immigrants in Mauritius. The act also stated that no emigrant was to be received from the emigration agent without a certificate, stating his/her name, father's name, and age. The act also made rules regarding the vessels used for carrying the labourers across the seas. It was imperative to have medical attendants and medical stores, and an appropriate number of women (forty women for hundred men, as decided by the colonial office in 1868) on every ship. The duration of the voyage from Calcutta was ten weeks during April–October and in November–December, eight weeks; the same from Bombay was five weeks in

April–September and six weeks during October–March.[94] The protector's salary was to be paid by the Government of India and he could be removed from office by the same. He also had to submit regular periodical reports to the Government of India.[95]

In 1843, when emigration from India came under systematized government superintendence, the imperial government showed real concern for the labourers and introduced a series of regulations, which the planters considered detrimental to their interest. The 'Free Labour Association' played an important role in the formulation of new rules and regulations for the indentured in the island. Certain regulations proposed by the Free Labour Association, were incorporated into these emigration rules (see Appendix 1).[96]

Ordinance 40 of 1844 of the Government of India made it obligatory for estate owners to provide lodging and hospital facilities for the labourers and regulate the articles of food to be supplied to them. In March 1844, the Government of India took over the supervision and management of the process of recruitment in an attempt to put an end to the abuse which had crept into the system. The number of labourers each planter could receive annually was fixed by government regulations. The contingent system introduced the first element of conflict for some planters who were not satisfied with their quota of coolies. In 1858, new regulations were introduced, which further reduced the quota. However, the contingent system was abolished and the immigration process was freed from arbitrary governmental restrictions. Planters in need of labourers were left free to indent any number of immigrants they wished, provided they furnished a good security amount for the payment of the cost of introduction.[97] Ordinance no. III of 1843, of the Government of Mauritius, sought to prevent the return of the immigrated labourers to India, and raised the indemnity for the return passage of the Indian labourers. It was believed that the number of able and practiced hands who would thus be retained in Mauritius would be greater in number. The immediate need of labourers in Mauritius in 1843, soon (1843) reached the 'saturation point'. It was estimated that 30,000 labourers would be enough to meet the demand of the plantations of Mauritius, and therefore, after 1 January 1844, it became necessary that further immigration be limited.[98]

By the Act XXI of 1843, the Government of India, on 1 January 1844, restricted emigration only from the port of Calcutta.[99] But it was discovered soon that Bengal alone could not meet the demand for labourers in Mauritius. Six thousand fresh immigrants were estimated to be the annual requirement in Mauritius. The Government of India therefore passed Act VIII of 1847, which permitted emigration from Madras on the same footing as from Calcutta.[100] Immigration into Mauritius from India was regulated from 1850 onwards by Act VII of 1847 (India). A labour law of Mauritius—Ordinance XXII of 1847—subjected the labourers to extreme hardships. Under the ordinance, it was not binding upon the employer to provide residence to his labourers. A labour was to be paid ten pounds and one shilling per annum in lieu of accommodation provided by the masters. Moreover, labourers absent from work without leave were to forfeit their wages and rations. Under this ordinance, offending labourers might even be given, under certain circumstances, a maximum of one month's imprisonment with hard labour.[101] Through the Act XIX of 1856, the Government of India once again suspended the emigration from India to Mauritius. This was due to a report from Mauritius that 284 out of 697, i.e. more than 40 per cent of the total number of emigrants on board the *Hyderre* and the *Futteh Mubarik*, had died due to gross negligence during the voyage to Mauritius.[102] In this context, the Government of India consolidated all of the nineteen existing laws on emigration in 1864. Act XIII of 1864 tried to systematize further the recruitment of indentured labourers from India. The Act also strengthened the power of the protector. It even provided power to the Government of India, under sections 64–7, to suspend the emigration of Indians to any British colony if the migrant labourers were not being provided with the passage. Besides, this Act protected the emigrants against the prevailing malpractices at the time of making contracts.[103]

Ordinance XXXI of 1867 (Mauritius) improved the position of the Indian immigrants to some extent. It made provisions for—(a) the issue of an employment certificate to each emigrant, (b) the cancellation of indenture on 'sufficient and satisfactory' grounds, (c) the discharge of infirm labourers and the cancellation of their contracts, and (d) quick recovery of wages of the labourers. The ordinance also defined the general rights of labourers. 'This ordinance and Act XIII of 1864 lifted the indentured labourers at least theoretically from the slough of slavery. It would be wrong to suppose, however, that the measures (the Act and the Ordinance) removed all the grievances of Indian labourers in Mauritius.'[104] By Ordinance no. 120 of 1878, the Government of Mauritius strengthened the power of the protector of immigrants and also made sure that the indentured got the free return passage to their country only after the completion of their tenure of five years.[105] During the 1880s, when there was a huge demand for Indian labourers in Mauritius, the government passed a memorandum about the scale of wages and sundry rules. It was circulated in India by the emigrant agency for the information of emigrants and others interested in emigration (see Appendix 2).[106]

The Indian population of Mauritius stood at over 350,000 in 1867.[107] The demand for fresh Indian labourers slackened in consequence. A crisis in the sugar industry in the same year was sought to be met by promulgating an ordinance, which adversely affected Indian labourers of all categories—indentured as well as non-indentured. The mildest form of punishment could be given to an indentured labourer under these laws for each day's absence. Punishment was also inflicted by the employers of indentured labourers themselves without reference to a court of law. If they went to the court, the magistrates could inflict one or more of the following penalties on the delinquent labourers: (a) a fine amounting to a maximum of a month's wages, which, on realization, was to go to the employer; (b) simple or rigorous imprisonment for not more than fourteen days; and (c) cancellation of the contract of service. These laws discouraged the free labourers and led to their grievous oppression. If Indians wanted to stay back, they would re-indenture themselves on the existing terms and conditions, or settle down as shopkeepers, artisans, or day labourers.

In 1851, a general meeting was held in Natal to discuss the issues of introducing Indians as indentured labourers in Natal.[108] The indentured system had already met with enormous success in Mauritius and other British and French colonies. The issue of introduction of the indentured in Natal was widely debated, and by 1855 the government was ready to introduce Indians as indentured labourers in the colony. Sir George Grey, a British official, made sincere efforts in this regard. However, initially, the Government of India did not accept this proposal, as it highlighted some of the unattractive features of the Natal Emigration Ordinance of 1855. There were primarily four reasons why the Government of India denied permission. First, there was a high demand for labourers in India, especially in the Bombay Presidency, resulting in Indians getting higher wages in their own country. Second, greater advantages were given to emigrants to the colonies of Mauritius and West Indies. Third, it was already difficult to meet the demands for supply of labour in Mauritius and West Indies. Fourth, the Government of India wanted precise and satisfactory information as to the rates of wages that were to be paid to the emigrants at Natal.[109] Thus, the

Government of India did not pass any law related to the migration of indentured Indian labourers to Natal.

As a result, the Natal government made serious attempts to provide necessary information about the indentured migrants' position in the colony. Finally, the Government of India accepted the Natal government's proposal and agreed to send the migrants only from the Bombay port.[110] The Natal government, in this Ordinance of 1856 (ordinance empowering Natal to import indentured Indian labour), raised the wages of the indentured migrants from five to six shillings a month, with provisions for 'ample rations'. However, the new wages were still very low when compared to what could be obtained in Bombay itself, where the demand for such labour was quite high.[111] The Natal government's request for migration of Indians from other ports like Calcutta was rejected on the grounds that Mauritius proved to be a more lucrative option for emigration. As regards the emigration of female labourers, this is what an emigrant agent of Calcutta had to say: 'Owing to the demands for female emigrants to Mauritius, viz., 33 per cent, it has been difficult of late to procure a sufficient number to meet the demand, and often times bands of men have been refused at the depot in consequence of there being no females with them.'[112] Due to the limitations of the Natal Emigration Ordinance (1855), the Government of India asked the Natal government to revise the rules according to the other plantation colonies. It also wanted more information about the emigrants' terms of service, contract of servitude, and the medical facilities that they would be receiving—in short, information on every measure essential for the comfort and welfare of the indentured in the colony. The Government of India further demanded that a fixed number of women should be maintained on the voyages.[113] It is evident that the Government of India was very keen on maintaining an appropriate number of women in proportion to the number of men, and the statement of the Bengal agent (mentioned earlier) shows that the recruitment of female labourers was a very crucial issue for the political economy in the colonial plantations.

The year 1858 saw a massive increase in the production of sugar in Natal, which led to an increase in the demand for labourers, leading to a national problem of shortage of labourers, since the supply now ran short.[114] A petition was signed by the planters and was submitted to the legislative council of Natal for the recruitment of Indians as indentured labourers.[115] Due to the high demand for labour and the Government of India's refusal to send indentured labourers from the other ports of the country, the Natal government passed the Natal Law of November 1859,—laws 13, 14, and 15 of which were based on St. Lucia's emigration ordination.

The three laws mentioned dealt with three separate issues. Law 13 was essentially the one concerned with the arrival of the new Asiatic immigrants to Natal. According to a part of Law 13, any indentured labourer could enter into a contract of service for any period, not exceeding three years. After these three years, he had to complete the five years' industrial residence. His wages, it was decided, would not be less than ten shillings per month. This law, with twenty-six clauses, can be briefly summarized as follows:

…Only a licensed authority could introduce (transport) immigrants into the colony (clauses 1–8). The Immigration Agent (later called the Protector of Indian Immigrants) after personal inspection and examination of the ship, had the power to issue a certificate to allow the ship and its passengers to land (clauses 9–12), while the master of the ship had to provide provisions (rations) for the 48-hour period immediately after landing for the immigrants. Thereafter the Protector's task was to issue every emigrant with a ticket of registration, record all necessary documentation in a separate register (clauses 13–14), allocate the immigrant to an employer (clause 15) and demand that every employer pay the required passage money and other traveling expenses of the immigrant (clauses 16, 17). A fine of £50 could be imposed on the master of any ship (or introducing agent) who failed to feed his passengers adequately or in any way abused or ill-treated such emigrants (clauses 18, 19). . .[116]

Law 14, with its forty-three clauses, was concerned with the rules and regulations for the immigrants, the conditions of the service and wages of the labourers, and the contract between the master and the servant, who was a bonded labourer for a period of five years. The Law 14 of 1859, was based on the Mauritian Act 15 of 1842. According to this Law, all expenses incurred by the Government of India in the hiring, employing, and maintenance of such emigrants during their passage, were to be paid by the planters. The Lieutenant-Governor of Natal also appointed an immigration agent, who was expected to maintain a register in which he would record the name and number of the immigrants, their age, sex, the place from which they had arrived, and also the amount of money advanced to each immigrant (paid in India), which was to be repaid by him out of his wages in Natal. In India, before their departure to Natal, the emigrants had to sign a contract at the depot, in which the name of their employer was mentioned. Otherwise intending recruits signed a bond to serve any employer to whom he would be allotted by the protector of Indian immigrants, on his arrival at Natal.

On arrival at Natal, the immigration agent was responsible for assigning the labourers to the planters or estates and finalizing a contract between the employer and emigrant for a period not exceeding three years. Employers had to provide the immigrants with proper and sufficient food, medical services, and lodging. However, if an employer neglected his duty and failed to provide these facilities to his employees, he would be fined ten pounds sterling for every offence. Failure to pay the fine resulted in imprisonment for thirty days.

After the expiration of their indentured contract, the immigrants had to complete an industrial residence of five years. During the indentured period, if an immigrant's assigned task was transferred, he was bound to continue to work for another employer, but with the consent of immigration agent. The labourer was bound to serve his new master for the unexpired term of his contract. In case of death of his employer, his service would be continued for the benefit of the heirs and executors of master. This law also stipulated that if any immigrant, without any lawful excuse, was absent from work, his two days' wages were to be deducted and in case no wage was due, the immigrant would be imprisoned with hard labour for any time not exceeding fourteen days. According to this law, every immigrant who had completed ten years in the colony, including five years of industrial residence, was permitted a free passage back to India. The immigrants had the right to exchange their return passage for a piece of land in Natal, equal in value to the cost of such return passage.[117]

Law 15 recommended that from the indentured wages, a sum of twelve shilling per annum was to be deducted for accommodation and medical services.[118]

In August 1860, the governments of Bengal and Madras approved the ratio of female to male as 35 per cent for the first year, 43 per cent for the second, and 50 per cent for the third and following years for Natal.[119] With the passing of this Act on 7 August 1860, the emigration of indentured Indians to Natal finally received approval. W. Gray demanded that the ports of Calcutta and Madras should also be opened, along with Bombay, for the transportation of new recruits from Indians for Natal.[120] As a result of this, the Calcutta and Madras ports were opened up for Natal soon after and these two areas became the main centres of indentured recruitment in India.

Meanwhile, the protector of emigrants in India advised the government of Natal to attract more Indians as indentured by offering them conditions of employment similar to those offered by the Government of Mauritius. For example, in Mauritius, the indentured were offered wages of 10 shillings per month for the first year, 11 shillings per month for the second year, and 12 shillings per month for the third, fourth, and fifth years; and there were no reduction in food, accommodation, or medical expenses, which in the case of Natal amounted to Rs.2 per month. Further, in Mauritius, the indentured received a suit of clothes every year and their contract was for a five-year period. As a result of these and other subsequent recommendations during the next fifty-one years, many of the clauses of Law 14 were constantly modified or revised.[121]

Emigration to Natal was finally sanctioned by Act XXXIII of 1860 (India). W.M. Collins, the Postmaster-General of Natal, was sent to Madras as an emigration agent in March 1860. As a result of the Natal Emigration Ordinance, the first ship *Truro*, from Madras, reached Natal on 16 November 1860 with 203 adult males, 87 adult females, 21 boys, 19 girls, and 10 infants.[122] The government's emigration agent at Calcutta for Natal was I.A. Firth. In the first ship from Calcutta, there were 225 men, 70 women, and 30 boys and 16 girls under ten years of age, counted as 15 and 8 adults respectively (two children under ten years of age were counted as equal to one adult). During the period 1860–6, there were 3,421 male, 1,269 female, and 747 children, indentured migrants from Madras; on the other hand, 695 males, 194 females, and 122 children; while went as indentured migrants from Calcutta.[123]

From 1868–73, emigration was stopped due to an economic crisis (caused by a depression in the sugar industry). By 1866, the two British colonies in South Africa were struggling to survive financially. These events, in turn, affected Indian emigration and in 1866, emigration of indentured Indians to Natal was stopped.[124] Also, on their return to India, the emigrants had complained of ill treatment by their masters. From the mid-1870s, the sugar industry of Natal experienced a reduction in the price of sugar, because of: international competition, the impact of the American Civil War, and the over-production of sugar in the colony. This was compounded by crop diseases, natural disasters, loss of soil fertility, and difficulty in obtaining credit.[125]

However, the situation improved over time, and the planters' demands for labour supply from India revived, largely due to the discovery of diamonds at Kimberley (1867), and gold at Pilgrim's Rest (1873).[126] This time, the Government of India refused to allow emigration on the ground that the migrants who had returned from Natal had complained of ill treatment by the planters. The complaints were mostly about non-payment of wages; physical assault and flogging by Messrs Lister, Kennedy, and others; bad quality of rations; deduction from wages for absence due to illness, which ranged from 1–2 shillings and was even as high as 2 shillings and 6 pence (25 cents) per day; extra working hours; and non-payment of the bonus of 10 shillings that they were promised upon their return to their country. Consequently, after fulfilling their tenure as indentured labourers, many of them returned in a 'state of poverty'.[127] They were dissatisfied with their rations, particularly the amount of meals in lieu of rice, poor medical services, and the treatment they received when they were ill.[128] But, due to the scarcity of labourers, the Natal government formed a 'Coolie Commission' for enquiry of these complaints and for reviewing the condition of Indians in the plantations of Natal. This commission included Mr Galley, the Attorney General, and Lieutenant Colonel Banastre P. Lloyd of the Bengal staff.[129] In 1872, a majority of the cases reported by the returning emigrants to the commission were those of being beaten up by the planters. However, no serious steps were taken against the white planters, who had committed such atrocities. These planters argued instead that the Indian labourers were responsible for causing disorder and chaos in the plantations. The commission submitted its report to the government and argued that the Indians were not ill-treated in Natal, and that their condition there was much better in comparison to the other colonial plantations. Further, the commission argued that the Indians had failed to understand the terms of the indentured contracts, and that they were never promised the bonus of 10 shillings on their return from Natal on the expiration of their contracts.[130] Reading through the commission report, it seems as Henning stated that … the Natal government had the situation 'under control'; as to their treatment of the labourers, the commission stated '…they are not and have never been subject to any systematic ill-treatment or oppression by their employers.'[131] The commission, in its report, argued that Indians were in a better position as compared to labourers in any corner of the world, including their own country.[132] Unfortunately, in the absence of any written records from the Indian indenture is about their ill-treatment, there is no foolproof way of highlighting the other side of the picture. The collection of evidences appears to be one-sided. In all of the thirty-six members who formed the commission: thirty were employers, three officials, and only three Indians labourers; these three Indians were very discreet in their condemnation of the system. The commission did, however, criticize the social system and they pleaded for the establishment of schools and temples, and for increasing the number of women among the indentured.[133]

The commission had also criticized the use of the word 'Coolie' for the Indian emigrants. According to them, 'This word in India is applied to the lowest classes only, and it is regarded as a term of reproach and in the nature of abuse.'[134] The word coolie originated from the Tamil word *kulie*, which referred to payment for menial work for persons from the lowest level in the industrial labour market. In this regard, Ashwin Desai and Goolam Vahed argued that '…In the transformation of *kuli* to coolie, the distinct humanity of individual Indians was appropriated and eliminated as the person collapsed/merged into the payment.'[135] The process led to the mass commodification of 'coolie' labour.

As a result of these complaints the Natal government was forced to make some improvements in the laws related to Indian indentured labourers. The Natal government also revised its legislation regarding the further introduction of Indian labourers into the colony. The Coolie Consolidation Law of 1869 became Law 2 of 1870. It was basically a revision as well as a 'tightening up' of Law 14 of 1859 (Natal Coolie Law).[136] Consequently, the indentured emigration again commenced in 1874 and continued till 1911. Interestingly, it might be noted that seventy-two women from the first batch of emigrants, who returned (1860) from Natal on the *Red Riding Hood*, out of whom thirty belonged to Madras and forty-two to Calcutta:[137] had no complaints about their living or working conditions. This raises certain imperative questions— did the women have no complaints, or did the colonial government never try to probe into their problems, or were the women's grievances generalized and represented by their male colleagues?

On the basis of the complaints mentioned earlier, the Natal government also restricted the emigration of indentured labour to some of the concerned plantations in future, and also made some rules for the protection of the indentured labourers in the colony. According to Law 2 of 1870, the immigration agent had to keep a register of all immigrants, and all the employers had to keep a 'wages book'. Medical care was also emphasized upon; an employer of more than twenty Indians had to provide a hospital, and the employers also had to send monthly medical report to the emigration agent. Any immigrant, who was unlawfully absent from work, had to forfeit a sum equal to 'half penny' for each shilling of his monthly wages for each day of absence.[138] Within two years, however, the Natal government passed a new law, the Law 12 of

1872, which was similar to the emigration ordinance of British Guiana.[139] This Law increased the contract period of the indentured from three to five years, with five years industrial residency in the colony. It made provisions that wages should be paid to the indentured weekly or fortnightly, as paid in Guiana and Trinidad, instead of only once in two months. A commissioner was appointed to inquire into the condition of Indians in Natal.[140] The colonial government also appointed a 'Protector of Emigrants', instead of an 'Emigrant Agent'. The protector's powers were extremely wide as regards to the Indian population.[141] According to the new law, the protector of emigrants would be responsible for performing all those duties, and looking into all those matters and things, which any law in the colony required the emigration agent to have done or performed. His salary was £500 per annum, showing the high status of this post. In 1872, Lt. Col. Lloyd was appointed as the first Protector of Indian Emigrants. Later, Capt. McLeod, Col. Graves, Louis Mason, and J.A. Polkinghorne were appointed to the post; and it was during Polkinghorne's term of office that the indentured system ceased, in 1911 in Natal.[142]

According to Section 11 of the Law 13 of 1872, powers of jurisdiction were given to the protectors in case of a tussle between the emigrants and their employers. Thus, the protector had all the administrative and judicial rights for the welfare and protection of the Indians in the colony. Further, the Natal government passed the new Law 19 of 1874, and it was believed that 'The provisions of the new act will adequately secure in all aspects the due protection of Indian immigrants, this law was particularly aimed at strengthening the legal powers of the Protector'. The law further clarified the protector's powers of jurisdiction; for example, in case of prosecution or in defense of an Indian, if there arose a difference of opinion with a local magistrate, then 'the decision of the protector shall prevail'.[143]

According to the Law 19, an employer may prosecute his employee (the indentured) for offences like: refusing to perform his stipulated work, or performing it negligently; damaging, by neglect or improper conduct, something entrusted to his care; behaving violently or insolently with his employer; scandalous immorality or even drunkenness; and desertion or other instances of gross misconduct.[144] For these offences, punishment may be awarded as imprisonment with or without labour for one month or a fine not exceeding five pounds. On the other hand, an employee could sue his employer according to Section 12 of this law only in two situations: non-payment of wages and breach of contract of service.[145] The protector may, in these cases, make an order for the payment of wages; a warrant of distrait may be issued, and failing recovery, the employer may be sent to prison for a month, or till the compensation or payment was made within the month.[146]

The colonial law was indeed oppressive and made the immigrants helpless. It played an imperative role in strengthening the sovereignty of the plantation economy and maintaining law and order. Although the laws were for both the plantation owners and the workers, these naturally worked in favour of the white planters. The rule of law was indeed discriminatory in the colonial milieu. Bernard S. Cohn rightly stated, '…this system of rule was to be run by Englishmen and had to take into account the British ideal of justice and the proper discipline, forms of deference, and demeanor that should mark the relations between rulers and ruled.'[147] Clearly, laws that were made for the protection of the indentured preferred the interest of the planters.

While Law 19 of 1874 was signed on 15 January, another very important law had been introduced three days earlier, namely, Law 20 of 1874, which was described as the Indian Emigration Trust Board Law, 1874.[148] The Indian Emigration Trust Board emphasized on the successful transportation of 'human cargo'. It emerged as a powerful business venture, whose main functions were recruitment, repatriation, employment, and the general welfare of the indentured Indians.[149] This law, followed by Section 4, Law 14 of 1875, imposed stricter regulations for the introduction of medical services.[150]

As thousands of emigrants departed annually from India, it became necessary for the Government of India to impose strict regulations such as those provided in Act XXXI of 1883. This act made provisions for just about every aspect of emigration of Indian citizens, particularly for the depots and the voyage itself. Additional and warmer clothes were provided to the emigrants who migrated to Natal. One compounder was appointed on each ship for every 500 emigrants. A female nurse was appointed for every twenty-five infants under two years of age. This Act was revised in 1897, in which focus was mainly given on the condition of the 'return emigrants', those who were returning as 'the sick and helpless'. On their landing, '…they shall be properly lodged and provided for until the Agent is in a position to arrange for their departure.'[151] As one can see, the government tried to give a charitable and humanitarian approach to the terms of the emigration law; however it is also important to note that the emigrants had to experience miserable conditions and even corporal punishment on the ships.

The colonial government at Natal used appealing slogans and promised the Indians that there would be no interference as far as their religion, caste, and creed were concerned. The following notice of 1874 is particularly interesting, since it throws light on the 'making of indentured':

NOTICE TO COOLIES INTENDING TO EMIGRATE TO NATAL

You will be taken free of expense to Calcutta, and while there, will be well fed and properly lodged until the ship sails, and should you be ill, the greatest care will be taken of you.

When the ship is ready you will be supplied with good clothing; the finest ships are selected, and the voyage takes about five or six weeks. The food, medicines, and other appliances too will be provided to you. The Indian government has appointed officers, who are most strict and vigilant in securing for you all these advantages.

On and after your arrival in Natal, there is a Protector of Immigrants ready to advise you at all times during your residence there. You will be located on an estate where a medical man is employed.

Your religion will be no way is interfered with, and both *Hindoos* and *Mohomedans* are alike protected.

You will find over 5,000 of your countrymen settled there.

You will have a house rent free to live in, with plenty of garden ground to cultivate at your leisure, and care is taken not to separate families and relatives.

The climate is remarkably healthy, and there is an abundance of good water, fruits, and vegetables. If you are ill, medical attendance, medicines, and nourishment are provided free of charge.

You will be required to cultivate sugarcane and to make sugar, rum, and molasses. Great verities of work, either for strong men or for women and children are available.

You will have to work for five years, six days in a week, for nine hours between sunrise to sunset, all Sundays and holidays excepted.

Besides rations the men receive for the first year, Rs. 5 monthly; for the second year, Rs. 5 and half monthly; for the third year, Rs. 6 monthly; for the fourth year, Rs. 6 and half monthly; for the fifth year, Rs. 7 monthly. The women are paid half wages and the children in proportion.

After five years you may return to India at your own expense, and after ten years you will be entitled to a passage back.[152]

From this example, one might become aware of the fact that migration to both colonies was not just the result of 'push' factors like poverty and starvation prevailing in India; rather, the Indians were enticed in the name of better housing and living conditions. The Natal government passed the notice in 1874 when there was the need of continuous and cheap labour from India. However, the colonial government consciously concealed the other side of picture in the notice. According to the actual agreement through which the Indians were employed, the planters could sue the indentured labour for not performing their work, or performing it negligently, or for immorality and misconduct. Further, the duties that the indentured were to perform were ambiguous in the provisions of the agreement, and the interpretation of these was left to the overseers, much to the disadvantage of the labourers. Also, nothing was said about the penal sanctions for the breach of contract.[153] The main aim of the notices was to attract the Indians. The colonial government deliberately masked the rules and regulations of the contract since it knew that the indentured, once trapped, had no way out of the situation. It should be further noted that there was a strict prohibition on the new arrivals to meet the settlers of Indian origin in the plantations. Thus, the indentured system was based on the tactics of control over the body and lives of the indentured labour.

In order to 'reform' the indentured migration, the colonial government published the contract in vernacular languages, for example Urdu and Bhojpuri mixed Hindi.[154] However, these contracts only mentioned the clauses related to wages, free rations, medical and living conditions, and also highlighted free return passage and some advance money before their departure, but this 'advance money' had to be paid back during their working years.[155] The miserable working and living conditions remained veiled in the contract. Moreover, as far as the question of women was concerned, they were not treated as individual 'labour unit' and in some cases, women were working without even signing the contract. The emigrants did not sign any 'contract' as such, but simply put their marks under a written statement which read: '…We the undersigned male adult emigrants do hereby agree to serve the employer to whom we may respectively be allotted by the Natal government, under the Natal Act 14 of 1859 and we all understand the terms under which we are engaged.'[156]

Condition of Indian Migrants in Colonial Mauritius and Natal

'Cheerful at morn he wakes from short repose,
Breathless the keen air and carol as he goes;
At night returning, every labour sped
He sits him down the monarch of a shed.'[157]

By 1866, a total of 339,706 labourers had migrated to Mauritius. Their numbers dwindled thereafter, until the traffic to Mauritius was finally halted in 1910. A summary of the arrival and departure of Indian immigrants from 1834 to 1910 is given in Table 1.3. Over the entire period (1834–1910), 451,796 Indians (346,036 males and 105,760 females) arrived in Mauritius, and 157,539 (128,761 males and 28,778 females, including children born in Mauritius) returned to India.

In this context, Bowman has observed that, '…the Indian proportion of the Mauritius population rose from 18% in 1839, to 43% in 1851 and to 67% in 1871.' Since then, it has remained almost constant. The tide of emigrants was enormous, and the population of Mauritius tripled during this time, from around 100,000 in 1834 to 310,000 by the census of 1861. The strongest multi-racial immigration decade was 1851–61, with the influx of a total of over 100,000 immigrants (see Table 1.3).

The Indian population, whose increase was at a peak, as denoted in the 1861 census, began to decrease, particularly after 1881, as shown in Table 1.4.

TABLE 1.3: Arrival and Departure of Indian Immigrants in Mauritius, 1834–1910

Year	Arrival	Departure	Net total in Mauritius
1834–40	25,403	1,103	24,300
1841–5	57,671	11,314	46,357
1846–50	36,019	16,174	19,845
1851–5	71,048	16,475	54,573
1856–60	113,007	25,679	87,328
1861–5	56,980	14,747	42,233
1866–70	14,312	14,919	-607
1871–5	26,651	14,641	12,010
1876–80	11,178	10,446	732
1881–5	9,903	9,934	-31
1886–90	9,275	7,570	1705
1891–5	4,226	5,444	-1218
1896–1900	3,968	4,639	-671
1901–5	10,409	2,715	7694
1906–10	1,736	1,790	-54
TOTAL	451,786	157,589	294,197

Source: R.R. Kuczynski, *Demographic Survey of the British Colonial Empire*, vol. 2, London: Oxford University Press, 1949, p. 796; cited in Bowman, *Mauritius*, p. 21.

TABLE 1.4: Indian Population in Mauritius

Year	General Population	Indian Population	Indo-Mauritian Population	Chinese Population	Total
1840	99,450	23,490	–	1,395	124,335
1846	101,017	56,245	–	1,200	158,462
1851	101,527	72,180	5,816	1,300	180,823
1861	115,864	172,425	20,209	1,552	310,050
1871	97,497	155,367	6,089	2,287	316042
1881	107,323	135,595	113,398	3,558	359,874
1891	111,517	99,329	156,591	3,151	370,588
1901	108,422	60,208	198,878	3,515	371,023
1911	107,432	35,396	222,301	3,662	368,791
1921	104,216	17,056	248,468	6,745	376,485

Source: P.S. Vivek, *From Indentured Labour to Liberated Nation: Public Policy and Small Planters in Mauritius*, Bangalore: Focus Press, 2007, p. 44.

The Indians who came to Mauritius at least until the 1860s, were drawn by the insatiable demands of the plantocracy for cheap labour. Under the terms of indenture, the emigrants signed an initial contract promising five years indenture, plus an additional five years of work (re-indenture); at the end of this ten year period, the immigrants were supposed to be entitled to free return passage home. But the right of return passage was limited; was altogether abolished in Mauritius after 1853 and thereafter, was only honoured for Indians who were sick or not fit.[158] The conditions of indentured labour in Mauritius were extremely harsh. Coolies were expected to work six days a week and then do unpaid labour on Sunday. The work was hard, in an oppressive climate, and flagging generally resulted in severe beatings.

Many of the Indians whose indenture period had expired settled on unoccupied and unclaimed lands on the high hills and earned their living independently. The planters, however, wanted even these Indians to work for them. Those who refused to work were sent to a special vagrant depot, built at Port Louis. Strict vagrancy laws were passed to help the planters hold workers onto the estates. After 1867, all labourers had to carry passes; the ones found without passes, or in a district of the island where they were not employed, were subjected to arrest and punishment. If the indenture-expired immigrants or the 'old immigrants', as they were called, remained firm in their decision to settle down as free men in Mauritius, they were treated like convicts.

An indentured would also have to take a ticket from the immigrants department.[159] No ticket was valid without a photograph of the holder of the ticket and two shillings were charged for the photograph. The loss of the ticket entailed other hardships. The fee for a duplicate one was £1, plus an additional charge of two shillings for a new photograph. The 'old immigrants' had to advertise in *The Royal Gazette* for a month before the issue of a duplicate ticket. A permit to work would be issued to him in the meanwhile, on payment of a fee of five shillings. A Mauritian regulation of 1865 made it obligatory for an 'old immigrant' to take out a license, originally fixed at four shillings per annum, which was raised to £1 subsequently. The person had to wear a badge on his arm with the words 'job-men' inscribed on it. Failure to obtain a license or to wear it was punishable with a fine of £2 or a week's imprisonment in default.[160]

Free Indian labourers were liable to be arrested, imprisoned, or charged heavy fines, if they failed to produce on demand at any time— the police pass, the portrait ticket, the certificate of employment, the day-labourer's license, or the return permission from the employer.[161] They had to carry each and every one of these documents with them whenever they went out. In the year 1869, for example, 30,824 persons in all were arrested for failing to produce on demand one or more of these documents. S.B. Mookherji, in his work, notes that 7,000, i.e. about 25 per cent of the total number were subsequently found to have been arrested unlawfully, 12,538 were sentenced to various terms of imprisonment, and the remaining 11,826 were left off with lighter imprisonment.[162] These vagrancy regulations compelled the 'old immigrants' to re-indenture.[163] Thus, 45,460 indenture-expired Indian labourers accepted work under their old masters in 1870, and 31,481 did so under new masters in the same year.[164] Responding to concerns expressed about the indenture labour system in Mauritius, the British government appointed a Royal Commission to investigate matters in 1872–3. The 'free' Indians or old immigrants filed their petition before the commission, in which they demanded for complete freedom like the other non-indentured inhabitants of the colony. The commission received about 500 petitions in writing or orally. The old immigrants reported their complaints about several issues, like harsh operation of the Ordinance no. 31 of 1867, the excessive fees charged for duplicate tickets at the immigration and the police offices, ill-treatment in the immigration offices, and arbitrary and vexatious conduct of the police in enforcing the law, among others.[165] However, this commission was of little help in solving the problems of the helpless Indian migrants, in spite of the fact that it was convinced of the genuineness of the Indian complaints and admitted that the condition of the Indian labourers was deplorable. Yet, in the opinion of some scholars, the Indians in Mauritius were more prosperous in their new homes than they had been in India. As regards their condition in Mauritius, an independent testimony had been made by the Indian officials of high standing. Mr G.M. Harriot, as a consulting engineer for irrigation in 1913, had written:

...I however cannot help feeling that the government of India has been entirely misled with regard to the condition of the Indian labourers in Mauritius. I have made inquiries from the labourers, and the well to do Indians in the island, and have observed the field labourers most carefully...I have without exception, been informed by the people that they are well paid, and cared for, and my investigation shows that this is the case. They have a much more prosperous appearance (men, women and children) than I noticed in Indian field labourers anywhere, and none of them seems to have any desire to return to India...[166]

However, the actual picture was very different from this description. Though the Indians settled there, they did not have much choices, as has been discussed already. During 1913, about 30 per cent of the total area under cultivation was in the hands of the non-indentured, free Indians, who had become smaller planters themselves. But even then, they had to face subjugation and exploitation at the hands of the big planters. The lands of the small planters were seized and forcibly sold when they could not pay their debts to the sugar estate owners, to whom the lands were mortgaged. The colonial government also did not come forward to help these people. Indians were out of the ambit of any political rights in the colony. The Royal Commission of 1909 remarked that:

...For about three quarters of a century it has been found possible for the Colonial Government to regard the Indian as a stranger...who must indeed be protected from imposition and ill-treatment and secured in the exercise of his legal rights, but who has no real claim to a voice in the ordering of the affairs of the colony.[167]

Mahatma Gandhi, who had taken up the issue against racism in South Africa and had launched a crusade for the rights of the Indians there, visited Mauritius in 1901. He addressed Indians and inspired them to fight for their rights. On 16 June 1915, Gandhiji wrote a letter to Jehangir Bomanji Petit (Secretary of the South African Indian Fund) that, '...the system of indentured emigration is an evil which cannot be mended but can only be ended...your committee should lose no time in approaching the Government of India with a view to securing entire abolition of the system for every part of the empire.'[168] After that, Dr Manilal and Sir Maharaj Singh arrived in Mauritius to enquire about the condition of the Indians in the colony. They saw the appalling conditions of the Indian migrants there and became their voice of protest, inspiring them to fight for their rights and for preserving their cultural heritage. On the basis of the Indians' social, political, and economic condition, Sir Singh, in his report, recommended that no future indentured emigration be permitted from India to Mauritius.[169] In this regard, it would be interesting to take a look at this extract from a letter in *The Mahratta* (Poona),[170] in which Dr. Manilal wrote to the editor of newspaper, warning his countrymen against migration to Mauritius.

EMIGRATION TO MAURITIUS (A WARNING)

To the Editor of *The Mahratta*

Sir, I have the honour to request you to be so kind as to give publicity to the following for the benefit of our poor countrymen, who may be possible victims of Indian touts in Calcutta and Madras:

1. There are too many Indian labourers in Mauritius, so many that in fact you will see hundreds of men and women starving to death near the Muslim's mosque and on the streets on account of want of work.
2. This colony is too small for any immigration.
3. The treatment of Indian labourers on sugar estates is really unhappy, though undeniably better than in Natal or the Transvaal.
4. Indian labourers under indentured are liable to be compelled to carry human excreta in the shape of manure to the fields—no matter what their caste may be.
5. During indentured if you are beaten or abused by your white employer, your Indian friends will either be afraid of your master or will be won over to his side by better pay, more rations or light work. By the bye, sometimes the quality of your rice and dhall may not appeal to your palates.
6. You may be set harder tasks than you can do—abler men (paid extra but without your knowledge) may be induced to work with you and do more work than you can finish within the same time. If you not do your allotted task—you may be charged with the offence and sent to jail with the help of Indian witnesses.

7. If you are ill, the dispensary steward may say there is nothing the matter with you, or give you such medicines and treatment as may cure your supposed idleness.

8. During the crop season you will be made to work day and night for a paltry extra.

9. If you have a good looking wife, your superiors, Indians, whites or semi-whites, may give you all the trouble in world to rob you of your prize.

   If you are about to complete your five years or any shorter period of your indenture—there may be prosecutions against you for idleness, illegal absence, not doing your allotted task, not returning agriculture implements belonging to the estate, etc.,—all such prosecution being liable to be withdrawn if you re-engage.

10. The protector of immigrants does not always find it easy or practicable or to his interest to protect you, howsoever well-disposed he may be at heart.

11. Mauritian stipendiary magistrates usually are related or connected or well-disposed towards your employers, and human nature being what it is, you have no great opportunities of proving your complaints against your masters, if you be so foolish as to waste your hard-earned starvation savings in litigation.

12. There are no ideal lovers of justice and humanity to espouse your cause among legal practitioners in this colony and if you have no money, defenseless you must go to goal and helpless your cases must end in smoke.

I have exaggerated nothing in what I have said above, I have only summed up the results of my personal information and if you came here as indentured labourers do not say that I did not warn you beforehand.

Port Louis	Yours truly
Mauritius	Manilal
8th June 1910	Barrister-at-law

The situation in Natal was somewhat different. Although there was a great demand for indentured labourers from India, they were not welcomed in Natal. It was believed that 'the Indian' was a 'problem', not a person.[171] Soon they became the subject of hatred amongst both the natives and the Europeans. Their behaviour towards the Indians reflected the colonial, racial attitude. *The Natal Mercury* recorded the landing of the Indians for the first time in Natal, and showed that they aroused curiosity among the natives and European settlers alike. *The Natal Mercury* described, in some awful words, the first boat that brought Indian emigrants to Natal—

…A very remarkable scene was the landing…They were a queer, comical, foreign looking, very oriental-like crowd. The men with their huge muslin turbans, bare scraggy and thin bones, and coloured garments; the women with their flashing eyes, long disheveled pitchy hair, with their half-covered well-formed figures and their keen inquisitive glances; the children with their meager, intelligent, cute and humorous countenances mounted on bodies of unconscionable fragility, were all evidently beings of a different race and kind to any we have yet seen either in Africa or England…[172]

The situation on the second indenture ship to Natal, *Belvedere*,[173] was an upheaval in practically every respect; when it reached Natal, the ship was placed in quarantine immediately. On the orders of the health officer, the clothing and bedding of the 351 survivors were destroyed. The colonists lived in constant fear of infection and resented the extra cost that the infections incurred.

The immigrants were seen as sources of venereal diseases in the overseas colonies, and for this reason they were separated from the settler communities. Thus, they had to face ghettoisation and isolation. Apart from these problems, the Indians also had to face racial discrimination in Natal and Mauritius, as pointed out by Edward Shils, who suggested that the Europeans possessed a basic antipathy towards people of colour. This is a hypothesis worth investigating in terms of psychology.[174] Thus, a different type of thought, action, and feeling, was adopted against the Indians. The gulf was further entrenched between the 'Orient' and 'European' and between the 'Orient' and 'Occident'.

As shown in Table 1.5, in the initial phase of migration, i.e from 1860 to 1866, about 6,445 indentured migrated to Natal. Then, after the period of prohibition from 1868 to 1874 was over, when migration started again, an estimate of 21,676 indentured migrants reached Natal in the period between 1874 and 1882. From 1883 to 1889, as many as 19,583 indentured migrated, and in the next eight years, i.e. from 1892 to 1900, the number was 35,184—which was a significant increase. But in the next decade, i.e. from 1901 to 1910, this number reached its peak when it rose to 64,311. Here, it is interesting to compare the statistics of migration and repatriation with the other overseas colony. Mauritius and Natal became areas where immigrants preferred to settle in relatively larger numbers (see Table 1.6).

During the initial period of sugarcane cultivation, when the Natal planters wanted a continuous supply of cheap indentured labour from India, the colonial government recommended Law 2 of 1872, in which it was mentioned that a grant of eight or ten acres of land outside Durban would be given to the ex-indentured Indians, in lieu of the return passage.[175] However, this situation changed later, due to the

TABLE 1.5: Number of Indian Migrants to Natal, 1860–1911

Period	No. of Ships	Total
Nov. 1860–July 1866	20	6,445
June 1874–Oct. 1877	17	8,206
Oct. 1877–Nov. 1878	17	6,477
Jan. 1879–Dec. 1882	20	7,003
Apr. 1883–Apr. 1885	20	6,601
Mar. 1886–Nov. 1889	20	5,480
Feb. 1890–Dec. 1891	19	7,502
Feb. 1892–Dec. 1893	17	6,147
Jan. 1894–Dec. 1895	18	6,352
Jan. 1896–Dec. 1896	10	3,952
Jan. 1897–Dec. 1897	14	6,052
Jan. 1898–Dec. 1898	15	5,942
Feb. 1899–Dec. 1900	16	6,739
Jan. 1901–Dec. 1901	17	7,346
Jan. 1902–Dec. 1902	16	6,491
Jan. 1903–Dec. 1903	14	5,117
Jan. 1904–Dec. 1904	18	7,691
Jan. 1905–June 1905	11	4,836
July 1905–Dec. 1905	7	3,078
Jan. 1906–June 1906	13	6,141
July 1906–Dec. 1906	12	5,512
Jan. 1907–Dec. 1907	1	6,489
Jan. 1908–Dec. 1908	7	3,173
Jan. 1909–Dec. 1909	7	2,487
Jan. 1910–Nov. 1910	12	5,860
Jan. 1911–July 1911	11	5,065
TOTAL (1860–1911)	384	152,184

Source: Surendra Bhana, *Indentured Indian Emigrants to Natal, 1860-1902: A Study based on Ships' Lists*, New Delhi: Promila & Co., 1991, p. 3.

heightened racial discrimination that was prevailing there. Apart from the indentured Indians, there were also other groups of Indian immigrants in Natal, known as 'passengers', and Muslim traders known as 'Arabs'. The whites and the 'natives' perceived these ex-indentured

TABLE 1.6: Number of Indian Immigrants in Overseas Colonies

Country	Total Emigration	Returned	Percentage
West Indies	534,109	149,054	28
Mauritius	466,018	168,747	36
Reunion	118,000	88,000	75
Natal	152,184	34,001	23

Source: C.G. Henning, *The Indentured Indian in Natal, 1860-1917,* New Delhi: Promila & Co., 1993, p. 23.

Indians as a major threat (discussed later). It should be pointed out that in Natal, political and economic factors were also different (such as the political threat posed by the natives [Africans]; the two Boer wars; and the emergence of different economic sectors in the colony, for example— coal, gold, and diamonds mines, and the hotel industry, among others) from the other overseas plantation economies, and these changes had an enormous impact on the condition of the Indian indentured in colonial Natal.

Indian immigrants, mostly Gujaratis belonging to the established trading castes of India, called 'passengers', came to South Africa for trading and commercial purposes. But they also faced discrimination at the hands of the colonists. However, they became an important part of the Natal economy. In this context, Mr Justice Wragg mentioned:

...Free Indians thrive in Natal. Their industrious habits cause them to prosper in nearly every occupation in which they are engaged. They do remarkably well as cultivators...They have converted wasteland and unproductive lands into well-kept gardens planted with vegetables, tobacco, maize and fruit trees. Those settled in the vicinity of Durban and Pietermaritzburg have succeeded in winning for themselves almost entirely the supplying of the local market with vegetables...Natal is admirably suited whether as a temporary or a permanent home to Indian immigrants...[176]

The Europeans felt that the free Indians were competing with them and their (the Indians') prosperity was regarded as a potential danger. They even felt that the Natal government, by allowing these free Indians to settle, was actually interfering in the economic rights of the European settlers. There was another fear of the whites, as Hilda Kuper has pointed out. Since the Indian population was mostly comprised of young people, the birth rate within them was higher as compared to the Europeans, and there was a possibility of Indians increasing more

TABLE 1.7: Population Structure in Natal, 1860–1911

Year	Europeans		Africans		Indians	
	Number	*%*	*Number*	*%*	*Number*	*%*
1861	12,538	8.2	139,625	90.9	1,512	0.9
1871	17,380	6.0	266,817	92.2	5,070	1.8
1881	28,483	7.6	329,253	87.1	20,196	5.3
1891	46,788	8.2	483,690	84.6	41,142	7.2
1904	97,109	8.8	904,041	82.1	100,918	9.1
1911	98,114	8.2	953,398	80.4	133,420	11.4

Source: Y.S. Meer, *Documents of Indentured Labour: Natal 1851-1917*, Durban: Institute of Black Research, 1980, p. 60.

rapidly in number than the Europeans and Africans. The higher birth rate was used as the basis of much anti-Indian propaganda by the whites, who constantly expressed their fear of being swamped.[177] This fear was not merely an imagination of the colonizers; the period witnessed a tremendous growth of the Indian population in Natal, as given in Table 1.7.

Thus, these people became a considerable part of the population, in a numerically and socially significant manner. This rapid increase in the Indian population in Natal became a major problem for the political economy of colonial Natal. At the same time, the number of free Indians was increasing day by day; once they gained freedom from their indentureship, they preferred to settle down elsewhere in the colony itself. The increasing population of free Indians (along with indentured Indians) in the colony, excluding the Indian traders (known as Arabs) –is shown in Table 1.8.

The other provinces of South Africa also blamed the Natal

TABLE 1.8: Number of Free and Indentured Indian Immigrants in Natal

Year	Category of Indians	
	Free Indians	*Indentured Indians*
1886	20,877	8,951
1901	47,599	25,000
1910	65,917	27,028

Source: Annual Report of the Protector of Indian Immigrants of the respective years, Revenue and Agriculture Department (Emigration Branch), NAI.

government for this rapid increase of Indians, which they considered to be hazardous.[178] They forced the government to introduce an 'Anti-Asiatic Bill' and put an end to the further introduction of indentured Indian immigrants. Consequently, Act 25 of 1891 saw a revision of the law pertaining to indentured immigrants. The grant of crown land to contract-expired Indian labourers, as per Section 51 of Law 2 of 1870, was now revoked; the aim was obviously to discourage Indians from migrating to Natal and then settling down there permanently.[179]

The white settlers of Natal discovered now that the Black (Zulu) population would be a cheaper source of labour. There would be no shipping expenses, no medical fees, less wages to provide, etc. Thus, the Indian and Natal governments passed a law according to which after 30 June 1911, no Indian emigrant would be introduced into Natal under the provision of Law 25, 1891. One of the first anti-Indian moves was the introduction of Act 25 of 1894, which sought to deprive about 251 Asiatic people of the parliamentary franchise. This however, had little effect on the 'free' ex-indentured Indians, as most of them were too poor to qualify for the franchise. But the Indian traders had to face these repercussions. Gandhi, at this point of time, started the movement for franchised rights for the Indians in Natal. However, the anti-Indian feeling became stronger with passing years. The Europeans demanded that if the 'free' Indians decided to stay back in Natal, their status should be reduced and they should carry an identity document, stating their freedom of movement and place of residence or proof of business. It was also recommended that the 'penalty upon residence' should be raised to £10, with some capitalists even suggesting £50, in order to discourage Indians from settling down in Natal.[180] In 1893, Mr Henry Binns, a member of the Legislative Assembly of Natal and Mr Louis Henry Meson, Protector of Immigrants in the colony of Natal, were sent to India to work out an arrangement for the indentured labourers' return to India after the expiry of their five-year contract, or stay in Natal through a re-indentured contract.[181] It was also during this time that the Natal government stopped issuing licenses to the Indians for trade, opening shops, and other independent occupations. According to the Act 17 of 1895, after completion of the five years of indenture, the immigrants had to either return to India or had to get re-indentured; but if they desired to stay in Natal, they were supposed to pay a 'penalty' of a £3 tax per annum, in addition to a £1 per annum tax for males.[182] In 1903, this tax was extended to girls aged thirteen and boys aged sixteen. In 1913, Gandhi started an agitation on this issue, against the iniquitous tax and unjust laws. Due to the strong agitation, the tax was withdrawn in 1914. While the law tried to restrict the entrance of Indians to the colony, the way in for the Indian immigrants' (already residing in Natal) wives and children became a very controversial issue in the history of migration in Natal.

The Natal government had separate policies for European immigrants. It passed the Act of 1894, titled, 'To amend the Law relating to the Management of European Immigration', to strengthen the position of the White settlers in the colony.[183] The government also provided them with opportunities for settling in the colony, like the opening up of new areas for residence. In the 1890s, there were pressures on the Government to open up reserved African lands, Zululand (which was under the control of Africans, and this became a cause for the second Boer war), for white settlers in Natal. The White settlers in the colony also had the right to sell and transfer their lands. These laws were only applicable to the British subjects from London or Southampton, residing in Natal. There were few categories of immigrants from the European subjects; they came as wife and family, female relatives, intended wife, female domestic servant, female shop assistant and clerk, dressmaker, governess, and agriculturist.[184] The government also accepted applications (for emigration) from persons not included in these categories, on their special merits, and there was an agent-general for the European migrants, who sanctioned their emigration in the colony.

Prior to this, during the early phase of the plantation economy in Natal, the government adopted a very strict policy towards native emigration into the colony. The government passed a law in 1855 to prevent natives being brought into the province. According to this law, the subjects of the 'native' chiefs residing beyond the boundaries of Natal should not be brought or encouraged to come into the province. But in 1859, the government introduced immigrants from the east of the Cape of Good Hope.[185] Like the indentured Indians, they also had to sign a contract under the supervision of the protector of immigrants—a verbal contract, for a period of not more than one year, or a written contract of service for not more than three years. Unlike the Indian indentured, however, the native emigrants' passage money and other expenses were not considered as a debt, and was not recoverable from them; on the contrary, in this case, the masters with whom the emigrants had signed their contracts had to pay all the expenses.[186] Like the Indian indentured, they too had to get a 'ticket of registration' from the protector of immigrants.[187] They also had to take a pass before entering or leaving the colony. The magistrate was responsible for issuing the passes, but inward passes could be issued by any authorized officer; however, no passes were to be issued until a prescribed fee was paid for this.

By the Law of 1884, the Natal government made a provision for regulating the entry of natives from the neighboring states and territories. According to the law, the term of service of these people was a year or two, and they had the freedom to choose it for themselves. The wages of the native immigrants were seventeen shillings per month for agricultural labour, and one pound per month for ordinary labour. In addition to their wages; rations, lodging, medicine, and medical attendance were also provided to them by their employers. Thus, unlike the hostile policies of prohibition towards the Indian indentured, the Natal colonial government, during the late-nineteenth century, considered the native people as a cheap and good source of labour, and thus adopted a favorable emigration policy towards them.

Thus, it can be said that the situations in Natal and Mauritius were very different from each other. In Natal, the Indians had to deal with the rigid discriminatory attitude of both the white community and the government, while in Mauritius, they had the opportunity to become a part of the larger society. In Natal, 'passengers' or free Indians became an economic threat for the white settlers, while in Mauritius, the free Indians became small planters (though they had to face a lot of hardships) and were not perceived as an economic threat by the European settlers.

Conclusion

The overseas colonial governments and the Government of India introduced a number of laws for both the employers and the employees of the plantations. These laws, though designed to protect the Indian immigrants in the colonies, were neither strictly executed nor enforced. In case of the overseas colonies, there were employers who interpreted the laws according to their own interests. As Revd W. Pearson[188] commented, '...the laws afford him (the indentured Indian) no adequate protection, either in principal or in practice.' It was also difficult for the illiterate indentured to understand the jargon of those laws. H.S.L. Polak considered the indentured system as 'temporary slavery'.

He further stated, 'The Indian labourer is often regarded by his employer as of less account than a good beast, for the latter costs money to replace, whereas the former is a cheap commodity.'[189] This comparison between the labourers and a beast reflects the level of degradation that the Indians had to face in the plantation colonies. Undoubtedly, the indentured were subjected to great hardships by their employers who had dehumanizing tendencies, and they also had to face petty prosecution, constant injustice, and appalling cruelty, which highly contributed to accelerated rate of suicides.

Notes

1. David Northrup, *Indentured Labour in the Age of Imperialism, 1834-1922*, USA: Cambridge University Press, 1995, p. 16.
2. Cited in Amit Kumar Mishra, *Mauritius*, Delhi: National Book Trust, 2008, p. 1. Mark Twain wrote this line in his travelogue *Following the Equator: A Journey Around the World*, in 1897.
3. Ranbir Singh, *Mauritius, the Key to the Indian Ocean*, Delhi: Arnold-Heinemann, 1980, p. vii.
4. Ibid., p. 13. The Mauritius government website claims the island of Mauritius started to emerge around 8 million years ago. For details see http://www.govmu.org/English/ExploreMauritius/Geography-People/Pages/GeographyPeople/Overview.aspx, accessed 5 December 2018.
5. Larry W. Bowman, *Mauritius: Democracy and Development in the Indian Ocean*, London: Westview Press, 1991, p. 2.
6. Ibid., p. 3.
7. Jitendra Kumar Mittal, *Mauritius*, Delhi: Rajpal & Sons, 1972, pp. 7–8.
8. Bowman, *Mauritius: Democracy and Development*, p. 4.
9. Mishra, *Mauritius*, p. 3.
10. Prahlad Ramsharan, *Mauritius Ka Itihas*, Delhi: Rajpal & Sons, 1979.
11. Mabel Palmer, *The History of the Indians in Natal*, Cape Town: Oxford University Press, 1957, p. 1.
12. Ibid.
13. Ibid., p. 2.
14. Mishra, *Mauritius*, p. 16.
15. Ibid., pp. 21–2.
16. Singh, *Mauritius*, p. 18.
17. S.B. Mookherji, *The Indenture System in Mauritius, 1837-1915*, Calcutta: Firma K.L. Mukhopadhyay, 1962, p. 8.
18. Ibid.
19. Ibid., p. 9.
20. Mishra, *Mauritius*, p. 40.

21. Percival R. Kirby, ed., *Andrew Smith and Natal: Documents relating to the Early History of that Province*, Cape Town: Van Riebeeck Society, 1955, p. 221.
22. Leo Marquard, *The Story of South Africa*, London: Faber and Faber Limited, 1955, pp. 218–19.
23. M. Reddy, 'Structural Adjustment Policies, Agricultural Growth and Rural Poverty in Fiji', *Journal of South Pacific Agriculture,* vol. V, no. 1, 1998, p. 61.
24. Mishra, *Mauritius,* p. 44.
25. Ibid.
26. Toussaint Auguste, *History of Mauritius*, tr. W.E.F. Ward, London: Macmillan, 1977, p. 63.
27. Bowman, *Mauritius: Democracy and Development*, p. 19.
28. P.S. Vivek, *From Indentured Labour to Liberated Nation: Public Policy and Small Planters in Mauritius,* Bangalore: Focus Press, 2007, p. 152.
29. Ibid.
30. Hugh Tinker, *A New System of Slavery: The Export of Indian Labour Overseas, 1830-1920*, London: Oxford University Press, 1974, p. 3.
31. Ibid., pp. 25–6.
32. Sidney W. Mintz, *Sweetness and Power: The Place of Sugar in Modern History*, New York: Viking, 1985, p. 71; cited in Bowman, *Mauritius*, p. 19.
33. Bowman, *Mauritius*, p. 19.
34. Mookherji, *Indenture System in Mauritius,* p. 39.
35. Helen Chapin Metz, ed., *Indian Ocean: Five Island Countries*, Washington: Federal Research Division, Library of Congress, 1995, p. 102.
36. Letter from the Protector of Indian Immigrants in Mauritius to the acting Colonial Secretary, titled 'Alleged Depression in the Mauritius Sugar Industry and its effect on Indian Labourers', Revenue and Agriculture Department (Emigration Branch) Proceedings, January 1886, no. 7, paras. 1–4, National Archives of India (hereafter NAI).
37. Vivek, *From Indentured Labour to Liberated Nation*, p. 159.
38. Ibid.
39. This refers to the Indian immigrants in Mauritius who have completed their indentureship of five years in the colony and had settled there as free people.
40. Vivek, *From Indentured Labour to Liberated Nation*, p. 159.
41. Ibid., p. 8.
42. Northrup, *Indentured Labor*, p. 133.
43. Palmer, *History of Indians in Natal*, p. 2.
44. Hilda Kuper, *Indian People in Natal,* Durban: Natal University Press, 1960, p. xii.
45. John Robinson, *Notes on Natal: An Old Colonist's Book for New Settlers*, Durban: Robinson & Vause, 1872.
46. Ibid., pp. 1–4.

47. Ibid., p. 30.
48. Ibid., p. 48.
49. Ibid.
50. Ibid.
51. Colin A. Lewis, 'The South African Sugar Industry', *Geographical Journal*, vol. 156, no. 1, 1990, p. 70.
52. Surendra Bhana, *Indentured Indian Emigrants to Natal, 1860-1902: A Study based on Ships' Lists*, New Delhi: Promila & Co., 1991, p. 87.
53. Peter Richardson, 'The Natal Sugar Industry, 1849-1905: An Interpretive Essay', *The Journal of African History*, vol. XXIII, no. 4, 1982, p. 518.
54. Natal Ordinances 6 and 7 of 1855; Natal Law 1 of 1867, Law 16 of 1875; Laws 2, 3, and 4 of 1881 and Law of 1886; cited in Richardson, 'Natal Sugar Industry', p. 518.
55. Order-in-council of September 1846; Natal Ordinances 6 and 7 of 1855; Law 19 of 1859; Law 11 of 1861; Law 13 of 1863; Law 1 of 1867; cited in Richardson, 'Natal Sugar Industry', p. 518.
56. Richardson, 'Natal Sugar Industry', p. 521.
57. Lewis, 'South African Sugar Industry', p. 70.
58. Thomas R. Metcalf, 'Indian Migration to South Africa', in *Studies in Migration: Internal and International Migration in India*, ed. M.S.A. Rao, New Delhi: Manohar Publications, 1986, p. 352.
59. Bhana, *Indentured Indian Emigrants*, p. 87.
60. Richardson, 'Natal Sugar Industry', p. 522.
61. Ibid.
62. Ibid.
63. Ibid., p. 525. This phrase appeared for the first time in the Natal Sugar Act of 1936.
64. Desai and Vahed, *Inside Indenture*, p. 107.
65. Lewis, 'South African Sugar Industry', p. 70.
66. Richardson, 'Natal Sugar Industry', p. 526.
67. Ibid.
68. Bhana, *Indentured Indian Emigrants*, p. 89.
69. Ibid.
70. Metcalf, 'Indian Migration to South Africa', p. 335.
71. Annual Report of the Protector of Indian Immigrants in Natal for the year 1902, Revenue and Agriculture Department (Emigration Branch) Proceedings, December 1903, nos. 3–5, NAI.
72. Ibid.
73. Annual Report of the Natal Emigrant Protector for the year 1901', Revenue and Agriculture Department (Emigration Branch) Proceedings, August 1902, nos. 16–18, NAI.
74. Commerce and Industry Department (Emigration Branch) Proceedings, March 1910, nos. 14–43, NAI.
75. Mookherji, *Indenture System in Mauritius*, p. 11.

76. Ibid., p. 12.
77. Singh, *Mauritius*, p. 37.
78. *Parliamentary Papers, India,* vol. XVI, no. 45, p. 1841.
79. Letter, *The Royal Gazette*, 18 June 1834, Bermuda; cited in David Aickin, 'From Plantation Medicine to Public Health: The State and Medicine in British Guiana 1838-1914', unpublished PhD thesis, University College London, UK, 2001, p. 29.
80. Enclosure no. 2, letter from Gillanders Arbuthnot and Co. to J. Gladstone, 6 June 1836; letter from J. Gladstone to Lord Glenelg, 28 February 1838; *Parliamentary Papers, UK*, vol. LII, pp. 1837–8.
81. Tinker, *New System of Slavery*, p. 63.
82. Vivek, *From Indentured Labour to Liberated Nation*, p. 79.
83. *Parliamentary Papers, UK*, 1837–8, document nos. (11), (180), (232).
84. Mookherji, *Indenture System in Mauritius,* p. 17.
85. *Parliamentary Papers, India*, vol. III, 1937–8, undated report of T.C. Scott; cited in Mookherji, *Indenture System in Mauritius*, p. 18.
86. C. Kondapi, *Indian Overseas, 1838-1949*, New Delhi: Indian Council of World Affairs, 1951, p. 8.
87. Mookherji, *Indenture System in Mauritius*, p. 21.
88. Ibid., p. 26.
89. Singh, *Mauritius*, p. 37.
90. Mookherji, *Indenture System in Mauritius*, p. 29.
91. Ibid.
92. Ibid., p. 142.
93. Ibid., pp. 30–1.
94. Geoghegan, 'Report on Coolie Emigration from India, 1874', *Parliamentary Papers, UK*, vol. 314, 1874, pp. 12–13; Letter from A.B. Clapperton, Master Attendant Office, to G.B. Greenlaw, Secretary to the Marine Board, Home Department (Public Branch) O.C., 20 April 1874, no. 4, para. 2, NAI.
95. Letter from A.B. Clapperton to G.B. Greenlaw, Home Department (Public Branch) O.C.
96. 'Plan of the Mauritius Free Labour Association instituted under the Sanction of Government', Home Department (Public Branch) O.C., 12 May 1841, no. 20, NAI.
97. Vivek, *From Indentured Labour to Liberated Nation*, p. 85.
98. Mookherji, *Indenture System in Mauritius,* p. 29.
99. Kondapi, *Indian Overseas*, p. 11.
100. Letter from Colonial Secretary, Mauritius, to the Secretary to the Government of Madras, Home Department (Public Branch) O.C., 21 December 1849, no. 17, NAI.
101. I.M. Cumpston, *Indians Overseas in British Territories, 1834-1854*, London: Oxford University Press, 1953, p. 176.

102. Geoghegan, 'Report on Coolie Emigration from India, 1874', paras. 4 and 5.
103. Mookherji, *Indenture System in Mauritius*, p. 47.
104. Kondapi, *Indian Overseas*, p. 13.
105. Mauritius Ordinance no. 1 of 1879, Home, Revenue and Agriculture Department (Emigration Branch) Proceedings, January 1880, nos. 24–6, NAI.
106. Ibid.
107. Mookherji, *Indenture System in Mauritius*, p. 48.
108. Y.S. Meer, *Documents of Indentured Labour: Natal 1851-1917*, Durban: Institute of Black Research, 1980, p. 22.
109. Ibid., p. 34.
110. Ibid., p. 29.
111. Extract from the letter from the Colonial Secretary of the Cape of Good Hope, R.W. Rawson, to the Colonial Secretary of Natal, cited in Meer, *Documents of Indentured Labour*, p. 32.
112. Letter from Secretary to the Government of Bengal to the Secretary to the Government of India, Home Department (Public Branch) O.C., 2 January 1857, nos. 11–12, part A, NAI.
113. Home Department (Public Branch) Proceedings, 31 March 1858, no. 44, part A, NAI.
114. Editorial, 'Critical Labour Situation', *The Natal Mercury*, , 24 August 1859; cited in Meer, *Documents of Indentured Labour*, p. 36.
115. Ibid., p. 37, document no. 14.
116. C.G. Henning, *The Indentured Indian in Natal, 1860-1917*, New Delhi: Promila & Co., 1993, p. 9.
117. Ibid., p. 15.
118. Ibid.
119. Meer, *Documents of Indentured Labour*, pp. 39–47, document no. 15.
120. Act no. XXXIII of 1860, Home Department (Public Branch) Proceedings, 7 August 1860, nos. 13–24, part A, NAI.
121. Henning, *Indentured Indian in Natal*, p. 16.
122. Abstract 'Truro', cited in Meer, *Documents of Indentured Labour*, p. 68.
123. Diary no. 55, Madras government notice no. 409, dated 26 May 1872, Agriculture, Revenue and Commerce Department (Emigration Branch) Proceedings, May 1872, nos. 13–19, NAI.
124. Henning, *Indentured Indian in Natal*, p. 38.
125. Desai and Vahed, *Inside Indenture*, p. 107.
126. Henning, *Indentured Indian in Natal*, p. 38.
127. Keate's dispatch of 21 Dec. 1871, no. 125, Agriculture and Commerce Department (Emigration Branch) Proceedings, October 1872, nos. 4–5, NAI.
128. Henning, *Indentured Indian in Natal*, p. 41.
129. Report of the Coolie Commission, in the letter from A. Musgrave, Esq.

Lieutenant-Governor of Natal to the Secretary of State, Revenue, Agriculture and Commerce Department (Emigration Branch) Proceedings, February 1873, nos. 16–19, NAI.

130. Ibid.

131. Ibid.

132. Ibid.

133. Ibid. Rangasamy, in his testimony, stated '…the scarcity of females caused many debauches, and in many cases they [the males] committed suicide.' He also held strong views on punishment for adultery.

134. Ibid.

135. Desai and Vahed, *Inside Indenture*, p. 13.

136. Henning, *Indentured Indian in Natal*, p. 53.

137. Diary no. 55, Madras Government notice no. 409.

138. Henning, *Indentured Indian in Natal*, p. 53.

139. Ordinance 12 of 1872, Revenue, Agriculture and Commerce Department (Emigration Branch) Proceedings, June 1873, nos. 5–7, NAI.

140. Ibid.

141. Ibid.

142. Henning, *Indentured Indian in Natal*, p. 54.

143. Ordinance 12 of 1872, Revenue, Agriculture and Commerce Department (Emigration Branch) Proceedings.

144. Ibid.

145. Revenue and Agriculture Department (Emigration Branch) Proceedings, June 1873, no. 6, file no. 58, NAI.

146. Ibid.

147. Bernard S. Cohn, *Colonialism and its Forms of Knowledge: The British in India*, Princeton: Princeton University Press, 1996, p. 61.

148. New Natal Law 14 of 1875, Revenue and Agriculture Department (Emigration Branch) Proceedings, April 1882, nos. 81–5, NAI.

149. Henning, *Indentured Indian in Natal*, p. 54.

150. New Natal Law 14 of 1875, Revenue and Agriculture Department (Emigration Branch) Proceedings.

151. Ibid.

152. Ibid.

153. Brij V. Lal, 'Labouring Men and Nothing More: Some Problem of Indian Indenture in Fiji', in *Indentured Labour in the British Empire*, ed. Kay Saunders, London and Canberra: Croom Helm, 1984, p. 128.

154. For example, see Appendix 3, 'Notice to the Intending Migrants for the Demerara Colony', CO 352/101, Notice to the Indian Immigrants, The National Archives of UK (Kew, London).

155. Letter from the Government of India to the Secretary of State for the Colonies, Government of India, Agriculture and Commerce Department (Emigration Branch) Proceedings, September 1873, nos. 16–22, NAI.

156. Meer, *Documents of Indentured Labour*, p. 4.

157. John Bolton, Half Yearly Report of the Inspections of Estates in Mauritius for 31 December 1911, Commerce and Industry Department (Emigration Branch) Proceedings, October 1912, nos. 24–5, part B, NAI.

158. Bowman, *Mauritius*, p. 19.

159. Geoghegan, 'Report on Coolie Emigration from India, 1874', p. 62.

160. Mookherji, *Indenture System in Mauritius*, p. 50.

161. *Report of the Royal Commissioners Appointed to Enquire into the Treatment of Immigrants in Mauritius*, London: William Clowes and Sons, 1875, p. 3 [C.1115].

162. Mookherji, *Indenture System in Mauritius,* p. 50.

163. Geoghegan, 'Report on Coolie Emigration from India, 1874', p. 88.

164. Ibid.

165. *Report of the Royal Commissioners*, p. 16 [C.1115].

166. Mauritius Immigration Report for the year 1913, Commerce and Industry Department (Emigration Branch) Proceedings, March 1915, nos. 3–5, part B, NAI.

167. Singh, *Mauritius*, p. 55.

168. No. 19, letter to J. B. Petit, Ahmedabad, 16 June 1915, *The Collected Works of Mahatma Gandhi*, vol. XV, New Delhi: Publications Division, Government of India (electronic book), 1999, p. 18. For the condition of Indian indentured in Natal, see Report Post from a 'Natal Correspondent', no. 100, 3 September 1900 and India 12 October 1900, *The Collected Works of Mahatma Gandhi*, vol. III, p. 370.

169. Ibid., p. 65.

170. *The Mahratta* was a newspaper started by the extremist nationalist Bal Gangadhar Tilak, in English. Letter from Dr. Manilal to the Editor of *The Mahratta*, Commerce and Industry Department (Emigration Branch) Proceedings, August 1911, no. 7, part B, NAI.

171. Kuper, *Indian People in Natal*, p. xvi.

172. Editorial, *The Natal Mercury*, 22 November 1860; cited in Meer, *Documents of Indentured Labour in Natal*, pp. 5–6.

173. Meer, *Documents of Indentured Labour*, p. 68–92, Document no. 26.

174. G.E.W. Wolstenholme and Maeve O'Connor, eds., *Immigration: Medical and Social Aspects*, London: J. & A. Churchill Ltd., 1966, p. 20.

175. Report of the Coolie Commission, in the letter from A. Musgrave.

176. 'The Wragg Commission Report 1885-87', see Meer, *Documents of Indentured Labour*, p. 321.

177. Kuper, *Indian People in Natal,* p. xii.

178. General Smuts, 'Africa for Whites: Closing the door on Asia', *Rand Daily Mail*, 29 January 1908, Johannesburg; Commerce and Industry Department (Emigration Branch) Proceedings, September 1908, no. 21, NAI.

179. Henning, *Indentured Indian in Natal*, p. 81.

180. Letter from G.E. Mahalingam Iyer to the Chief Secretary to the Government of India, Revenue and Agriculture Department (Emigration Branch) Proceedings, March 1894, nos. 7–17, NAI.
181. Ibid.
182. Ibid.
183. 'Laws and Regulations in force in Colonies under Responsible Government", *Parliamentary Papers, UK*, July 1904, p. 68 [Cmd. 2105].
184. Ibid.
185. Ibid., p. 71.
186. Ibid., p. 72.
187. Ibid., p. 78; cited in the 'African Immigration Notice', Natal government notice no. 25, 1889. For more details see Appendix 1.
188. Revd W. Pearson was sent by the Government of India to Natal in 1914, to act as an 'observer' of the Indian emigrants in Natal. See W.W. Pearson, 'Report on my visit to South Africa', *The Modern Review*, June 1914, p. 637; cited in Henning, *Indentured Indian in Natal*, p. 107.
189. H.S.L. Polak, *The Indian of South Africa: Helots within the Empire and how they are Treated*, Madras: G.A. Natesan and Co., 1909, p. 6; cited in Henning, *Indentured Indian in Natal*, p. 107.

CHAPTER TWO

Making 'Suitable' Indentured Labour
On the Depots of Calcutta and Madras

...after examination of the Indian emigrants landed from [this] vessel, we have pleasure in reporting that they were a very healthy lot of men and very compact and muscular in build. We have pleasure in stating that none of these men had to be allotted conditionally. We are of opinion that great care had been exercised by the surgeon superintendent in the selection of the immigrants and also in his treatment of them on board ship.

—DR G. P. STAMTON, Annual Report of the Protector
of Indian Immigrants in Natal for the year 1898

The plantation economy primarily focused on good physique and masculinity as a crucial element and sign of efficient labour power. The recruiting agent was expected to recruit 'able-bodied' agricultural labourers having 'good health'. The focus was more on the physical appearance and the body of the indentured. First slave, then convicts, and after that, indentured labourers were employed for working in these overseas plantations. Medical knowledge regarding 'the Indian body' was utilized to recruit the fit and weed out the frail and sickly. Anil Persaud, in this context, has argued that the indentured labourers were recruited not only on the basis of their physical strength, but also because of their ability to work as agricultural labourers.[1] In support of his argument, he gave an example of recruitment areas and 'hardy agricultural races'. Further, while comparing slavery and indentured labour, he argued 'whereas slavery invested the black body with strength; indentured invested it with varying forms of knowledge, such as knowledge of wages and contract, moral uprightness, knowledge of agriculture and then there was "knowledge" carried in their blood in the form of immunity and suitability.' To some extent it is true that for an indentured, 'agricultural knowledge' was the first criterion; but a strong and healthy body was considered to be equally important during the recruitment process. In the course of this chapter, we will see that Persaud's argument can be considered acceptable for the initial phase of indentured recruitment; but during the latter period, particularly after 1870s, there was a shift in this attitude, when a kind of tussle began between the 'British Raj's knowledge and the indentured body' for their survival. Persaud argued that labour's 'suitability' made them beneficial for the plantation economy;[2] but he did not deal with a number of the governmental policies that made the labourers' bodies 'suitable' for the same. The planters and the white doctors adopted a general definition of health that measured an indentured person's worthiness according to the market value and potential for productive and long-lasting labour. The objectification of indentured health extended beyond the body, and included measures of character and skill as well.

In this chapter, I would like to deliberate upon this process of making indentured labour 'suitable' for these colonies—how modern science, technology, new knowledge, and medicine helped the colonial government to fulfil its purpose and how this scientific and medical knowledge affected the recruitment process of indentured labourers. Further, I would also like to delve into the migrants' interaction with this scientific knowledge and medicine on the depots and how this interfered with their lives. This chapter will also highlight the everyday practices of migrants and their resistance against the imposition of this newly developed science and medicine.

Recruitment of 'Hard' Hands and 'Healthy' Bodies

The recruitment of indentured labour was the most important issue for the colonial plantations, and the recruiter played an important role in this process. He decided the criterion of recruitment. Thus, he focused more on the physical appearance and 'body build' of the recruits. Generally, the recruiters at the top level were all European officials, but at the local level, the *arkaties* and *duffadars* were reportedly from the ranks that supplied 'sepoys, *chaprasis*, and domestic servants', who acted as scouts for the regular recruiters. Major Pitcher's report shows that most of the men employed were bearers, cavalry men, infantry men, policemen, sepoys, *chaprasis*, and others. Very few of them could read or write.[3]

Recruiters were generally imagined by the coolies as schemers, liars, and even as 'kidnappers' of female recruits. Their work was to inform the emigrants about the nature of work, destination, and terms of indentured contract. However in reality, they mostly misinformed the recruits. Gaiutra Bahadur, in her recent work, stated: '...They gave recruits the false impression that they could return home from their jobs for the weekend; they promised work as easy as sifting sugar; and they exaggerated the gains to be had, inflating wages and conjuring lands of milk, honey and gold.'[4]

By the 1870s, a well-organized recruitment system under the aegis of the emigration agent of the colonies had been established. Under the emigration agent, the actual recruiting was done by the head recruiters or subagents assisted by the recruiters, the clerks, the food contractors and several hangers-on.[5] The emigration agent appointed subagents in the headquarters of the main recruiting districts, who, in turn, employed a set of recruiters. Recruiters were broadly of two types, viz., licensed and unlicensed. The subagents and the recruiters were licensed by the protector of emigrants. The formal system of recruitment was however buttressed by proliferating numbers of unlicensed recruiters and subcontractors who worked under the licensed subagent and the recruiters. The unlicensed recruiters were universally known as *arkaties*. Major Pitcher and G. Grierson found that a licensed recruiter was always a man, while an unlicensed recruiter could be either a man or a woman. Licensed recruiters included the head recruiters, commonly known as subagents, and ordinary recruiters who may be subordinated either to a head recruiter or to someone working independently.[6] The recruiters were paid both on a contract basis and in a regular salary system. However, the head recruiters were always paid on a contract basis, i.e. price per coolie introduced into the emigration depot at the port of embarkation (like Calcutta or Madras). The price for a coolie varied according to the distance of the main depot from the place of recruitment. The expense of travelling was the main item of difference. The subordinate recruiters were paid by the head recruiter, while the head recruiters and independent recruiters were paid by the emigration agent.

The main function of the licensed recruiters was to gather the intending emigrants, get them medically examined and register them with the magistrate before sending them to the main port for embarkation. The unlicensed recruiters were often the main agents for gathering intending emigrants for the licensed recruiters. The unlicensed female recruiters were very active in the process of recruitment of female labourers. Major Pitcher described the female recruiters in the following words: 'They are unlicensed, of no character, and entirely beyond government control, they are without exception degraded specimens of their sex, and the mischief they do can easily be imagined.'[7]

The recruiters favoured certain castes and regions, and disfavoured those who they did not consider as good labour.[8] They were directed to recruit only muscular, healthy, and able-bodied labourers. They were also directed not to recruit males above forty-five years and females over thirty-five years, unless they formed the part of a family.[9] On the one hand, certain classes of Indians, such as priests, beggars, weavers, ex-policemen, clerks, barbers, tailors, shopkeepers, discharged convicts, goldsmiths, persons suffering from infirmity, brahmins, *baniahs*, fakeers, and *kyesths* (Kayasthas) were not to be recruited; on the other hand, the order for women for the agents was: 'You may pass all females of 18 years and over, no matter whether Mohammedan or of any caste than the lowest caste, provided, they have reasonably hard hands and are not beggars, devotees, dancing girls or prostitutes.'[10] The reason behind this unquestioned recruitment of women was that they were not considered as a reliable agricultural labour force, and therefore, there was no need of weeding out the 'disorderly' or 'not suitable' women. During the late 1870s, planters considered that *Madrasee* labourers had proven to be better as compared to the *Kalkatyia* labourers. Consequently, there was a time when no applications were filled by the planters for *Kalkatyia* labourers.[11] As the protector of immigrants in Mauritius remarked in his annual report, '...Planters seem of late to show a preference for Madras coolies. The cost of their introduction is less than that of others'.[12] The medical superintendent, while emphasizing on the physical qualities of the coolies, remarked, 'the Madras men, generally speaking, were a mixed lot as regards physique, altogether a considerable number were of good muscular development. Nevertheless, they should, I think, prove a serviceable body of labourers.'[13]

Women participants were essential for the plantation for production as well as reproduction purposes. Their importance can be seen in the recruitment process, where a subagent received Rs.22 per male and Rs.33 per female. The subagents were getting a higher amount for recruiting female emigrants, because of the scarcity of females and the difficulty in recruiting them.[14] Apart from this, the emigration agents also considered the possibility that without women, the Indian men might just refuse to migrate to Natal. In this context, the Natal Emigrant Agent, Mr. Firth, remarked to his subagent—'Whenever men were sent without the proper proportion of females they would be returned.'[15] Therefore, a law was made according to which each batch of hundred emigrants had to include at least forty women. The pressure of this law can be seen in a statement of Dr Payne, a medical surgeon of Mauritius at the Calcutta depot, who excused the presence of 'aged' persons, physically weak individuals, and 'hill men' (among whom deaths at sea were frequent on the *Adelaide*, as the result of instructions for a large number of women) citing—'the latter [law] has left me no choice, but to accept some men, whom I should otherwise have rejected, since they have been accompanied by women who could not be replaced.'[16]

The recruiters' agents were primarily responsible for the quality of emigrants. Once the medical surgeon declared that the emigrant was medically fit to embark, the recruiters would get two-third parts of their commission; and, if they successfully embarked at their destination, then the recruiters were eligible for getting the rest of their commission. If the emigrants were medically rejected, they were sent to their home districts at the recruiter's expense.[17] Recruiters got nothing if the coolies were rejected medically or by the protectors in the Calcutta or Madras ports. If a coolie absconded from the depot, changed his or her mind, or died, then the recruiters got half of their rates. This commission system thus put a huge check on recruiters to make them get medically fit and disease-free labourers.

The experience of labour trade and transportation, along with medical knowledge, forced the emigration authority to initiate new regulations regarding the recruitment of indentured labour in India. The high sickness and mortality rates during the sea voyages, along with the agitations by the anti-slavery groups, forced the government to take steps regarding the recruitment of labourers. Apart from this, the pressure from the planters in order to 'maximize the profit' and 'minimize the loss' was also an important motivation. As a result, the Government of India, in 1883, established an enquiry committee under the supervision of Major Pitcher and Grierson. This committee came up with instructions for the surgeons, which the latter had to follow while examining and selecting emigrants for the overseas colonies.

Surgeons were instructed that intending emigrants had to be free from contagious diseases and should be in a fit state to be able to undergo the voyage of three months; they should also have ten years of experience in field work (decided possibly on their physical appearance).[18] Their chest should be round and well developed, and flat-chested men should be rejected. Their hands should have calluses on the palm at the base of the finger, showing that the emigrants were accustomed to hard work. Cases of hernia, hydrocele, and enlarged testicles should be discovered and rejected, as these diseases were usually prevalent in the colonies. Bad cases of ophthalmia or diseased eyelids should be rejected. People with slight ophthalmia may be retained for treatment until cured. If a person had lost an eye from this disease or from any other cause, on no account should he be accepted.[19] Further, they were instructed that emigrants with slight anaemia or malarial fever might be passed if it be considered that a few weeks of good feeding and careful treatment would help them in regaining their vitality. Cases of enlarged spleen and chronic anaemia were to be rejected outright.[20] Dwarfs and scarecrows were to be removed, but short stature or slim build was not a fatal objection if the emigrant was wiry and tough, and was able to handle agricultural implements well.[21] Finally, the height and weight of indentured were also a matter of measure. Recruiters were directed that the weight of the males should be nearly proportionate to the height that was 8 stone 3 lbs. for 5 ft., and an addition of 5 lbs. for each inch over 5 ft. Those who were suffering from slight bowel complaints should be detained till they were cured. The abdomen should not be flat or attenuated from chronic looseness, nor inflated from habitual indigestion. All cases of chronic bowel diseases were to be carefully sought and rejected. They were strictly instructed that opium-eaters and smokers, and *ganja*-smokers should also be rejected. Contagious diseases, measles, and smallpox had hitherto proved most troublesome, and every suspicious case was instructed to be carefully examined.[22] The slightest signs of leprosy, varicose veins in any part of the body, ulcers on legs or feet, and syphilis in any form were regarded as sufficient to justify rejection. Cases of enlarged goitre were undesirable. Sickly children were also regarded as troublesome. Not infrequently, a large family had been kept back month after month at successive embarkations on account of a weak child. All such children were rejected, most possibly with their family members as well. There was also the provision that no emigrant should be passed without vaccination.[23] Here, it is important to note that colonial medical gaze typified and categorized the Indian body, weeding out the frail, redundant, and the idle. Some of the ex-indentured had to pay their own way when they wanted to leave India again, because they were physically too weak to qualify for a new indentureship.[24] Thus, the legal and scientific idea of 'healthiness' created a definition of health that was remarkably supple, and at the same time, severely limiting. The definition of healthiness incorporated subtle variations of age, skill, gender, fecundity, physical strength, mental acuity, and character.

During the 1840s, a number of missionaries, anti-slavery groups, and the Opposition party in the British Parliament criticized the condition of labourers on the voyages and the high mortality and sickness rates during these journeys. They were against the indentured labour system in general; consequently, the recruitment of indentured labour from India to Mauritius was stopped in 1842, till further improvement in the Coolie Law. These agitations forced the government to provide basic medical facilities to the indentured during the voyages. The protector of emigrants at Calcutta had proposed under Section VI of Act XV of 1842, Clause 3, that before sending emigrants to Mauritius Island, the government needed to regulate their medical examination, and also check the medical stores and medical attendants on the voyages.[25] Further, under the same Act, in a modification of Clause 2, which was related to vaccination, the deputy governor suggested that— 'It would be the duty of the superintendent to fulfill the work of vaccination of the intending emigrants in the colony.'[26] The marine surgeon, with a salary of 600 per mensem, or his assistant, would be responsible for certifying to the emigrant agent that the work of vaccination was duly performed in the presidencies.[27] At this point, the medical officers raised an issue regarding the new imposed duty on the marine surgeon and his salary. Medical board officers raised the objection that:

…The situation of marine surgeon even before the recent order did not appear to us by any means over paid and it cannot be denied that they have imposed upon him a great extent of additional duty of the most disagreeable kind…this is very labourious and irksome duties against him as marine surgeon in connection with native emigration to the Mauritius.[28]

The marine surgeon, M.M. Thompson, in his letter to the secretary of the medical board, stated that: '…I have been called upon to perform during the whole course of my service independent of the fatigue which I am compelled for several hours to undergo after I return have weary and exhausted from visiting my patients.(*sic*)'[29] He further stated that, '…I am occupied four or five hours every day except Sunday in examining and granting certificates to the emigrants…in addition to this I have also to examine the supply of medicine and to grant a certificate to each vessel before it sails.'[30]

Medical officers, those who were involved in the indentured's recruitment, wanted a salary equal to the army medical officers. They argued that the salary of Calcutta's medical servants was not acceptable to them, since it was considerably less in comparison to the army medical officers, because they had the advantage of the private practice. The medical officers who were involved in the indentured's recruitment could not spare any time for private practice. In this context, Iams Mutchinson stated in a letter to the medical board that: '...I beg to be allowed to point out that I am in a great measure deprived of this advantage, by having so much of my time daily occupied in examining the emigrants.'[31] It can be argued that like the British army, indentured labourers too were important for the stability of the British Raj. Just as the army was the basis of British conquest and stability in the colonies, the indentured too became the basis of strengthening their rule in the overseas colonies. The colonial government established indentured populations in the colony as their 'own controlled' people, which in its way was a form of territorial expansion. The colonizers learned that for systematic economic gain, as well as for strategic security, organized and controlled manpower was necessary.

Medical practitioners were also aware of the importance of their role in the selection of emigrants. On this basis, they tried to negotiate with the government in order to get a greater share of profit. This led to the 'professionalization' of the whole system. The marine surgeon (Mutchinson) stated: '...from last two months I am doing this disagreeable, enormous and troublesome duty, and the annoyance myself and family are subjected to by my house and premises being eroded by the emigrants for several hours daily where the noise and the effluvium from their persons combine to render it a most so [*sic*] disagreeable office.'[32] Further, he stated that, '...I have not yet applied to the government for any remuneration for the onerous and responsible duty I have performed, but I trust that no objection will be raised to compensation, which the Mauritius merchants are willing to pay, as it is entirely for their own profit and advantage.'[33] The marine surgeon also wrote a letter to the Government of Mauritius, in which he mentioned the importance and the problems of recruitment and selecting an 'able', 'disease free' labour.

Indentured migrants, before their departure, had to go through three stages of medical examinations: the first one was in their own districts, the second at their arrival in the depot by a 'native' doctor, and finally on boarding the ship by a European doctor. By 1892, it was made mandatory that the recruited emigrants would be medically examined in the sub-depots before they signed the indentured contract.[34] This was done in order to avoid the unnecessary expense that were spent on returning the rejected emigrants to their homes. The duty of the medical examiner was to examine the emigrants and to ensure for the planters that the emigrants were suitable for (hard) labour and 'free from all bodily and mental diseases':

...All single men are first examined by the native doctor, to see that they are not suffering from syphilis, gonorrhoea, hernia, or any other disease about the genital organs; those that he considers fit subjects are then marked with a stamp, and brought before me. I usually feel their pluses, look at their tongues, take their general appearance into consideration, examine for pits of smallpox,... married men and women do not undergo the native doctor's examination alluded to above.[35]

In order to receive a labour force with good physique, the overseas colonies paid 8*an.* for each emigrant's medical examination, including infants in arms, whether passed or not, to ensure as far as possible the selection of eligible people.[36] For each coolie passed by the medical officers in Calcutta and Madras, agencies paid the former two rupees and the latter one rupee.[37] Those who were suffering from diseases were sent back by the agencies, as it was believed that they were not fit to emigrate. The government also made a new legislation, according to which no certificate would be regarded as authentic if the marine surgeon had not signed it. The marine surgeon, in turn, was free to decide whether the presenter of the certificate was the real owner of it; he had right to destroy the certificate if he thought otherwise.[38]

The emigrants who were of 'obviously robust health were passed at once', while those who were suffering from sickness or fatigue were given a chance to recover. They were at times remanded at the depot for future recruitment. Those who were rejected by the medical examiners were permanently declared unfit to work as labourers. In 1894, six people were rejected by the medical inspector in Calcutta because of insanity, epilepsy, and excessive intake of opium.[39] These people were regarded as a 'burden' on the plantations and employers were not willing to bear the cost of these 'unfits'. In 1894, about fifty to sixty people were rejected as medically unfit by the Natal Emigrant Trust, which was responsible for recruiting medically fit people.[40] However, the Surinam and Trinidad authorities recruited these people as indentured labour.[41] This shows the relative understanding of health and body in the medical discourse of the day.

The processes involved in medical examination should be examined critically here. What social, political, or economic processes were involved in medical recruitment? Was any compromise made on the part of the colonial government regarding the medical examination of labourers, especially when there was serious scarcity of the same? Moreover, why did the rules regarding recruitment differ from colony to colony?

Under the new Act XXI of 1883, a provision was made for the compensation of rejected emigrants. Section 50 of the Act stated that all rejected emigrants were entitled to compensation, from 8*an.* in the case of children to Rs.3 or more in case of adult males.[42] The purpose behind this regulation was, as Dr J. Grant had stated: 'It has also been observed that the colonial emigration officers might with advantage bring some pressure to bear upon their employees in the interior to send down only fit and able-bodied labourers, and if this were done, a great deal of unnecessary harassment would be avoided.'[43]

The colonial emigration agencies protested against this new law; they argued that in the Act, the award of the compensation was purely optional, while the protector of emigrants apparently considered all rejected emigrants entitled to compensation. The emigrant agent of British Guiana and Surinam argued that—'The loss accruing from rejection is one of the principal factors in the heavy expenditure now incurred in connection with the recruitment of emigrants, and we are apparently to be called on still further to increase this by paying what in the peasant's native village would be more than a month's wages.'[44] In answer to these, the Protector of Emigrants J.G. Grant argued that his procedure had been misapprehended. The compensation was meant only for those labourers who had been—firstly, irregularly recruited, or had been induced to execute contracts under coercion, under influence, fraud, or misrepresentation; secondly, to those who, by execution of contracts, had been definitively engaged by an agency through its recruiters for service in the colony, but were ultimately rejected by that agency (not medical inspector), for no fault of theirs, but in consequences of the emigration agent having decided, for some reason of his own, not to accept them; and thirdly, to those whose ill-treatment or neglect on the journey to the depot was satisfactorily established.[45] It was made clear that no compensation was to be given to the labourers who may be finally rejected by the medical inspector on the medical grounds. Dr Grant considered that unsatisfactory medical examination was a separate issue. He remarked that the remedy lay with the agents themselves, by arranging to hold the medical officers, who were employed as examiners, responsible for the consequences of any neglect or carelessness in the performance of duties for which they were being paid. The rule of compensation was an acceptable technique to pressurize the colonial emigration officers to send only fit and able-bodied labourers. Acquired data shows that about 12 per cent, quite a high number, of the emigrants were rejected at the depot every year. In 1904, this rejection cost Mauritius over Rs.13,000.[46]

The Indians wanted to escape from poverty, and their deteriorated conditions in India pushed them to migrate. However, the new medical norms of fitness became an obstacle. Consequently, they tried to hide their sickness. They were aware of the fact that if their sickness was discovered, they would not be allowed to embark. In order to escape from this medical regime and board the ship, sometimes these rejected persons took the help of the *duffadars*. The *duffadars* helped them for extra commission and income. The intending emigrants paid them two to three rupees for their certificates.[47] The marine surgeon complained that these rejected emigrants—'present themselves several times in the hope of eluding my attention', and stated that 'the only remedy I am suggesting for this very serious fraud, is to re-examine the men after they are all on board, but this would be attended with great inconvenience, trouble and loss of time'.[48] Carter stated, '…the increasing sophistication of frauds led to the use of caustic solutions—marking migrants on the thumb nail or even on the face. Such practices were criticized in the reform press, as they caused some distress to the recruits.'[49] The overseas colonial agencies recommended that the local medical officers in the overseas colonies were better judges of the standards of fitness necessary for satisfactory performance in the plantations. They recommended that in order to avoid disappointment and unnecessary expense, greater strictness should be observed in passing the intending emigrants as 'fit' at Calcutta and Madras.[50]

In order to reduce the number of rejected labourers in the main depots, emigration agents showed their interest in getting the coolies medically examined upcountry, as rejection at this stage saved them the cost of the coolies' return railway fares and other expenditures. But in return of their services, the agents were not ready to pay the upcountry doctors more than 8*an*.[51] This resulted in the denial of service by the local civil surgeons, none of whom were ready to do this troublesome work for such a meagre amount of money.

The issue of a large number of rejections of emigrants on medical grounds at the depots again became an important issue in Calcutta in 1899, when the local government dwelt on the large number of rejections of emigrants passed as fit on medical examination in the districts of recruitment. The protector of emigrants and his agents considered that it was due to the carelessness and the perfunctory examinations that had been made by upcountry civil surgeons.[52] Most of these rejected emigrants were from the districts of Allahabad and Oudh; therefore, the the civil surgeons of these regions were held responsible for this carelessness. However, further enquiry in this matter showed that these emigrants were rarely brought before civil surgeons in the districts of recruitment, and so, it could not be attributed to any neglect of duty or carelessness on the part of the local medical authorities.

The chief secretary of North-Western Provinces and Oudh argued that neither the Emigrants Act XXI of 1883 nor the rules imposed upon the civil surgeons the duty of examining the intending emigrants upcountry, though a provision had been made for the same in Section 42 of the bill.[53] So, there was nothing in the Act or the rules to prevent a recruiter from passing his coolies straight to the port of departure. If the agencies gave the recruiter instructions to secure a medical certificate for the coolies upcountry, he was at liberty to take them either before a civil surgeon who agreed to the terms, or to a private practitioner as he liked.[54] Therefore, to prevent the large number of rejections, civil surgeons were nominated by the emigration agents as the only examiners of emigrants. The inspector-general of civil hospitals of North-Western Province and Oudh suggested that—'the medical examination of emigrants before proceeding to Calcutta or other port of embarkation be conducted by civil surgeons only, and that no responsibility will attach to the district local authorities if the examinations were conducted by private practitioners with or without the requisite recognized medical qualifications.'[55]

The Civil Surgeon of Allahabad claimed that: '…I rejected such a large number of intending emigrants, after which they made some other arrangements for having them examined…I believe the certification of emigration is now done here by the private medical practitioners of the L.M.S. class.'[56] Further, he argued that, '…if the agents of the different colonies will only [circulate] to the Civil Surgeons a description of the class of emigrant they require, giving a list of the defects that would cause rejections, I cannot see why the Civil Surgeons of these provisions should pass men other than those desired.'[57] The agencies circulated among the medical officers the points on which a certificate was required; and these were, among others, that the intending emigrant should be free from any contagious disease, should be able to bear a voyage to the colony, and should be able to work there for ten years.[58] He argued that in a good harvest season, there were a good lot of men and agents in Calcutta selected from among them only the very best of the lot, returning the remainder as 'rejected'. When there was no requirement of labourers, the coolies were rejected on the ground of being unfit.

In plantation economy, thus, each and every 'body' was important. Agents were instructed to recruit labourers with only 'fit', 'strong', and 'able' bodies. Those who did not fit the criteria were discarded and seen as the cause of 'spreading of the diseases', and hence, attempts were made to separate the 'good' from the 'bad'. But there were also a lot of people who posed a great threat to the agents' program of 'recruitment of hard hands and healthy body'. These fitness criteria had their own compromises and strictness according to the need, demand, and supply.

The Depot: Making the Indian Body 'Suitable'

The 'body' that arrived at the depot was often regarded as not 'suitable'. Therefore, it needed to be nourished in accordance with the need of the plantation colony. Most of the people who came as intending emigrants were weak and frail. The work of the depot was to provide good food, shelter from bad weather, and medicines to make them 'strong' and 'fit' for the voyages. Making them 'suitable', 'healthy', and 'clean' on the depot and voyages became an important issue. The atmosphere and facilities provided in these places made them different from 'the other' Indians. Once the intending emigrants entered in the depot, they could not move out of it. Their surroundings were isolated areas, and new norms of discipline and order were exercised on the lives of these people.

In order to reach the embarkation point for the overseas colony, emigrants had to pass through many local depots and sub-depots on their way to the central depots in Calcutta and Madras. Coolies were kept at the depot till there were sufficient numbers to form a batch.[59] In the early days, the journey to the port area was an ordeal, because the intending emigrants had to travel hundreds of miles by foot. The journey from upper provinces, i.e. the districts of Banaras and Patna, took about thirty to forty days. The travellers arrived in Calcutta, after having gone through forced marches, and the women and children were footsore. Those who finally reached the destination and passed the initial examination, therefore, proved to be in good physical condition. The development of railways simplified the transfer of labourers to a great extent. The journey took no more than two days, the emigrants being squeezed together in third class compartments. Calcutta was the central port for northern India, and Madras for southern India. In a broader sense, Calcutta covered Orissa, Bengal, Central Province, Eastern Province, Behar, North-Western Province, Oudh, central India, Punjab and its dependencies, Nepal, and other 'native' states. Madras, on the other hand, covered the whole of south India and Bombay.[60]

These two ports in India thus became almost medical centres. The prevailing view among medical officials was that the healthcare of migrants could best be improved prior to embarkation by their removal and isolation from their habitual medical and dietary regime. In order to strengthen the recruits and prevent the outbreak of diseases in the depot and voyages, the Mauritius emigration agent advocated limited contact with the local people around the depots, and complete detention inside the depot compound. In the Madras depot, emigrants were prohibited to consume; 'highly objectionable' and 'frequently injurious' readymade food which were 'constantly hawked about in the streets'.[61] H.N.D. Beyts, the newly appointed protector of emigrants was in favour of extending these reforms to the Calcutta depot as well. In 1883, Major Pitcher and Grierson suggested that—'Giving the food instead of money at the local depot would be best. If coolies were given money, they will try to save it and starve themselves in so doing. Besides this, coolie wandering about the bazaars to purchase food would be liable to contact contagious diseases, and sow the seeds of them in the depot.'[62]

The depots became places where medical officers tested the physically weak population and tried to maintain their health for the journey forward. The emphasis on isolation from local people at the depots increased the duty of the medical staff; they needed to ensure that only medically 'fit' people were admitted and entered therein. The official reports show that there were some restrictions but complete detention was never imposed on the coolies.[63] It was also regarded as dangerous for the recruits to come into contact with people from outside the depot, as it could lead them to change their mind and eventually leave. Major Pitcher argued: 'Complete confinement could not be imposed for a very obvious reason that the subagents feared public reprisal or even a riot, if it was discovered that people were kept against their will.'[64] Marina Carter throws some light on the lives of these recruits in the Mauritius depot. She describes that 'many emigrants were kept in the private establishments of recruiters, and only transferred to the colonial depot shortly before embarkation, because it was more economical when shipping was not available, or demand was low. They were often kept under lock and key.'[65] She discussed the case of Pratap Singh of Orissa, who complained of being held for fifteen days and not being allowed to go out unless the *duffadar* (local recruiter) accompanied him. Eighteen recruits from Madras had similar complaints.[66]

At the main depots such as Calcutta and Madras, where emigrants had contracted to emigrate, a copy of contract of the emigrants was shown to the medical inspector as soon as was convenient, after the arrival of the emigrant at the depot. A medical inspector was appointed by the local government at each port of embarkation. The Government of Bengal appointed a medical inspector of emigrants in 1862 to visit each of its depots at the port. Mauritius officials retained, in addition, the exclusive services of their own medical staff, and Natal had its own trust board for the same purpose. According to Act VII of 1871 (Sections 10–13), it was the duty of the medical inspector and the protector of emigrants to inspect and approve the license of the depot for the reception and lodging of the emigrants it. The depot was supposed to hand over approved license to the emigrant agent; and without the depot's license, the emigrant agents of the various colonies were not entitled to recruit labourers for their respective colonies. In the absence of their own depot, they were required to get permission from the emigrant protector to use another colony's depot for the same purpose. For every license, an emigrant agent had to pay a fee of fifteen rupees to the protector. The medical inspectors were supposed to issue a depot's license on the basis of cleanliness; accommodations for the married, single men, and women; hospital arrangements and provisions for the exclusion of cases of contagious diseases; and provision for proper separate, latrines for on the depot for males and females. The protector had the authority to cancel the license if he considered that the depot for which it was granted was unhealthy, or had in any respect become unsuitable for the purpose for which it was established.[67] It was also the duty of the medical inspector and emigrant protector to inspect the depots from time to time, and at least once in every week, examine the state of the depots and the manner in which the emigrants therein were lodged, fed, clothed, and attended to. The medical inspector was also required to submit an annual report to the protector of emigrants. He was responsible for reporting to the protector about any circumstance that might come to his knowledge, pointing to the unsuitability of the depot.[68] According to Act III of 1876, Section 25, the medical inspector had the authority to isolate or exclude any person from the depot if he thought that an emigrant was suffering from a disease which was likely to be dangerous to his neighbours. In such cases, he recommended the suffering person to be shifted to a hospital for proper treatment at the expense of the emigration agent.[69]

'During the busy season…every recruiting dwelling of any kind is converted into a depot until the time arrives for the departure of the ship, when new arrivals from the recruiting districts take the place of these who have embarked.'[70] The local depots were managed by the subagents, the recruiters, the clerks, the food contractors, and the hangers-on.[71] Recruiters generally had a contract with a neighbouring *baniah*, who supplied uncooked food, which the recruits cooked for themselves in the depot. The interest of the owners of the depots, i.e. the head recruiters or the subordinate recruiters, was to keep the recruits in good health and *khush* (happy). The depots were simply familiar among the recruits as company *ghur* (house). Apart from the emigration agents who lived generally within the walls of depots, the rest of the staff, comprising doctors, clerks, watchmen, sweepers, etc., were Indian. There were never more than three to four separate depots in Calcutta though there were a number of emigration agencies (ten in the 1880s). These three or four depots were simultaneously utilised by multiple agencies. Earlier there was only one depot at Bhowanipur for Mauritius, followed by Garden Reach for Demerara, and others at Ballygunj and Chitpur. Until 1859, there were no depots at Madras and the coolies were lodged in the contractors' godowns; thereafter, an independent Mauritius depot acquired a godown with three large sheds to accommodate the emigrants.[72] Other colonies like Natal, Malaya, and Fiji did so too. A contractor was brought in to arrange two meals a day on the premises. The depot was located in the residential centre of Vepery, but the Beyts Report criticized it as being 'surrounded by impurities' with cesspools, latrines, and a tank with stagnant water nearby, along with sepoys' lines and huts of poor people. The depots (at Calcutta and Madras) were maintained to accommodate at least two shiploads of coolies. In 1859, the Government of Mauritius was authorized to establish a depot at Bombay; but it was not until the visit of the Protector of Emigrants, Beyts, that a temporary establishment was rented in 1861. Heavy mortality on ships proceeding from Bombay in 1864–5 led to the proposal for the improvement of the depot and the allotment of a space of 24 by 12 feet per emigrant, to prevent overcrowding. This proposal was made for the depot at Madras as well. It might be mentioned here that during the time of the declining demand of labourers (in around 1865), Bombay was suspended from emigration, and no further migration of labourers took place from there.

The duration for which the coolies stayed in these depots was normally between one and three weeks.[73] When there was no coolie ship in the Hugli River, the emigrants had to wait for a long time in the depot, sometimes up to three months, in the dark, overcrowded sheds with palm-leaf roofs, ant-eaten walls, and mud floors.[74] These depots were regularly raided by the police in search of wanted men, and also women, as some Indians complained about their missing wives, daughters, and sisters.[75]

Before 1870, during the boom period of Mauritius emigration, there were shipments for Mauritius throughout the year. Later, the time period between September and February was allotted to West Indies and Fiji, in order to get the best of the weather at sea, while Mauritius and Natal were allotted the remainder of the year.[76] The higher mortality and sickness rate on the voyages forced the Natal government to pass a resolution in September 1892 that stated: '...Indians be not embarked from India, for Natal during the months of July, August and September', which were known as cholera months.[77] Beyts made observations on the weather and the outbreak of diseases. He concluded that diseases were rampant each year between mid-February and mid-April, probably because of the warm and rainy climate. He thus advised the agencies to reduce recruitment during this risky period.

The medical officers had to prepare an annual report about the sanitation condition of the depots. The following citation from one of the reports would be helpful to elaborate on the functional architecture of the depot and facilities to protect the indentured from insanitary conditions:

...Sanitation: The general sanitary arrangements of all the depots have been satisfactory throughout the year. Every possible measure is taken to improve the general condition of the emigrants, and to make their well being attended to.

Accommodation: The accommodation is sufficient for all wants in all the depots, and is in accordance with the regulations.

Food: The food issued to the emigrants was frequently examined by the medical inspector. It was found to be well–cooked, sufficient in quantity and in every respect suitable for those for whom it was intended.

Water-supply: All the emigrants' depots draw their supply of water from Calcutta Mains.

Clothing: The articles of clothing were inspected by the Medical Inspector as well as by the Surgeon-Superintendent of each emigrant ship and were always found to be satisfactory. The clothes issued to the emigrants are sufficiently warm and comfortable.

Latrines: At all the depots the latrines are well looked after, being well flushed and kept clean.

Hospitals: At all the depots, the hospitals are kept sufficiently supplied with drugs and instruments. The buildings are satisfactory, allowing a proper amount of cubic space for each patient, and the ventilation is good.

The medical treatment of both the sexes is carried out in separate wards, and at the depots special arrangements are made for lying-in women.

In charge of the hospitals of the various depots there are Indian doctors, who work satisfactorily, are kind to the sick, and take a keen interest in their patients.

Serious cases are brought to the notice of the depot surgeons who visit the depots twice or thrice in a week. No sick person is ever neglected.

All the depot hospitals keep in stock medical comforts of various kinds which are issued to the sick as required. Infants and small children along with pregnant women and mothers have a special ration of milk every day.

Vaccination: All the emigrants were vaccinated or re-vaccinated on their arrival at the depots.[78]

These were the conditions that were considered ideal for an emigrant depot in order to make the indentured body 'suitable' for the plantation economy. It should however be taken into account that these reports were not accurate. Medical inspectors often criticized the quantity and quality of food, accommodation, water supply, hospitals, and sanitary conditions in their annual report. The water supplied to the depot was usually not of good quality. When medical knowledge had acknowledged that impure or polluted water was the main cause of cholera in the depots and the surrounding area, steps were taken to supply and store clean drinking water on the voyages and in the depots for the future labourers. The source of this clean water was the Calcutta municipality water tanks. However, Beyts, in his report, stated that:

...the water supply to the depot for the emigrants was not as 'isolated' as it was expected to be. At Calcutta, the drinking water supply of the Mauritius agency's depot was shared with that of the native lunatic asylum. The water was used by *sudder* court, and a neighboring bazaar for bathing purpose of these establishments. Also cholera was not effectively checked until depots were linked to Calcutta's piped water system in 1890s.[79]

As far as food for the intending emigrants was concerned, it was a matter of high importance, as it was to be nutritious and healthy, because most of the indentured were either ill or in weak physical condition. The emigration agents thus focused specifically on the issue of the emigrants' recovery and tried to make them 'able bodied'. The question regarding the indentured's diet recurred and haunted colonial emigrant officials constantly. They tried not only to control emigrant food habits, but also tried to regularize it. The Coolie Law also decided in terms of what the indentured should get as their food, and even decided the quantity of their food. As I have mentioned earlier, each depot had its own system of providing food to the emigrants—some depots provided rations, while some were satisfied in giving the recruits money instead of food. But this question (regarding diet) recurred each time the issue of health emerged. For example, the Trinidad and Jamaica recruits were getting 2*an.* per adult and 1*an.* per child for purchase of food, and each was allowed to cook for himself/herself separately or in a group.[80] Grierson had enquired into this matter and found that:

...a man was kept in the depot, who alone supplied foods of a certain quality, at bazaar rates. The coolies were not given cash, but tokens, which only allowed them to pass for the current food with the particular *modi* [shopkeeper], and hence, the coolies could get only the food of the best quality. Restrictions were also placed upon the kind of food which [the] indentured bought: for instance, if it was found that a coolie bought too much sweetmeats and not sufficient nourishing food, they would put a stop to it.[81]

On the other hand, in the French depot, coolies were provided food according to the *bhandara* system. Reports do not, however, talk about the preparation and serving of food to the recruits. The *bhandara* system was familiar to the Indian culture, and most of the community feasts in India followed the *bhandara* system. Major Pitcher explained this system in his report; and Mr. Firth, the Emigration Agent defended it on the following grounds:

...The food is thoroughly cooked.
The food consumed is good and wholesome.
The meals are regularly issued and partaken of.
Greater contentment and fewer desertions.
Better control of people, more perfect discipline, and greater facility for detecting disease in its early stage.
Less risk to life.
Cleanliness and neatness of depots [maintained].
It prepares the emigrants for life on board ships.
Trains cooks for employment at sea.
Less expense for repairs of sheds.
It allows more time for healthy recreation.[82]

On account of all these reasons the *bhandara* system was preferred by the emigration agents and the protector. Discipline, sanitation, healthiness was better maintained and thoroughly controlled in this way.

J.G. Grant, the Protector of Emigrants at Calcutta, raised questions regarding the quality of food provided by the Mauritius depot to the recruits. The Mauritius and Demerara depots issued daily rations to the intending coolies according to the scale no. 1, which included 147 grains of nitrogen and 4,237 grains of carbon in the meals of every recruit (see Table 2.1). The depots also used different menu charts for rice and flour eaters, according to the scale no. 2, which included 147 grains of nitrogen in both cases and 5,344.50 grains of carbon for rice-eaters and 4,494.25 for flour-eaters in the meals of each adult recruit (see Table 2.2). Apart from this, curry items often included tamarind, garlic, onions, and an all-important anti-scorbutic item for improvement of the emigrants' health. In this context, Dr Grant observed:

…The scale of daily allowances, however, was not perfect: though subject to the control of the medical officer in charge, it should be complete in itself, independent of extras. Accepting the physiological dictum that in a state of idleness one requires *at least* 4,300 grains of carbon and 200 grains of nitrogen daily; so, it follows that the daily scale here was deficient, especially, in nitrogenous food. Therefore, if a daily scale be used, I would suggest the adoption of scale no. 2, for rice and flour eaters respectively, especially as it is virtually the same as that which Dr Patridge has himself recommended for emigrants on board [ships]. Thus, if the scale now submitted, and the other about to be recommended for the voyage, be approved of, the coolies while in depot will not only be ensured good feeding, but will be gradually prepared for nearly the same diet provided for them on board.[83]

There was a separate menu for mothers, pregnant women, and for children. Pregnant women and mothers were supposed to get more nutritious foods like *soojee*, oatmeal, sago and arrowroot.[84]

The intending emigrants were given food twice a day at the depots; a meal in the morning which was served at 9 a.m. and one in the afternoon at 2 p.m. Nutritious food items like ghee and mutton were decided to be served once in a week. However, in reality, these rules were baseless. Emigrants were not given good food, and sometimes they, along with the medical surgeon and the protector, made complaints against the quality and quantity of food. One of the major reasons behind the high death rates among indentured and their children was the shortage of quality food and clothes.

The connection between the soldiers and the indentured labour has already been discussed. A short comparison in terms of ration would

TABLE 2.1: Scale 1 Diet Schedule for the Coolies in the Depots

Articles	In Ounces							In Grains		Remarks
	Quantity	Water	Albumen	Starch	Sugar	Fat	Salts	Nitrogen	Carbon	
	Oz.	Oz.	Oz.	Oz.	Oz.	Oz.	Oz.	Grs.	Grs.	
Rice	20	2.6	1.26	15.32	0.08	0.14	0.1	85	3,415	'Curry stuffs' often include tamarind, garlic, onions—all capital anti-scorbutics.
Dholl	4	0.6	0.92	2.22	0.08	0.08	0.1	62	675	
Mustard oil	0.5	0.07	–	–	–	0.43	0.5	–	147	
Salt	0.5	–	–	–	–	–	–	–	–	
Curry stuffs, &c.	0.5	Variable, not estimated								
TOTAL	25.5	3.27	2.18	18.04	0.16	0.65	0.7	0147	4,237	

Demerara

Vegetables   4 to 6 oz. are issued three times a week.

Fish or flesh   2 oz. only are issued twice a week.

Flour, ghee, and milk for infants, &c.   and other extras are issued irregularly as desired or ordered.

The scale used in the depot for Mauritius is the same as the above, except that—

Mauritius

Vegetables   4 oz. are issued daily.

Dholl   3 oz. are issued daily.

J.G.

Source: Home Department (Public Branch) Proceedings, 21 May 1870, no. 137, NAI.

TABLE 2.2: Scale 2 Diet for the Rice and Flour Eaters, showing Daily Allowances for each Adult

Articles	In Ounces							In Grains		Remarks
	Quantity	Water	Albumen	Starch	Sugar	Fat	Salts	Nitrogen	Carbon	
	Oz.	Oz.	Oz.	Oz.	Oz.	Oz.	Oz.	Grs.	Grs.	
For Rice Eaters										
Rice	20	2.6	1.26	15.32	0.08	0.14	0.1	85	3,415	
Dholl	6	9	1.38	3.32	0.12	10.13	0.15	93	1,012	
Ghee	1	0.15	–	–	–	0.83	0.02	–	403.5	
Mustard oil	0.5	0.07	–	–	–	0.43	–	–	147	
Vegetables	4	3.89	0.05	0.22	0.09	–	0.03	3.47	70	
Fresh Fish or flesh	3	1.9	0.46	–	–	0.12	0.12	29.5	297*	
Salt	0.5	–	–	–	–	–	20.5	–	–	
Curry stuffs, & c.	0.5	Variable, not estimated								
TOTAL	35.5	9.41	3.15	19.36	0.29	1.65	0.92	210.97	5,344.5	
For Flour Eaters										
Flour	16	2.4	1.73	10.6	0.67	0.32	0.27	116	2,700	
Dholl	4	10.6	0.92	2.22	0.08	0.08	0.1	62	675	
Ghee	1.5	0.23	–	–	–	1.25	0.03	–	605.25	
Mustard oil	0.5	0.7	–	–	–	0.43	–	–	147	
Vegetables	4	3.89	0.05	0.22	0.09	–	0.03	3.47	70	
Fresh Fish or meat	3	1.8	0.46	–	–	0.12	0.12	29.5	297*	J.G.
Salt	0.5	–	–	–	–	–	20.5	–	–	
Curry stuffs, & c.	0.5	Variable, not estimated								
TOTAL	30.0	8.99	3.16	13.04	0.84	2.20	1.05	210.97	4,494.25	

Source: Home Department (Public Branch) Proceedings, 21 May 1870, no. 137, NAI.
Note: * The nutritive value of only 2.5 oz. has been given, as one-sixth has been deducted for loss, on account of bone, & c.

help in elaborating it further. In 1867–8, the basic daily issue to the soldiers was 1 lb. (454 g.) meat, 1 lb. bread, 1 lb. vegetables, ¼ lb. rice, and 2½ oz. sugar. This, however, changed during the First World War.[85] Apart from these, coffee, chocolate, jam, and dried fruits were also available to them. Sumit Guha argued that there was no deficiency in the diet in terms of calories and protein and milk and other products were adequately available in terms of vitamins and minerals. Also, his study showed that the worse-paid and worse-provisioned Indian sepoys suffered more from diseases like scurvy. However, in case of the indentured labourers, this difference was even more glaring. This difference was maintained on racial and climatic grounds. The official discourse tried to naturalize the colonizer's idea of minimum requirement of food for the Indians on the grounds of climate. They considered that the tropical climate of India minimized the need of food for the Indian race and hence, maintained the low standard of living of the intending emigrants.[86] According to them, Indians could survive in harsh conditions to which they were already accustomed to, while the Europeans could not survive without a proper standard of living.

The diet scale was an important issue not only for the army and the indentured labour, but at the same time for the prisoners, lepers, those of unsound mind, and patients, in the jails, asylums, and hospitals respectively. Proper diet scale of these institutions became important to fulfil the British government's policy of provisions for 'justice to the darker race'[87] and for management of the empire as well as these institutions. David Arnold stated that prison provided a critical site for observation and experimentations of much wider utility.[88] The high death rate and rate of sickness in prisons forced the Government of India to improve the diet of the inmates. Dr Mouat, who wanted to turn prisons into industrial workshops in order to reduce the financial burden, was not ready to compromise on the sound physical condition of prisoners.[89] Arnold argued that it was the experiments on Indians done in prisons, which provided the standard for the minimum requirement of food for the survival and labour of Indians.

In the depots, in order to maintain good health of the indentured, the emigrant agent (British Guiana) insisted that the coolies take interest in a reasonable amount of health oriented exercises. The agent of British Guiana was in the habit of encouraging them to organize amusing exercises among themselves, such as running races in the compound, doing gymnastics, and stimulating them for exertion by giving prizes ranging from Re.1 to Rs.3 at a time.[90]

The intending emigrants were supposed to work in the depots, pre-embarkation. Once a Calcutta emigrant agent brought into the notice of the Government of Mauritius the work done by the intending emigrants and directed it to pay to the coolies a remuneration at the rate of one and a half pice for each hour's work. The colonial secretary of Mauritius, in reply to this guidance, stated that:

...after careful consideration of the subject, that, as the slight labour and assistance which are exacted from the coolies in the morning and evening are merely such as may fairly be expected from them in their own interest as being conducive to the preservation of health and the maintenance of cleanliness and order in the Depot...and such kind of measure would entail additional expense to this colony.[91]

After such suggestions, they sanctioned the rule that every intending emigrant would be liable to work on every weekday for a limited time of two hours, in return for the food and lodging with which they were supplied, and if they would perform extra work apart from this, they would be entitled to a pecuniary remuneration.[92]

The Indian nationalists constantly attacked of the indentured system. The Indians had this notion that the government was anxious to export the population in the interest of colonial and metropolitan capitalism. They were also suspicious that the government was exporting the men for slavery and the women for prostitution purposes. *The Pioneer* (India) called it 'an Indian slave trade'.[93] Therefore, the government decided to provide every facility to the recruiting agents to attract emigrants by 'legitimate means'.[94] This forced the emigrant agents to paint a glorious picture of the depots. This was important because a shoddier picture of the depot could have had a bad impact on the recruitment process. Dr Scott, the government medical inspector of emigrants, wrote on the plight of the intending emigrants—'...that the people on embarkation are starved skeletons, that they are received in the depot as such and not being liberally fed while there, they do not improve until after embarkation'.[95] In the reaction to this statement, S.B. Paritridge stated:

...suffice for me to assert (an assertion which I am certain you can corroborate) that the emigrants are not shipped in a weak and debilitated condition—a condition which I suppose Dr Scott means to imply by the extraordinary expression 'starved skeleton', and that when, as much necessarily occasionally happen, they are received into the depot in a weak state, they do most manifestly and rapidly improve under the liberal treatment of the emigrant agent, and are [not] suffered to embark until restored to health and vigour.[96]

It is important to note that at different levels, different authorities were responsible for maintaining the 'fit' condition of labourers.

Whenever a group of new intending emigrants arrived, the first action for them was to take a bath; and then they received new clothes. For instance, giving a *dhoti* to a woman in rags helped in attracting the attention of other migrants. Major Pitcher highlighted an interesting example that:

…many of the women arrive at the depot in a state bordering on nudity, many of the women enter the depot in a garment of filthy rags, which can hardly be said to cloth them, the grant of dhoti (in cost one rupee) greatly popularizes recruiting…a new dhoti to each women would go far to diminish the chance of disease germs being conveyed on shipboard.[97]

After the disinfection of their earlier clothes, the next important step was the medical inspection by the Indian doctors, in the case of men, and by a skilled Indian nurse in case of women.[98]

The men had to strip to the waist, and were checked for sight and hearing. The women, however, received a much more superficial examination. The general belief was that any attempt to enforce a rigorous medical standard for the females would scare away other potential recruits. The medical inspector of Natal claimed that as a consequence, many of the women were passed as 'fit' even when they were infected with venereal diseases.[99] Some undeveloped cases of VD had passed during the medical examination while recruiting indentured in the depots itself. The main cause of this was that the women migrants were examined by an unprofessional person [the nurses were not considered professional doctors], in probably a less efficient manner than that of the men, who were passed by a duly qualified medical practitioner.[100] The whole issue of examination of women became an important subject, because male medical officers were not allowed to examine the female migrants. Here, it is also important to highlight the fact that migrants at times resisted against the medical intervention by the depot staff. For example, at Bombay, trouble broke out when married women would not submit to the 'close examination' by the port surgeon, and 'they agreed only for vaccination; at Karaikal and Pondicherry, the examination of female recruits was abolished, following strong objections from migrants.'[101] This, to some extent, had a negative impact on the process of recruitment.

Till the 1870s, the nurse's examination of the female recruits was still absurdly superficial, but by the end of the nineteenth century a proper procedure was established. After the men were passed by the Indian doctor, they had to appear before a European depot surgeon, and also before a government doctor nominated by the protector of emigrants. The only person who was to scrutinize the recruits rigorously, was the surgeon superintendent. This examination of the intending emigrants took place three and four days prior to sailing. However, since there was a great rush and many other formalities had to be completed, the surgeon superintendent was forced to pass many for embarkation, who otherwise were not to be passed. Medical Surgeon M.M. Thompson stated, '...Four or five hundred unknown Indians would be passed before me at a steady speed, with assurances from the depot surgeon that all had been inspected and certified as of "sound limb". If I identified a man as doubtful, it was likely that half a dozen other would pass by while I checked the suspect.' He would be told that it was natural for people from that particular part of India to appear frail; he would even be told, if an obviously sick man stepped up, that a little good feeding and sea air would put him right.[102] This pressure forced them (these medical officials) to pass a lot of people, including those who otherwise would be categorized unfit. The circumstance of demand and supply of labourers forced the suppliers to compromise the medical interventions.

Architecture of the Depot: Sickness and Mortality

The depot was always a site of infections and it could turn into a 'valley of death'. In order to maintain proper sanitation in the depots, the architecture of the same became important (see, for example, Plate 2.1). The depots were surrounded by high walls to prevent contact with the outside world and unrestrained comings and goings of people. The depots had a number of barracks with bungalows for the staff; for instance, most of the head recruiters lived in a fine European building with a large compound.[103] The report of the protector of emigrants at Calcutta described the coolie depot as: '...it usually consisted of a pretty large house in the native style, with separate accommodation for men and women, along with a well and latrine arrangement.'[104] This was, however, not the same situation with each depot; some were in worse condition. As Major Pitcher and Grierson gave a description of the Trinidad sub-depot—'It is in the bazaar and is dirty, there is no separate accomodation for men and women and only one latrine…there is no well, the inmates being supplied with Ganges water'.[105] The facilities which were provided to the recruits in these depots had their own limitations, apart from being irregular. The architectural structure underwent changes from time to time. We have examples of the Natal and British Guiana's depots, with which it would be helpful to do a comparable study—between the old and the new depot structure.

In the annual report, the protector of emigrants at Calcutta mentioned that '…between October 1908 and May 1909 the building of this depot, comprising sleeping sheds, feeding sheds, bath-houses, kitchens, latrines, urinals, *babu's* quarter, *darwan's* quarters, depot office

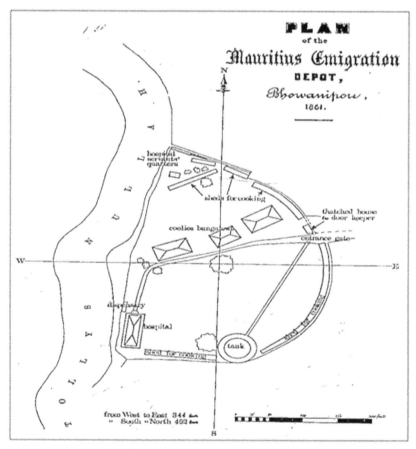

PLATE 2.1: The Mauritius Emigration Depot at Calcutta

Source: Bengal Revenue and Agriculture Department (Emigration Branch) Proceedings, May 1887, no. 41, NAI.

and store godowns, were entirely demolished and new buildings of more modern design erected.'[106] This report further highlighted that the 'old sleeping-sheds, with their rammed-mud floors, and fixed sleeping platforms, had been replaced by structures built on solid brick and cement flooring, with removable platforms, resting on masonry-piers well raised from the ground, roofs with skylight, and wire-panelled openings at fragment intervals in the walls'.[107] The report of the protector of emigrants at Calcutta for 1909 (the closing year of the indentured system), mentioned:

…The walls of the new depot were higher than before, the roofs were thrown out at a wider angle and were so designed as to make provision for a much better circulation of air and increased light: while the seven ill-lighted and poorly ventilated sheds which previously existed had been transformed into eleven cool, well-lit sections with a liberal open-air but roofed-in space between each.[108]

On the issue of sanitation, the report emphasized that:

The main latrine had been rebuilt in toto and was now a clean, sanitary, well ventilated masonry building with all necessary equipments for washing facilities, adequate drainage and entirely separate accommodation for the sexes. The urinal was removed from its former site, which had been undesirably close to the depot hospital, to a more suitable spot near the main latrine.[109]

Further, the same report emphasized that:

…the feeding shed had been rebuilt on solid masonry flooring, and its extent had been doubled. A new bath-house was erected for the use of the emigrants, and arrangements were in place now for a constant supply of both hot and cold water for them. The kitchen had been reconstructed with a masonry floor, and the old, open boilers were replaced by the modern iron-kitchen range, now in use in the government jails throughout India, with all necessary accessories, such as covered rice-coolers, strainers, distributing trays, etc. Masonry drains had been constructed throughout the depot premises. A filtered water supply from the Calcutta mains has been laid on, with storage tanks, cisterns, etc. The dispensary was rebuilt on much improved lines. New quarters (including kitchen and latrine) had been built for the depot's native staff on healthier sites than before, and a new and spacious store 'godown' had been constructed for the depot sweepers, etc., outside the depot enclosure.[110]

These changes were made in the depot structure in order to reduce the unsanitary conditions and sickness rates at the depot. However, the annual report of the depot medical surgeons revealed a contrary situation. Despite these changes, there wasn't any decrease in the sickness and mortality rates in the depots. In 1908, it was 0.55 per cent, while in 1909, it was 0.71 per cent.[111] The major cause for this increase in the death rate was a cerebrospinal meningitis epidemic, which alone was responsible for the forty-four deaths at the Calcutta depot.[112] This shows that the spread of an epidemic in a depot could turn the whole depot into a 'valley of death'. In the annual report of the medical inspector of the Calcutta depot, it has been stated that—'I found that there were a few diseases on the depot which were the main cause of the death among the recruits, such as cholera, smallpox, chickenpox, fever, cerebrospinal meningitis, measles, mumps, respiratory diseases, venereal disease, etc.' The medical inspector, in his report, mentioned the number of the recruits that was admitted to the depot hospital every year, what the cause for their admission was, the number of people who were discharged from the hospital, and the number of deaths recorded during the year, including the reasons for the deaths.[113] The necessity to decrease the number of sick and the mortality rate at the depots and to continue the flow of indentured, forced the Government of India to invest money on the sanitary conditions of these depots and coastal areas.[114]

Many commissions were appointed to investigate the causes of higher mortality at the depots. It should be noted that whenever this death rate crossed 1 per cent, it raised an alarm among both the government officials and planters. Though the data of Mauritius and Natal is missing for the year 1909 in Table 2.3, it is important to notice the classification of diseases in the medical records of various depots, which caused much trouble for the recruitment of desirable labourers.

Garden Reach and Bhowanipur were two important depots in Calcutta—the former was for British Guiana and Trinidad, and the latter for Jamaica and Mauritius. During 1872–3, the mortality rate recorded at these places was 0.42 per cent and 0.66 per cent; while in 1874–5, it was 1.03 per cent and 1 per cent: respectively. A commission was appointed to investigate the causes of the higher mortality rates. Its report mentioned that '…The mortality and privation suffered by the coolies in their long journey from the village to Calcutta and in some cases previous distress from famine, exhaustion inevitable from the hardships of travel during south-west monsoon, and insufficient rest at the depot to recover from exhaustion.'[115] Apart from this, a major cause that was considered by the commission was the insalubrious condition of Garden Reach, Calcutta, which appeared to have been caused by the then recent event of residence of the king of Oudh. Mr Jones, the Commander of the *Forkshire*, in his evidence says:

...Garden Reach was considered a healthy suburb until the King of Oudh, with about two thousands of most filthy habitants, took up his residence there. A lot of wealthy residents had abandoned this locality in consequences of the nuisance created by his majesty and his retinue that their compounds had become jungle filled with filthy putrid pounds. In the centre of this is the Demerara emigration depot.[116]

One can relate this with the political situation of India after 1857, which also shows the negative and racist mindset of the Europeans against Indians. It also reflects the attitude of refusal to take responsibility and blaming Indians for their situation. Tolley's Nullah near the Mauritius depot was, according to Thomas Caird (emigrant agent for Mauritius at Calcutta), in a 'filthy state' giving out a 'noxious effluvia' (polluted air) into the surroundings. Garden Reach also contained: '... large tracts of abandoned and undrained land, which became stagnant pools in the monsoon. Drinking water was taken out from wells, tanks, or ponds in the vicinity, and was quite unpalatable to the upcountry newcomers: it resulted in diarrhoea, dysentery, and sometimes cholera.'[117] The brief period of cold weather in Calcutta was fairly healthy, but from February to April, diseases like cholera were rife. These circumstances led to an increase in the death rate or sickness in depots.

It was recorded that the upcountry people were more inclined to sickness than a 'native' of Calcutta, and a proposal to move emigration establishments away from Calcutta was part of an ongoing debate on the means of reducing the shipboard mortality of indentured labourers. Dr Scott, in his letter to Dr Grant, stated that: '...large aggregations of people are more or less liable to sickness in proportion to the perfection or imperfection of the sanitary arrangements of the place in which they live.'[118] In order to avoid sickness in them, some officials made this suggestion that these people should keep out of Calcutta or they should board the ship as soon as possible.[119] They also suggested the opening of a new depot in Oudh (for the recruits of the nearby area), which was however rejected because of two reasons. First was the expenditure, and second, the officials argued that if they had to find out the germs of the infectious disease in the blood they must give it time to reach the maturity level. Therefore, it was necessary to keep the intending emigrants away from their homes for some days, or at least for some hours.[120] Therefore, the travelling time from Oudh to the Calcutta depot or residency there, was notified to the new recruits prior to their

TABLE 2.3: Causes of Sickness and Mortality in different Depots and Outside Hospitals for the year 1909

	Demerara				Trinidad				Jamaica			
	Sickness		Death		Sickness		Death		Sickness		Death	
Diseases in Depots	Number	Percentage	Number	Percentage	Number	Percentage	Number	Percentage	Number	Percentage	Number	Percentage
1	2	3	4	5	6	7	8	9	10	11	12	13
Cholera	–	–	–	–	3	0.09	1	0.03	–	–	–	–
Dysentery	19	0.61	–	–	2	0.06	–	–	5	0.34	–	–
Diarrhoea	1	0.03	–	–	1	0.03	–	–	–	–	–	–
Fevers	54	1.74	2	0.06	35	1.08	–	–	33	2.26	–	–
Cerebro-spinal meningitis	17	0.55	8	0.25	25	0.77	15	0.46	14	0.96	9	0.61
Measles	–	–	–	–	–	–	–	–	–	–	–	–
Smallpox	–	–	–	–	–	–	–	–	–	–	–	–
Chickenpox	–	–	–	–	3	0.09	–	–	–	–	–	–
Respiratory diseases	35	1.13	8	0.25	33	1.02	7	0.21	33	2.26	4	0.27
Venereal diseases	70	2.26	–	–	43	1.33	–	–	31	2.12	–	–
Mumps	–	–	–	–	–	–	–	–	–	–	–	–
Other diseases	36	1.16	3	0.09	16	0.49	–	–	3	0.2	–	–
Total of —1909	232	7.5	21	0.67	161	4.9	23	0.71	119	8.16	13	0.89
—1908	192	8.79	16	0.73	169	5.24	10	0.31	31	4.95	1	0.15

Diseases in Depots	Natal				Fiji				Surinam				Total			
	Sickness		Death		Sickness		Death		Sickness		Death		Sickness		Death	
	Numbers	Percentage	Number	Percentage	Numbers	Percentage	Numbers	Percentage	Numbers	Percentage	Numbers	Percentage	Numbers	Percentage	Numbers	Percentage
	14	15	16	17	18	19	20	21	22	23	24	25	26	27	28	29
Cholera	–	–	–	–	–	–	–	–	–	–	–	–	3	0.02	1	–
Dysentery	–	–	–	–	–	–	–	–	10	0.4	–	–	36	0.31	–	–
Diarrhoea	–	–	–	–	–	–	–	–	3	0.12	–	–	5	0.04	–	–
Fevers	–	–	–	–	5	0.48	–	–	52	2.1	6	0.24	179	1.58	8	0.07
Cerebro-spinal meningitis	–	–	–	–	8	0.77	3	0.29	13	0.52	9	0.36	77	0.68	44	0.39
Measles	–	–	–	–	–	–	–	–	1	0.04	–	–	1	0.04	–	–
Smallpox	–	–	–	–	1	0.09	–	–	–	–	–	–	1	–	–	–
Chickenpox	–	–	–	–	–	–	–	–	–	–	–	–	3	0.02	–	–
Respiratory diseases	–	–	–	–	18	1.74	3	0.29	8	0.32	2	0.08	127	1.12	24	0.21
Venereal diseases	–	–	–	–	24	2.33	–	–	6	0.24	–	–	174	1.54	–	–
Mumps	–	–	–	–	–	–	–	–	–	–	–	–	–	–	–	–
Other diseases	–	–	–	–	8	0.77	1	0.09	14	0.56	–	–	77	0.68	4	0.03
Total of —1909	–	–	–	–	64	6.21	7	0.67	107	4.33	17	0.68	683	6.05	81	0.71
—1908	96	8.78	12	1.09	331	7.19	23	0.5	308	9.02	22	0.64	1,127	7.44	84	0.55

Source: Annual Report of the Protector of Emigrants at Calcutta for the year 1909, Commerce and Industry Department (Emigration Branch) Proceedings, August 1910, no. 9, part B, NAI.

departure. The emigrant agent at Calcutta argued that it was admitted that those arrangements in the Calcutta depot (in terms of accommodation, sanitation, hospitals, food, etc.) were far from people even in great cities in Europe. They (intending emigrants) could scarcely, therefore, be expected to be better in any part of India. On the basis of these points, he suggested that it would be better to invest only on one depot rather than on two depots in order to get better results. The debate shows that depots were sites of observation as well. Their (the intending emigrants') quality of being labourers made them different from the rest of the population of India. Some of the facilities and provisions that they received were not available to the common people in even some of the big cities of Europe at that point of time.

The body of the indentured became so important that emigrant agents considered that it was necessary to save it from every one and at every step, from impurity to infectious diseases. There was also a complaint by the surgeon superintendent of the Madras depot about the disadvantage of the depot being located far away from the place of embarkation. The agent general, in his letter to the colonial secretary, mentioned that: '…the passengers having to walk some three miles from the depot through crowded street to the custom house where they were inspected by the protector of emigrants before being embarked: the risk of infection being largely increased thereby.'[121] This statement of the surgeon shows that by entering into the depot, this large group of Indians became separated from the 'other' people of India. The distance of three miles and the crowded street of their own town became fatal for them.

When an epidemic spread in the Presidencies, the situation and condition of isolation of the depots became more hostile. Some major diseases emerged in different parts of India from time to time, which forced the government to adopt new rules and regulations to prevent the intending emigrants from infection. These diseases, which broke out in the 1850s, the 1880s, and then in the 1890s, posed a great threat to the indentured trade and the empire as a whole. For example, during the 1880s, a large number of cases of cholera were reported from all over India. Consequently, the alarmed officials took steps to save the intending emigrants in the depots and the sub-depots. A number of questions were also raised by the depots' authority, such as: (a) should coolies be allowed to embark as emigrants from a depot in which cholera existed? (b) if coolies from such a depot were not to be allowed to embark, then at what time from the date of the last case of death, or the discharge from hospital, of the last case of cholera should the coolies be allowed again? (c) if, from a cholera-infected depot, coolies are not allowed to embark, what is to be done with them? Are they to be allowed to remain in the depot?[122] In search of the answers to these questions, in 1889, the Government of India passed the Public Health Act 1 (BC) of 1889, and new rules were implemented for the cholera patients and the places which were affected by cholera. Every emigrant agent and related officials were responsible for keeping an eye on the cholera patients. It was their responsibility to take out suffering patients from the hospital and keep the whole group, to whom the patient belonged, in the sheds which were made for the same purpose. All managers of the depots and the rest houses were also responsible for taking out the cholera patients from the hospitals. He was also responsible for disinfecting the clothes and belongings of the whole group that was staying with him in the same hospital. Whether the patient belonged to the same group or not, the manager had to supply them with new and sanitized clothes and get them admitted into segregated sheds.[123] If even one case emerged in a depot, it was the duty of the manager of the depot to thoroughly clean and disinfect the woodwork, floor, and other parts of the sheds. He was also responsible for making arrangements for light and fresh air in the sheds. It was his duty to dig the floor and disinfect the floor mud or burn it or pitch its surface.[124] Those who were kept in these segregated sheds were not allowed to leave the premises until the emigrant officers allowed them. The segregation period was for five days after the emergence of a fresh case of cholera. The emigrant agent would not permit any emigrant to enter the depot or the sub-depot, until he fulfilled the criteria for the segregation period. During the segregation period, it was the duty of the manager or officials to provide every emigrant with two meals, as was provided to other intending emigrants. The uninfected population of the depot was kept separate from the infected population. Enormous measures were adopted for safeguarding the uninfected people.

Once the intending emigrants entered the depot, they became the property of the emigrant recruiting agency. The latter required a healthy and suitable labour force, and so they had to pay for the former's treatment at the Indian depots. The rule set out that: the treatment of every patient costs 8*an.* per day, which was to be given by the concerned officials or by the manager of the depots. The admission of a patient into a hospital would cost Re.1 per person, to be paid by the emigrant agent or by the manager of the depot where the patient stays. Further, it was mentioned in the rules: that 'If any patient died from cholera the whole expenditure of his burial was to be paid by these officials…if somebody tried to violate the rules he would be liable to pay a fine of rupees five hundred.'[125]

Apart from cholera, there were many other infectious diseases in the Indian subcontinent, which haunted the empire. In consideration of Sir John Woodburn and Holderness's notes, the Indian government passed a Prohibition Notification on 6 March 1897. The main purpose of this Act was to save Calcutta from infection and to stop the movement of the population from an infected depot to an uninfected one. This Prohibition was applied for the first time against Bombay, because of the plague that had spread in the city. In the Emigration Act of 1901, there was a sanitary clause in which rules were mentioned for prevention of spread of plague from one region to another and for those departure depots which were dealing with the poorer class of labourers.[126] The Prohibition Notification was intended partly to lessen the chances of plague spreading to Calcutta and partly to prevent the spread of plague to other countries by parties of infected emigrants.[127] The Government of Bengal was terrified of the plague and tried to stop the flow of population from Bombay. There was also another objective of this Prohibition Notification, and that was to control, by this indirect means, the flow of 'free' or 'uncontrolled' emigration into Natal and avert a politico-economic danger to the white population of that colony.[128] On the basis of these, emigrant officials suggested that during the spread of plague, the government should restrict the emigration of people not only from the port of Bombay but from other ports too. Under the regulations made by the Epidemic Diseases Act of 1897, Indian jugglers, dancers, and circus attendants were also prohibited from embarking on a journey to any other country.[129] Even after the plague came under control and no longer posed a threat, Bombay was still under the prohibition of embarkation. After much debate among the authorities, was granted conditional withdrawal of the prohibition in Bombay. The condition was that the notification should be modified so as to prohibit the departure of a native of India from Bombay as an emigrant or labourer, who until now had been subjected to a strict medical examination and his clothes and bedding had been thoroughly disinfected.[130] Under the Epidemic Diseases Act, the government prohibited the emigration of those who were staying in the Bombay Presidency since January 1897; this prohibition was not only for indentured labourers, but also for other emigrants or movable population.

Another disease which posed a major threat in the depot, and was discovered in the later period of indentured recruitment was anchylostome. Some medical theories of the nineteenth century claimed that Indian coolies were the transmitters of this disease the overseas colonies. Experiments and investigations were carried out in different regional prisons to find out the carrier of the disease. Arnold opined that prisons provided a place where medical science acquired knowledge about the Indian body and its behaviour and applied it on the plantation labourers.[131] Measures were adopted to prohibit the emigrants suffering from this disease from entering into the colonies. The protectors of emigrants at Calcutta and Madras suggested to the sanitary commissioners to treat them with thymol.[132] Further, the protectors suggested that their treatment should be done on board the ships or after the emigrants had reached their destination. They argued that if this treatment is done on the depot, it could have a negative impact upon the process of recruitment, since it was unpopular among the coolies and resulted in disturbances and even stampedes. Marsden, the emigrant agent of British Guiana, in this context, pointed out that: '... An attempt to introduce the treatment in the depot during the year 1907, resulted in disturbances by the coolies which led to its abandonment.' Major Simon, the Medical Inspector of Madras, considered the treatment as 'nasty, drastic and rigorous'.[133] He referred to an incident in 1909, when the introduction of the treatment in the Madras depot was so very unpopular that it had to be abandoned. A coolie threatened the emigrant agent saying that if the treatment was to be imposed on them forcefully, they would leave the depot in groups. The general cry amongst the coolies then was: '...Have you brought us here to kill us'.[134] The major cause of this agitation was that the coolies did not consider themselves as 'sick', because at the earlier stages, the symptoms were not very developed. Colonel Pilgrim observed in his letter (to A. Marsden, Emigrant Agent for British Guiana) dated 25 March 1903:

...The administration of thymol in large doses frequently gives rise to unpleasant, though not dangerous, symptoms; and occasionally to distinctly dangerous symptoms, and even to death. It must be admitted that this depleting treatment would hardly be a good preparation for a voyage through the Bay of Bengal in monsoon.[135]

After these agitations, the officials decided that they would provide the treatment for this disease in the overseas colonies, once the emigrants reached there. Beta-naphthol was selected as the drug which gave the best results, causing the least amount of constitutional disturbance to the coolies. Also the Calcutta and Madras emigrant agents were instructed to reject the people suffering from this disease on medically unfit grounds.[136]

Thus, the whole story of recruitment of emigrants, and their stay in the depots, shows that medical scrutiny and facilities had an important role in the system. The existing historiography shows that the intending emigrants were not just passive victims of the medicalization process. On their arrival at the depots, if they were not satisfied with their surroundings and treatment, they did not hesitate to show their displeasure and refused to emigrate. Moreover, the huge distance between the destination and the depot, rejection of relatives or friends on medical or other grounds, outbreak of diseases—all added fuel to the fire. The emigrants could only be restrained by moral persuasion, as the sepoys and *darwans* who guarded them were not regular soldiers or policemen, and therefore, were unable to utilize sufficient physical force against the fit and able-bodied labourers in the event of riots or desertions. The emigrant officials themselves accepted that any attempt to submit the coolies to a drastic medical treatment, as in the case of curing ankylostomiasis, would only result in riots, desertion on a large scale, or, a general stampede. A simple Indian peasant who believed he was in good health and felt no pain could not be persuaded to understand that he was ill, and would not willingly submit to a treatment of starvation and purging accompanied with nauseating medicine, such as thymol, which he considered quite unnecessary to take, as it weakened him. The principal reason for a 'coolie' wishing to emigrate was domestic trouble and starvation. If he was recruited for the latter reason, he expected, on arrival at the depot, ample amount of food and not to be deprived of it for two days—as required for the ankylostomiasis treatment, purged, and then followed by doses of thymol, which is particularly nauseating.

Conclusion

John Kelly has remarked that the British did not recruit 'coolies'; rather, they made 'coolies'.[137] Recruiters recruited people from all castes and classes, such as gardeners, palanquin-bearers, goldsmiths, tanners, boatmen, soldiers, and even priests to meet the demand for labourers in the plantations. The indentured system turned them all into a degraded mass of plantation labour. They lost their caste taboos and family ties. The main aim of the recruiting agencies was to select a fit body and make it suitable for not only the hostile conditions of the voyages, but also for the plantation economy. The long-term experience of indentured trade and the demands of the plantation economy made the concerned authorities adopt stringent measures in the selection of the indentured body, on the basis of medical grounds. But the study of these measures shows that the criteria for selection was more or less a flexible one. It depended on the demand and supply of the indentured labourers. When there was a shortage of labourers, indentured were supplied even with unsuitable medical condition; while on the other hand, when there was an overwhelming number of intending emigrants, strict medical fitness criteria was followed for the recruitment. The female migrants, because of the shortage of women in the colonies, were often passed with unsuitable conditions. The male labourers who were with women, despite their unfitness, passed because of the latter. Thus, the recruitment agencies were often forced to make compromises with their own rules and regulations. Depots were established in order to make the 'fit' indentured body further 'suitable' for labour, by giving them proper food, western medicines, and proper medical treatment. But the resistance of the intending emigrants towards these medicines, treatment, and the 'process of making them suitable', forced the government to make some compromises. The shifts and changes in the rules and regulations reveal the story of these resistances by the Indians and adaptations by the emigration officials. The officials adapted the measures and policies suitable for the smooth trade of transportation of labourers.

Notes

1. Anil Persaud, 'Transformed Over Seas: "Medical Comforts" aboard Nineteenth-Century Emigrant Ships', in *Labour Matters: Towards Global Histories*, ed. Marcel van der Linden and Prabhu Mohapatra, Delhi: Tulika, 2009, p. 22.
2. Ibid.
3. Major Grierson and Pitcher Report, Revenue and Agriculture Department (Emigration Branch) Proceedings, August 1883, nos. 16–18, part A, para. 42, NAI. They were appointed by the Government of India to enquire about the malpractices in the indentured recruitment system in northern India. The report prepared by Pitcher and Grierson provided information

about the depot's medical facilities, recruitment system, conditions of recruits in the depots, malpractices, and kidnapping of recruits, especially the women.

4. Gaiutra Bahadur, *Coolie Woman: The Odyssey of Indentured*, London: Hurst & Company, 2013, p. 38.

5. Major Grierson and Pitcher Report, Revenue and Agriculture Department (Emigration Branch) Proceedings.

6. Deputation of D.G. Pitcher enquiry, Revenue and Agriculture Department (Emigration Branch) Proceedings, April 1882, nos. 64–73, NAI.

7. Grierson and Pitcher Report, Revenue and Agriculture Department (Emigration Branch) Proceedings.

8. Thomas R. Metcalf, *Forging the Raj: Essays on British India in the Heyday of Empire*, India: Oxford University Press, 2005, p. 223.

9. Ashwin Desai and Goolam Vahed, *Inside Indenture: A South African History, 1860-1914*, Durban: Madiba Publishers, 2007, p. 119.

10. Metcalf, *Forging the Raj*, p. 229.

11. The Protector of Indian Immigrants in Mauritius in his annual report, highlighted that there was no requisition received for labourers from Calcutta. See Annual Report of the Protector of Indian Immigrants in Mauritius for the year 1886, Revenue and Agriculture Department (Emigration Branch) Proceedings, December 1887, nos. 12–15, NAI. There was no recruitment from Calcutta for Mauritius during the years 1885, 1886, and 1887 (NAI).

12. Annual Report of the Protector of Indian Immigrants in Mauritius for the year 1879, Home, Revenue and Agriculture Department (Emigration Branch) Proceedings, May 1880, no. 20, NAI.

13. Natal Law 25 of 1891, Revenue and Agriculture Department (Emigration Branch) Proceedings, August 1895, nos. 5–6, NAI.

14. Major Pitcher Report, Revenue and Agriculture Department (Emigration Branch) Proceedings, February 1883, nos. 1–12, NAI.

15. Ibid.

16. *ARI*, 1860, Appendix H; cited in Marina Carter, *Servants, Sirdars & Settlers: Indians in Mauritius, 1834-1874*, Delhi: Oxford University Press, 1995, pp. 86–7.

17. Metcalf, *Forging the Raj*, p. 239.

18. Major Grierson and Pitcher Report, Revenue and Agriculture Department (Emigration Branch), see appendix IV.

19 Ibid.

20 Ibid.

21 Ibid.

22. Ibid.

23. Ibid.

24. India Office Records, Emigration Proceedings, vol. 5442, 1898, cited in P.C. Emmer, 'The Meek Hindu: The Recruitment of Indian Indentured

Labourers for Service Overseas, 1870-1916', in *Colonialism and Migration: Indentured Labour Before and After Slavery*, ed. P.C. Emmer, Dordrecht/Boston/Lancaster: Martinus Nijhoff, 1986, p. 197.

25. The proposal was raised at the meeting of the Supreme Council of India by G.A. Bushly, Secretary to the Government of India, Home Department (Public Branch), O.C., 21 December 1842, no. 1, NAI.
26. Ibid.
27. Ibid.
28. Extract of a letter from Medical officers to the Medical Board, letter no. 23, Home Department (Public Branch) O.C. April 1843, no. 12, p. 336, NAI.
29. Ibid., p. 341. Extract from a letter from Marine Surgeon M.M. Thompson to the Medical Board, letter no. 23.
30. Ibid.
31. Extract of a letter from Iams Mutchinson, Marine Surgeon Officers, to the Medical Board, no. 23 Home Department (Public Branch) O.C., April 1843, no. 12, p. 336, NAI.
32. Ibid.
33. Ibid.
34. Emmer, 'The Meek Hindu', p. 191.
35. Persaud, 'Transformed Over Seas', pp. 23–4.
36. Letter no. 2615, letter from the Emigrant Agent of British Guiana to the Secretary to the Government of Bengal, Revenue and Agriculture Department (Emigration Branch) Proceedings, February 1887, no. 12, NAI; Also see Madhwi, 'Recruiting Indentured Labour for Overseas Colonies, *circa*1834–1910', *Social Scientist*, vol. 43, no. 9–10, 2015, pp. 53–68; also available at www.jstor.org/stable/24642373, accessed 20 February 2019.
37 Extract from a letter from Marine Surgeon M.M. Thompson to the Medical Board, p. 341.
38. Ibid.
39. Annual Report of the Protector of Indian Immigrants in Natal for the year 1895, Revenue and Agriculture Department (Emigration Branch) Proceedings, July 1894, nos. 107–19, part B, NAI.
40. Ibid. Also see Madhwi, 'Recruiting Indentured Labour for Overseas Colonies, *circa*1834–1910'.
41. Annual Report of the Protector of Indian Immigrants in Natal for the year 1893, Revenue and Agriculture Department (Emigration Branch) Proceedings, July 1894, nos. 31–2, part A, NAI.
42. Letter no. 2614, letter from Dr J. Grant, Protector of Emigrants at Calcutta, to the Secretary to the Government of Bengal, Revenue and Agriculture Department (Emigration Branch) Proceedings, February 1887, no. 12, part A, NAI; Also see papers related to Emigration Act XXI

of 1883, Legislative Department Proceedings, December 1883, nos. 107–246, NAI.

43. Ibid.

44. Letter no. 2615, letter from the Emigration Agent of British Guiana and Surinam to the Secretary to the Government of Bengal.

45. Letter no. 1146, letter from Dr J. Grant, Protector of Emigrants at Calcutta, to the Officiating Secretary to the Government of Bengal, Revenue and Agriculture Department (Emigration Branch) Proceedings, February 1887, no. 12, part A, NAI.

46. J. Wilson Report on Emigration from the port of Calcutta for the year 1903, Revenue and Agriculture Department (Emigration Branch) Proceedings, August 1904, nos. 1–4, NAI.

47. Extract of a letter from M.M. Thompson to the Medical Board, p. 336.

48. Ibid.

49. Carter, *Servants, Sirdars & Settlers*, p. 125.

50. Letter no. 42, letter from the Secretary of State of India to the Government of India, Revenue and Agriculture Department (Emigration Branch) Proceedings, June 1896, no. 24, NAI.

51. Letter no. 937, letter from the Chief Secretary, Government of the North-Western Provinces and Oudh to the Secretary to the Government of India, Revenue and Agriculture Department (Emigration Branch) Proceedings, April 1901, nos. 14–15, NAI.

52. Notice no. 154, from the Government of Bengal, Revenue and Agriculture Department (Emigration Branch) Proceedings, May 1901, no. 13, NAI.

53. Letter no. 937, letter from the Chief Secretary, Government of the North-Western Provinces and Oudh, to the Secretary to the Government of India; Also see Major Grierson and Pitcher Report, Revenue and Agriculture Department (Emigration Branch) Proceedings.

54. Letter no. 937, letter from the Chief Secretary, Government of the North-Western Provinces and Oudh, to the Secretary to the Government of India.

55. Ibid.

56. Letter no. 369, letter from the Civil Surgeon, Allahabad, to the Inspector-General of Civil Hospital, North-Western Province and Oudh, Revenue and Agriculture Department (Emigration Branch) Proceedings, April 1901, nos. 14–15. NAI.

57. Ibid.

58. Major Grierson and Pitcher Report, Revenue and Agriculture Department (Emigration Branch) Proceedings.

59. Ibid.

60. Revenue, Agriculture and Commerce Department (Emigration Branch), February 1876, Appendix C, NAI.

61. H.N.D. Beyts Report, 1861; letter no. 188/66 within the proceeding to

Secretary to the Government of Madras, 21 May 1862; Home Department (Public Branch), 15 October 1870, NAI.

62. Major Grierson and Pitcher Report, Revenue and Agriculture Department (Emigration Branch) Proceedings.
63. Ibid.
64. Ibid.
65 Carter, *Servants, Sirdars & Settlers*, p. 80.
66 Ibid.
67. The Indian Emigration Bill 1880, Home, Revenue and Agriculture Department (Emigration Branch), May 1881, NAI.
68. Ibid.
69. Ibid.
70. Caird on p. 119 to the Secretary to the Government of Bengal, 17 February 1862; cited in Carter, *Servants, Sirdars & Settlers*, p. 82.
71. Carter, *Servants, Sirdars & Settlers*, pp. 86–7.
72. Hugh Tinker, *A New System of Slavery: The Export of Indian Labour Overseas, 1830-1920*, London: Oxford University Press, 1974, p. 142.
73. Ibid., p. 137.
74. Robert Mitchell to the Government Secretary of British Guiana, 17 March 1904, CO 111/543, Colonial Office Correspondence, Public Record Office, TNA.
75. Ibid.
76. Major Grierson and Pitcher Report, Revenue and Agriculture Department (Emigration Branch) Proceedings.
77. Annual Report of the Indian Immigration Trust Board, Natal, for the year 1893, India Office Records, IOR/L/PJ/6/364, British Library.
78. Annual Report of the Protector of Emigrants at Calcutta, Revenue and Agriculture Department (Emigration Branch) from 1871 to 1914, NAI.
79. Beyts Report, cited in Ralph Shlomowitz and John McDonald, 'Mortality of Indian Labour on Ocean Voyages, 1843-1917', *Studies in History*, vol. VI, no. 1, 1990, p. 31.
80. See Major Grierson and Pitcher Report, Revenue and Agriculture Department (Emigration Branch) Proceedings; Also, introduction of a revised scale of diet for the coolies at the emigration depots at the port of Calcutta, see No. 137, letter from Dr J. Grant, Protector of Emigrants, to A. Mackenzie, Junior Secretary to the Government of Bengal, Home Department (Public Branch) Proceedings, May 1870, nos. 60–2, NAI.
81. See Major Grierson and Pitcher Report, Revenue and Agriculture Department (Emigration Branch) Proceedings.
82. Major Grierson and Pitcher Report, Revenue and Agriculture Department (Emigration Branch) Proceedings.
83. Introduction of a revised scale of diet for the coolies at the emigration

depots at the port of Calcutta, No. 137, letter from Dr J. Grant to A. Mackenzie.

84. Annual Report of the Protector of Indian Immigrants in Natal for the year 1908, Commerce and Industry Department (Emigration Branch) Proceedings, September 1909, nos. 1–4, part A, NAI.

85. Sumit Guha, 'Nutrition, Sanitation, Hygiene, and the Likelihood of Death: The British Army in India c.1870-1920', *Population Studies*, vol. 47, no. 3, 1993, pp. 385–401.

86. David Arnold, 'Vagrant India: Famine, Poverty and Welfare under Colonial Rule', in *Cast Out: Vagrancy and Homelessness in Global and Historical Perspective*, ed. A.L. Beier and P.R. Ocobock, Ohio: Ohio University Press, 2008, p. 121.

87. James Patterson Smith, 'Empire and Social Reform: British Liberals and the "Civilizing Mission" in the Sugar Colonies, 1868-1874', *Albion: A Quarterly Journal concerned with British Studies*, vol. XXVII, no. 2, 1995, p. 270.

88. David Arnold, *Colonizing the Body: State Medicine and Epidemic Disease in Nineteenth-Century India*, Berkeley: University of California Press, 1993, p. 111.

89. Ibid., p. 112.

90. Letter from Captain C. Burbank, Protector of Emigrants at Calcutta, to J. Geoghegan, Junior Secretary to the Government of Bengal, letter no. 178 in the proceedings, 8 May 1866, Home Department (Public Branch) Proceedings, July 1866, no. 31, NAI.

91. Letter from F. Bedingfeld, Colonial Secretary of Mauritius, to the Secretary to the Government of Bengal, letter no. 101A, 18 January 1866, Home Department (Public Branch) Proceedings, July 1866, no. 31, NAI.

92. Ibid.

93. 'An Indian Slave Trade', *The Pioneer*, cited in the letter from Robert G.W. Herbert, Undersecretary of State for the Colonies, to the Undersecretary of State for India, dated 25 May 1871, Revenue and Agriculture Department (Emigration Branch) Proceedings, August 1871, nos. 30–3, NAI.

94. Major Pitcher Report, Revenue and Agriculture Department (Emigration Branch) Proceedings.

95. Introduction of revised scale of diet for the coolies at the emigration depots at the port of Calcutta, letter no. 137, letter from Dr J. Grant to A. Mackenzie.

96. Ibid.

97. Major Grierson and Pitcher Report, Revenue and Agriculture Department (Emigration Branch) Proceedings.

98. Annual Report of the Protector of Indian Immigrants in Natal for the year 1885, Revenue and Agriculture Department (Emigration Branch) Proceedings, October 1886, nos. 8–9, NAI.

99. Ibid.
100. Annual Report of the Protector of Indian Immigrants in Natal for the year 1887, Revenue and Agriculture Department (Emigration Branch) Proceedings, September 1888, nos. 16–17, NAI.
101. See Carter, *Servants, Sirdars & Settlers*, p. 125.
102. Extract of a letter from M.M. Thompson to the Medical Board, p. 341.
103. Major Grierson and Pitcher Report, Revenue and Agriculture Department (Emigration Branch) Proceedings. See the description of the French sub-depot at Danapur.
104. Annual Report of the Protector of Emigrants at Calcutta for the year 1874, Revenue and Agriculture Department, Bengal Government (Emigration Branch) Proceedings, August 1876, nos. 17–18, part A, NAI.
105. Major Grierson and Pitcher Report, Revenue and Agriculture Department (Emigration Branch) Proceedings. See the description of the Trinidad sub-depot.
106. Annual Report of the Protector of Emigrants at Calcutta for the year 1909, Commerce and Industry Department (Emigration Branch) Proceedings, August 1910, no. 9, part B, NAI.
107. Ibid.
108. Ibid.
109. Ibid.
110. Ibid.
111. Ibid.
112. Ibid.
113. Letter from the Agent-General of Emigration to the Honourable Colonial Secretary, Commerce and Industry Department (Emigration Branch) Proceedings, January 1912, nos. 3–6, part A, NAI. In his letter, the agent general mentioned:

   …The Protector of Emigrants at Calcutta is a medical man, and holds I think no other appointment, but in Madras the Protector of Emigrants is also the 'Collector' of Madras and he has many important duties. The Protector at Calcutta submits an annual report to this government, which contains interesting and useful information on the subject of the various depots, and on recruiting during the year. I do not know whether the Protector at Madras prepares a similar report, but if so, a copy has not at any time been supplied to this government, and we are also wholly in the dark in respect of emigration from Madras to other colonies.

114. Introduction of a revised scale of diet for the coolies at the emigration depots at the port of Calcutta, No. 137, letter from Dr J. Grant to A. Mackenzie.
115. Mortality on board the *Forkshire* from Calcutta to Demerara, Revenue, Agriculture and Commerce Department (Emigration Branch) Proceedings, November 1875, no. 23, NAI.
116. Ibid. An ousted Indian king, the Nawab of Awadh (Oudh), had set up

his court-in-exile at Garden Reach after the British removed him from power in 1857. For three decades, poets and courtesans thrived there under the aegis of the Nawab, the host of many decadent parties. When the king died in 1887, however, the landscape was transformed. Jute factories and dockyards replaced the gardens. During the monsoon season, water stagnated on tracts of undrained land, which led to the breeding of mosquitoes and consequently, spreading of malaria. The king's palace was razed, and the mansions of his ministers were sold to clear his debts. The houses of his ministers became the headquarters for the government agency sending workers to British Guiana. See Bahadur, *Coolie Woman the Odyssey*, p. 43.

117. Tinker, *A New System of Slavery*, p. 141.
118. Introduction of revised scale of diet for the coolies at the emigration depots at the port of Calcutta, No. 137, letter from Dr J. Grant to A. Mackenzie.
119. Also see Emmer, 'The Meek Hindu', pp. 192–3.
120. Introduction of revised scale of diet for the coolies at the emigration depots at the port of Calcutta, No. 137, letter from Dr J. Grant to A. Mackenzie.
121. Letter from the Agent-General of Emigration to the Honourable Colonial Secretary.
122. See letter from Surgeon H.C. Cutcliffe, Inspector of Emigrants, to Dr J. Grant, the Protector of Emigrants at Calcutta, regarding the restriction of emigration from depots where cholera prevails, Agriculture, Revenue and Commerce Department (Emigration Branch) Proceedings, January 1872, nos. 21–3, NAI.
123. Rules for the treatment and segregation of infected emigrants in Bengal, Revenue and Agriculture Department (Emigration Branch) Proceedings, March 1900, no. 23, NAI.
124. Ibid.
125. Ibid.
126. Proposed modification of the Home Department, notification no. 836, dated 6 March 1897, under the Epidemic Disease Act, prohibiting emigration from India, Revenue and Agriculture Department (Emigration Branch) Proceedings, February 1901, no. 17, part A, NAI.
127. Ibid.
128. For details, see chapter one of this volume.
129. Telegram from the Government of Bombay, no. 24 M., dated 22 April 1900, Department of Revenue and Agriculture (Emigration Branch) Proceedings, May 1900, nos. 20–7, NAI. A circus company, named Professor Devel's Circus, consisting of about sixty people, along with elephants, lions, and tigers, proposed to go to Egypt for a month and then to the Paris exhibition. Indian nationalist leader Motilal Nehru had also

written to the Emigrant Protector at Bombay, seeking his permission for the embarkation of the performers and artisans for the Paris exhibition.

130. Proposed modification of the Home Department, notification no. 836, dated 6 March 1897, under the Epidemic Disease Act, prohibiting emigration from India, Revenue and Agriculture (Emigration Branch) Proceedings, February 1901, no. 17, part A, NAI.
131. Arnold, *Colonizing the Body*, p. 107.
132. Note of the Sanitary Commissioner, dated 12 May 1911, Commerce and Industry Department (Emigration Branch) Proceedings, June 1911, nos. 2–3, part A, NAI. Thymol is a natural monoterpene phenol derivative of cymene, $C_{10}H_{14}O$, isomeric with carvacrol, found in oil of thyme, and extracted from *Thymus vulgaris* (common thyme) and various other kinds of plants as a white crystalline substance with a pleasant aromatic odour and strong antiseptic properties.
133. Ibid.
134. Ibid.
135. Memorandum on ankylostomiasis by A. Marsden, Colonial Civil Service, Officiating Govt. Emigration Agent for British Guiana, Commerce and Industry Department (Emigration Branch) Proceedings, December 1911, nos. 1–4, part A, NAI.
136. Note of the Sanitary Commissioner, dated 12 May 1911.
137. John Kelly, *A Politics of Virtue: Hinduism, Sexuality and Countercolonial Discourse in Fiji*, Chicago: University of Chicago Press, 1991, p. 29.

CHAPTER THREE

Transporting 'Bodies'
Shipping Indentured Labour to Mauritius and Natal

> It must be borne in mind that Indian labourers who have never been at sea before, and who are accompanied with their wives and children, require much more attention and care on board ship than troops, who have their officers to look after them.
>
> —Extract from a letter from the Emigration Agent, 9 March 1843, Home Department (Public Branch)

The comparison between British troops and Indian indentured labour shows the importance of labour, which determined economic development as well as territorial expansion. This comparison also shows two types of mobile population—the indentured on one hand, who went through hostile conditions at sea during voyages, and the British army on the other hand, travelling with well-prepared officers with the experience of being a superior naval power in the world.[1] According to Partha Chatterjee, the British achieved superiority as an empire by the myth of the 'Empire of the Seas'.[2] Indian labourers did not have any experience of sea travel before their departure as coolies to the overseas plantation colonies. The transportation of the indentured labourers in these colonies started in 1834 with the beginning of sugar plantations in Mauritius. In the beginning, 'hill coolies' were selected for working as labourers, but soon they became the victims of the harsh condition of voyages, resulting in diseases and a high death rate. The hostile situation and pressure from anti-slavery groups forced the government to adopt measures to prevent sickness and mortality during the voyages. The hill coolies were soon replaced by Indian labourers who were from the plains. In the previous chapter, the importance of the 'depot' on the basis of which the government sought to create an

PLATE 3.1: Memorial Plaque of Indentured Workers on the Bank of River
Hooghly, Kolkata Port Trust, Garden Reach[3]

Source: The author.

able-bodied labour force has been discussed. This chapter would discuss
the spatial significance of the ships used for transportation of the
indentured. It would also delineate the efforts made by the government
to preserve and maintain the 'health' and 'body' of the migrants.

Historians have explored the multi-layered connection between the
voyages and indentured trade, and also the importance of voyages for
the making of new social relationships. Keeping these in mind, my
attempt is to move further and explicate the medical and sanitation
processes associated with indentured voyages. It begins by referring to

the technological developments and its effect on the ships during the journey over the seas. It intends to enquire the role of the ship surgeons, who treated sick labourers on the vessels transporting the indentured. It aims to explore the surgeons' professional credentials, their motivation, and especially the medical services they provided to the recruits. The chapter also deals with diseases on the voyage, the methods of their treatment, and the efforts to reform the medical and other aspects of the trade. An attempt has also been made to examine the everyday lives of the recruits on the ship, along with their experiences, taking into account seasickness and the new rules and regulations of food, sanitation laws, and medical environment.

Shipbuilding: Voyages and Modern Technology

In September 1834, thirty-six Dhangur nomadic tribal male labourers (hill coolies), who belonged to the Nagpore-sambhg village of Bihar, came to Calcutta port for migration to Mauritius.[4] In the initial period of indentured trade, there was no separate ship for the migrants. They were made to travel in the cargo ships. There was a great demand for Indian rice, wheat, and other consumer goods by planters and traders in Mauritius. The captains of the cargo ships provided travel arrangements for 150–200 passengers at a subsidized rate.[5] Thus, the transportation cost of the labourers was cheaper for the planters in Mauritius. Labourers travelled on these cargo ships as deck passengers. Planters found this arrangement both beneficial and cheap.

From September 1834 to December 1835, fifteen cargo ships with indentured labourers travelled from India to Mauritius.[6] These cargo ships were, however, not suitable for carrying humans, and the mortality rate was quite high during these voyages.[7] This type of transportation soon became a hassle for the authorities. The anti-indentured lobby became active in the late 1830s when the details of abuses related to the unregulated transportation of Indian labourers, were exposed.[8] The Indian press and reformists depicted emigration as the 'Indian slave trade' and petitions were submitted demanding the abolition of indentured trade. As a result, emigration was temporarily suspended in 1839. This decision also brought about various reforms in the nature of the indentured trade. Both the concerned officials, as well as various groups of planters like the 'Free Labour Association',[9] were forced to adopt reform policies regarding transportation of the coolies. J. Prinsep, one of the members of the Calcutta Enquiry Committee, stressed that

PLATE 3.2: River Hooghly, Kolkata Port Trust, Garden Reach Road,
West Bengal

Source: The author.

migration should be actively encouraged as a 'powerful agent of
civilization'.[10] On the pretext of greater benefit of the Indians, as
suggested by the Free Labour Association and the planters lobby, the
Government of India, once again, in 1842, started the recruitment and
transportation of Indians. A Passenger Act was passed in the same year
to regulate the transport of human cargo from India to the various
colonies. This act was already in use for the transportation of soldiers to
different parts of the empire, and the European migrants to the US and
Australia.[11] The Colonial Land and Emigration Commissioners,
appointed by Lord John Russell in 1840, were also required to oversee
the practice of Indian migration from 1842. At least on paper, a number
of rules and regulations were made to cover every aspect of indentured
migration in detail. Later, chartered ships were also appointed for the
indentured trade.

A typical slave ship sailing from the European ports to Africa and
the West Indies was not a special vessel in the eighteenth century;
rather, it was just a wooden cargo vessel.[12] In the mid-eighteenth
century, vessels from the merchant fleet of the country were in use.
Shipbuilding became a complex task. Every ship was in its way a work
of art, of complexity, joinery, and design, in which different types of
wood were combined. It was as if the shipwright had been a cabinetmaker!
All ships were subject to damaging attacks by barnacles or shipworm;

beginning only in the late eighteenth century were ships of northern Europe given copper-sheathed hulls as innovation, which not only protected vessels from shipworm but increased their speed too.[13]

The Act XV of 1842 redefined the indentured system for the first time, as it laid down new structures for recruitment of the indentured and regulation of the voyages. The high death rate on the voyages, and accidents at sea due to storms, fires, and navigational errors demanded new safety measures and structural changes in the passenger ships. This new demand provided opportunities to the European, and specially, the British shipbuilding companies, to introduce new ships with advanced technology, which were bigger and had higher speeds, to the indentured trade.[14] In order to protect the interest of the metropolitan economy, the British Navigation Acts of 1814 and 1823 ensured that all trade to and from the colonies was carried out exclusively in British vessels, sailing in and out of British ports.[15] These vessels soon replaced the old country-built sail ships, which were earlier being supplied from Bombay, Cochin, or Moulmein and had shown themselves fully capable of competing with their British counterparts.[16] Most of the country-built ships was usually of teak construction, were small, and less efficient when it came to speed. The recognized causes of higher mortality on the ships were overcrowding, dampness in the ship, ill-defined amount of space for individual travellers on the ship, and long duration of the journey. The new ships were intended to solve all these troubles, making them more efficient and ensuring swift transport of labouring bodies to the colonies.

After 1870s, the rules for the departure of the coolie ships were more comprehensively and more efficiently enforced, as compared to other passenger ships.[17] The British India Steam Navigation (BISN) Company introduced steamer services which soon took over the routes to Mauritius and Natal. It cut short the duration of the journey to various colonies. Ralph Shlomowitz and John McDonald, in their studies, show that in the late 1870s and by the mid-1880s, most immigrants were being transported by steamships, which reduced the length of the voyages to less than two months.[18] They mention that this also had some effect on reducing the death rate among the infants, for example, from one-quarter to one-twelfth.[19] But some of the emigrant agents were not in the favour of these steamers; they thought that a long journey was good for the recruits as it would provide them with adequate time to rest and put on weight, which would be beneficial for the labour body.[20] Again, according to them, the long journey would be helpful for the expiration of the normal period of incubation before they reached their destinations. The Trinidad Agent-General on the other side, had a different thought; he mentioned in his annual report after the arrival of a group of indentured labourers on the new steamer— 'Struck…by their bright and cheerful expression, so different from the usual stolid, stupid looks of those who for nearly a hundred days had had nothing to do except eat, drink and sleep, and this I attributed to the shortness of the voyage.'[21]

The protector of immigrants in Jamaica was also in favor of the new steamer ships. He mentioned in his report that the employment of these ships was a great success, as the death rate had been reduced to a minimum, and this also added to the certainty of the immigrants arriving within a fixed time, amply justifying the extra expenditure incurred.[22]

A report from the Emigration Commissioners, related to the overcrowding of certain emigrant vessels dispatched from Bombay sailing to Mauritius in 1864, came with the suggestion for establishing a uniform system of measuring emigrant vessels.[23] The size of the ship became an important aspect in this regard; after a long discussion and several experiments, the concerned authorities finally came to the conclusion that 'Sterling's rule' [the British law regarding space allocation] should be adopted in India for measuring the emigrant vessels.[24] It was only in 1871 that Sterling's Formula for measuring emigrant ships was adopted, after having 'been in force in England for a long time', and this brought uniformity to the way emigrant ships were measured, i.e. a uniformity between the ships leaving from India and those leaving from Britain.

Subsequently, the Government of India also directed the other colonies involved in the indentured trade to adhere to this formula.[25] All the three presidencies in India—Calcutta, Madras, and Bombay— were instructed to follow the same rules for the measurement of passenger decks of the emigrant vessels.[26]

The space which was provided to the emigrants on voyages was very narrow; they were tightly packed in the paddle steamers in allotted spaces of six feet by two feet. In order to avoid the high death rate on the voyages due to overcrowding, a new rule was implemented, which defined the number of passengers for every ship. According to this rule, a ship was allowed to carry only 347 emigrants (under the then present allowance of 12 sq. ft.).[27] The protector of emigrants, along with the medical surgeon, were responsible for the enforcement of these rules. A difference in the measurement of deck of ships according to the prevailing rule and Sterling's rule is given in Table 3.1.

TABLE 3.1: Comparison between the Old (prevailing) Rule and Sterling's Rule for Measurement of Emigrant Vessels

Name of the ships	Area in square feet of deck according to old rule of thumb	Area in square feet of deck according to Sterling's rule
Alnwick Castle	5,400	4,812
Newcastle	6,026	4,995
Clarence	5,400	4,954
Ganges	5,807	4,278
Atalanta	5,310	4,188
Belvidera (sic)	3,820	3,361
Canning	4,620	4,079
Lincelles	5,107	4,166

Source: Letter from the Officiating Master Attendant to the Emigration Agent for Mauritius, no. A1247, dated 4 March 1869, Home Department (Public Branch) Proceedings, 26 June 1869, nos. 18–19, NAI.

There were also provisions in the Act XV of 1843 for the construction of berths on the indentured voyages, because during the voyage, it was impossible to keep the decks clean and dry. A medical surgeon mentioned in his report: '...seawater was almost every day washing over the ship'.[28] The Calcutta emigrant agent discussed in his report that berths were not sufficient to prevent dampness during the voyages, apart from not being suitable for the warm climate. In order to prevent the danger of wet decks on the voyages, suggestions were made for the construction of a platform for each emigrant, instead of berths, which was already in use in the ships *Surat Merchant* and *City of London*.[29] Dampness was a prime cause of several diseases; therefore, provisions were made on the ship for an emigrant to sleep on a wooden platform raised about 2.5 ft. above the floor, which would of course remain perfectly dry.[30] Provisions were also made to provide a platform on the lower deck of every ship for the comfort and health of the emigrants. Platforms were added to the lower deck, creating in effect a second tier of housing. The 'platforms are of bamboo-work, closely arranged, and raised about three feet from the deck.' While several captains approved of the platforms and considered them, 'wholesome', there were others who found them to be source of diseases.[31] For example, Captain Wright, Assistant Protector of Emigrants: '...does not approve of platforms, thinks they impede air circulation, prevent the cleaning of the decks, interfere with free ventilation, and cause those sleeping under the tubes to lie in draughts, which renders them very sickly.' There were no platforms in the ships leaving from the Madras port.

There was a provision that every emigrant would get a sleeping space of 6 ft. by 2 ft.[32] The platform was arranged in such a way (see Plate 3.3) that it would be both firm, and at the same time, be easy to remove in order to clear away any filth that might accumulate under it. So, the 20 sq. ft. of superficial space allotted to each indentured labourer on the deck as their home for twenty-one weeks was not an arbitrary allotment. It took almost thirty years of debate to reach and finalize, this decision over space.[33]

The need to maintain the health of the indentured passengers on board ships forced contemporary science to come up with new technologies. One of the major causes of inconvenience on the ships, besides the humid environment, was the absence of proper ventilation. Smell on the ships was compounded of sweat, urine, excrement, and vomit; and the smell was leached so deep into the timber that it became almost ineradicable. It was the first thing that the emigrants encountered once on board the ships.[34] In the late 1870s, one of the major inventions was: Mr Theirs's self-acting ventilator. A long debate between the authorities and the medical surgeons culminated in the conclusion that the use of Theirs's self-acting ventilator was to be made compulsory on the ships carrying indentured labourers.[35] Besides the great success of

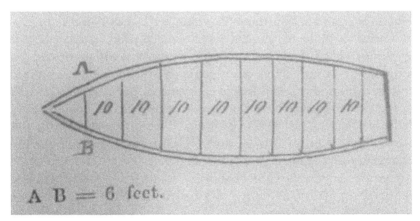

PLATE 3.3: Sketch of the way Platforms were Arranged on Ships

Source: Extract from a letter from the Emigration Agent, dated 9 March 1843, Home Department (Public Branch) Proceedings, 26 April 1843, no. 8, NAI.

this ventilator in the European countries, especially in warships and merchant ships from London, Crown-Agent Richard Assheton Cross wrote in his letter to the colonial office secretary that this ventilator was also useful in curbing, to some extent, the loss of indentured lives during the outbreak of epidemics like cholera and measles in the course of the voyages.[36] The self-acting ventilator was first used in India on the *Malabar*, and the commander of that ship highly appreciated the apparatus and expressed his experience in these words:

…During the hot weather there was always an offensive smell of foul air from the porter-room, fore-hold and lower deck but this time there has been an entire freedom from anything of the kind, which I attribute entirely to the working of the ventilators. The action of these ventilators is easily seen by their effects on the flame of a candle at the extremities of the terminal pipes below as well as by the current of heated and foul air forced up through the discharge pipe on the upper deck, which is readily perceptible to the hand and nose; I am therefore of an opinion that they might be fitted with advantage to the other Indian troop-ships or any vessels in her majesty's service.[37]

Therefore, the Government of India, in 1878, came up with this decision, under rules 1 and 7 of Schedule B, Act VII of 1871,[38] that it was compulsory to use this self-acting ventilator, a fog alarm, and a bilge pump on every ship involved in indentured trade.[39]

This decision was, however, not welcomed by the planters of the overseas colonies, who thought that it would increase the expense of transporting the indentured labourers to the colonies. The governor of Mauritius argued in his letter to the colonial secretary that the presence of ventilators on the voyages did not have much effect on the death rate as compared to the former voyages without ventilation, and '… introduction of ventilation, the expense of which "about doubles" the cost of the introduction of Indian emigrants to this island, and would, in fact, act as a prohibition almost as complete as if emigration from India to Mauritius had been suspended'.[40] The total expenditure on this element was calculated as 1,800 cents.[41] The emigrant agent of Mauritius also argued that in this season (1891–2) the death rate on the emigrant voyage was comparatively low and the duration of journey was also shorter from Calcutta (thirty and a half days) and Madras (twenty-seven and a half) as compared to other overseas colonies, which also received indentured emigrants. There was also a demand from the Protectors of Immigrants of Mauritius and Natal that steam vessels should be exempted from the use of artificial ventilation from the safety point of view. The surgeon superintendent who was serving

S.S. Congella of Madras port, mentioned that the ventilators were always available on the ship, but they never used them, and that natural ventilation was always available and good for the recruits' health.[42] Consequently, after the suggestions made by the medical superintendent of emigrant voyages, and by those who had already served many ships of England and West Indies, and were now serving the pilgrimage ships (like *Jedda*), the steamer ships were exempted from the use of the automatic ventilation.[43] As a result of long-drawn debates among the authorities, Mauritius and Natal ships were also exempted from the compulsory use of Theirs's self-acting ventilator. The majority of emigration surgeons had proved the ventilator as a failure. In the annual report on emigration from the Calcutta port to the colonies for the year 1883–4, the causes of this failure were explained; it was shown that the apparatus was inactive when natural ventilation was absent.[44] Dr Grant also found it to be unnecessary, in spite of the fact that it was quite inexpensive. Therefore, in order to keep cost of transportation low, most of the ships to Mauritius and Natal were exempted from the compulsory use of this ventilator.

The loss of ships on the seas and other accidents, such as the fire on board the *Shah Allum* in 1859 causing the death of 399 Indians; led to overhauling of the provisions for new safety equipment like lifeboats, lifebelts, lifebuoys, rafts,[45] and others.[46] This ship had sailed from Calcutta on 25 May 1859 for Mauritius with a general cargo, 349 emigrants, and a crew of about 75 men. C.W. Brebner, ship captain for Mauritius, noted this case in his account:

…All went well till noon of the 27th of June, when an alarm was raised that the ship was on fire. The *Shah Allum* was at the time in lat. 12° S. and long. 75° E., Mauritius bearing V.V. S.W., 1,100 miles. The ship continued burning from noon of the 27th till noon of the 30th, which at latter time was abandoned. After the boats left her she continued burning till 8 p.m., when the flames were no longer seen by those in the boats; the vessel having doubtless sunk. Out of nearly 500 souls that were on board previous to the outbreak of fire only 64 were saved in two boats, the launch and the gig. Out of these 64, only one was an emigrant. The others comprised of an officer, a doctor, a gunner, and about 12 of the crew, with at least 60 or 70 coolies who were drowned by the swamping of the cutter and jolly boat. About 200 to 250 coolies were set adrift on three rafts, the remainder perished either on board of the ill-fated vessel or were drowned alongside.[47]

After the evidence given by the master of the ship was fully corroborated by the chief and second mates, the Marine Board of Mauritius passed the following remark on the whole tragic affair:

...It is difficult, on learning for the first time that of all the people saved in the launch one only was an emigrant, to divest oneself of a certain painful suspicion that the master, officers, and crew must have rather exerted themselves for the preservation of their own lives than in doing their duty with regard to the unfortunate coolies; but when it is discovered in the course of examination that during nearly three days and nights every effort was made not only to extinguish the fire, but to provide for the safety of all on board in the event of an abandonment becoming unavoidable, suspicion gives place to a feeling of admiration at the coolness, courage, and perseverance displayed by the master, and those under his orders, in a situation of peculiar peril and difficulty from the moment the alarm was first given to the hour it became necessary to abandon the vessel, and with the exception of some 30 unfortunate wretches paralyzed by fear, the master, mate and crew were the very last that left her. The whole proceedings are, in the opinion of the Board, marked by great judgment, prudence, and forethought.[48]

Once again this matter generated a heated argument among the different countries' emigrant agents to provide safety against all risks to be incurred by the emigrant vessels. A meeting was held to decide on the number of such safety equipment on each vessel, against the number of passengers carried by the same. The authorities were also concerned about keeping a low rate of transportation of indentured labour to overseas countries. The Emigrant Agents of Natal and British Guiana wrote in their respective letters to the Calcutta agent—'...the proportion which the number of lifebelts should bear to the number of emigrants carried on emigrant vessels...should be determined by an actual experiment on a batch of emigrants selected haphazardly.'[49] Apart from this, the emigrant agent of Surinam argued that—'the number of lifebelts should be about one-third of the number of male emigrants carried on board of emigrant vessels.' He also wrote in his letter that:

...Should an emigrant vessel be wrecked on the high seas, I very much doubt if a single life would be saved through the agency of a life-belt, even if ready to their hands; but suppose they did, in that case most likely they would not know how to make use of them; in all probability one and the same lifebelt would be wanted by several emigrants, resulting in fights if not worse. To be brief, the very lifebelts would make confusion worse confounded, and instead of saving life, would bring about the very reverse.[50]

The Indians were thought of as illiterate and less efficient in handling complicated modern technology. On this ground, authorities suggested that there was no need to introduce these technologies on the voyages, as that could make transportation more expensive and complicated. If the Indians were entitled to use these apparatuses at all, it would be compulsory for them to be under the guidance of a white superior. The emigrant agent of Trinidad, however, had a different thought on this matter, which is reflected in his letter—'I would recommended that the board of trade statutory rules should be adopted in their entirety.' He further argued:

...I am strongly of opinion that, in the event of an emigrant vessel floundering in mid-ocean, either through stress of weather or after a collision, or being burnt at sea, the loss of life would inevitably be very great, no matter what life-saving appliances are provided. Still I don't see why all emigrants should not have an equal chance afforded to them, even though this involves the provision of a lifebelt for each person.[51]

This ideological difference gradually led to the authorities coming up with the decision that every emigrant ship was entitled to have these life-saving apparatuses for a percentage of the total number of passengers.

These modern technologies became the tools for the effective transportation of indentured to the colonies. An improvement in the apparatus of the transportation trade also pacified the anti-indentured groups to some extent, who were earlier raising questions, from time to time, about the inhuman conditions of the indentured system. Though these issues were discussed and some reformatory measures were put in place, most were never implemented in reality. Rules and regulations were adopted on paper, but the safety equipments carried in the vessels were not sufficient for the passengers. During accidents and cases of emergency, the ship authorities and crew members were given the priority of using these equipments first, in order to save their lives. The period after 1850s saw a tremendous increase in the demand of indentured labourer due to the expansion of the world plantation economy. This demand pushed the need for making the transportation process of indentured labour safer and more secure. In spite of the availability of these modern apparatuses, mortality figures in voyages were regularly increased by accidents at sea, when storms, fires, or navigational difficulties led to the wrecking of ships and loss of lives.[52] There was, however, a decline in the mortality rate after the 1870s, when stringent measures were taken to provide better food, accommodation, and healthcare on the ships.

The advent of newer technologies provided opportunities to the Western capitalist companies that found the migrant population to be a bunch of consumers. Official record shows growing competition among the different European companies who wanted to monopolize voyage consumers. The British government provided the opportunity to European companies to maintain their right of trade, pointing to the idea of 'common benefit of the human race'.[53] Indentured migration to different corners of the world also provided an opportunity to the European capitalists to 'work' for the welfare of the Orientals (which was only a façade which the former used to cover their profit-making motive). So, the British government assisted their agents for the capitalists to hold the trade on the sea voyages of migrants. Thus, money and power came together to rule over a vast empire. An example of the attempt to monopolize transportation can be cited in the fact that voyages were only allowed to keep the 'Baker's plantation microscope', which was introduced in 1907.[54]

The plantation economy was also involved in providing the financial aid as well as opportunities to the new medical research facilities in exchange of capital benefit. During the 1880s, for example, the profit margin for British traders in Bengal was two to three times higher than what they would have obtained in Britain. The aforementioned Calcutta medical firm suddenly got thousands of consumers in the form of emigrants. In the 1883 Emigration Act, the Cow's Head brand of condensed milk was included in the medical comforts list for the emigrants after recommendation of the experts. Earlier condensed milk from brands like Anglo-Swiss or Nestlé was in use on the voyages. Regarding the Cow's Head brand, the inspector-general of the civil hospital stated that—'It has been subjected to a practical test as regards its keeping qualities, and that it has been reported on favourably by the chemical examiner'. He added that '...the milk is rather richer in proteins than the "first Swiss" variety, which is one of the brands already recognized by the rules, and this is an advantage'. In these circumstances, the lieutenant-governor recommended that the brand of milk in question may be included in the list of medical comforts.[55] This was not only the case with condensed milk, but other medical products too, such as products for disinfection. These products further helped in the medicalization of the emigrant voyages.

It was only in the twentieth century, near the end of the indentured system, that science and technology acquired some control over the hazards of coolie transportation. Meteorological observations in Mauritius (1892) and India (1890), discussions over the nature of winds and weather (particularly over the Indian Ocean in 1853), and certain rules and regulations for sailing directions to avoid collision at sea, lights and their order, etc., helped in controlling disasters during voyages to a great extent.[56] In 1890, the meteorological reporter to the Government of India published a *Handbook on Bay of Bengal Cyclones*. Brebner, in the preface to his account of observations on Mauritius cyclones, stated—'I consider it a great boon to those who have to navigate the Bay.'[57] Brebner's own account provides a detailed account of his experiences and also provides information on sailing in the Indian Ocean to the future navigators and researchers.

Preserving the Health of Indentured Labour over the Voyages

'Your sailboats crawled
Through the equatorial torpor. Grim
Stop-overs at the Cape and St Helena;
Epidemics engendering emaciated death
In quarantine at the isle of the Saints
Prolonging the 100-day passage from India to the Caribbean.
I say voyage between pumpkins and salted fish
Snoek chutney and fish curry.'[58]

(K. Torabully, *Chair Corail Fragments Coolies*, p. 61)

The emigrants were subjected to regimented sanitary and medical control over the voyage. During the long journey of three months, often some new diseases like seasickness, certain heart diseases, bronchitis, phthisis, cholera (Asiatic), venereal diseases and diseases like diarrhoea, mumps, itch, and ringworm, etc., affected the emigrants. In order to keep the labouring body alive and fit despite these diseases, the ships were often transformed into hospitals. Also, as Anil Persaud rightly argued, they became a type of laboratory where experiments to find 'minimums' were conducted: minimum space, minimum diet, minimum light, minimum air, etc.[59] Thus, the emigrants on a ship were entering into a new medical regime, in which they, for the first time in their lives, encountered allopathic medicines and colonial science. Here, they were required not only to know their body, but also how to describe it in ways that science understood it.[60] Seaborne populations were at greater risk than the ones at the depots on land, because if an infectious disease was brought aboard a vessel at the time of embarkation or caused an outbreak during the voyage, it would rapidly spread among the passengers and crew in the confined space of the vessel. A latent role of medical science was to observe the manifestation of diseases that developed on the sea and affected the labourers. Shlomowitz and McDonald argued that 'nineteenth century health officials usually interpreted diseases in terms of the then prevailing 'miasma theory' of disease. Whereas the modern germ theory holds that a specific living micro-organism (such as a specific virus) is responsible for a specific disease (such as measles): whereas the miasma theory held that miasma (poisonous chemicals), when associated with certain atmospheric conditions, caused diseases.'[61] The emigrants' report had shown that the lack of knowledge could not protect emigrants from sickness, and the number of diseases and the mortality rate remained very high. Shlomowitz and McDonald, in this context, rightly stated:

…Not only was the testimony of nineteenth century health officials informed by an incorrect theory of disease, but their ascription of mortality to specific diseases must also be treated with caution. Diagnostic abilities in determining the specific cause of death were limited, and it was not until 1869, for example, that typhus and typhoid were separated in the nosology adopted by the Registrar-General of Vital Statistics of England and Wales.[62]

Ship mortality rates were closely monitored in the nineteenth century as an indication of the effort to organize the indentured system and look into the well being of the recruits. Various commissions and medical surgeons were appointed for the purpose of enquiring into the matter. Their conclusion on the high death rate among the coolies was more about discovering the progress of medical science and its effect on indentured trade. When the colonial state failed to diminish the high rate of mortality among the indentured, it blamed the emigrants for their condition. The most prominent cause identified by the enquiry commission was the psycho-cultural cause. Apart from psychological factors, other factors responsible for the high rate of mortality and sickness were regional epidemiology, environments, gender, age, and racial differences of the migrants. The enquiry commission's report of 1842 disclosed that the eccentric environment on ship, and the fear of the emigrants of losing their caste or religion were the main causes for the high rate of sickness.

The enquiry committee also compared the death and sickness rate between the coolies from Madras and those from Calcutta. Dr Bakewell in his report of 1869 mentioned that 'for Calcutta migrants in particular, life on the vast plain of Hindoostan amid miasmatic poison…must in the course of ages, have greatly deteriorated the race...on the other hand, Madrasis were simply less "fearful" of sea travel than migrants from North-Eastern India.'[63] The comparison also describes the differences between the two groups in these words:

...The 'Madrassee' [those who belong to the southern part of India] is a lively singing fellow who delights in remaining on deck, seldom stays below if he can help it, day or night is always ready to bear a hand in pulling on ropes or other work...and is much less troubled with prejudices of any kind...the 'Bangalee' [i.e. the man from upper India] is so much given to remaining below that compulsion is necessary to bring him on deck. He rapidly gives way to seasickness; when taken ill always imagines that he would die; and remains in an apathetic state of torpid indifference.[64]

This categorization of Indian labour into two groups, one from the south and the other from the north, can be understood in the wider context of the event of 1857 and its impact on colonial rule. Meena Radhakrishna argued that—'post-1857 was the era of classification and categorization into warrior or martial races and criminal tribes, agricultural or professional castes, and so on, in order to sort out the loyal from the disloyal group within India.'[65] This categorization (north and south) further extended to the physical qualities of the rice-eaters versus the wheat-eaters. The Bengalees were considered to be lazy people with effeminate bodies, as compared to the robust bodies of labourers from south India. The Bengalees were also described as timid and prone to suicide. Madrasee labourers were thus the most desirable labourers for the planters.

Clare Anderson, in her book, shows the enormous symbolic appeal of transportation to the colonial authorities and the Indian people in the context of convicts. Colonial officials in Mauritius saw great public advantage in the use of a near continuous supply of convicts as labourers to build roads, bridges, and basic infrastructure. In this context, Anderson refers to the significant penal connections between India and Mauritius. During 1815–37, about 1,500 convicts were transported from India to the island.[66] After 1853, the Government of Mauritius, after consultations with Indian officials, liberated the few who remained on the island, though they were not given permission to leave the island.[67] She also states that the authorities believed that the 'Hindus', 'elite Muslims', and others of high social standing, feared the prospect of a voyage across the *kala pani*, or 'black water' on the grounds of losing caste and religious purity. She further added: '...the forced intimacy of sharing cooking pots and food, water, and latrines was horrifying to them.'[68] The general picture on every ship during the initial few days of boarding was that there was a combined feeling of horror, confusion, nervousness, and anxiety on the face of the recruits. Some people called these ships: 'floating caravans of barbarian tourists', while some *girmitiyas* remembered them as floating funeral processions: '*chalta, firta, jeeta, jagata janaza*'.[69] Brij Lal argued that—'The ship became the site of a massive social disruption. All ship travellers ate together in a *pangat*, seated single file, drank water from the same container, shared and cleaned the same toilet, and took turns sweeping, hosing, and cleaning the deck.'[70]

European medical surgeons were of the opinion that there were inadequacies in the Indian diet and lifestyle. The captain of one of the ships opined that an exclusive vegetable diet was responsible for dysentery during the voyages and suggested salt-fish instead of vegetables for the indentured.[71] The new diet schedule also recommended biscuits, but later it was found to be problematic as the emigrants were not habituated to those. They also believed that seasonal variation in the climate of Calcutta was also responsible for the occurrence of diseases, especially between February and April. During these months, cholera was prevalent, and the river water which the migrants drank was mostly brackish. Another major cause which the authorities identified as a cause of sickness among the indentured was the long duration of journey on the river Hooghly and on the sea. Again, seasickness and mortality rates were higher among the Indian travellers, as compared to the European travellers. The reason behind this was that India had a much more epidemiologically hostile environment than Europe; and it was much less nutritionally secure than Europe to.[72] Apart from these causes, the medical surgeons found that the mortality rate on ships was accentuated due to deaths among women, pregnant women, and infants. The weak bodies of the females and the infants were most liable to contract diseases and they were often unable to survive in the harsh atmosphere of long voyages. In 1855, a booklet of instructions to surgeons of vessels was issued, which provided details of the vaccination and for the selection of cooks, sweepers, and crew members. In 1857, the Lieutenant Governor of Bengal appointed Dr F.J. Mouat to enquire into the causes of death aboard emigrant ships.[73] The latter focused his enquiry on various issues, such as: the selection of recruits, their physical condition before they embarked, food and living conditions, and health conditions during the sea voyages. In this process, he found that the previous records of healthcare had not been kept. Dr Mouat, after interviewing the ship captains and surgeons, came to know that the emigrant ships were of different sizes, and all carried cargoes of rice, cereals, sugar, and jute, along with the emigrants. From this, he concluded that this was the main cause of inconvenience for the emigrants, since it led to the formation of 'mal-air' and spreading of diseases among the passengers, as per the belief in those days. Dr Mouat, in his report, also recommended a reduction in the proportion of women recruits on the voyages from 33 per cent to 11 per cent, which was, however, ignored by the authorities.[74] Women and their poor maternal care were held responsible for the high rate of mortality among the infants. In his report, the Medical Inspector of Mauritius asserted that: '...Child mortality on the ships was testimony to the perfect indifference which prevails among Indian mothers as to the lives of their infants when from sickness or other care, they become troublesome to them'.[75] In some cases, the report also held the emigration agent, surgeon, and officers of the voyages responsible for neglecting the criterion of fitness in their selection of persons for the voyages. In this context, the diary entry of one Captain Swinton can be cited: '...May 3, a woman died of dysentery. This makes seventy dead. It is dreadful mortality: still anyone who had ever sailed with them would not wondered at it, as they are so badly selected at the depot and so many diseased sent on board...'[76]

On shipboard, it was the responsibility of the medical surgeon to keep the emigrants fit and able-bodied for labour. Even their pay and future employment depended on the number of coolies who were, in the harsh terms of business, 'landed alive'. Due to this reason, a great check was put on emigrants and also on the ship members. It was also emphasized that no officer, crew member, engineer, stoker, firemen, or any of the passengers should have any sickness on board.[77]

Dr Mouat also recommended separate accommodation for men and women. Earlier they were lodged together in the lower deck. As a result of Dr Mouat's enquiry, the government made separate accommodations on the ship for three types of emigrants: the ones with family, single women, and single men.[78] The single women were allotted the rear end of ships, the single men were accommodated on the other side, and the married couples (or families) were placed between these two sides.[79] This arrangement was made to prevent easy access of women to the accommodations of the single men and vice versa. The dispensary was placed on the top deck and aft (rear part of the ship); the hospital was located amidships and forwarded the galleys or cookhouse. There were

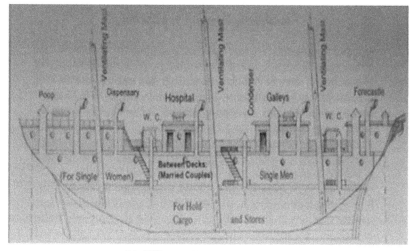

PLATE 3.4: Vessels in the 1850s

Source: Leela Gujadhur Sarup, *Indentured Labour: Slavery to Salvation: Colonial Emigration Acts, 1837-1932*, Calcutta: Aldrich International, 2004, p. 108.

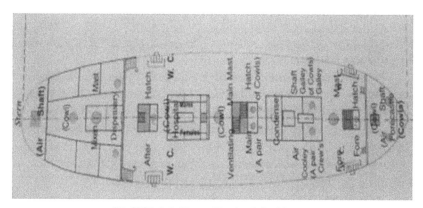

PLATE 3.5: Upper Deck of the Vessels

Source: Gujadhur Sarup, *Indentured Labour*, p. 108. Also see Revenue and Agriculture Department (Emigration Branch) Proceedings, December 1884, no. 4, NAI.

separate wards in the hospital for the male and female recruits as even one for the males on the fore part of the main deck, the other for the females on the after part. Regulations for indentured trade from the Calcutta ports to other colonies laid down that hospital accommodations must be increased on the ships; it should not be less than six bunks.[80] These ships were the world for the emigrants for many months.

The protector of emigrants was instructed to maintain a ship register of emigrants on each and every voyage. These ship registers had great potential for building up a quantitative picture of transportation flows—where the emigrants were from, their social origin, patterns of inoculation against smallpox, biometric analyses of their heights, and even their tattooing practices.[81] These records thus revealed a great deal about the lives of the emigrants and also had an enormous potential for reconstructing indentured's lives over the voyages. The data was introduced in these records through a number assigned to an individual migrant. These registers also recorded their conduct or behaviour on shipboard, status of their health, sickness and its cause, marriage, and if the case be, death. After 1874, medical surgeons were instructed to maintain medical registers. These registers were in use in the Army Sanitary Commission and in the European and native hospitals throughout India.[82] In order to minimize the effect of any contagious disease on the voyages, the master and the surgeon of a ship were instructed to forward a full report of unusual occurrences that were seriously affecting the health and safety of the emigrants at any point of time.[83] They were instructed to maintain proper and sufficient records, which also focused on the caste and the class of people who were more likely to fall sick. These registers were maintained to discover the nature and causes of various shipboard epidemics and whether the diseases were brought on board by the emigrants from the depots or they occurred in the course of the voyage due to the circumstances in which the emigrants were placed.[84] The adherence of contemporary government officials to the miasma theory explains their continuing debate over the cause of shipboard deaths. These explanations were considered to be mutually exclusive. Shlomowitz and McDonald stated in this context,—'We now know, that disease cannot be spontaneously generated, but has to be brought aboard a vessel, either in contaminated water and food, or by infected passengers and accompanying animals.'[85] Conditions on board, such as an overcrowded and unsanitary environment, could then promote the spread of the disease, and poor nutrition on the voyage could lower the resistance of the body of the infected passengers.

Ship officers were responsible for providing all kinds of basic facilities, like well-cooked and nutritious food, suitable clothes, clean drinking water, latrines, hospitals and medical facilities, etc., to the passengers. During 1864, it was discovered by medical science that the spread of cholera on ships was due to the consumption of impure water, though the germ theory was controversial in the nineteenth century, and opposed by the accepted theory of 'spontaneous generation'.[86] Consequently, it was decided that the easy and sure-shot way of ensuring the purity of water on shipboard was the direct transmission of drinking water from the Calcutta municipal hydrant to the ships. According to the Emigration Act of 1871, water for the use of emigrants in ships was stored in tanks loaded on the voyages, after acquiring a certificate from the health officer of the municipality that it was pure, filtered, and was supplied by the municipality.[87] Earlier, water was ordered to be brought from Fulta and taken into boats via valve openings through a filtering medium, which was controlled by the crew of the boat, and the water was often found to be impure. This method used for the transportation of water was inconvenient, and caused delay in the departure of the ships, and also left the water vulnerable to accumulation of impurities. J.G. Grant stated that in the new method, all the vessels would be able to fill their tanks directly through the hose provided by the municipality. This method was not only the simplest and the fastest, but insured the water against risks of impurity that were inseparable from the use of the tank boat.[88] The medical surgeons were responsible for regularly checking the quality of drinking water on board the ship. Surgeon Superintendent W.J. Jackson's note can be cited as an example in this context—'I examined the tanks, they were clean and smelt sweet.'[89] In the circumstances of high mortality and sickness rates, drinking water became a subject of careful inspection in order to maintain the health of the indentured on the voyages.

As far as food for the emigrants was concerned, it was the most important issue, and it was recommended that food should be nutritious and healthy, because most of the indentured were of weak and ill disposition. The slave ships were also entitled to provide food to the captured Black body to keep them alive for future labour.[90] Feeding the slaves on voyages was a terrible exercise, especially when captives refused to eat. Sometimes, it was necessary to force slaves to eat, to prevent them from committing suicide by self-starvation. For those who were recalcitrant, a special pair of scissors or 'speculum oris' was used.[91] The blades were forced between the teeth of the rebel, and then the attached thumbscrew was turned in order to force the jaws apart. However, the slave ships always remained short of food. Meals on English ships were usually given twice a day, at ten in the morning and at five in the evening. Captain Phillips (on an English slave ship) recalled that—'The first meal was large beans, boiled with a certain quantity of Muscovy lard which we have from Holland…the other meal was of peas, or of Indian wheat, to which salt, palm oil, and malaguetta (pepper) were

added to relish.' It was thought that malaguetta pepper would give '…
our negroes in their messes [something] to keep them from the flux
[that is acute diarrhoea] and dry bellyache'.[92] On slave ships, meals were
usually distributed to the slaves in tens in '…a small fat tub, made for
that use by our coopers…each slave having a little wooden spoon to feed
himself handsomely…'. Captain Phillips recalled that these meals were
held on the main deck and forecastle, so '…that we may have them all
under command of our arms from the quarterdeck in case of any
disturbance; the women eat upon the quarterdeck with us, and the boys
and girls upon the poop'.[93]

The plantation officials took specific actions for recovering the
emigrants in order to make them able-bodied. They not only tried to
control emigrants' food habits, but also tried to regularize it. The coolie
law decided the terms of their diet as to not only what they should get
as their food, but also the quantity of their food. The emigrants were
given food on the ship thrice a day; a meal in the morning was served
at 9 a.m. up on the top deck, if the conditions were fair, the afternoon
meal was served at 2 p.m., and another meal followed from 5–6 p.m.
Medical officers were supposed to examine and invariably satisfy
themselves that the food was properly cooked and fairly distributed.
Emigration rules laid down that stale food should not be kept by either
cooks or emigrants, and that all utensils be cleaned out and shown to
the medical officer after each meal. Provisions were also made for the
motherless infants (whose mothers had died on board) to provide them
with suitable and freshly prepared food such as milk, soup, sago, etc.,
every three to four hours.[94] In case of an emergency or deteriorating
health condition of the indentured, the surgeon superintendent was
allowed to bring changes in the fixed diet that was recommended. From
the Madras port, a contractual system was implemented for feeding
emigrants on board. In this case, the captain of the ship was responsible
for providing food to the labourers. For this, he charged Rs.3 per person
for two meals per day. This new arrangement had a positive effect on
the health of the recruits who had recently boarded for the Strait
Settlement.[95] Medical research on the diet of emigrants led to the
conclusion that food for emigrants on voyages, which made no difference
between the rice-eaters and the flour-eaters, had a prejudicial effect on
the health of the coolies.[96] In 1870, Dr Grant and Dr Palmer (Medical
Inspector of Emigrants) suggested—

…There should be a slight change in the existing dietary scale in which main
difference in the substitution of preserved or fresh mutton or dried fish in both

the rice and flour dietary scales, a reduction in the quantity of salt, and a slight increase in the allowance of *dhall* [pulses] in the rice diet and of flour and ghee in the flour diet. The additional expense involved in these changes will be about one cent per adult.[97]

But Dr Grant and Dr Palmer did not think that the expense would be so high. They thought—

...The additional proposed diet schedule is far within what the colonial authorities would seem to be ready to accept, and looking to the advantage that may be expected from the arrival of the coolies in good physical condition and in sound health, ready for immediate work, the small additional expenditure may well be borne by the colonies.[98]

During bad weather, emigrants on board were supposed to have dry food, because cooking was impossible in such conditions. Sometimes, they had to continue eating this kind of food for several days at a stretch. This had ill-effects on the health of the migrants, sometimes even leading to death. On a particular occasion, even the *London Times* joined in, accusing Caird (Medical Surgeon) of causing deaths during the passage from India by giving the travellers impure water from the Hooghly and biscuits, which were alien to the Indian diet.[99] Instead of biscuits, to which Indian villagers were not habituated, *choora* (flattened rice) was recommended as dry food on the voyages, especially during bad weather.[100] It was also mentioned that *choora* as dry food should be given to emigrants on Sundays as a one-time meal, so that the cook could have some rest and the cleaning of the store would be possible. During bad weather, in order to boost emigrant health, the emigrants were supposed to get twenty gallons of rum, wine, and brandy in a fixed amount. Medical surgeons of the emigrant ships argued that instead of bad quality port wine, the emigrants could have ten gallons of good quality wine from Jamaica or good quality rum.

On the voyages, it was recommended by the Surgeon Major D.R. Thompson, M.D., C.I.E., Medical Inspector of Emigrants, that no preserved mutton should be taken from the port for use during the voyages. Instead, four live sheep per hundred emigrants was suggested. This ensured a supply of fresh meat on the voyages. Apart from that, he also recommended that forty gallons of lime juice would be enough for hundred adult emigrants.[101] These provisions were especially made for the Madrasee coolies: for their fitness. Dr Grant also made a new suggestion regarding the adopting of 'curry-stuff' in the food for emigrants, which he found useful because it consisted of tamarind, which was antiscorbutic. He also suggested reducing the amount of salt in the food. This suggestion was, however, not accepted by D.R. Thompson on the ground that 'Madras coolies suffer very much from the round-worm, which predispose them to bowel disorders, such as diarrhoea and cholera; the free use of salt is a protection from these parasites; it is therefore necessary that the coolie should have enough of it to put into their food.'[102] One of the chief druggist firms of Calcutta had stated that they were prepared to supply medicines on the new scale at a cost not exceeding the total amount then paid to those on the existing scale.[103] Some new medical equipment were included in the new scale, with increased quantity for each group of hundred emigrants (for details see Appendix 6, Statement of Instruments and Appliances for Hospital and Dispensary). These suggestions were made on medical grounds to ensure good health of the Indian recruits on voyages.

Diseases and Treatment on the Voyage

…June 7: Infant died, and many sick found who are afraid to take our medicine. Doctor gave me his list…and makes 110 [dead] all told, or about 80 adults deceased to date. Fearful![104]

The diaries of medical personnel and ship captains provided the 'fearful' picture of the diseases in the everyday lives of emigrants on voyages. Sometimes an entire ship was turned into a hospital. The radical spread of diseases on voyages also led to depression among the emigrants. The medical personnel who were there to help the sick, often found themselves helpless on the indentured voyages. Cholera was the most prominent among contagious diseases on the voyages which affected the health of the emigrants. Cholera caused more than 2,200 deaths in 1859.[105] In 1861, *Auguste* set out from Pondicherry with 339 coolies instead of 309 (the maximum capacity of the ship) and was struck by an epidemic of cholera. An inquest later revealed that some of the sick had been thrown into the sea while they were still alive, and that the passengers had been deprived of water and food, and had also been whipped by the officers.[106] Shlomowitz stated that the higher average death rates on voyages from Calcutta, particularly the mortality peaks of 1856–61 and 1864–6, were mainly due to cholera.[107] This disease, during 1872–1906, killed more than 400 Indian coolies while on voyage.

Studies also show that apart from cholera, measles and its sequelae, such as bronchitis, was another major cause of death among the recruits on ships. It killed more than 837 indentured labour during 1872–1906.[108] For most of the nineteenth century, medical knowledge could not do better than diagnose cholera and typhoid as diseases caused due to filth and impure air.[109] This notion changed in 1884, when Robert Koch identified the comma bacillus as the source of cholera. It was not surprising that the uprooted coolies, who were quite incapable of coping with communal and city existence, became victims to this disease. In 1892, the Calcutta depot was connected to the city's water pipes system; consequently, cholera remained in control and thereafter, occurred only in occasional and isolated incidents. When research proved that bad ventilation was not one of the causes of mortality and cholera, medical persons discovered that most other diseases were either latent in the body of the emigrants or were concealed by them prior to their embarkation on the voyages. These diseases, after boarding the ships, were aggravated by seasickness, listlessness, and delay in seeking medical advice—because being natives, the emigrants were averse to European medical treatment. This discovery led to new research works and experiments on the Indian soil, the source of the emigrants. Generally, emigrants did not have faith in the European doctors, their methods of treatment, and the medicines which were alien to them. It was generally observed that the first fortnight of the voyages had the maximum chance of proving fatal to the emigrants. It needs to be mentioned here that the coolie doctors (Indian doctors) were able to make more successful voyages, as C.G. Conram mentioned in his letter—'…the coolie doctors, who knowing the language and the habits and manners of the emigrants, attract recruits' confidence, and who for the first fortnight are most watchful in detecting disease and most assiduous in healing them'.[110] Therefore, doctors of Indian origin were employed on the ships under the title of 'coolie doctor(s)' as agents of the European medical system. Medical science also discovered that the passengers of Indian coolie vessels, because of their life in a tropical region, were in many respects peculiar and could not be treated on the same lines as the passengers of European emigrant ships or any other ordinary passenger boats. Medical experts on voyages also emphasized on the documentation of emigrant health and diseases.[111] They considered that proper, detailed medical reports would be helpful in knowing the cause and origin of particular diseases, and thus could be used to cure patients at the right time. The voyages' doctors used Dr Patrick Manson's: *Tropical Disease* for many years for the treatment of emigrants on the voyages.

Emigrants on voyages were a mobile population; and there was a belief that these mobile populations carried diseases with them from one place to another. In order to acquire knowledge about the diseases, researches were carried out on these groups. Experiments were conducted on various groups from different parts of India to confirm the symptoms and origins of the diseases. For example, experiments were done in hospitals and jails in order to enquire which groups of Indian natives were liable to be affected from a particular disease. Thus, a 'filtration theory' (separation of sick from healthy) was applied to acquire information about which group of people from which part of the country suffered from a particular disease.[112] After the experiment, the medical officials came to the conclusion that people from up-country and from the Central Provinces, from where the larger group of recruits belonged, were more prone to diseases. For example, it appeared that the variety of round worms called anchylostoma had been especially noticed in the Cuttack and Darbhanga jail hospitals.[113] Ships also became laboratories for new research; medical experts found sailing vessels as confined places with limited resources that were a complete laboratory for the proper preservation of the essential specimens. Some medical experts recommended that the medical surgeon on the vessels should carry out these researches during the voyages. However, most of the medical surgeons on the ships refused this proposal on grounds of overwork. They emphasized that—

…The surgeon superintendent and his assistants already have their time very fully occupied with the care of the several hundred people under their charge, who require constant attention and supervision both day and night, and that the question of adding to their manifold duties is one for serious consideration, for it is not to be expected that they could devote the time and attention requisite to so intricate a research except at the expense of their regular work amongst the emigrants.[114]

The confined space of the vessels provided an opportunity to the medical personnel to continue their research on diseases like anchylostome, which was infamous among the recruits and created agitation among the emigrants in the depots of Madras. The advantage of carrying out research in the ships was that the recruits had less opportunity to resist against treatments.

The situation deteriorated further on the voyages of returning indentured (those who had fulfilled ten years of residential stay in the colony). These voyages recorded a higher death rate, overcrowding, lack of ration water, and lack of medical facilities; and sometimes these plantation colonies did not hesitate to send back insane Indian migrants and Indians suffering from infectious diseases (such as leprosy) on the return voyages.[115] The *Watkins* left Port Louis on 28 November 1843 and arrived at the Hooghly (Calcutta port) after a slow voyage on 20 February 1844. The conditions in this voyage and the ill-treatment of the migrants raised questions on the indentured system. A report was sent to Calcutta by telegraph about the 'alarming mortality' on board and a steam tug brought the ship to Calcutta, in which 44 out of the 149 embarked had died, including the captain. Captain Rogers told a court of inquiry that the *Watkins* had accommodation for only 86 passengers. The Indians also complained of water shortage, though according to the chief mate they were put on short supplies only after the ship had lain becalmed for two weeks. When the Mauritius authorities were asked about overcrowding, they replied that they did not consider themselves bound by the order in council as regards to the return passage.[116] Moreover, many Indians were unfit for travel and they had been sent on board directly from the hospital in Port Louis. The Protector of Emigrants 'Anderson' laid the blame on the Indians themselves, who wanted to travel back in spite of their bad health. There were many such other cases of return passage in which overcrowding of ships was very common, and the agents did not sympathize with the condition of emigrants.[117] The Calcutta emigrant agent took this neglecting behaviour very seriously and stopped indentured recruitment for Mauritius from India. It was started again only when the Governor of Mauritius gave ample ensurance that in future all the necessary regulations would be followed to secure the health, comfort, and safety of the labourers on the return passage. It is also to be noted that the returning emigrants lost their identity as labourers, and thus were not entitled to get facilities on the return voyages from the colonial planters. This might have been one of the ways of discouraging the return of the migrants.

Law and order on the return ship was a matter of concern; the returning coolies were commonly inclined to resist against authority and give them trouble. The general behaviour of the returned coolies on board was thus almost always a matter of complaint for the surgeon superintendent. For instance, a ship surgeon from British Guiana complained that—

…The labourers who leave British Guiana after making their fortunes, have generally been accustomed to a certain amount of freedom and independence, soon turning into sauciness and insolence which cannot be tolerated at sea, and has to be checked at once to avoid further and more serious consequences. It is their belief (and they openly express it) that they are at liberty to do what they like on board, without the least regard to discipline, good order and cleanliness.[118]

Medical surgeons were suggested to be prepared to take strict means if necessary in order to preserve order and law. Generally the returning coolies had grievances against the planters, government, sirdars, plantations' law and disciplinary regulation, and against the medical personnel. Their experience in the colonies made them rebellious on the return voyages.

In the 1870s, the Government of India raised questions about the return of the 'lunatics' (mentally unstable) and lepers from the colonies. These unfit labourers were hunted by the police in the colonies and shipped back to India directly from the hospitals. In order to get rid of them, the Government of Mauritius allowed them to spend few days on the depot before being sent back to India. On the ships, there was no provision for separate wards for these patients.

Suggestions were made by the overseas colonies that 'harmless and ordinary' lunatics should be allowed to go back to their home. But here the question that emerged was the criteria for—'harmless and ordinary'. In 1875, Mauritius Central Board of Lunacy passed fourteen men and five women as fit people to be entrusted on board as ordinary invalids, but further enquiry reported that they were '…not fit and proper persons to be allowed to be at large in the colony."[119] This transportation of mentally unsound Indians shows that there was a continuous increase in the number of Indian lunatics in the colony. The Government of Mauritius was thus in a hurry to reduce the number of mentally invalid labourers in the colony and in the mental asylums, which were overcrowded.[120] It was also common that a lunatic, who was quiet and tractable when embarked, sometimes became violent and unmanageable on board. In such a case, he also became a source of trouble, if not danger to his fellow passengers.

On 22 September 1900, the surgeon superintendent of the voyage *S.S. Erne* made the following remark on Kalika, who was mentally unstable—

Kalika is more troublesome and will no doubt have to be chained up soon. He defies all authority, curses the *Sirdars* and their wives, and will get a beating no doubt soon. Lunatics should never be sent with other emigrants in a crowded ship with no means of restraint. I objected but was assured they were cured… Since writing the above Kalika was has been violent again, he was found sharpening a knife and had been cursing people copiously and threatening them. As many on board go in fear of injury from him, I determined to restrain him, and so the leg-irons were put on him, amid much cursing and threatening to kill when he got out.[121]

The emigrant agent of Calcutta stated,—'I quite concur with the surgeon's remarks as to the inadvisability of sending lunatics to sea in emigrant vessels. They cannot possibly express their wish for repatriation. On arrival here, they are a source of endless trouble under escort on the way to their homes up country. There is frequent reference to this man throughout the surgeon's journal. Some of the other lunatics also gave much trouble.'[122] Thus, the mentally unstable and the lepers on the return voyages were the main threat for the medical surgeons. Moreover, the Government of India was also not ready to undertake the burden of maintenance of the mentally unstable individuals, on their shoulders. It would be interesting to note here that Kalika, who had a grudge against *sirdars*, did not forget even in the state of lunacy, his prime exploiter, who supervised indentured work on the estates.

The transportation of patients suffering from leprosy was recommended on the grounds of better care at their homes with their family and friends. *Gurjun* oil, which was used for the treatment of lepers in the colonies, was transported from India. The treatment of leprosy with this oil was proved successful in the hands of Dr Dougall at Andaman. The medical surgeon of the colonies opined that the condition of these unfortunate people might be ameliorated by the medical care of their own country.[123] The repatriation of lepers from British Guiana encouraged the Government of Mauritius in the subsequent year to seek permission for the transportation of nineteen mentally unstable coolies to their own country. The Secretary of India stated that the two matters were very different materially, as he said, '... the repatriation of lepers from British Guiana [was] allowed on the grounds that those unhappy persons had a chance of being cured in India by *gurjun* oil treatment, and that in any case they would have the consolation of ending their days among their friends and in their native country.'[124] Also, the Government of India was only ready to receive these people when they had first ascertained that their family and friends were willing to undertake the responsibility of their care, or were ready to pay for their maintenance in an asylum.

The Indian Emigration Act of 1883 came with the regulation for the voyages of returning emigrants. Regulations mentioned that mentally unstable emigrants were to be prohibited on the return voyages and people with contagious diseases were not to be allowed in the absence of separate wards for them on board. The medical surgeon soon came to the conclusion that there should be a twenty per cent increase in the amount and number of medical facilities on the return voyages. Ship captains were soon informed that the increase would be almost ten cents extra per hundred adult emigrants. E.E. Black in his letter suggested to J. Nourse, contractor, who was asked to bear this extra cost, that '…you should not forget that the passage money which you would get depends on the lives of these coolies, therefore we hope that you will feel able to agree to provide such extra medical comforts in the case of return vessels without any increase in your contract rate.'[125] However, the contractor refused to provide extra medical comforts at his own cost. The Act XXI of 1883 was revised in 1897, in which they focused mainly on the condition of 'return emigrants', who were returning as 'the sick and helpless'. On their landing, 'they shall be properly lodged and provided for until the Agent is in position to arrange for their departure.'[126] The Section 80 of Act XXI of 1883 provided a long list under Form 32(c), of hospital and dispensary medical instruments and appliances, which included major instruments for purposes like postmortem—to ordinary equipment like nipples to feed infants on the voyages.[127] Natal followed the same schedule for medical store (stock of medicines on voyages) and ration, which was entitled to Mauritius; but the journey to Natal was longer than the one to Mauritius. In 1879, on the basis of Dr Grant's recommendation, the schedule for the medicine became liberal for the Natal voyages. Ships were not allowed to depart without sufficient stock of medicines and rations. According to the official records, voyages were well looked after and checked for stocks of drugs and modern medical instruments.[128] But these records also show that in most cases, the European medical surgeons failed to find out the reason behind the illness of the emigrants. Apart from this, the higher death rate on the voyages was a strong point to explore the actual achievements of this 'medical-regime'.

Doctor's Duty on the Voyages

…A young man, who has no immediate prospect of settling in his profession, is often lured by fair promises to become a surgeon of a Guinea ship; but there long the bright prospect vanishes, and he finds that he has been cruelly deceived, and deplores, when too late, his degrading situation. If he possesses sensibility, his feelings are constantly on the rack; if his constitution be weak, his health is ruined, and he narrowly escapes with life. His attention to the poor creatures under his care must be unremitted.[129]

On the ship, the surgeon superintendent was the main person on whom the health and happiness of the Indians depended. Lt Colonel D.G. Crawford, in his pioneer work, *The History of Indian Medical Service 1600–1913*, stated that the first medical officers in the employment of the East India Company were surgeons on board ships.[130] The surgeons were also employed on the slave ships. The British Slave Trade Act of 1788 required that every British slave ship had to carry a doctor who was supposed to keep with him common medicaments, such as gum camphor, pulverized rhubarb, cinnamon water, mustard, and bitters; also, he was always involved in major decisions about the voyages. An order was passed that the doctor and supercargo checked the mouths and eyes of the slaves every morning.[131] Several surgeons, such as Alexander Falconbridge or Thomas Trotter on the *Brookes*, or William Chancellor on Philip Livingstone's sloop, *Wolf*, in 1750: contributed priceless information as to how the slave trade worked. The surgeon, the most important member of any ship's company, received the same salary of four shillings as a first mate or carpenter on an English ship. But it was not legally necessary to carry a surgeon; and many slave ships economized by choosing not to have one, including the ones from the United States.[132] Hugh Thomas, in his work, stated that the surgeons had to undergo medical training, which meant that they came from a background different from the generality of common seamen. By the end of the eighteenth century, it was necessary for the Liverpool ships that a ship's surgeon should have been trained at the Liverpool Royal Infirmary, the medical school from which the University of Liverpool developed later. These medically trained surgeons strengthened the coolie trade.

In the eighteenth century, it has been observed that grossly incompetent men, with little or no medical training, were appointed as medical men for services on the ships. In order to avoid this, the East India Company ordered that every applicant for appointment as surgeon on board ships had to undergo an examination as to their fitness for the post.[133] In 1836, the East India Company stated the qualifications for the recruitment of such medical men. Applicants needed to produce a certificate of having diligently practised as physicians at some general hospital in London for six months, or at some dispensary in London for twelve months, or at some general hospital in the country (within the UK) for six months, provided such provincial hospital contained at least, on an average, one hundred in-patients, and had attached to it a regular establishment of physicians as well as surgeons.[134] A surgeon was required to have a diploma in surgery or a degree in medicine, a certificate of having attended a course of lectures on midwifery, and of having conducted at least six labour nativity cases. In 1848, the surgeons were required to get a nomination letter and certificates from the Court of Examiners of the Royal College. These certificates and letters were considered as testimonies of their qualifications.[135] In 1855, the candidates, who provided all these certificates of their qualification, needed to appear in the examination. The examination included questions about surgery, medicine (including the diseases of women and children), therapeutics, pharmacy and hygiene, anatomy and physiology (including comparative anatomy), and natural history (including botany and zoology). The selected applicants for the medical services needed to appear for written and practical examinations, followed by a viva voce. The practical examination included operating on dead bodies. The best qualified person in all respects was appointed as an assistant surgeon in the service of the East India Company.[136] These criteria set up by the East India Company for the selection and appointment of surgeons were followed in other British colonies as well. In 1873, the French, German, and Hindustani languages were added as optional or extra subjects in the examination.

The captain of a coolie ship, unlike a slave ship, was required to follow the surgeon's order, because his continuation as the captain depended on the surgeon's report. In the event of an adversely negative report by a surgeon, there were chances that the captain and the ship were excluded in the future from coolie traffic.[137] In order to encourage the doctors to be zealous in their duties, an allowance of eight rupees and four rupees five cents was paid to them on arrival in Mauritius and Natal respectively, for each person who landed alive; and nurses received a single payment of ten cents per person.[138] After 1857, the surgeon superintendent got ten cents per head on the first voyage, eleven cents on the second voyage, and twelve cents on every subsequent voyage.[139] Tinker opined that initially, on the relatively short voyages to Mauritius and Malaya, the ship's doctor was often an Indian or Eurasian trained in the Calcutta Medical School, probably looking for experience and a little capital. There was difficulty in obtaining a good medical professional, especially for Mauritius, because the journey was short and pay was low, as compared to the West Indies' and the Australian service.[140] The protector of emigrants at Calcutta, in his letter to the Government of Bengal, mentioned that, '...I do not think that generally speaking the doctors we get here could be trusted'.[141] But after some tragedies on the long voyages, the emigration commissioners and the colonial agents took great care to appoint doctors from Britain with proven qualifications to the post. Dr Payne observed that medical officers were appointed on a temporary service and the best qualified did not come forward to work on board ships. Finally, the decision was taken to employ the ship surgeon on a permanent basis and offer them all the advantages and privileges to which the officers of the civil services were entitled. The mortality rate was high on the voyage to the West Indies during 1856–60. But after 1862, there was a slight reduction of 5 per cent, which was attributed to the allocation of surgeons from Australia. Out of the 27 ships sailing from India, 17 carried 'Australian' surgeon superintendents.[142]

The debate over who should be the medical incharge of emigrants also revealed one of the ways in which race influenced science. It is important to know that due to racial discrimination, the colonial government only recruited white doctors with qualifications from Europe, for attending the Indian indentured. However, the problem of language and unfamiliarity with the Asiatic diseases hindered the work of surgeons and forced Dr Mouat to recommend that medical officers should have, '...some knowledge of the treatment of the disease of natives of India, and of such only as are capable of understanding the coolies'.[143] There was also a different opinion of some of the officials who argued that—'young surgeons fresh from Europe, and youths who have just completed their professional education should not be employed in this duty.'[144] This debate about the racial discrimination in the recruitment of doctors for emigrant voyages moved a little further when French emigrant authorities in 1861 questioned the required race of the surgeon. They questioned that the British authority asked—'whether the words of a European Surgeon, contained in section XIV of Act XLVI of 1860, are intended to be interpreted literally to the exclusion of a Eurasian Surgeon'.[145] In response to the question raised, the Governor-General recommended that the surgeon need not be a European. If a non-European had acquired a collegiate training in the European system of medical science, then he was considered to be qualified for the post.[146] On the question of the recruitment of female nurses on the ships, surgeon Lewer argued that, '...I do not think that a European woman superintendent or a Eurasian would be of any advantage in looking after the women immigrants on board ship.'[147] The surgeon recommended that on the Natal immigrant ships, the most motherly of the female immigrants was selected and paid to act as a nurse. However, the 'native' doctors became victims of racial discrimination during the process of recruitment for a higher and profitable position; and thus the situation did not prove very favourable for them. Even if someone was able to reach that stage, the working conditions were not easy for him. Roger Jeffery, in his articles 'Recognizing India's Doctors: The Institutionalization of Medical Dependency, 1918–39', argued that in the 1920s, in order to maintain the quality of the medical service and medical education, the higher levels of the Indian Medical Service (IMS) remained in the hands of the British.[148] The Indian graduates occupied only the subordinate posts. Until 1913, Indians composed only 5 per cent of the IMS; by 1921 their numbers had risen to comprise 6.25 per cent.[149] The ratio of Indians in senior positions increased slowly; only to about 3 per cent by 1905.[150]

The authority, which was white, was not ready to work under the supervision of the brown body, whom they considered efficient enough to give command. The employment of an Indian doctor on the long voyages was rare, and Dr A.C. Dutt was the first Indian medical superintendent to take coolies to Surinam. However, mid-voyage, Dutt (who had his wife and children with him) was put ashore on Ascension Island. The master Captain Bevan accused him of inciting the Indians to mutiny. He alleged that Dutt had placed the ship in 'imminent danger'.[151] On return, Dutt alleged that Bevan was appropriating the stores, and also accused the third officer, John Evans, of seducing two female emigrants. But Dutt, who had been put ashore with fifty cents to get his family back to Calcutta, obtained no further redress.

The colour of the Indian body played a significant role in discrimination against the doctors; they were considered as untrustworthy. The authorities always tried to recruit a White body with European education, morality, and genteel temperament, which were supposed to be absent in native doctors with brown bodies. The reason behind it that T.W.C. Murdoch gave (emigrant agent), in 1871, was that, '…it is clear that a native surgeon, whatever his professional qualifications, would lack the moral weight with officers and crew, probably also with the coolies that a European surgeon would possess.'[152] The authorities were aware about the deficiencies of recruiting a European for treating the poor and illiterate indentured Indians; but they could not trust even a qualified Indian doctor.[153] So, the emigration commissioner and the emigrant agent took great care to appoint doctors from Britain with proven qualifications to the post.[154] Due to this discrimination against native doctors, the lives of indentured Indians were surrendered at the hands of the inexperienced European doctors who were unable to understand Indian languages and diseases.

In the initial days of transportation, the medical man was appointed as the emigrant protector; but soon they realized that there should be a separate post for a medical surgeon. However, the lonely, monotonous, and at times arduous and dangerous post of doctors on emigrant voyages; did not attract the best candidates. A different kind of man was attracted to the work, very often the loner, the unconventional, the misfit; also, there was another category who wanted the challenges, the responsibility—who was authoritarian and paternalistic, and who proved to be a strong pillar of the British Empire. Some of the doctors were recruited from the Indian civil medical service, including men who had worked in jails, while some were former regimental or naval doctors. Later on, surgeon superintendents who worked at the job for twenty years or more were built up as regular cadres. The great attraction of this job was the space between voyages, when these men were able to live as they pleased, free from the daily chores of the ordinary English doctors on call night and day.[155] On a voyage, the surgeon superintendent was assisted by his own staff. He had two 'compounders'—Indian or Eurasians with some medical qualifications—and a nurse.[156]

During the initial period, for the treatment of female emigrant patients, some female emigrants were engaged in nursing work. Those who were unskilled and inexperienced were recruited without payment. A compounder was appointed for every hundred emigrants on the ship. A female nurse was appointed for every 25 infants under two years of age.[157] One compounder was permanently in charge of the sick bay or ship's hospital, while another was in charge of cooking arrangements. The compounders were given a gratuity of 16 cents per ship. They were supposed to follow the commands and orders of the surgeon superintendent, and were responsible for dispensing medicines and maintaining order and discipline among the emigrants. In case of Natal, the compounders were entitled to get 7 pounds sterling per month, in addition to a gratuity of 9 pence per person landed alive at Natal. They were also entitled to a free passage to the colony and back to India at the expense of the ship, second class cabin accommodation, and ration from the cabin table.[158] However, their salary and gratuity were payable only if they were successful in acquiring a certificate from the surgeon superintendent that they had performed their duties in a satisfactory manner. The third officer was also entitled to assist the surgeon and issue supplies of food and clothing.

Doctors were employed on slave transport voyages as well, and they earned a pretty good amount for successful transportations. But in case of the transportation of indentured labour, a migrant body became a countable asset and they began to be registered in the ship register with a particular number. This number became their identity in the official records.

The medical structure on ships was hierarchical, and the rank in the hierarchy played an important role. The experience of social discrimination was real and tangible not only for the juniors but also for the senior Indian medical officers.[159] The loyalty and morality of Indians became the subject of suspicion of the British government. At the lower end of the hierarchy, the crew members, nurses, and compounders with *topazes* (word for sweepers in Lashkari language)[160] had to face the most discriminatory behaviour of the colonial officers.

Sanitation, Discipline, and Morality over the Voyages

…The privies have been constantly washed and disinfected, even during the night, when they were cleaned every four hours; the between decks have been dry, holystoned daily by fifty men, and whitewashed eight times during the voyages. As for the cleanliness of the persons of the immigrants, I have found them unwilling to use water, hot or cold, fresh or salt.[161]

…the crew and ship were in bad state of order and discipline, it appeared to me that the mates were afraid of the coolies…there were two or three bad characters who sold bhang (hasish)…there were also women of bad character… who made a great deal of money among them by prostitution.[162]

James, pilot on the *Edward*, described the conditions on board in these words. In order to turn the recruits into perfect able bodies, authorities focused on some aspects of physical exercise. The look of the labourers were important; they were forced to look happy, pleasant, and able-bodied. The ships' surgeons encouraged emigrants to participate in singing, dancing, and physical activities.[163] New medical regimes enforced new measures for sanitation, morality, and discipline, which were considered essential for a 'disease free body'. On the voyages, emigrants were forced to obey a regular routine, which consisted of some exercise; officers also taught them lessons on physical chastisement.

Dr Whitelam recommended that during the voyage, emigrants should take bath at least once a week and oil themselves with coconut oil twice a week.[164] The 'objectification' of the indentured health left the emigrants experiencing pain, diminishment, and violation.

The emigration rules also provided the medical officers the right to search the bundles of recruits for any indigestible food, grains, or gold rags, all of which should be thrown overboard or burned either in the engine furnaces or on shore in his presence. A man going to Natal was allocated three dhotis, one jacket, one cap, two 'Patna made' blankets, while the warm clothing included one guernsey (or *banian*) and one cap. On the other hand, a woman received three saris and two blankets. According to Act XXXI of 1883, additional and warmer clothes were provided to the emigrants who migrated to Natal. The emigrants' clothes also became a matter of inspection by the medical surgeon on the voyages at least twice a week. They also received an aluminum plate, and *lotahs* (lota) for drinking water and soup. Some ships even issued a wooden comb to the ladies.[165] These articles were all that the emigrants could call their own on the ships. Suddenly, these materials became so precious in their lives after leaving everything behind that these petty things became the cause for the continuous clashes and disturbances among the emigrants. Dr J.E. Dyer narrates the everyday experience in these words—'most of them complained that they lost their *lotahs* or plates, accusing others of having stolen them, with two or three people claiming for the same article.' In order to avoid these quarrels, he recommended the numbering of these articles.

The surgeon superintendents were instructed to keep a daily journal of their proceedings during the voyages and were asked to keep a note of every event and the time of its occurrence. These registers were also supposed to clearly mention the dates when the docks were scrubbed or cleaned, the ship fumigated, the blankets of recruits dusted and aired, and the bathing and washing days of the emigrants. The superintendents were instructed that they should state every day the nature of the weather, the latitude and longitude, and should note the crossing of the tropics and of the lines (of latitude and longitude). They should also enter any noteworthy instances of good or bad conduct of those on board, or of the working of the regulations for their discipline, and copies of any letters they might have written or received on service. At the end of the journal, they were to place together all these general observations made on the voyage, mentioning every objection that might be seen as reason to be added to the regulations, or any other part of the arrangements. The Emigration Act of 1883 clearly mentioned that a surgeon superintendent should bear in mind that the journal was a very important document of which he was in charge, and that it should be a faithful record of the occurrences on voyages. Surgeons were instructed that the record of each day's occurrences should never be done on the basis of their memory or loose memoranda.

In order to 'discipline' these recruits, officers frequently used power and; '...their prejudice against Indians often directed the exercise of their power'. Cases of flogging and other harsh punishments used against the Indians recurred frequently in eyewitness reports and official correspondences.[166]

In 1855, published instructions for surgeons of vessels and regulations were made, for the promotion of recruits' health and comfort over the voyages, and the surgeons were directed to strictly and regularly follow them. These were also translated in Tamil, to aid the south Indian recruits. These rules were—

- The male emigrants to be divided into three batches, being always on the upper deck; but they were not required to assist in the duties of the ship beyond washing decks.
- All the emigrants, male and female, including children (those who were not sick), to be required, in moderate weather, to come on the upper deck daily at a certain hour, which would be fixed by the commanders, and to remain on deck for at least an hour.
- A fatigue party to be formed from the male emigrants daily, for the purpose of cleaning the lower deck.
- The lower deck to be fumigated at least once a week.[167]

Each day, the emigrants were raised early. Their kit was supposed to be rolled up while the decks were holystoned and disinfected. The decks were also whitewashed every alternate Saturday. At least half the coolies were supposed to be on deck at all times during the day. There was a clothing inspection every week on the voyages. The officers often complained about the dirty, and at times filthy, habits of the coolies. The major trouble for the authorities was to keep a check on the consumption of narcotics such as *bhang* (marijuana), opium, and tobacco. These were not only considered as injurious to health according to European medical treatment, but were also a cause of indiscipline and misbehaviour among the recruits on the voyages. There was a constant demand among the recruits for these things, to which they were habituated in their own country. According to the Emigration Act, these narcotics were not allowed to be transported on the indentured ships, but were always available among the recruits, *topazes*, and other Indian employees. Eventually, after 1871, tobacco was included among the list of transport materials on the ships. Dr J.E. Dyer had given a narrative saying that scarcely a day passed that the officers of the ships and himself had not been besieged by a coolie asking for *sooka* (dry tobacco).

The hostile conditions on the ship forced recruits to rebel and act violently; and at times, some of them even tried to escape from the ships. In order to control these disillusioned and terrified recruits, the Calcutta agents never hesitated to use 'gentle coercion'. Further, to have a hold over the recruits, laws were made to strengthen the officers' hands. Emigrants were constantly trying to hide their diseases, as they had objections on the European mode of medical treatment, and they also knew that if they were discovered as 'sick', then they would not be allowed to embark. Thus, there was a constant tussle between the emigrants' 'body' and the colonial 'medical-regime'. The archival official record shows that prolonged seasickness, the miserable conditions on board the voyages, and the 'medical-regime' forced some of the emigrants to commit suicide. These accounts reveal the colonial government's failure to provide these people with a safe environment during the journey. The protector of immigrants in Natal mentioned in his report that, '...during the last voyage Umovati, from Madras, a girl aged sixteen committed suicide by throwing herself overboard. The conduct of this girl appears to have been such as to render it necessary to place her under restraint; and the means adopted by Captain Reeves for this purpose, namely that of putting her in irons in the, '...tween decks,...is of opinion that the case was of suicide, for which the captain in no way be held responsible.'[168] The report further revealed that the colonial government used all kinds of restraints on the emigrants. Another interesting case revealed the ship's excruciating situation, where the protector writes, '...during the passage Sophia Joakimill one of the women attempted to jump overboard but was fortunately prevented. I enquired into the circumstances and she did so when much upset by seasickness, was the only reason there could have been for it.'[169] One of the 'disturbing souls' who raised his voice against the captain and some crew members' misbehaviour with the recruits, became the victim of flogging by the captain, on the deck.[170] It is recorded that they tied him for the whole day and the night without food and water; the next day he was not present on board, and after that no one ever heard of him.

Thus, the emigrants were constantly kept under strict control and were subjected to severe punishments. The colonial authority, in turn, argued that corporal punishment was necessary for the control and discipline of troops, convicts, and indentured labour, especially when on active services. However, the colonial authorities came under heavy criticism from various humanitarian lobbies in Britain, denouncing severe practices in the colonies; and the pressure from those advocating abolition steadily increased with the progress of the century.[171]

Although on board the ships all possible care was taken to preserve and subsist the indentured in the interest of the planters, brutality was neither normal nor inevitable. It was the legacy of slave voyages, and as John Newton was convinced, slave trade ruined the sensitivities of all the crew.[172] Slave trading was a dangerous, corrupt, and filthy industry, and its nature remained more or less unchanged even during coolie trade. The terror, brutality, filth, disease, and abusive language was a part of the identity of the coolie's voyages.

It was not as if only the indentured labourers became the victims over the voyages; subordinate crew members too were a part of this victimization. In order to secure safety from both points of view, i.e. safety from Indian agitation and health, it was made compulsory that all employees on the indentured voyages must be Europeans. If it was not possible to get Europeans for the post, then in that case *lascars* could be employed under the control of the *serang* (bosun),[173] but in limited number—not more than five.[174] A prohibition was implemented against the employment of 'Negroes' and natives of the West Indies on the emigrants' ships. This effort of complete ban on the employment of Negro seamen failed because of practical business interests. Most of the subordinate crew members were hired from China, South Asia, and India (mainly low caste Indians) to perform the 'dirty-works' on board. However, when the *topazes*, who were all from India, themselves were sick, filth accumulated everywhere, causing a lot of nuisance on the voyages. The nature of work and the terms of their wages always remained a matter of discussion in the coolie trade. James Mariners stated, '…the crews are not human beings but things, "manufactured men"…their permanent condition is sordidness.'[175] It is as Amitav Ghosh has mentioned—'they were the first to travel extensively, participated in industrial processes of work and the first to adapt to clock-bound rhythms of work time by the invention of the watches and new technologies.'[176] In this regard, they were the first to become the subjects of victimization of the modern world. On the slave ships, the crew members were treated inhumanely and even worse than the slaves by their superiors.[177] Even during the later period, when modern forms of control (such as equality before the law, police control, legal action, and enquiry commissions) were established: flogging and washing wounds with salt water were very common punishments on these voyages.

As Emma Christopher argues, part of the reason that the rule of a ship was often based on terror or the threat thereof, rather than more modern forms of control, was the circumstances that prevailed in deep-sea trades. Geographically distant from any other authority, while a ship was at sea, the surgeon and captain had practically absolute power in their hands. Their word was the law, and that law was to be upheld as they saw fit. A sailor's contract stated that he had to obey the officers' commands, and to not do so constituted behaving—'in a riotous and disorderly manner'.[178]

Another major source of trouble for the authorities was the female emigrants and their personal hygiene. Women's issues were sensitized, where morality was constantly evoked, since it helped the colonizers in asserting and reasserting various patriarchal norms. Indentured migration historiography at large has overlooked this facet—where the labour regime invoked the rhetoric of women's 'dangerous' sexuality and how this rhetoric was crucial in shaping labour conditions. Colonial discourse portrayed Indian emigrants as: 'unhealthy', 'unclean', and 'dirty'; but as compared to males, the females were considered even more: 'unclean' and 'dirty'. On shipboard, women were considered as a source of venereal and other diseases. So, they became chief subjects of sanitary issues and medical check-ups. The colonial government even tried to control the free movement of the females on board by taking certain steps, as one of the records shows—'at night single women were lodged in their own compound, and will be precluded from leaving it, the depot and ship medical officer is hopeful that these additional precautions, preventing, as they are designed to do intercourse of the sexes, will have the effect of stopping the spread of venereal diseases in the depot and ship.'[179] Dr Whitelam recommended that—'...the decks below be well lighted, especially the female section on the board, to prevent promiscuous intercourse', though the lights in the men's section could be dimmed after eight in the evening.

Female emigrants on the ship had to face various types of assaults in the name of civilization, and law and order. They were often sexually exploited by their fellow male emigrants and also by the ship's crew. On one voyage, the surgeon in charge was arrested; 'for rape, attempted rape, or indecent assault against female emigrants'. [180] A ship's captain reported in 1885, '…considering the number of emigrants and the closeness in which they are herded together immorality is very small'. He said that some precautions were taken—single women were put in the hind part of the ship, with the married people and single men in the fore part; but there is nothing, if they have a mind, to prevent a single man from going to a single woman or vice versa. There was a *sirdar* at watch all through the night, at each of the four hatchways, but the aforementioned captain also went on to say, '…in spite however, of all care, it has happened that I have had complaints made against my crew by the *sirdars* that something was going wrong.'[181] Colonial officials mentioned that they could force males into obeying the law, but it was difficult to control women, who were also held responsible by the new medical regime for being filthy, chaotic, and immoral. Official discourse also portrayed female recruits as careless in the handling of their infants, resulting in a high death rate among the latter. In order to protect their daughters from sexual abuse, the emigrant parents on the ships married off their girls at an early age.[182]

The next issue which made the emigration office a little warm was the question of arrangement of the privies for women on the voyages. It had taken several years to decide the position of privies on the voyages. Lack of proper privy facilities for women on the voyages was the main concern among the authorities that led them to portray the women emigrants as dirty and immoral. In 1852, the ship captain complained to Mouat that the Indians were: 'dirty' and 'disorderly'; for example, it was difficult to force the women and children to use privies on the deck. Suggestions were made for the construction of privies for females on the afterparts of the ships to provide isolation for the female recruits.[183] In 1886, a report came into light on the ship *Sheila* from India to Trinidad. In his letter, W. G. Wilson, the Emigrant Agent at St. Helena, wrote to the crown agents for the colonies that—

…I must note my very strong objection to the new form of women's water-closets. When a door is opened, and a woman is squatting in the next compartment, anyone can see her and the mere fact of a woman having to back into the water-closets in view of the whole ship is an indignity to which no coolie should be subjected. If a canvas screen is hung in front of, and distant two feet from, the water-closets, this will be obviated.[184]

This suggestion was accepted and self-acting hinged doors were fitted on each compartment. Latrines on indentured ships served as a bizarre portal to the women aboard, where 'puddings' were occasionally left as sad enticements for sexual favours.[185]

Although all these facilities were arranged, women were still found not using these facilities. The authorities thus stereotyped women as being 'immoral' (responsible for immorality on voyages, source of venereal diseases, and also responsible for the high mortality rate among children, due to lack of proper care) and having filthy habits. Official records mentioned that the privies made for women were well looked after, being well-flushed and kept clean.[186] The emigration board in England suggested that 'the distilling apparatus shall be so arranged that the waste warm seawater can be made available for washing, or when not required for washing purposes for cleaning the privies.'[187] But evidence shows that they were not cleaned and not properly looked after, as emigrants avoided using them. There's no mention of the risks women took by going to wash, though incidents abound of women being assaulted while going to or coming from the privies. On the voyage to British Guiana in 1871, a female migrant became the victim of ill treatment by a crew member, when she was going towards the water closet alone. Dr J. Carroll described the behaviour of the crew towards female recruits as being one with 'unbridled license'.[188] This statement created a heated argument among the authorities and he faced several problems due to his remark. Captain W. Owen objected to this statement, arguing that, '...I must state that I cannot agree with the statement, for I never saw any impropriety practiced, and I took every possible precaution to prevent the crew interfering or taking notice of the women and specially mustered them on leaving port and told them that the coolies were to be treated as passengers in every respect, and not to be molested in any way...there was a strict look-out and of seeing that there was not any communication between the ship's company and the coolie women, and I had the ship's galley locked up at night to prevent any of them congregating...'[189] R.B. Cooper (Assistant Secretary to the Emigration Board) bellowed at Dr Carroll on how he could use such a harsh statement against his general crew members for such a minor incident like that. In the explanation of this incident, Dr Carroll wrote an apology and clarified—'the expression quoted was an unfortunate one', and mentioned, 'I have already explained that it must have been used in a moment of irritation.'[190] These cases show that there was a constant check on each and every action to preserve and maintain the good image of the indentured trade. Those who were involved in the trade and benefitted from it could not afford a criticism of it under any circumstances. In this scenario, the British Guiana emigrant agent recommended to change the location of water closets for women on the ship; but this suggestion was not accepted. Evidences also suggest that the enclosures of the privies were deliberately ill-maintained and the 'lack of facility' forced women to avoid it. Despite the rules and captain's order (captain warned his officers and crew to never go to the side of the ship reserved for women after dark), there were several cases showing that there had been many attempts to assault the women on the voyages. One of the crew members, named Albert Stead, on the British Guiana ship was caught several times in the women's toilets, smoking or simply lingering.[191] In order to reach the toilet, women had to pass from one end to the another end of the ship, where the sailors and crew members waited to get hold of them.

On the voyages, emigrants constantly became the victim of their superiors' behaviour and their racial discrimination. On the voyage of *Christopher Rawson*, one of the Indian doctors, Abdullah Khan, mentioned an incident in which the captain, for his comfort, had put many lives in danger. He explained the incident in these words, '...there was a great crowd on deck, where the Captain and his lady were accustomed to walk and to get quit of them, he ordered them down below...the gunner remonstrated with the captain and told him the men would die.'[192] Sometimes, in order to force sanitation measures, surgeons and authorities went beyond the limit and even violated the sentiments and customs of recruits. For example, once on a voyage, Captain Edward ordered Abdullah Khan to cut the hair of all the emigrants, including the women. Later on, an enquiry commission was established in Calcutta to enquire into the matter, and as a result, Captain Edward was held responsible. He was subsequently questioned before the enquiry commission—

...Question: Was it under your order that the hair of the men and women was cut off soon after they embarked?
Answer: ...the causes of this order was the preservation of cleanliness. It is evident that no persons so closely stowed together ought to have hair a yard long...
Question: Did any of them object strongly to having their hair cut off?
Answer: They did object and some of them on religious grounds, as they said; but I insisted and it was done.[193]

Marina Carter argued that in theory, respect for the culture and religious needs of the migrants was built into the shipping legislations. Yet, the European crew members subjected the migrants to indiscriminate humiliation and the women in particular to sexual harassment and abuse. For example, in one instance, a doctor gave wine to an indentured woman and made fun of her. In this case, the doctor was held guilty of ill treatment.[194] In another case in 1886, the emigrants made grave allegations against the surgeon superintendent, both of assault and of improper relations with the female emigrants during the voyage as well as at the quarantine station.

The case of the medical officer on the *Nimrod*, which sailed from Calcutta to Mauritius, is a striking example. On the arrival of the ship, several Indian women complained that Dr Browne had publicly pulled off their saris and forced them into his cabin. This was confirmed at an enquiry by the chief officer of the vessel and the assistant doctor.[195] Browne was also accused of raping a young Indian woman named Champa. He simply stated that '…she is a woman of bad character'. The steward confirmed the continuous presence of women in his cabin. The case of Jhunnea, who claimed to have been publicly stripped and her wrists tied to the rigging, which was confirmed by her husband. In his defense, Browne stated that, '…I invariably promote amusements, especially dancing amongst the emigrants, and I have frequently caught hold of those who appeared depressed or downhearted, in order to make them dance and rouse them up'.[196] In exoneration of his general behaviour he stated that:

…No one who has not actually been in charge of [Indian emigrants] can form a proper idea of the difficulty that a surgeon has to contend with in preserving cleanliness and order amongst them…the surgeon who stands in ceremony with them is not a man who can discharge efficiently his duties. They are exceedingly dirty in their habits and unless cleanliness is rigidly enforced, there is every likelihood of disease breaking out amongst them.

W. Buckmaster, the chief officer who was enquiring into the allegations against Dr Browne, came to this conclusion that this was an incident of a—'medical officer causing serious disturbances amongst the emigrants; taking liberties with them whilst under the influence of brandy.'[197] As a result of these complaints, Dr Browne and his assistant were dismissed from the service.

As a result of all the medical and sanitary measures, there was always a tussle and distrust between the Indian emigrants and European authorities on the voyages. The emigrants, who were travelling in groups united by kin, village, or north and south Indian identities ties, were in a position to protect themselves as a group. As the case of *Nimrod* showed, the emigrants did not tolerate abuse unresistingly. The chief officer of the ship reported: '…the coolies one day seemed disposed to be mutinous'. Some of them said: '…the doctor is a bad man, we shall either thrash him or jump overboard…'[198] James Smart, piloting the *Edward* down the river Hooghly in the 1830s, portrayed a vivid picture of discontented migrants and a fearful crew who could do little to prevent the nightly escapes or the threats of revolt. Muskets and pistols were loaded and the pilot was warned: '…we must arm ourselves, for the coolies would rise and put every white man to death.' Smart described the migrants' reaction in an incident when the captain had attempted to take a female passenger into his cabin by force—'The natives were so angry that they threatened to kill the Europeans…it appeared to me that the mates were afraid of the coolies; indeed it was stated that the coolies thrashed them both.'[199]

The physical appearance of the indentured body was very important; they should not only be of good build and health, but look cheerful, amused, and pleased too. This was paradoxical, and in the hostile situation of the ship, the travelling emigrants were forced to look appeased and cheerful. Earlier too, in case of the slave trade, slaves were forced to dance, sing, and their body was policed before their sale in the market, so they would look healthy and their owner could get a good amount.

PLATE 3.6: Slaves Being Forced to 'Dance' on Board a Ship

Source: International Slavery Museum, Liverpool, available on http://www.liverpoolmuseums.org.uk/ism/slavery/middle_passage/, accessed 3 January 2013.

Conclusion

To sum up, one can say that voyages played a crucial role in preparing the indentured for the lifestyle in the plantation colonies. The floating space on the Indian Ocean changed the lives of the indentured; they became 'subject' and 'sample of experiments'. The European notion of civilization, morality, chastity, and purity became part of the medical science, which they enforced on the indentured body. Science and medical research played an important role in fulfilling the requirements of the colonial society, which acted according to the social and cultural needs of their society. Emigration rules and regulations made several provisions for the comfort and benefit of the indentured over the voyages; but most of the time these remained only as unfulfilled promises. The management and organization of the ship transformed from being a slave ship to a coolie ship. During slavery, it was said that the trade was 'founded in blood', which legitimized violence by making it a part of everyday life; but during indentured period, this brutality was hidden behind the modern ways of control and discipline, and cases of brutality were not recognized in the official discourse.

Although medical science and advanced technology had somewhat of a hold over disasters, in reality, these could only become useful in the beginning of the twentieth century, i.e. the closing years of the indentured system. Various welfare approaches were also adopted on paper to appease the liberals and anti-indentured groups in Britain and India. These welfare approaches were adopted towards the recruits only until they were under the bind of contract as indentured labourers. The situation was worse on the return voyages with the coolies, when plantation colonies did not think it necessary to spend anything on returnees.

Coolie voyages emerged as a new notion of 'floating space' in the imagination of recruits, as a beginning of new physical and psychological journey. Their confusion, anxiety and distrust against the 'coolie voyages' brought them closer to one another. The voyages were also great levellers of hierarchy and status. Once aware of their condition, some of them protested and resisted; while others tried to cheat their way through or bypass the normal channels; but to no avail. In this hostile and rigid disciplinary and discriminatory atmosphere, new cultural ties, such as Bengalee, Madrasee, and *jahaji bhai* were formulated among themselves. These new relationships have also been mentioned by Brij Lal. The *jahajis* treated one another like kin, with all the obligations and responsibilities that such relationships entailed.

Notes

1. Many Africans thought that the Europeans were people who had no country, and who lived in ships. One slave who later did tell this story was Olaudah Equiano, a slave captured by the British and carried to the West Indies in the 1760s. He wrote:

   ...The first object which saluted my eyes, was the sea and a slave ship, which was then riding at anchor...These filled me with astonishment, which was soon converted into terror, when I was carried on the board. I was immediately handled and tossed up, to see if I were sound, by some of the crew, and I was now persuaded that I had got into a world of bad spirits and that they were going to kill me. Their complexions too differing so much to ours, their long hair and language they spoke...united to confirm me in this belief. Indeed, such were the horrors of my views and fears at the moment that, if ten thousand worlds had been my own, I would have freely parted with them all to have exchanged my condition with that of the meanest slave in my own country.

   See Hugh Thomas, *The Slave Trade: The History of the Atlantic Slave Trade, 1440-1870*, London: Papermac, 1998, p. 408.

2. Partha Chatterjee argued that:

   ...The peculiarity of the English (later British) ideology of empire lay in its reconciliation of a critique of continental empires as land-based absolutist tyrannies with its own possession of overseas territories. This was achieved by the myth of the 'empire of the seas'—a constellation of far-flung territories and outposts held together not by the might of armed forces but rather by commerce, producing, it was maintained, an imperial system that was entirely consistent with the requirements of liberty.

   See Partha Chatterjee, *The Black Hole of Empire: History of a Global Practice of Power*, Princeton: Princeton University Press, 2012, p. 52; Professor Nilesh Bose is of the opinion that Chatterjee claims the history of the Empire is best understood through a coherent faithfulness to a certain type of *mythos*. See Neilesh Bose, review of *The Black Hole of Empire: History of a Global Practice of Power* by Partha Chatterjee, *Reviews in History*, August 2012, review no. 1307; see http://www.history.ac.uk/reviews/review/1307, accessed 19 November 2014.

3. Gaiutra Bahadur considered the importance of Garden Reach in these words—'Garden Reach became the point of departure for the emigrants, the place where they said goodbye—forever, for most to the land their families had called home for centuries. It was also the place their metamorphose began.' See Gaiutra Bahadur, *Coolie Woman: The Odyssey of Indenture*, London: Hurst & Company, 2013, p. 42.

4. Dharmendra Prasad, *Hind Mahasagar Ka Moti: Mauritius*, Delhi: Pustakayan, 1993, p. 34.

5. Ibid.

6. Ibid., p. 35.

7. Ralph Shlomowitz and McDonald in their study stated that during the period of 1850–73, the death rate was 19.8 per cent per month per 1000 of the population. See Table 1, Ralph Shlomowitz and John McDonald, 'Mortality of Indian Labour on Ocean Voyages, 1843-1917', *Studies in History,* vol. 6, no. 35, 1990, p. 9.

8. RC (series petition) Report 37, 1837. Following these revelations, the suspension of migration was voted in the British Parliament in 1838. *The Times* described Indian emigration as a 'novel abomination', 12 and 29 July 1838; cited in Marina Carter, *Servants, Sirdars & Settlers: Indians in Mauritius, 1834-1874,* Delhi: Oxford University Press, 1995, p. 20.

9. Ibid. Free Labour Association defended the indentured system; they claimed that importation of Indians was not materially different from the resettlement of Europeans overseas.

10. *Parliamentary Papers, India,* 1841, vol. III, no. 43, Minute of Prinsep, 9 May 1841. In the Island, the issues of introduction of Indians as indentured labour became a matter of argument among the authorities, reformists, and planters. In Mauritius, one group of planters supported Indian importation to the Island on the basis of its useful influence on the apprenticed population. Henry Taylor explained that the indentured would compel the emancipated Negroes to compete with the industrious Indians for subsistence. Others were not in favour of introducing Indians in the colony. As James Stephen warned, the introduction of a large migrant workforce would be likely to—'throw a great mass of people out of profitable employment', believing that Indians had been brought for the express purpose of rendering the proprietors independent of the existing supply of labour. The anti-indentured lobby depicted emigrants as the victims of deception,—'inveigled to Calcutta, sold, resold, and shipped off to countries they have never heard of.' The planters lobby soon raised their voice and supported the Indian migration to the colony on the pretext of benefit of Indians. Marina Carter argues that the destitution of the indentured labourers in their native country was used to uphold the notion that all parties would benefit from indentured: Indians would be able to earn higher wages, India would be relieved of a proportion of her 'superabundant population', the empire would benefit from 'an increased production of sugar and augmentation in custom dues', and planters would be saved from 'total ruin'. A committee of enquiry appointed in Calcutta to investigate emigration in 1838 contested such attempts to place indentured at par with the European settlement. The Governor-General of India, Earl of Auckland, agreed with those who believed that Indians could not be considered akin to free, voluntary European migrants because of their limited knowledge of their destination. In its anti-emigration stance, the Calcutta Commission was also supported by local capitalists who looked upon the plantation colonies as competitors in production and rivals in the recruiting ground. Carter, *Servants, Sirdars & Settlers,* pp. 20–1; Also see

Michael Adas, *Machines as the Measure of Men: Science, Technology, and Ideologies of Western Dominance*, Ithaca and London: Cornell University Press, 1989, p. 2. He asserted that the ships represented an area of technology in which the Europeans had few rivals by the fifteenth century and in which they gained the supreme position by the seventeenth. Sailing ships with superior maneuverability and armament permitted the Europeans to explore, trade, and conquer all around the world.

11. Carter, *Servants, Sirdars & Settlers*, p. 23.
12. During medieval times, a warship was usually equipped with a multi-deck, castle-like structure in the bow. This was used as a platform for archers to shoot enemy ships, and also as a defensive stronghold in case the ship was boarded by the enemy. At the aft end of the ship was made a similar but usually much larger structure, called the aftcastle. This structure often stretched from the main mast to the stem of the ship.
13. Thomas, *Slave Trade*, p. 302.
14. Even sugar planters of various overseas countries were involved in the introduction of new and advanced ships for the transportation of Indian indentured to the colony. Sandbach, Tinne and Company, who began as sugar planters and merchants in Demerara, introduced the iron ship *Pandora* in 1864, and it gave tough competition to other shipping companies such as the Nourse Line, the principal carrier of coolies at that time. For details, see Hugh Tinker, *A New System of Slavery: The Export of Indian Labour Overseas, 1830-1920*, London: Oxford University Press, 1974, p. 146.
15. Chatterjee, *Black Hole of Empire*, p. 53.
16. Tinker, *New System of Slavery*, p. 146.
17. Ibid., p. 145.
18. The emergence of Britain in the Victorian period as the world's most powerful trading nation was the direct result of the process of industrialization that had transformed the country since the latter part of the eighteenth century. This economic and social revolution had been driven by many elements, but the most significant by far was the widespread application of steam technology. On sea, Britain dominated the industrialized world both in tonnage and distance: the British India Steam Navigation Co., established in 1856, became the largest shipping line in the world, eventually connecting India to South-East Asia, the Far East, the Persian Gulf, Britain, East Africa, and Australia. For details see Paul Atterbury, 'Steam & Speed: Industry, Power & Social Change in 19th-Century Britain', *The Victorian Vision*, 2001. Available at http://www.vam.ac.uk/content/articles/s/industry-power-and-social-change, accessed on 19 November 2014.
19. Ralph Shlomowitz and John McDonald, 'Babies at Risk on Immigrant Voyages to Australia in the Nineteenth Century', *The Economic History Review*, vol. 44, no. 1, 1990, p. 89.

20. This theory regarding the long journey was also adopted for the plague affected Bombay Presidency pilgrims who wanted to go to Puri. They were allowed to go via Calcutta instead of going to Puri directly. The reason for this, as Biswamoy Pati stated, was that 'this journey would be "so long" that the normal period of incubation will have expired before they reached Calcutta'. See Biswamoy Pati, '"Ordering" "Disorder" in a Holy City: Colonial Health Interventions in Puri during the Nineteenth Century,' in *Health, Medicine and Empire: Perspectives on Colonial India*, ed. Biswamoy Pati and Mark Harrison, Delhi: Orient Longman, 2001, pp. 270–98.

21. Annual Report of Trinidad Agent-General of Emigration for the year 1901–2, Revenue and Agriculture Department (Emigration Branch) Proceedings, August 1903, nos. 33–5, NAI.

22. Employment of the steamer for the conveyance of emigrants, Revenue and Agriculture Department (Emigration Branch) Proceedings, April 1882, nos. 63, NAI. Dr Grant had compared the death rate from Calcutta and Madras ships, in which he found that the mortality rate from Calcutta was higher, and suggested that the use of steamers could reduce this higher death rate. Diary no. 94, from the Government of Bengal, dated 27 March 1882, file no. 58; Employment of steamers for the conveyance of emigrants, Revenue and Agriculture Department (Emigration Branch) Proceedings.

23. Adoption of a uniform system of measurement of emigrant ships in the three Presidencies.

24 Earlier, the French law was in practice. The difference between the two was that—'the French law stipulated for no particular space to be allocated to each emigrant. It only admitted one emigrant to each ton of the vessel's registered burthen. The English law likewise restricted the number with reference to tonnage, the proportion being one adult emigrant to every two tons.' Extract from a letter (no. 29) from J.J. Franklin, Esq., Colonial Emigration Agent, to T. Pycroft, Esq., Chief Secretary to the Government of the Fort Saint George, dated 14 January 1858, Public Nos. 26/31, Home Department, Public Consultation, June 1858, Government of India.

25. Adoption of the Sterling's Rule for the measurement of emigrant vessels, Agriculture, Revenue and Commerce Department (Emigration Branch) Proceedings, January 1872, no. 1, NAI.

26. Adoption of the Sterling's Rule for the measurement of emigrant vessels, Home Department (Public Branch) Proceedings, April 1871, no. 102, NAI; Also see letter from the Officiating Master Attendant to the Emigration Agent of Mauritius, no. A1247, dated 4 March 1869, Home Department (Public Branch) Proceedings, June 1869, nos. 18–19, NAI.

27. Sterling's Rule for the measurement of emigrant vessels, Home Department (Public Branch) Proceedings.

28. Report of W.J. Jackson, Surgeon Superintendent; Annual Report of the Protector of Indian Immigrants in Mauritius for the year 1890, Revenue

and Agriculture Department (Emigration Branch) Proceedings, November 1891, nos. 15–16, part A, NAI.

29. Extract from a letter from the Emigration Agent at Calcutta to the Emigration Agency of Madras, Dated 9 March 1843, Home Department (Public Branch) Proceedings, 26 April 1843, no. 8, NAI.

30. Annual Report of the Protector of Emigrants at Calcutta for the year ending 30 June 1894, Revenue and Agriculture Department (Emigration Branch) Proceedings, February 1895, nos. 6–7, part A, NAI.

31. In the interviews conducted by Dr F. J. Mouat, the captain of the *Shah Jehan* said he: '…approves of the platforms, and considers them wholesome'. The captain of the *Adelaide*: '…considers the platforms to be useful at the sides of the ship, but to be useless amidship'. Mr Chennell, surgeon of the *Wellesley*: '…approves of the platforms, and considers them wholesome'; and Captain Parish of the *Wellesley* stated: '…I consider them useful'. Dr Mouat's report is contained in the *Papers Relating to the West India Colonies and Mauritius* (1858) and the British mortality data is in the *Reports Relative to the Mortality on Board Certain Emigrant Ships* (1854). See IOR/L/PJ/6/105, File no. 1452, August 1883; also see IOR P/188/49, January 1858, BL.

32. Extract from a letter from the Emigration Agent dated 9 March 1843.

33. Anil Persaud, 'Transformed Over Seas: "Medical Comforts" aboard Nineteenth-Century Emigrant Ships', in *Labour Matters: Towards Global Histories*, ed. Marcel van der Linden and Prabhu Mohapatra, Delhi: Tulika, 2009, p. 25.

34. Amitav Ghosh, *Sea of Poppies*, Delhi: Viking, 2008, p. 143.

35. Introduction on board emigrant vessels of the self-acting ventilator, Revenue Agriculture and Commerce Department (Emigration Branch) Proceedings, September 1878, nos. 3–4, NAI.

36. Ibid.

37. Ibid.

38. Rule 1: Ventilation of the between-decks—Besides hatches, there must be provided air shafts, cowl-headed funnels or tubes, and one of Theirs's automatic ventilators with 10 in. cylinder, and such other additional means for affording light and ventilation to the space intended for the accommodation of the emigrants as the Protector and Medical Inspector of Emigrants may consider necessary. If there are any stern-port or side scuttles provided between decks, they must be glazed, well fitted, about 14 in. apart, and as close to the upper decks as possible.

Rule 7: Ventilation of the hold—Except in vessels fitted with ventilating masts, in which case a proportionate reduction may be allowed, there should be five steam pipes solidly and strongly put together, of stout metal or wood, and airtight, each at least 9 in. in diameter, fitted with cowl-heads, and leading from the hold to the open air on the upper deck. There must be a Theirs's automatic ventilator with 10 in. cylinder for the ventilation of the hold; and the automatic ventilator, as well as the ventilating masts and steam pipes, must be conveniently placed and so arranged as to carry off the steam from the cargo quite clear of the between-decks. For details see Home, Revenue and Agriculture Department (Emigration Branch) Proceedings, May 1880, nos. 47–53, NAI.

39. Letter no. 83, dated 10 April 1876, from Captain F. Kelly, R.N. Commander, Her Majesty's ship *Malabar*, to the Director of Transport Service, Revenue, Agriculture and Commerce Department (Emigration Branch) Proceedings, August 1877, nos. 41–3, NAI.

40. Adoption of Theirs's automatic ventilator on board emigrant vessels; proposed exemption of vessels for the Mauritius from the rule requiring the use of the ventilation. Revenue and Agriculture Department (Emigration Branch) Proceedings, October 1881, nos. 1–2, NAI.

41. Letter from Secretary to the Government of Bengal to the Secretary to the Government of India, and the Protector of Emigrants at Calcutta to the Officiating Under Secretary to the Government of Bengal respectively, Revenue, Agriculture and Commerce (Emigration Branch) Proceedings, August 1877, nos. 41–3, NAI.

42. Diary no. 222, of the Government of Madras, amendment of the rules regarding artificial ventilation on emigrant vessels, Revenue and Agriculture Department (Emigration Branch) Proceedings, July 1892, nos. 1–6, NAI.

43. Ibid.

44. Related to the compulsory use of artificial appliances for ventilation on board vessels carrying emigrants from India, Revenue and Agriculture Department (Emigration Branch) Proceedings, February 1887, nos. 1–3, NAI.

45. The rafts were constructed of spare topmasts, topgallant masts, jibboom, drivergaff and boom, studding sail booms, and yards. All the hencoops, the long boats cover—in fact, everything capable of floating that could be made available for the purpose of saving lives, was used for these rafts, which were firmly lashed together with small running rigging unrove for that purpose. See C.W. Brebner, *The New Handbook for the Indian Ocean, Arabian Sea and Bay of Bengal: With miscellaneous Subjects for Sail and Steam, Mauritius Cyclones and Currents, Moon Observations and Sail-Making*, Bombay: Times of India Press, 1898, p. 145, British Library (hereafter referred to as BL), London, UK.

46. Tinker, *New System of Slavery*, p. 146.

47. Brebner, *New Handbook for the Indian Ocean*, p. 145.

48. Ibid.

49. Letter no. 375, 22 July 1903, from Robert W.S. Mitchell, Emigrant Agent for Natal and British Guiana, to the Protector of Emigrants at Calcutta,

Revenue and Agriculture Department (Emigration Branch) Proceedings, February 1904, nos. 3–7, NAI.

50. Ibid.

51. Ibid.

52. In 1866, the *Fusilier* dragged its anchors and went ashore at Port Natal, where 26 of the migrants perished by drowning or due to the weather, and the *Eagle Speed* was wrecked on the Multan bank in the river Hooghly, where 262 out of 479 of her emigrants died. See Tinker, *New System of Slavery*, p. 146.

53. Chatterjee, *Black Hole of Empire*, p. 34.

54. Annual Report of Protector of Emigrants at Calcutta for the year 1908, Commerce and Industry Department (Emigration Branch) Proceedings, September 1909, nos. 4–7, NAI.

55. Inclusion of the 'Cow's Head' brand of condensed milk in the list of medical comforts prescribed in the rules under the Indian Emigration Act 1883, Revenue and Agriculture Department (Emigration Branch) Proceedings, August 1904, nos. 4–8, NAI.

56. Brebner, *New Handbook for the Indian Ocean*, p. 145.

57. Ibid.

58. Cited in Marina Carter and Khal Torabully, *Coolitude: An Anthology of the Indian Labour Diaspora*, London: Anthem Press, 2002, p. 40.

59. Persaud, 'Transformed Over Seas', p. 46.

60. Ibid.

61. Shlomowitz and McDonald, 'Mortality of Indian Labour on Ocean Voyages', p. 5.

62. Ibid., p. 7.

63. Bengal Emigration Proceedings, 432/21, letter from Murdoch to Rogers, Emigration Board, 16 July 1869; extract from a report of Dr Bakewell on 'the causes of the sickness and mortality in coolie ships, June 1869', cited in Carter, *Servants, Sirdars & Settlers*, p. 127.

64. F.J. Mouat, Inspector of Jails in Bengal, and formerly a Professor of Medicine at the Calcutta Medical College, 'Report on the Mortality of Emigrants Coolies on the Voyage to the West Indies in 1856–57', India Public Proceedings, October 1858. IOR/L/PJ/6/105, file no. 1452, August 1883; also see IOR P/188/49, January 1858, BL.

65. Meena Radhakrishna, 'Of Apes and Ancestors: Evolutionary Science and Colonial Ethnography', *The Indian Historical Review*, vol. XXXIII, no. 1, 2006, p. 8. Also see Tayyab Mahmud, *Colonialism and Modern Constructions of Race: A Preliminary Inquiry*, Miami: University of Miami L. Rev., 1999, pp. 1219–46. See http://digitalcommons.law.seattleu.edu/faculty/501, accessed 21 December 2014.

66. Clare Anderson, *Subaltern Lives: Biographies of Colonialism in the Indian Ocean World, 1790–1920*, Critical Perspectives on Empire, Delhi: Cambridge University Press, 2012, p. 23.

67. Clare Anderson, *Convicts in the Indian Ocean: Transportation from South Asia to Mauritius, 1815–53*, Great Britain: Macmillan Press, 2000.

68. Anderson, *Subaltern Lives*, p. 25.

69. Brij V. Lal, *Chalo Jahaji: On a Journey through Indenture in Fiji*, Suva, Fiji: Fiji Museum, Prashant Pacific, 2000, p. 29.

70. Ibid.

71. Bengal Emigration Proceedings, 432/17, Report of the Committee on *Shah Jehan* in Colonial Secretary to the Secretary to the Government Bengal, 6 January 1866, in Beyts Report enclosure no. 4; cited in Carter, *Servants, Sirdars & Settlers*, p. 127.

72. Shlomowitz and McDonald, 'Babies at Risk on Immigrant Voyages to Australia in the Nineteenth Century', p. 3.

73. Dr Mouat was at that time the only competent officer available, according to the authorities. He was the Inspector of Jails and General Dispensaries in Bengal, and had already carried out similar inquiries in the past. He also visited Mauritius in 1851.

74. Mouat, 'Report on the Mortality of Emigrants Coolies on the Voyage to the West Indies', IOR/L/PJ/6/105, File no. 1452, August 1883; also see IOR P/188/49, January 1858, BL.

75. Carter, *Servants, Sirdars & Settlers*, p. 127.

76. From the citation of the diary of Captain Swinton on the *Salsette*, who drowned with the same voyage, published by his widow after his death, revealed the story of death of emigrants on the voyages. See Tinker, *New System of Slavery*, p. 158.

77. Annual Report of the Protector of Indian Immigrants at Mauritius for the year 1890.

78. According to the Report of 1853, on a ship, every emigrant should get 15 superficial ft.; the married couples' berths were 6 ft. long and from 3 ft. 1 in. to 3 ft. 4 in. wide; those for the single men were 6 ft. long and 1 ft. 9 in. wide. See letter from the Calcutta Emigrant Agency to the Land and Emigration Commissioners, chaired by T.W.C. Murdoch, dated 11 February 1853, Home Department (Public Branch) Proceedings, July 1853, no. 24, NAI.

79. Annual Report of the Protector of Indian Immigrants in Natal for the year 1887, Revenue and Agriculture Department (Emigration Branch) Proceedings, September 1888, nos. 16–17, NAI.

80. Proposed issue of a revised set of rules for regulating emigration from the port of Calcutta, Home, Revenue and Agriculture Department (Emigration Branch) Proceedings, August 1879, nos. 17–26, NAI.

81. Anderson, *Subaltern Lives*, p. 28.

82. Letter no. 272, dated 1 August 1874, from Arthur Howell, Deputy Secretary to the Government of India, to the Secretary to the Government of Bengal on the adoption on all emigrant vessels of a register of cholera

cases, Revenue, Agriculture and Commerce Department (Emigration Branch) Proceedings, August 1874, nos. 1–3, NAI.

83. Letter no. 2782, 11 December 1869, from A. Mackenzie Junior Secretary to the Government of Bengal, to E.C. Bayley Secretary to the Government of India, Home Department (Public Branch) Proceedings, 29 January 1870, nos. 44–6, NAI.

84. Letter no. 272, 1 August 1874, from Arthur Howell to the Secretary to the Government of Bengal.

85. Shlomowitz and McDonald, 'Mortality of Indian Labour on Ocean Voyages', p. 39. Shlomowitz and McDonald argue that the average death rate on Indian indentured labour voyages exceeded that of the equivalent population in India. Even though the shipboard population contained a smaller proportion of those sections of the population who were mostly at risk (namely, the very young and the very old) than the population on land, it was not until after 1906 that the annual equivalent shipboard crude death rate declined to the level of the crude death rate on the mainland, estimated at 40 to 50 per 1,000 per annum sickness on the voyage (ibid., p. 55). The higher average death rate of the shipboard population can be explained by their low nutritional status, the stress of migration, their vulnerability to new diseases to which they lacked immunity. Infants and children were at great risk on the voyages, and the birth of underweight babies and a reduction in the period of breast feeding may be attributed to pregnant women and nursing mothers being under stress due to the process of migration and seasickness on the voyage (ibid., pp. 55–7, Table 4).

86. The more formal experiments on the relationship between germs and diseases were conducted by Louis Pasteur between the year 1860 and 1864. He discovered the pathogen of the puerperal fever and the pyogenic vibrio in the blood, and suggested using boric acid to kill these microorganisms before and after confinement. But the view was controversial in the nineteenth century, and opposed the accepted theory of 'spontaneous generation'. A transitional period began in the late 1850s with the work of Louis Pasteur. This work was later extended by Robert Koch in the 1880s, and by the end of the decade, the miasma theory was struggling to compete with the germ theory of disease.

87. Proposed issue of a revised set of rules for regulating the emigration from the port of Calcutta, Home, Revenue and Agriculture Department (Emigration Branch) Proceedings, August 1879, nos. 17–26, NAI.

88. J.G. Grant, Protector of Emigrants at Calcutta, to the Secretary to the Government of Bengal, on supply to emigrant ships sailing from the port of Calcutta of water from the municipal hydrants of the town, Home Department (Public Branch) Proceedings, 17 September 1870, nos. 55–8, NAI.

89. Annual Report of the Protector of Indian Immigrants in Mauritius for the year 1890.

90. The 'Black body' referred to an African slave's body. Between 1492 and 1870, approximately 11 million Black slaves were carried from Africa to the Americas to work on plantations, in mines, or as servants in households. The marketing of Black slaves was probably the first profitable 'outcome' of the costly African expeditions. The Iberian countries, in the sixteenth century, established a huge colonial empire outside of Europe. To obtain cheap manpower, they began to bring in African slaves, who had proved their worth in Europe as capable and handy workers; to the New World. They were working largely in the mines and plantations and helped Iberian countries preserve their colonies. The development of capitalism in Europe helped Holland, France, and Great Britain in their rise. They established their colonial empires in Asia, Africa, and in America. The rapid development of the West Indies and the American colonies would have been impossible in that period without the mass employment of cheap manpower in the form of African slaves. For details, see S.U. Abramova, 'Ideological, Doctrinal, Philosophical, Religious and Political Aspects of the African Slave Trade', in *The African Slave Trade from the Fifteenth to the Nineteenth Century: Reports and Papers of the Meeting of Experts Organized by UNESCO at Port-au-Prince, Haiti, 31 January to 4 February 1978*, vol. II, The General History of Africa Studies and Documents, Paris: United Nations Educational, Scientific and Cultural Organization, 1979, pp. 17–18.

91. Thomas, *Slave Trade*, p. 418.

92. Ibid.

93. Ibid.

94. Rules under the Assam Labour and Emigration Act VI of 1901, Revenue and Agriculture Department (Emigration Branch) Proceedings, April 1902, no. 36, NAI.

95. Diary no. 131, file no. 71, from the Government of Madras, notice no. 247, dated 29 April 1881. Rationing of coolies to the Strait Settlements during their voyage from Madras, Revenue and Agriculture Department (Emigration Branch) Proceedings, June 1882, nos. 10–11, NAI.

96. Letter no. 90, 11 July 1881, from Edward Wingfield to Under Secretary of State for India, proposal for regulating the diet on board emigrant vessels according to the class of coolies embarked, Revenue and Agriculture Department (Emigration Branch) Proceedings, September 1881, nos. 22, NAI.

97. Notification no. 2473, dated 19 July 1870, regarding the adoption of the revised scale of dietary medical comforts and medicines for ships carrying emigrants from Calcutta to British and French colonies, Home Department (Public Branch) Proceedings, October 1870, nos. 165–8, NAI.

98. Ibid.

99. *Port of Spain Gazette*, 18 August, also 20 February and 15 May 1858, cited in Rattan Lal Hangloo, ed., *Indian Diaspora in the Caribbean: History, Culture and Identity*, Delhi: Primus, 2012, p. 79.

100. Letter no. 210, from C.W. Bolton Under Secretary to the Government of Bengal, General Department, Revenue and Agriculture Department (Emigration Branch), December 1883, nos. 1–3, NAI. *Choora*, or flattened rice (also called beaten rice) is dehusked rice flattened into light, dry flakes.

101. Letter no. 295, 17 November 1831, from R.W. Barlow, Acting Protector of Emigrants at Madras, to the Chief Secretary to the Government of Madras, on revision of the scales of provisions, medicines, etc., prescribed for vessels carrying emigrants, Revenue and Agriculture Department (Emigration Branch) Proceedings, January 1882, nos. 25–9, NAI.

102. Ibid.

103. Notification no. 2473, 19 July 1870, adoption of revised scale of dietary medical comforts and medicines.

104. From the citation of the diary of Captain Swinton on the voyage *Salsette*. See Tinker, *New System of Slavery*, p. 158.

105. Mouat, 'Report on the Mortality of Emigrants Coolies on the Voyage to the West Indies', IOR/L/PJ/6/105, File no. 1452, 25 August 1883; also see IOR P/188/49, January 1858, BL.

106. Cited in Hubert Gerbeau, 'Engages and Coolies on Reunion Island: Slavery's Masks and Freedom's Constraints', in *Colonialism and Migration; Indentured Labour Before and After Slavery*, ed. P.C. Emmer, tr. Bernard Delfendahl, Dordrecht, Boston, Lancaster: Martinus Nijhoff Publishers, 1986, p. 209.

107. Shlomowitz and McDonald, 'Mortality of Indian Labour on Ocean Voyages', p. 12.

108. Ibid., pp. 59–61, see Table no. 14. Annual Report of the Protector of Emigrants at Calcutta for the years 1874–1907, NAI.

109. Mouat, 'Report on the Mortality of Emigrants Coolies on the Voyage to the West Indies', IOR/L/PJ/6/105, File no. 1452, August 1883; also see IOR P/188/49, January 1858, BL.

110. Letter no. 88, 18 February 1886, from C.G. Conram, M.D. C.C.S., Mauritius Emigration Agent, Madras, to the Protector of Emigrants, regarding the use of the artificial appliances for ventilation on board emigrant vessels, Revenue and Agriculture Department (Emigration Branch) Proceedings, June 1886, nos. 8–13, NAI.

111. Letter no. 47, 28 February 1873, from A.O. Hume, C.B. Secretary to the Government of India, to the Secretary to the Government of Madras, on the maintenance by surgeons on board emigrant vessels of a record of facts of diseases, Agriculture, Revenue and Commerce Department (Emigration Branch) Proceedings, February 1873, nos. 46–7, NAI.

112. Letter no. 628, dated 23 February 1903, Dr W. Forsyth, F.R.C.S., Protector of Emigrants at Calcutta, to the Secretary to the Government of Bengal, regarding the provision for the supply of microscopes on emigrant vessels, Revenue and Agriculture Department (Emigration Branch) Proceedings, July 1903, nos. 4–11, NAI.

113. Ibid.

114. Ibid.

115. Repatriation from Surinam, Mauritius, and Fiji of British Indian lepers and lunatics, Revenue and Agriculture Department (Emigration Branch) Proceedings, May 1903, no. 51, NAI.

116. Tinker, *New System of Slavery*, p. 79.

117. Several distinguished scholars have recently shown that there was no close relation between 'tight-packing' and mortality. A meticulous analysis of statistics suggests that tightly packed ships in fact did not have a significantly larger number of deaths than the more humanely stored ones: 'the number...taken on board in itself did not relate to [the] mortality experienced by 'African slaves' during the crossing. The disadvantage of overpacking was not, it seems, that it in itself led to a greater incidence of diseases, but that it was usually accompanied by a reduction in the space available for storing food for the voyage; and that of course, caused malnutrition. An epidemic would, after all, sweep through even a lightly loaded ship; and if there were no epidemics, and the captain was clever as well as fortunate, he might be able to land most of his cargo even in case of a tightly packed vessel. See Thomas, *Slave Trade*, p. 414.

118. Permission to lepers to return to India from the West Indies, Revenue, Agriculture and Commerce (Emigration Branch) Proceedings, August 1875, nos. 3–7, NAI.

119. Transfer of lunatic coolies from Mauritius to India, Revenue, Agriculture and Commerce Department (Emigration Branch) Proceedings, June 1876, nos. 6–8, NAI.

120. Ibid.

121. Prevention of the embarkation of immigrants for repatriation to India who have been confined in lunatic asylums, Revenue and Agriculture Department (Emigration Branch) Proceedings, May 1901, nos. 18–19, NAI.

122. Ibid.

123. Permission to lepers to return to India from the West Indies, Revenue, Agriculture and Commerce (Emigration Branch) Proceedings.

124. Transfer of lunatic coolies from Mauritius to India, Revenue, Agriculture and Commerce Department (Emigration Branch) Proceedings.

125. Letter no. 977, J & P, dated 16 July 1891, from E.E. Block, Crown Agent for the colonies to J. Nourse, Contractor, regarding revised scale of

medicines, etc., for emigrant vessels, Revenue and Agriculture Department (Emigration Branch) Proceedings, August 1892, no. 27, NAI.

126. New Natal Law 14 of 1875, Revenue and Agriculture Department (Emigration Branch) Proceedings, April 1882, nos. 81–5, NAI.

127. Notification no. 2271, Revision of scales of medical stores required to be put on board emigrant vessels by the colonial emigration rules, Commerce and Industry Department (Emigration Branch) Proceedings, December 1907, nos. 8–13, NAI.

128. Annual Report of the Protector of Indian Immigrants in Natal for the year 1908.

129. Thomas Winterbottom, *An Account of the Native Africans in the Neighbourhood of Sierra Leone; to which is added, an Account of the present state of Medicine among them*, vol. II, London: Charles Whittingham, 1803, p. 43; cited in Richard B. Sheridan, *Doctors and Slave: A Medical and Demographic History of Slavery in the British West Indies, 1680–1834*, USA: Cambridge University Press, 1985, p. 98.

130. D.G. Crawford, *A History of the Indian Medical Service, 1600-1913*, vol. I, London: W. Thacker & Co., 1914, p. 2. Crawford stated—'Dr John Woodall, the Surgeon of the East India Company in 1614, in January 1617–18, recorded his directions as regards preservation of health on board ships to be delivered to the commanders of all the Company's ships, and by them observed on the voyage. This was a reference to the first edition of *The Surgeon's Mate* published in 1617'; He further emphasized, in the court minutes of 26–7 March 1618, that his salary from the East India Company was increased from 20 pounds to 30 pounds a year. For details, also see Crawford, *History of Indian Medical Service*, p. 19.

131. Thomas, *Slave Trade*, p. 416.

132. The fact that so many Liverpool ships carried trained doctors led to the growth of the tradition of tropical medicine there, which, in turn, led eventually to the Liverpool school of that science, and therefore, indirectly, in the late nineteenth century, to Sir Ronald Ross's identification of the mosquito as the agent of malaria. See Thomas, *Slave Trade*, pp. 307–8; Also see Emma Christopher, *Slave Ship Sailors and their Captive Cargoes, 1730-1807*, New York: Cambridge University Press, 2006, p. 39.

133. D.G. Crawford, *A History of Indian Medical Service, 1600-1913*, vol. II, London: W. Thacker & Co., p. 488.

134. Ibid., pp. 514–15.

135. Ibid., p. 515.

136. Ibid., p. 520.

137. Tinker, *New System of Slavery*, p. 147.

138. J. B. Brain and P. Brain, 'The Health of Indentured Indian Migrants to Natal, 1860-1911', *South Africa Medical Journal*, vol. VI, 1982, pp. 739–42.

139. Tinker, *New System of Slavery*, p. 147.

140. Carter, *Servants, Sirdars & Settlers*, p. 144.
141. European surgeon on emigrant vessels, Home Department (Public Branch) Proceedings, May 1861, nos. 32–3, NAI.
142. Report from the Emigration Commissioners, 'Return of Emigration to the West Indies, 1861–62', dated 3 October 1862, NAI.
143. Mouat, 'Report on the Mortality of Emigrant Coolies on the Voyage to the West Indies', IOR/L/PJ/6/105, File no. 1452, August 1883; also see IOR P/188/49, January 1858, BL.
144. Letter from C. Beadon to A.R. Young, 23 September 1858, Home Department (Public Branch) Proceedings, 1858, nos. 25–9, NAI.
145. Letter dated 23 April 1861, Home Department (Public Branch) Proceedings, April 1861, nos. 32–3, NAI; Also see Persaud, 'Transformed Over Seas', p. 37.
146. Letter dated 17 May 1861, Home Department (Public Branch) Proceedings, April 1861, nos. 32–3, NAI. Letter no. 37, 16 January 1872, from J.G. Grant, Protector of Emigrants at Calcutta, to the Junior Secretary to the Government of Bengal, regarding qualification of Dr Sinclair of the emigrant ship *India*, Agriculture, Revenue and Commerce Department (Emigration Branch) Proceedings, February 1872, nos. 2–3, NAI.
147. Wragg Commission of 1885–7, cited in Y.S. Meer, *Documents of Indentured Labour: Natal 1851-1917*, Durban: Institute of Black Research, 1980, p. 371.
148. For details see Roger Jeffery, 'Recognizing India's Doctors: The Institutionalization of Medical Dependency, 1918-39', *Modern Asian Studies*, vol. XIII, no. 2, 1979, pp. 301–26.
149. Pratik Chakrabarti, '"Signs of the Times": Medicine and Nationhood in British India', *Osiris*, vol. XXIV, no. 1, 2009, p. 192.
150. Jeffery, 'Recognizing India's Doctors', p. 311.
151. Letter dated 23 April 1861, Home Department (Public Branch) Proceedings.
152. Revenue and Commerce Department (Emigration Branch) Proceedings, December 1871, no. 4, NAI; Also see Tinker, *New System of Slavery*, p. 150.
153. In 1872, Dr Grant stated that 'at present the supply of medical men whose antecedents best fit them for the coolie emigration service is a limited one'. The best qualified were those employed by the emigration commissioners, but they were lacking in knowledge of Indian languages. Recruiting doctors in India would solve this problem but, if 'natives' of India were admitted, they would be less qualified professionally. Revenue and Commerce Department (Emigration Branch) Proceedings, December 1871, no. 4, NAI.
154. These doctors were highly qualified. For example, Major H.W. Pilgrim, I.M.S., M.B. London, F.R.C.S. (England), was appointed as a senior

surgeon to the General Hospital, Calcutta and as the Depot surgeon to the Emigration Agency of British Guiana.

155. Tinker, *New System of Slavery*, p. 148.
156. Revenue and Commerce Department (Emigration Branch) Proceedings, December 1871, no. 4, NAI.
157. New Natal Law 14 of 1875, Revenue and Agriculture Department (Emigration Branch) Proceedings.
158. Letter from Natal government Emigration Agency, Garden Reach, Calcutta, 9 February 1899, to S. Doud Ali (appointed as compounder for Natal ships), India Office Records, IOR/L/PJ/6/505 file 584, BL.
159. W. Ernst, 'The Indianization of Colonial Medicine: The Case of Psychiatry in Early-Twentieth-Century British India', in *NTM International Journal of History & Ethics of Natural Sciences, Technology & Medicine*, vol. XX, no. 2, 2012. p. 70. Ernst argued that the process of Indianization of the Indian medical service started in the early twentieth century, initially at the provincial level, in 1919. She argued that the Indian medical officers had to suffer racial discrimination. The senior Indian officers' wages were low as compared to the British officers and their accommodation was inferior to the British officers, who were staying in the 'red houses' as a 'paradise'.
160. Amitav Ghosh, 'Of Fanas and Forecastles: The Indian Ocean and some lost Languages of the age of Sail', *Economic and Political Weekly*, vol. 43, no. 25, 2008, pp. 56–62.
161. Conditions of the ship returning with coolies from British Guiana, Revenue, Agriculture and Commerce (Emigration Branch) Proceedings, August 1875, nos. 3–7, NAI.
162. Annual Report of the Protector of Indian Immigrants in Mauritius for the year 1890.
163. Letter no. 44, dated 17 April 1873, Secretary of State for India to the Government of India, regarding the 'ill treatment of female emigrants on board the ship *Dover Castle*', Agriculture, Revenue and Commerce Department (Emigration Branch) Proceedings, May 1873, no. 5, NAI.
164. Extract from a letter from the Emigration Agent dated 9 March 1843.
165. C.G. Henning, *The Indentured Indian in Natal, 1860-1917*, New Delhi: Promilla & Co., 1993, p. 5.
166. Chief Medical Officer's report, 18 January 1860, on *Shah Allum*, cited in Carter, *Servants, Sirdars & Settlers*, p. 143.
167. Extract from a letter from the Emigration Agent, dated 9 March 1843.
168. Annual Report of the Protector of Indian Immigrants in Natal for the year 1882, Revenue and Agriculture Department (Emigration Branch) Proceedings, May 1883, no. 7, NAI.
169. Annual Report of the Protector of Indian Immigrants in Natal for the year 1885, Revenue and Agriculture Department (Emigration Branch) Proceedings, January 1886, nos. 15–17, NAI.

170. Ibid.
171. David Killingray, '"The Rod of Empire": The Debate over Corporal Punishment in the British African Colonial Forces, 1888-1946', *The Journal of African History*, vol. XXXV, 1994, p. 201.
172. Thomas, *Slave Trade*, p. 309.
173. A *serang* or bosun is a ship's officer in charge of equipment and the crew. *Serang* was the highest rank a *lascar* could hope to reach.
174. Notification no. 1950/447, 15 October 1902, from the governments at Madras and Calcutta, proposing prohibition of the employment of Negroes on emigrant vessels, Revenue and Agriculture Department (Emigration Branch) Proceedings, March 1903, nos. 21–3, NAI; Also see 'Employment of Negroes sailors on ships conveying coolies between India and colonies', 30 July 1894, file no. 1333, L/PJ/6/378, Public and Judicial Departmental Papers, India Office Records, BL; The racist attitude about the seamen of African origin is best captured in the words of a Protector of Immigrants in Jamaica, who wrote in 1891—'on account of their generally incorrigible addictedness to sexual intercourse, Negroes, if employed, should be in a minority in a coolie emigrant ship."
175. C.L.R. James, *Mariners, Renegades and Castaways: The Story of Herman Melville and the World we live in*, London: Allison and Busby, 1985, p. 22. Cited in Christopher, *Slave Ship Sailors*, p. 21.
176. Ghosh, 'Of Fanas and Forecastles', p. 58.
177. James Morley, once a cabin boy on the *Amelia* of Bristol, in his answer to a question posed at a House of Commons inquiry, 'How have the seamen been generally treated on board the Guiana Ships in which you have sailed?' replied, 'with great rigour and many times with cruelty'. He recalled how he had once accidentally broken a glass belonging to Captain Dixon and the consequences that he faced for that: 'I…was tied up to the tiller in the cabin by my hands, and then flogged with a cat [cat-o'-nine-tails], and kept hanging there some time'. Most seamen, Morley thought, slept on the deck: 'They lie on the dock and die on the dock.' Cited in Thomas, *Slave Trade*, p. 309.
178. Christopher, *Slave Ship Sailors*, p. 96.
179. Annual Report of the Protector of Indian Immigrants in Natal for the year 1885.
180. Ibid.
181. Meer, *Documents of Indentured Labour*, p. 5.
182. Marriage Law of Natal, Revenue and Agriculture Department (Emigration Branch) Proceedings, May 1883, nos. 36–9, NAI. During the voyage, new relations of brotherhood emerged among the different sections and castes of society. This was also the centre where many new matrimonial relations developed among the emigrants. These marriages were of two types, one that was between the single women and single men, and the other in

which the parents of young girls married them off in order to save them from abuse.

183. Communication from the Government of Bengal with enclosures regarding the construction of privies in the afterparts of emigrant ships, for the use of females and children. Home Department (Public Branch) Proceedings, May 1868, nos. 119–20, NAI.

184. New forms of water closets adopted for the use of the women on board the *Sheila* on her voyage to Trinidad in 1886, Revenue and Agriculture Department (Emigration Branch) Proceedings, February 1887, no. 11, NAI.

185. Ibid.

186. Annual Report of the Protector of Indian Immigrants in Natal for the year 1908.

187. This became the part of the emigration rule in 1871, No. 4853, 13 October 1868, regarding certain modifications in the rule for the utilization of warm seawater from the distilling apparatus on board emigrant ships, Home Department (Public Branch) Proceedings, 9 January 1869, nos. 83–5, NAI.

188. No. 44, 17 April 1873, Secretary of State for India to the Government of India, regarding the 'ill-treatment of female emigrants on board the ship *Dover Castle*'.

189. Ibid.

190. Ibid.

191. According to the clause; the standard for charters with indentured ships: 'the master shall prevent by all means in his power any intercourse whatever between the officers and the crew and the female emigrants.' A copy of the contract is enclosed in 'Mutiny on *The Main*', 29 August 1902, CO 111/535, Colonial Office Correspondence, Public Record Office, TNA; Also see 'Report on the Voyages of the ship *Main*', 10 May 1902, file no. 928, L/PJ/6/600, Public and Judicial Departmental papers, India Office Records. BL.

192. Calcutta Commission Enquiry report regarding the evidence given by Abdullah Khan; cited in Carter, *Servants, Sirdars & Settlers*, p. 143; Heavy mortality on the *Antony Anderson* was reportedly caused by the confinement of the migrants below decks with all the hatches closed, on account of bad weather.

193. Ibid.

194. Annual Report of the Protector of Indian Immigrants in Natal for the year 1888–9, Revenue and Agriculture Department (Emigration Branch) Proceedings, December 1890, nos. 1–6, NAI.

195. Mr William Lawry, the master of the vessel, states in his deposition, that Dr Browne, on one occasion, at eleven o'clock in the night, took a woman into his private cabin to examine her, alleging that she had gonorrhea.

This was confirmed by the chief officer and assistant doctor, who conducted the woman to the doctor's cabin. Dr Browne, on being questioned by W. Buckmaster, Colonial Secretary of Mauritius, as to the reasons which justified his examining the woman at that hour of the night, said that his justification rested on medical grounds, which, however, have not been explained. Complaints made by the emigrants on *Nimrod* against Dr Browne, Agriculture, Revenue and Commerce Department (Emigration Branch) Proceedings, May 1873, nos. 6–8, NAI.

196. Complaints made by the emigrants on *Nimrod* against Dr Browne, Agriculture, Revenue and Commerce Department (Emigration Branch) Proceedings.
197. Ibid.
198. Ibid.
199. Calcutta Commission Enquiry report regarding the evidence given by Abdullah Khan; cited in Carter, *Servants, Sirdars & Settlers*, p. 145. Cases of Indians throwing themselves overboard were particularly frequent in the 1830s;—evidences of Revd Garstin, James Rapson, Captain Edward, Bengal Public Proceedings, 13/28, Prinsep to Calcutta Commission of Enquiry, 3 October 1838; *Parliamentary Papers, India*, 1840, vol. 37, Dick to Secretary to the Government of Bengal, 18 August 1838; cited in Carter, *Servants, Sirdars & Settlers*, p. 145.

CHAPTER FOUR

Fit Body, Fit Labour
Hospitals, Doctors and Resistance

'Improvements continue gradually to be made in the matter of housing and barracks accommodation on all the estates, and employers are learning that the more care they take in questions affecting the welfare of the Indian labourers, his health and comfort, the more likely are they to get from him the maximum of work.'

—Annual Report of the Protector of Indian Immigrants in Natal for the year 1901, Revenue and Agriculture Department (Emigration Branch), August 1902

These words of the protector of Indian immigrants in Natal show that to continue the indentured system and to extract maximum work from the indentured labourers, it was very necessary to keep the labourers healthy. Many plantation colonies adopted the model of healthcare which was created by Governor Grant of Jamaica. Governor Grant placed plantation medical officers on government payroll. The reason behind this move, as James Patterson Smith mentioned, was that this removed the profit motive and brought the responsibility for coolies' health directly in the government's hands.[1] But here one needs to understand that in order to ensure long-term profits, these reform tools were adopted by the governments with the consent of planters themselves. Thus, the medical facilities given to the indentured migrants were neither simply motivated by the 'control' aspect nor completely motivated by the 'reform' agenda. In the plantation economy, its main purpose was to put a control on the epidemic diseases which were a major cause of death of the larger proportion of the labour force. Moreover, the white settlers considered these epidemics a big threat to their own population as well. The investment by the government as well as the planters, on immigrant health and sanitary issues was similar to capital investment; the purpose behind this investment was to extract maximum work or to restrict the proportion of mortality with less investment. It is also remarkable to note that the indentured labourers were able to get the medical facility, which was important to keep them alive in a hostile situation.

Government intervention like this was unprecedented at home. Even though the liberals sought to build colonial social peace through fairer systems of justice, they were still quite sure that police and armed forces were also required. British experience in India and Ireland reinforced these conclusions. In the non-white empire, Arthur Mills was sure that—'...when our sceptre can no longer be supported by our sword, the days of our dominion will be numbered.' James Fitzjames Stephen, a member of the Indian Viceroy's Council from 1869–72, compared the position of the British in India to a bridge over which natives passed from brute violence to peace and industry.[2] One pier supporting that bridge was justice; the other was military power.[3] Patterson Smith saw these medical comforts and facilities as the matter of justice; but by doing so, he neglected the methods of application and the terror behind these mechanisms of justice, for which the emigrants were not ready. Sometimes, they were forced to accept these medical facilities. The overseas government used police, punishment, and terror to impose these reform measures in the colonies.

In the last chapter, I had discussed recruits as a mobile threat to the new overseas colonies. In this chapter, I will trace their transformation from a mobile population to confined workers. I would also explore the relationship between the indentured system and plantation capital society, through the lens of medical facility. The colonial government, through the welfare approach, 'forced' planters to provide medical facilities to the indentured labourers, though they were actually acting on behalf of the profit of planters. This chapter focuses on the plantation economy of two colonies and how the newly transported indentured labourers were treated at their workplace, how they were assigned the labour work, and how they were affected by the new environment. The last section of this chapter focuses on the nature of the resistance of the indentured against these reform measures.

From the Immigration Depot to the Quarantine Station

The devastation by white ants have rendered the buildings most dangerous... the building is utterly unprovided with cooking places and privies...it allows the immigrants to escape from it…and many who have profited by this latter facility are now wandering about the colony without having been registered at this office.[4]

In the early days of the indentured system, the emigrants directly landed at the immigrant depot of the destination colony and were simply handed over to the planters on whose behalf they had been recruited and transported. In 1838, under the pressure of the prohibition of transportation of the indentured from India, a scheme was framed by the planters to establish a depot in Mauritius, where disembarked labourers would be given lodging, food, and medical attendance prior to their allotment to planters.[5] In 1843, the immigration duties which had earlier been carried out by the police, were formally handed over to the protector of immigrants, and provisions were made for accommodating and inspecting the freshly arrived Indians.[6]

Immigrants were provided one pound of rice with a little salt. When the doctor proposed giving them vegetables and fish, the colonial secretary refused by stating, '…the immigration depot was not a place of entertainment for maroons…'[7] In 1844, in New Moka Street, Port Louis was accepted as a depot site. It was built on the ruins of an old building from the French period, close to the civil and military hospitals. However, the condition of the depot was not suitable for human habitation, and periodic complaints were registered from time to time in the immigrant protector's records. Those who were sick within forty-eight hours in the depot were sent to the civil hospital, and expenses for treatment were taken from the immigration fund. In 1850 and 1853, the leaky roof of the depot was reconstructed and the building was enlarged and improved subsequently. In 1859, a depot magistrate and surgeon were appointed, and in 1860, a depot medical officer was appointed, whose duties were to examine inmates and new arrivals, vaccinate those who required it, and report deaths in the depot. High walls were built around the depot to prevent the newly arrived from deserting. A depot photographer was appointed in 1869. Policemen and peons were also appointed to keep order and discipline on the depot, especially when the depot was busy and tense with planters and *sirdars* competing for the new labourers. In 1886, provisions were made for the supply of clean water from the municipal canal, supply of fresh air along with the light, ventilation, and the drainage system which was also improved. This depot was the first place where the white officials started to 'civilize' the Indians. The medical officers wanted to change 'the dirty practice of Indians sleeping on the naked earth'. Dr Barraut believed,

'...it would be well for the Indian, on his first initiation to Mauritian customs and manners to have before his eyes more refined habits than he has been accustomed to see in his own country'.[8] In order to civilize and discipline Indians, the peons often used rattan sticks as their tool.

The depot was also a waiting place and shelter for those who had completed their contract and were returning to their country; for women who were helpless and had no financial support; for people who had lost their health; and invalids, orphans, and lepers. It is only after the 1860s, when more space was available, that lepers were kept in a separate shed and their belongings like plates, clothes, and *lotas* were separated. Earlier, they were housed in the same shelters with other healthy Indians.[9] Sometimes, they had to wait for several months to find a place on board.

In the case of Natal, when the first ship of indentured labourers reached Durban, they were forced by the police force to herd together into the unfinished barracks surrounded by pools of stagnant water. Their condition was such that in contrast to the destination depot, the ships appeared a better place. There was no cooking arrangement, but the new arrivals were asked to cook for themselves; also, there were no privies. They were exposed to the soggy, mosquito-spawning terrain of the Natal bay. Consequently, they were soon hit by many diseases such as dysentery, cold, cough, and fever. In spite of all these problems, *The Natal Mercury* reported the luxuriant picture of coolie accommodation in the depot, which was presented as being made for the convenience which they were used to in India.[10] In order to prevent the absconding and absence of Indians at the time of their allotment to the planters, high walls had been built around the barracks.

As the system refined with time and due to the fear of their spreading contagious diseases across the colony, Indians first became the subject of medical check-ups and were confined in quarantines, for medical examination and clearance before being passed to the depot. If the medical surgeon had any hint of epidemic diseases on a ship by which Indians had arrived, they did not allow them to disembark, and so the emigrants had to spend some more days on the ship, and sometimes even weeks.[11] Here, it is also to be noted that the climates of Mauritius and Natal were unsuitable for the Indians, being far colder and changing more frequently than that in their native country.[12] In the case of Mauritius, Indians were treated in the nearby civil hospital. In 1868, a dispensary was opened at the depot (at Mauritius) and a compounder dresser (*infirmier*[13]) was appointed there. Preference was given to those who were trained in government hospitals and who spoke

PLATE 4.1: Indian Indentured Landing in the bay of Port Natal, 1860

Source: Local History Museum, Durban.

Indian languages. In the early 1880s, for a short period, a medical practitioner was appointed; but soon the post was cancelled because the civil hospital was very close to the depot, and it would also increase the financial burden on the immigration board.

In 1856, a cyclone broke out in Mauritius, and as a result of the poor shelter provisions at Lazaret, and subsequent lack of care, the newly arrived Indians suffered tremendously, which led to a high mortality rate. During the subsequent four months, 280 out of 703 Indians died. The chief medical officer, in his special report, justified the accident in these words—

...unremitting efforts were made to supply the unfortunates with every requirement...inclement weather made the tents an inadequate shelter...the first doctor appointed, Dr. Finlay, proved unequal to the crisis, both from want of energy and the total absence of order and regularity...he was replaced by Dr. Finnimore, the military assistant surgeon...no one had foreseen that tents would be inadequate material and workmen were sent to build wooden huts, and measures are underway to build permanent structures, although there have not been commenced because the island is perpetually in quarantine and artificers from alarm of contagion, are refusing to work there.[14]

The Government of India reacted by declaring a suspension on further migration until a more suitable quarantine site was chosen. As a result, Mauritius opted for Flat Island or Gabriel Island, while in Natal, emigrants first landed at 'The bluff' quarantine station.[15] The Natal government had to wait through ten years of negotiation with the Government of India for the recruitment of indentured labourers. The Government of India had refused the recruitment twice on the basis of indentured welfare and security. As a result of this delay and the Government of India's experiences in other indentured receiving countries such as Mauritius and West Indies, the Natal government was saved from taking unnecessary experimental measures and was able to adopt a more refined and advanced indentured system. The role model for the Natal indentured coolie law was Mauritius and British Guiana. In Natal, the average stay of newly arrived Indians in the quarantine was ten days in the normal conditions; but in case of epidemics, it could be extended as required.[16] For example, in case of measles, it was twenty-four days.

The permanent staff of the quarantine stations in general included a pilot, three lighthouse keepers, a storekeeper, a signalman, and a number of servants. The Natal coolie law recommended that the emigrants would not be assigned to any employers or planters for

PLATE 4.2: Flat Island Quarantine Station

Source: Andrew Balfour, *Report on Medical Matters in Mauritius, 1921*, Mauritius: Authority of the Governor P.G. Bumstead, 1921, accessed at WTL.[17]

three weeks. Within this period, it was observed whether the emigrants were affected by diseases or not. As a preventive measure, the quarantine system was established based on the theory of contagion of disease. In order to stop the spread of diseases from ship to the mainland, Mauritian authorities introduced strict regulations of quarantine. The Quarantine Committee of Mauritius also set an example as the most stringent quarantine authority in the world, and also served as a guide to other British possessions and foreign countries. C.W. Brebner, in his account, states that the Quarantine Committee at that time would have been unanimous in sacrificing ship and cargo rather than violate even one of their quarantine laws.[18] A yellow flag was waved on ships that were being quarantined, and was removed when the ship was allowed to pratique in order to land passengers.

An incident in the quarantine station of Flat Island (Mauritius) had an important impact on the history of Mauritius' indentured system and other overseas colonies engaged in the system. The recruits, who reached from quarantine to Port Louis quarantine station on *Shah Jehan* from Calcutta on 30 March 1873, saw a large number of deaths and outbreak of diseases among them because of the cold. They were kept there for no less than thirty-five days on the grounds of measles that had appeared and affected some of them.[19] Consequently, an enquiry showed that the quarantine station, where the emigrants landed first, was not properly maintained in terms of sanitation and medical facilities. The emigrants there had constantly complained about the quality of water. The high rate of sickness and death among the recruits in this incident forced the Government of Mauritius to appoint an enquiry commission under the supervision of Dr Payne. The report of this enquiry played an important role in the history of indentured labour, which defined the rules and regulations for the quarantine stations in overseas colonies. Dr Payne, in his enquiry report, stated the miserable condition of the quarantine station and the indentured labourers. In the case of the ship *Merchantman*, the report stated that—

...Mr. Romaine, the medical officer of the *Merchantman* and Captain Lawery who commands the ship, recommended that her people were landed at Flat Island in good health with two exceptions only. Eight or ten persons died on the Island, and three or four become blind there, who had no infection of the eyes when they left the ship, and this in a period of twenty-one days. Mr. Romaine heard that the water shown to him was the only water supplied to the coolies. He observed also that the landing place was unsafe, so much so that both Captain Lawry and he felt surprised that no accident occurred. Not a word was said to Mr. Romaine at Port Louis on this occasion about the deaths at Flat Island, nor any objection that hinted at the condition of the people on leaving the ship. Captain Lawry's evidence is even more emphatic with reference to the arrangements for landing. The water seemed to him brackish and was 'nasty' in taste, being inferior to that used on board ship. He drew Mr. Romaine's attention to it. The people suffered from cold. Captain Lawry adds: 'I saw the people after they left the Island, and though the superintendent seemed to say that they had recruited their strength there, they seemed to me to attribute the deaths at Flat Island to weak and ineffective persons shipped at Calcutta, and he spoke in the same tone of recent arrivals generally. Some persons left Flat Island blind who were not so when they landed here!'[20]

This incident attracted the attention of the authorities and provoked them to take measures to ensure the safety of the quarantine station in the colony. The colonist lived in fear of infection and resented the extra cost that the calamity had incurred.[21] In this case, the earlier medical officers in charge of quarantine at Flat Island on four occasions, viz., Dr Esnouf, M.R.C.S. London, and Dr Dubois, M.R.C.S., Edinburgh; both positively affirm in their letters that the well water was not used for drinking purpose, and Dr Dubois even declares that he himself saw the water issued twice a day from the tanks. In the enquiry, it was alleged that the water supplied to coolies in quarantine at Flat Island was bad and unhealthy; that those who disembarked there from the *Shah Jehan* in May 1859, suffered much from cold, and that the landing place on the island was unsafe.

There was another group among the authorities who considered that water was not the cause of sickness and mortality on the island. They argued that the well water of Flat Island (which was slightly brackish) was only used for washing. The drinking water, used by the coolies and the permanent residents, was rainwater collected in large tanks. The station had also been provided with a powerful Normanby's distilling apparatus since 1859, capable of supplying 1,000 gallons a day. They further argued that the permanent staff of the quarantine station never complained about impure water supply or any sickness occasioned by drinking water. Dr Gillespie, who was a resident medical officer for five years, never reported any ill-effects of the water that were now being attributed to it.[22]

These two groups of people were representing two governments and authorities that were performing different types of duties in two different countries—India and Mauritius. The deteriorated condition of recruits on the ships placed responsibilities on the ship authorities and; Calcutta authority while the sickness on the Island was blamed on

PLATE 4.3: Underground Rainwater Tank at the Quarantine Station

Source: Andrew Balfour, *Report on Medical Matters in Mauritius.*

the negligence of the colonial government. The two types of arguments mentioned were the results of this differentiation. In this particular case, the responsibility was that of the Mauritian authorities. It was evident that the coolies made complaints about the quality of water and they had no alternative; and that on one occasion the superintendent promised to send for water from a different source, but did not do so. The authorities at Calcutta stated that—

...These are the most important allegations. The mortality on Flat Island must, I think, attract attention here before long, and, whether true or not, it is better that the evidence be reported to His Excellency's Govt., and inquiry here be anticipated at Port Louis. It has been found easy by the immigration officer in the colony to explain to their own Govt. untoward events, by a charge of neglect against its distant servant here, but of late it has seemed to me that the Govt. has not been very ready to adopt their conclusion, so much so, indeed that I should not have considered this communication very necessary of the care and attention devoted to the service here: but there are other officers who are responsible for the working of the Calcutta system, and therefore interested in its just vindication; and they, sitting in corrective judgment on all that is done, and owing no allegation of service to the colonial government, will find at once their duty and their justification in drawing the attention of the government of Bengal to anything that may be reported defective in the provision for the health and reasonable comfort of the coolies at Port Louis.[23]

The year 1897 is a memorable one in the history of Mauritius quarantine. The bubonic plague in India brought many changes, one of them being the quarantine law, which interested merchants, and shipowners and masters. Brebner recalled his experience of quarantine laws in these words:

…The breaking out of the bubonic plague at Bombay caused an unnecessary panic. To quote the words of an old writer, who said—'the fear of death tended at times to cause unreasonableness in man' is justified by the extremes to which the Mauritians have this year carried their anti-plague precautions. No doubt quarantine for a small Island like Mauritius, where Asiatics are in majority, is necessary to a certain extent. The plague scare was brought about by a few leaders who excited the people in such a way that it would have been dangerous for a shipmaster, just admitted to pratique, to walk about the streets of Port Louis if it was known that a simple case of fever existed on board his ship.[24]

The fear of the spread of diseases on the island always kept the authorities anxious. An observer mentioned in his article, 'Friends of India' in an Indian newspaper: '…if a coolie or a lascar on board has an attack of diarrhoea, if a man becomes delirious with drink, the island goes mad'.[25]

The Government of Mauritius passed various laws and regulations regarding quarantine stations. Ordinance no. 3 of 1857 defined the duties of the surgeon superintendent and the management of the quarantine stations. The management was responsible for all the activities on the stations, like medical examination, keeping records, etc. The surgeon superintendent was responsible for providing food, accommodation, and new clothing to the Indians after the quarantine period, which was twenty-one days, after the last fatal case. He was also responsible for maintaining order and discipline among the new arrivals and prisoners who were sent there for manual work. A proper number of policemen and soldiers were kept by the management to maintain discipline. Apart from them, sufficient number of peons and washermen were also employed. No one was allowed to leave or enter the premises during the quarantine period. Ballast was used to sink the dirty clothes of the Indians in the sea, and lime was used to whitewash the walls and bury the dead. The fear of the spread of cholera was so hyped that there was an opinion among the officials to change the site of for quarantine station. A choice was available in the form of Rodrigues Island, but it was very far and so, administration would be difficult. Therefore, the Quarantine Committee recommended that Flat Island should remain the cholera quarantine station and Ile aux Benitiers was to be retained as the one for small pox.[26] The problem was that the authorities always thought that the Indians were responsible for the spreading of these diseases on the island, which did not exist in the colony before they entered.

Further, in Mauritius, the fundamental law on quarantine was established through Articles 27, 28, and 32 of Ordinance no. 6 of 1887. The first two articles dealt with the quarantine of infected vessels and vessels coming from infected ports. Article 32 dealt with fumigation and disinfection of the vessel and cargo. The first four articles of the regulations refer only to the between decks, forecastle, and other parts of the vessel used either for shipping or other purposes by native passengers or crew. It prescribes the burning of sulphur and the washing of the woodwork with a solution of carbolic acid. These articles refer only to the fumigation of that part of the ship which is used by the persons on board, and not to that part of the ship used for cargo. The abandonment of this practice became a legal offence, punishable by fines and imprisonment.

Though the resources related to Mauritius provide detailed information about the quarantine system as an institution, these records fall short of providing adequate information about the condition and treatment of inmates inside the station. On the contrary, we do not have much information about the establishment of the quarantine station as an institution in Natal, but it provides valuable details about its impact on newly arrived Indians, which was also recorded in the annual report of the protector.

In the quarantine station of the destination colony, men were checked by two male medical officers while women were checked by a skilled female nurse.[27] At times, some undeveloped cases of venereal diseases were passed during the medical examination of the recruiting indentured in India itself. The main cause of this, as officers argued, was women migrants, because they were usually examined by an unprofessional person (female) who was probably less efficient than the duly qualified medical man who passed the men.[28] Thus, here the whole issue of examination of female migrants became an important one, because male medical officers were not allowed to examine the female migrants. The Medical superintendents' reports help us to some extent, to understand the process of medical check-ups and treatments of these

Indians. But these reports do not throw light on the methods of treatment. However, one can get information about the depth of the medical examination of these people as reports mentioned the name of the diseases and their symptoms. The following reference of the *pongale* ships (from India to Natal) by a medical officer would be helpful to understand the examination and categorization patterns: '…Good deal of VD amongst them in one form or another, of the women, six we found to be suffering from syphilis, and eleven had vaginal discharge of a suspicious nature'.[29]

In the 1890s, the Natal medical surgeon's report mentioned that in all, about thirty women should (for precaution's sake) be kept back under observation, or till cured. One of the women had a rectovaginal fistula, and another one, a fibroid enlargement of the uterus. Neither of these women were allowed to submit to operations at that time.[30] Thus, in colonial discourse, emigrant bodies, especially women, were subject to tight scrutiny.

When Indian emigrants reached the depot, they were first re-vaccinated. The quarantine became the place where the officials separated the 'healthy' and the 'sick'. Those, who were considered as 'unhealthy', but the colonial medical regime hoped that they could recover, were kept back in the quarantine station.[31] The selection process of emigrants in the quarantine station emphasized that the interest of the colony could not be overlooked in the selection of indentured labourers. Both the colonies established a sanitary department to deal with the sanitation issues of the Indians. Sanitary authorities were supposed to carry out disinfection of the new arrivals' clothing and belongings. During the time of the spread of epidemics in the colonies, the emigrants were subject to higher scrutiny. Those who would not be able to perform their indentureship to the optimum were weeded out and were shipped back to India. After the quarantine period, they had to wait for a minimum period of forty-eight hours up to a maximum of six weeks or even more, depending upon the demands of the planters in the immigration depot. The natives and European settlers did not come into contact with these people as they thought that the Indians brought some diseases which could also affect them.[32]

The inmates who were admitted to the quarantine station received cruel and inhuman treatment. The lack of facilities and the unwillingness of authorities were the main causes of this kind of treatment. An eyewitness—Mrs Christie, widow of Captain Christie who died on the ship *Shah Allum* (1863), described: '…the treatment they received here on the quarantine station of Rodrigues, was the most remarkable and inhuman, and was rendered doubly so in view of the prostrate condition of the survivors'.[33] Dr F. Mouat also described the quarantine law as a 'monstrous absurdity', 'selfish', barbaric, and remorseless; which also caused great expenses and delays. Some of the local practitioners also expressed their opinion against this rigorous form of control. Beaton stated: '...no regulations, however strictly enforced, will ever be sufficient to ward off cholera from this colony.' It has become the fashion of the late years to ascribe all the disease in the colony to the influx of coolie immigration, instead of to the poor sanitary conditions in Port Louis.[34] Inmates expressed their protest in various forms against these ruthless quarantine laws. Even after the Government of India observed the abuses of the quarantine system, the Mauritius and Natal governments continued with these practices.

Classification of Labourers: 'Able', 'Non-able', and 'Invalid'

James Patterson Smith argued that in order to maintain economic benefit in plantation colonies, the colonial government adopted a more civilized, liberal method of control. He mentioned that 'from the perspective of the Colonial Office civilizing the barbarian made him more governable'. He further stated that government activism in the non-white empire and initiatives in colonial religion, education, health, justice, and labour regulation demonstrated a surprisingly liberal bent. However, the riot in Morant Bay, plus a series of smaller indentured coolie-labour riots in British Guiana and threats of such disturbances in Mauritius, made it clear that there was a direct relation between the social health of the sugar colonies and Britain's ability to retain them safely and cheaply. Enlightened policies promoting justice, order, and security were essential to attract new investments that might prevent further economic deterioration. Where the local planter-elites had failed to produce stability, London would have to act. James called these new policies and interferences of England as 'Englandism'. Moreover, because reform would also serve the interests of the masses of colonial subjects, humanitarian groups at home would welcome it.[35] Injustice had provoked bloody clashes in Jamaica and threatened to give Britain a negative reputation that would make it difficult to get cooperative black labour elsewhere. 'Justice to the darker races' would prove more effective than repression in maintaining the empire and promoting trade. Economic as well as social considerations thus demanded government action.[36] As a result, the colonial state came up as a surveillance state to its subject in order to maintain a more civilized and urbanized society.[37]

The physical fitness and health of the immigrants remained the most important issue throughout the indentured period. Recent historiography seems to agree with the official discourse, which showed that the earlier emigrants were not properly recruited, often not physically strong enough, and almost always suffered from bad health, because of which they were considered unfit for work. David Arnold argues that the study of tropical medicine during the nineteenth century was based on race theory, which argued 'different constitutions demanded different treatment...Indians it was said, being constitutionally weaker, could not stand such "heroic" measures as Europeans and accordingly were more likely to succumb to the onslaught of disease'.[38]

In Natal, the newly arrived indentured labourers were classified into two separate groups on the basis of their bodily qualities. The Natal Emigrant Protector Lt. Col. Banastre Pryce Llyod, in 1877, recommended that indentured labourers should be classified into 'able bodied' and 'non-able bodied', and that rate of wages should be fixed accordingly for each group.[39] This categorization into one class or another was not flexible, and required the certificate of a medical man. The upgradation from one class ('non-able' bodied) to another ('able' bodied) only took place after an enquiry was made by the immigrant protector.[40] This classification was supported in the colony for the benefit of the planters on the argument that these planters were forced to pay the same amount to their non-able bodied workers as they paid their best hands. Authorities argued that this kind of classification would also bring benefit for the comfort and well-being of the weak and delicate labourers. Generally, there was some work reserved for women only, that is, the kind of work that suited her 'fragile body'. But some unfortunate, delicate, and 'non-able bodied' men were forced by the protector to do the work reserved for women.[41] In return, they acquired half of the wage that the other men got, that which was fixed for women. This also threatened the masculinity of these male labourers. As the protectors claimed, '...by this kind of process these unfortunate people would be able to recognize their place.'[42] Therefore, the workers were divided not only on the lines of sex, but also on the line of their physical stature and working capability.[43] The notion of 'weak body' had a greater psychological and cultural impact upon the immigrant settlers, which also placed them in the hierarchal set-up of their society. In Mauritius, there was no discrimination on the basis of bodily ability, where 'able' and 'non-able' bodies worked together to fulfil their allotted task. But in both the colonies, the sick and weak labourers were often victims of exploitation by their master, overseers, and *sirdars*. There was a lack of sympathy for Indians of weak and sickly constitution; while the strong and robust, who could work hard, were well treated. Those who were unable to perform their allotted duties due to bodily infirmity or illness were quite neglected or harshly treated.[44]

This type of discrimination based on the body ability produced the concepts of 'degraded masculinity', 'marginal masculinity', and 'socially and culturally disqualified masculinity'.[45] The discourse of exclusion emphasized the collective as the bearer of social inequities. Some forms of social exclusion did envisage distinction 'flowing' from individuals to groups, located within a 'structure' of shame and degradation, representing a social and cultural nadir. The authorities of the Natal colony were well aware about the consequences of this kind of classification, which degraded the non-able body to an economic burden. This might have also encouraged competition among the Indians for well-paid work as well as social status. In the plantation economy, the limited number of women also created a competition among the male indentured for prospective partners. Able-bodied male labourers with higher income attracted more women than the non-able bodied labourers who could not earn enough for themselves. The 'sexual-jealousy' theory of the plantation economy revealed a number of cases in which women left their partners in search of material security.

Here, an example from the work on coolie women by Gaiutra Bahadur would help to strengthen this argument further. Ramautar killed Lutchminia, a seven months pregnant female migrant, in British Guiana. She had left him more than once, the first time for an Indian who grew plantains on the farm where she was killed. But that man became too ill to work, and he could not afford to keep to her any longer. So Lutchminia returned to Ramautar, who ranked low in the plantation hierarchy. He worked as a weeder on Nonpareil, eight miles from Enmore. Weeding was the least-paid job on any plantation, one usually reserved for women. Ramautar was so poor, he owned only one shirt. After the killing, he discarded his shirt, because it was stained with Lutchminia's blood. The author raises the question as to why she left him twice. Was it because, scrawny and pock-marked, he was not terribly heroic as far as avatars of Ram go? Or, did he call her *randi* to her face? With a son to feed and another child on the way, Lutchminia no doubt worried how they would all survive. Because she was pregnant, the plantation eventually stopped giving her work. A month before her murder, she moved in with a man who lived in a same barracks. He was in a shovel gang, which was the best paid gang. These men were generally the strongest, most muscular men on the sugar estates. The author anticipates that the weeder, who owned only one shirt, must have paled in comparison.[46]

Mauritius was the only sugar colony that imported Indian women as wives, not as workers. Women in Mauritius became more vulnerable to exploitation because they lacked contractual guarantee of plantation work, which was available in other plantations, albeit on discriminatory pay. In Natal, women were given lower wages than in other overseas colonies. In Fiji, an indentured male got one shilling for each day, while for women, it was nine pennies.[47] A small portion of Indian women in Mauritius had independent incomes as *ayahs* or domestic servants, but the majority did the unwaged work at home such as raising children, tending to cows and gardens, and selling milk and produce. They also provided casual and seasonal labour to the plantation. During the crop-time, women were able to get work in the plantations at six pence per day with rations. Since they were not employed under the terms of a contract, employers were not entitled to provide them other facilities such as housing and medical facilities. In some estates, planters recruited married women with their husbands at a price of two shillings per month. This was because they wanted to stop the desertion of wives, and by offering work to these women on low wages, they tried to keep the husband and wife together; they also did so because it was usually asked for by the husbands.[48] Thus, the economic position of women in the colonial plantations determined their social as well as legal positions. The secondary economic position of immigrant women in the plantations strengthened their dependency on the male members.

In Natal, there was a provision in coolie laws for females that—'... women should provide only lighter varieties of labour as such female immigrants were fitted for'.[49] However, till 1909, the law did not define the work which women should do. As a result, women were engaged in all kinds of work; but ideologically, this led to differences or variations in terms of wages, because their work was considered 'light'. Women's physical qualities led to their discrimination while getting jobs in high paid sectors, such as in the railways and coal mines. These higher income sectors were reserved for male workers only.

In the coal mines, where a number of hazards were involved, the workers were offered 2 shillings extra a month for working on the surface and 5 shillings extra a month for working underground, in addition to the usual wages given for agricultural work.[50] The women who were employed in coal mines were engaged in surface work, such as picking and storing the coal. Law made the provision that no boy under the age of twelve years, and no female of any age, shall be employed underground.[51] Interestingly, mining also became the metaphor for male sexuality. In other words, it reflected the domain reserved for the muscular and powerful men only.[52]

According to the laws of Mauritius and Natal, like any other indentured-receiving country, they were to provide free medical facilities and comforts to the labourers disabled from work because of their sickness. But soon it was noticed that sickness was a major cause of absenteeism and thus caused a loss of labour force. An enquiry committee was set up, which concluded that emigrants in their first year in the colony experienced constant illness and diseases; while after spending a year in the colony the sickness rate decreased to some extent.[53] This absenteeism soon became a cause of much concern in the colonies, as has been stated by J.F. Trotter, the Protector of Indian Immigrants in Mauritius, '…the fever months in Mauritius were January to May, the absenteeism from illness due to this cause is a source of serious loss to agriculture, upon which the very existence of this colony depends.'[54] The coolie immigration report noted that during 1834–44 in Mauritius, 11 per cent work loss was caused by absenteeism (3,850 men), 8 per cent by sickness (2,800 men), 6 per cent by desertion (2,100 men), and 2 per cent by change of masters (700 men).[55] Authorities in the plantation were strongly of the opinion that Indians were making 'sickness' an excuse to avoid their assigned tasks. The Coolies Immigration Council of Mauritius highlighted—'there is abundant evidence to prove that a large number of men feign sickness to escape from work, which they can do with facility, as there are no means of proving that imposition, except on the occasional visit of the medical attendant; nor of obliging the men to work under such circumstances.'[56] However, one cannot deny that indentured labourers had no other means to escape; they had to resort to the method of 'feigning sickness' as a weapon for excuse and negotiation. The protests of the labourers were hidden in their everyday resistance through various 'weapons of weak'[57] like—absenteeism, insubordination, theft, flight, malingering, feigning illness, destruction of property, and neglect of duty; they did not threaten to 'overthrow the authority at the workplace but constantly undermined it'.[58]

Though the law provided free medical facilities to the sick indentured, it did not assure accurate wages for the period of absence. In Natal, Coolie Law 14 of 1875 made a provision according to which six pence would be deducted from the wages of the indentured for every day of absence due to sickness. The Bengal lieutenant-governor and protector of emigrants soon raised this point—'the wages of the coolie during his first year in Natal are less than six pence a day, and that the Law practically amounts to an indemnification of the employer during the period of the coolie's engagement in which he is most liable to sickness, and is least able to afford any deduction from his earnings.'[59] In Mauritius, emigrants were to get double-cut (deduction of two days' wages, under Article 113 of the Labour Ordinance 1878) for each day's absence from work during their sickness, and no ration would be provided.[60] In Natal, the ration was not payable to the unlawfully absent labourers. Those who were ill or bodily infirm, not caused by his or her own act (which was again not rare), they were entitled to get ration and shelter from their masters. Plantation authorities characterized Indians generally as sick, and particularly as lazy and idle.

Mauritius authorities were looking for alternatives to deal with the supposedly lazy and idle nature of the labourers. Soon, the masters made it a debatable issue in Mauritius if a coolie could be refused rations on the grounds of his laziness.[61] Coolie laws were reformulated so as to provide the planter with the power, under Section 165 of the Mauritius Ordinance no. 12 of 1878, to deduct from the ration issued in advance to the indentured labourers per week, for each day he was absent from work.[62] For a 'habitual idler', who was unlawfully absent for fourteen days in a month or fourteen consecutive days in two months, the punishment was decided as three months' imprisonment and the employers were not bound to pay wages and give rations.[63] Also, disobedient and lazy coolies were liable to be fined one month wages and given a month's imprisonment. This 'habitual idler' (those who chose not to work and starve to death) posed a great threat to the plantation economy's disciplinary mission. The authorities were not able to cope up with the high mortality rate, which was being questioned by the Government of India. For example, the Madras government showed that during 1903, the death rate among the new arrivals was extraordinarily high in some of the estates in Mauritius. The medical inspector of Mauritius gives one probable reason for this, as he says—

...as for the last three batches of immigrants from Madras; that when he inspected them soon after landing he was struck with their fine physique and good condition, but with few exceptions they turned out a set of lazy good-for-nothing habitual idlers and deserters—they therefore received no pay and were seldom entitled to any rations—they soon found starvation starting them in their face, and when the malaria season set in they soon fell victims to the attacks of the disease, as they did not possess sufficient vital energy to resist them. In other words they were practically starved to death.[64]

This kind of resistance was very common not only in Mauritius, but in other countries that received coolies too. It has been seen that during the slavery period, the captured opted for starving to death rather than being a property or economic asset for his or her owner. These resistances by the indentured and, pro-malarial climate of Mauritius, forced the authorities to make some arrangements in terms of food for the newly arrived indentured migrants in the colony.

Apart from this, there was also an arrangement to send those who were classified as 'invalids labourers' back to India. Between October 1901 and July 1911, a total of 3,800 (7 per cent) people out of 54,053 indentured were deported back to India from Natal as invalids. Ashwin Desai and Goolam Vahed stated: '…this included large numbers who contracted phthisis in the coal mines.'[65] The indentured labourers who were mentally ill, blind, or suffered from diseases like phthisis, leprosy, heart and liver diseases, chronic bronchitis, or general debility, were repatriated to India as invalid labourers. The twenty-four-year-old Doorgiah (Coolie 1379)[66] was forced to go back to India on the grounds of having lost his leg and being thereby declared unfit for service.

…After having been in his service for about a year, he was rendered unfit for service by the scar on his leg which seems to have been neglected and after three months it become so bad that he was sent to hospital, when the doctor found it necessary to amputate it. On his leaving hospital he returned to Mr. Middleton's where he was put to light work such as women usually do. After six months he again became ill, when his masters said he was shamming, and gave him a thrashing and he was fined £1 by the magistrate. Mr. Middleton, who told him that he must return to hard work or pay him £ 10 to buy-off his unexpired term of services as he was unable to do hard work. His friends among the coolies raised the £ 10 to pay Mr. Middleton and thus he left. Since his departure he has been living about amongst his friends.[67]

So, at the age of twenty-five, Doorgiah returned to India as an invalid and a burden. In another case, Mewa Ram Bhagirath (128337), who was indentured to Thomas Robinson's estate. His job was to sell five bottles of milk per day. Unable to sell the milk one day, he returned with bottles of unsold milk. An irate Mrs Robinson threw the milk all over him whilst Robinson himself violently assaulted the poor man. The man managed to crawl away to the barracks, and eventually to the Indian market in Grey Street, Durban, where he was found in an exhausted condition. Dr Nanji, an Indian medical practitioner, referred him to the protector who, in turn, referred the matter to the Umlazi magistrate. Mewa Ram was sent to the depot hospital where he spent five to six months, recuperating. Certified a cripple, he was shipped to India in October 1907. He had married Gangajali (128349) while on board, and a few days before the assault she had given birth to a child. Mewa Ram returned home disabled, and without his wife and child.[68]

Plantation colonies were determined to provide hospital treatment to those who really needed it and had the scope to recover in order to benefit the colony. But again, it was very difficult to select the invalids, because a large number of labourers presented themselves as invalids daily.[69] Once an indentured decided to return home as an invalid, he worked very determinedly to fulfil his purpose, and it frequently cost him his life before his purpose was achieved. The medical inspector of the depot hospital of Mauritius, A.H. Wheldon, M.D.C.M., mentioned in his annual report about these willingly invalid labourers, and said—

…he will starve, vagabondize till he is taken up and punished as a vagrant, and then tamper with his eyes by irritating them with lime or some other irritants till he frequently loses them, or irritating any little scratch on his body till it becomes a large sloughing ulcer, frequently ending in death or requiring amputation. If he lives to return to the depot, he generally is in a pitiable state, and much needs invaliding.[70]

This type of resistance was very common among the labourers in the colony; if they failed to become an invalid body, they opted for suicide. Those who were sent back to India on grounds of misconduct or inability to work had to pay one rupee per month for return passage, till they paid off the total expenditure of their departure.[71] Crime and suicide were two major causes of tension in the plantation economy. Indentured labourers were very well aware of the importance of their labouring body in the plantation economy. Mauritius, Natal, and Fiji were the places where the highest rates of suicide among the Indians labourers were reported. The official discourse openly accepted that physical suffering (willingly, injury by self or naturally, known as the 'act of god') was one of the major causes for suicide among the Indians; with the other ones being jealousy and destitution.

Reform Measures and Laws:
Maintenance of Estate Hospitals

...It is a large airy building of wood with a wide verandah round it. The bedsteads are all of iron, and the bedding is clean and ample. Beside each bed there is a good small washstand, fitted with basin, jug, and cup; and at the head of the bed there is a small wooden shelf for the convenience of the patients—every part of the establishment having the advantage of being quite new and in high order. At a few paces from the hospital is the dwelling of the Attendant and the dispensary, the latter being provided with all requisite medicines, splints, and other appliances necessary for simple surgical operations. The hospital attendant was trained in Civil Hospital at Port Louis, receives 25 dollars per mensem and his food and dwelling, and devotes his time exclusively to the hospital.[72]

The Royal Commission Report of 1872 stated the estate hospital in Mauritius as outstanding; they hardly found any other building suitable to be called a hospital. Twenty-five estate hospitals were introduced in Mauritius to tend to the indentured labourers, and the number rose to forty by 1938, under the care of twelve doctors. The French Governor Bertrand-Francois Mahe de La Bourdonnais set up the very first hospital at Port Louis for the treatment of sailors and inhabitants. He established two more hospitals for the treatment of soldiers. There were three main hospitals during the period of the French East India Company (1721–67)—one at Port Louis, another at Grand River North-West, and a third one at Grand Port. The white masters and their slaves on the plantations were treated by moving practitioners as and when they were required. A few large estates had small hothouses or a hospital for their slave population.

The Mauritius Coolie Immigration Report of Council of 1845 came up with the conclusion that during 1834–44, in the ten sugar estates of the colony, there were 8,667 Indians, including women and children who died on the island. Consequently, it was suggested that this proportion was very small and it would not be appropriate to apply the theory of proneness to a high death rate to the whole colony, because of the deaths that had occurred during the last three months of the year due to an epidemic.[73] The report also deduced that the absence caused by sickness in the colony averaged to 8 per cent. In order to control the absenteeism of labourers and high death rate among the indentured in the colony, coolie laws were further revised and reformulated. The high death and sickness rates in the colony also raised questions about the medical knowledge and capabilities of the officials, especially when the cause of the diseases such as malaria was still unknown. Till 1844, the medical facilities and attendance that were provided in Mauritius estates to the labourers proved to be inadequate. The Labour Enquiry Commission of 1838 also reported that government intervention was essential to look into the accommodation, medical treatment, and meal timings allotted to the labourers. There was however, much opposition to official enquiries by the planters in certain districts. Planters were always against any enquiry and reform policies related to the indentured labourers, which they saw as detrimental to their own interest and benefit. In consequence of the enquiry, Ordinance no. 40 of 1844 was framed to regulate medical care, lodgings, and food for the Indian indentured, more efficiently. The necessity to build a district or central hospital for the special treatment of acute epidemics in the colony was realized.

In Mauritius, the epidemic fever of 1844 and the high mortality rate among the indentured Indians raised several questions. An enquiry committee was set up to enquire about the condition of the medical facilities in the colony—like the number of medical practitioners and the average number of persons under his service, the total expenditure on the medical facilities, etc.[74] The fear of the epidemic also led to a rising demand for public hospitals in each district of the colony. The total Indian population in Mauritius during 1844 was 440,532, residing in the nine districts of the island. The Government of Mauritius had employed a total of 37 medical practitioners for the entire Indian population. Out of these 37, the number of practitioners residing across the country districts were 25; and the rest of the 12, apart from being stationed at the towns, gave their attendance in the districts of Moka, Plaines Wilhems, Black River, and Pamplemousses South.[75] In the district of Moka, 7 medical practitioners were employed for every 808 labourers employed in different estates; in Plaines Wilhems, this proportion was 9 for every 4,155 labourers; in Savanne, 3 for every 4,085 labourers; in Grand Port, 2 for 5,187 labourers; in Flacq district, 3 for 8,159 labourers; in Riviere du Rempat, 3 for 8,901 labourers; in Pamplemousses North, it was 5 for 5925 labourers; and in Pamplemousses South, 8 medical practitioners for every 4,590 labourers.[76] The last three districts were managed by the same medical practitioners; it seemed that they were managing, at the same time, a total of 18,786 people. The committee came to the conclusion that except the district of Moka, where an extra medical practitioner was required, in all the other districts, the labourers were abundantly provided with medical attention. The committee in fact stated that the number of individuals falling under the charge of each medical man was below the capacity which he had in his power to attend. The medical men resided in the immediate neighbourhood of their allotted estates, so that they were able to give the promptest attendance when required. They were also allotted a carriage for travelling to the adjoined area by roads. The committee also decided that there was no need to establish public hospitals in the different districts of the colony; rather, they recommended that each proprietor was obliged to maintain a suitable hospital on his or her estate. Each estate hospital needed to acquire an approval from the Civil and Medical Authorities of the districts.

Committee estimates showed that the total yearly expense on the appointment of medical practitioners and their helpers for the nine districts of the Island would be 14,373 pounds. The committee took into consideration that the contagious diseases, which attacked the Indians, had disappeared completely from many estates; therefore, the public hospitals were no longer required for the indentured. The committee was also of the opinion that these would increase the expenses, as the report says, '…it would be manifestly useless because in all probability, the planter possessing a suitable hospital upon his own estate and the service of a medical practitioners in whom he has confidence, would not send his invalid labourers to the public hospital'.[77] Till this time, the government was not ready to spend money for the benefit of the non-labour body, including the natives and the free and invalid labourers. Medical facilities were provided only to those who were beneficial to the state economy. As such, no government district hospital was established until the end of the nineteenth century. The notion of public health emerged in the colonies during the late nineteenth and the early twentieth century, when the knowledge of the spreading of diseases through air and water; from one person to another, became popular.

In order to secure the health of the indentured labourers, the Government of Mauritius passed three ordinances, namely: Ordinance 6 of 1845, Ordinance 29 of 1865, and Ordinance 12 of 1878. As the enquiry committee of 1844 noted, the hospitals for the use of labourers on the estates were small, less in number and inefficient. In 1838, Magistrate Anderson wrote—'The hospitals on the establishments which I have seen, are generally more calculated to increase disease than to alleviate its sufferings…'[78] Ordinance no. 40 of 1844, titled 'Hospitals,

Lodgings and Articles of Food to be Supplied to Labourers on Rural Estates', defined for the first time the laws for the estate hospitals in Mauritius. This required that on every estate, which employed forty or more labourers, the proprietors were required to set a convenient place in the form of a building, properly enclosed and fit for the use as hospital, for the treatment of labourers.[79] The revised version of this ordinance was passed as Ordinance no. 6 of 1845, after the removal of the word 'retention' of Indians at the hospitals. It was required that labourers should be supplied with all necessary medicines and treatments by these hospitals, failing which they would be liable to pay a fine of hundred shillings. The fitness of the site and building, intended to be used as an estate hospital for the labourers, needed to acquire a fitness certificate from two government medical officers—one from the assigned district, and another from the adjoining districts. In case of difference of opinion of two medical officers, the matter would be transferred to another medical officer appointed by the chief medical officer of the Island. The fitness certificate cost one pound sterling. In case of failure to produce this certificate on demand, the estate owner was liable to pay a fine of five pounds sterling, and ten pounds sterling on failing to do so for the second time. The ordinance also recommended that no labourer should be confined to the hospital without proper reference of the medical inspector. A proper register of records, such as the admission and release of inmates and nature of their diseases, was to be maintained by the medical officers. The inclusion of this particular article into the ordinance showed that inmates were often forced to remain within the four walls of the hospital without their consent. In 1840, the Supreme Court of Mauritius sentenced one estate owner for having confined a group of Indians for forty hours, by locking the doors; on the instructions of the doctor. The Mauritian newspapers published the local opinion about this confinement, which held Supreme Court's decision as wrong and stated that sick Indians had to be confined in order not to spread diseases among other inhabitants.[80] The ordinance asserted that the labourers could be examined only after their consent, except in the case of insanity and contagious diseases.

However, in spite of all these regulations, the health of the indentured labourers on the estates did not improve. Although a number of laws were passed and estate hospitals were established for providing better treatment and medical facilities to the Indians, the government authorities could not force planters either to keep their labourers in healthy condition or to make them abide by the contract.

Thus, the hospitals were usually neglected by the planters and avoided by the labourers; and consequently, these buildings soon turned into animal sheds, where very sick people were left to die.[81] The Indians always complained about the treatment and the facilities that they received in these hospitals. Thus, the system of estate-managed hospitals failed to cope up with the high rates of sickness and death among the labourers on the island. The hard, back-breaking working conditions at the sugar plantations contributed to the increasing prevalence of diseases such as bronchitis, pneumonia, and heart diseases. According to Tinker, thus, '…the plantations brought sickness and premature death'. Sickness and hard labour soon turned the young able bodies to non-able and old, bodies.

Twenty years after failing to achieve its target of Ordinance no. 6 of 1845, the Government of Mauritius came up with another regulation, Ordinance no. 25 of 1865, related to the medical care of the labourers on the estates. This was the time when the demand for more labourers was prevalent, with the extension of the indentured contract period from one to three years and finally, in 1863, from three to five years. In order to stop the return of the indentured to India after the completion of their contract period in the colony, the right of their free return passage was removed. Only those who were not considered, 'suitable' labour bodies and held as a burden in the colony, such as the—old, widows, orphans, invalids, and lepers: were allowed a free return passage. There was a strong opinion among the authorities and planters that large numbers of people returned to their country after saving a good amount of money and those who were left in the Island were mostly unfit to work. [82] Therefore, necessary laws were reformulated and reconstructed to control the 'able body' labourers. This 'control' agenda came with more action on the part of the governments, bringing in better and stricter medical and sanitary facilities with the motive of getting a continuous labour force.

The 1850s were marked by various diseases that killed hundreds of inhabitants in the colony, and health conditions here, deteriorated considerably. In 1858, the government appointed the Medical Charity Commission (MCC) to find out the causes for inferior health of the inhabitants.[83] The MCC recorded their dissatisfaction with the conditions and facilities of the civil hospital. It emphasized that the civil hospital was very too small to cope with the present population; and also that the present location of the hospital was not suitable, as it was close to the harbour and thus exposed to pollution. The current conditions of the hospital showed that it was not well kept, and the pharmacy was neither clean nor supplied with sufficient medicines.[84] The attendants of the hospital were mostly rejected labourers, who were illiterate and with no experience in nursing. The MCC proposed to build a new hospital building, recruit qualified hospital attendants and also the 'sisters of charity', who were more experienced nurses, to take care of the patients. They also recommended cleaner wards, a larger kitchen, better privies, and baths suitable as per the habits of the Indians. Recommendations were also made for a better diet. The Indians who did not consume beef because of religious scruples, were proposed goat's meat. The most important recommendation that was made was the establishment of a medical and a surgical school at the civil hospital to provide training to the staff. A scheme was also presented to build a government hospital in each district for the Indians and the Creoles. Dr J.A. Finnimore, Government Medical Officer, suggested the construction of district hospitals, where Indian labourers could be treated for serious diseases, the treatment of which was difficult in the estate hospitals. All of these recommendations were appreciated by the government; and some measures were also taken regarding the location of the civil hospital, now shifted to Plaine Lauzun in the western suburb of Port Louis. The MCC was seriously against the construction of the district hospitals, as it thought that the centralization of the sick at one place would be harmful for the community. Another problem was about the expenditure, emoluments, and loads of responsibilities of the practitioners. Thus, as a result of all these constraints, no serious consideration was given by the government and planters to any of the recommendations made by the MCC.

During 1867, the outbreak of malaria in the colony raised alarm and terror among the authorities. Dr Henry Rogers, Senior Assistant Surgeon to the civil hospital, stated that: '...the year 1867 will long be remembered in Mauritius as one of the most disastrous in the annals of its history.'[85] At the same time, there was a tremendous change in the ideology of the new government officials, who now wanted some improvement in the living and working conditions of indentured labourers in India and abroad. Several enquiry committees were set up to investigate the condition of the labourers in overseas colonies and in Assam. As a result, the Government of Mauritius passed Ordinance no. 29 of 1865, in order to modify the law concerning hospitals and medical attendants on the estates. The governor openly admitted that the law was of a stringent nature, explaining the need to invest the executive

Plate 4.4: Ward at Maberbourg Hospital: Small Windows for Ventilation closed
by Shelter Authorities

Source: Andrew Balfour, *Report on Medical Matters in Mauritius.*

government with a more effectual power of supervision over the estate hospitals.[86] The main object of this ordinance was to deal with epidemics, such as malarial fever, in the colony. It made the provision that each estate or even job contractor, employing or having thirty labourers or more, had to make arrangements to provide access to a hospital to the labourers. This ordinance also introduced two major changes. First, it provided the right to the immigrant protector to visit any estate at any time and provide a full report about the condition of labourers, provisions of hospitals and medical facilities, etc., to the governor. But it could not operate for a long period as the planters saw this step as an unnecessary interference that put an extra financial burden over them; therefore, it was withdrawn in 1868. The second major provision was that any labourer refusing to enter the hospital could be classed as illegally absent, and employers were given the right to force their labourers to enter the hospital.[87]

This ordinance defined the architecture and size of the estate hospital for the betterment of the patients. It recommended that a hospital should be situated on a convenient site, built of stone and planking roof with tiles or slates; its size was required to be 60 sq. ft. as per imperial standard measures, and 500 cu. ft. respectively for each bed.[88] On failing to provide these facilities, the estate owners and job contractors were liable to be fined between two and ten pounds sterling. The medical facilities extended its boundary from indentured labourers to their wives and children as well; but it was only through the Labour Law of 1878 that separate wards for males and females were provided.[89] The ordinance also made a provision according to which the practitioners had to visit the estates with less than two hundred labourers, once a week and twice a week for estates exceeding two hundred labourers.[90] It further made the provision that estate practitioners had to reside within 10 mi. from the hospital. In order to know the causes of diseases in the colony, the need for the proper documentation of health was realized. Despite many loopholes, the annual report of the medical department continued to publish favourable accounts of healthcare in the colony. The Ordinance no. 25 of 1865 emphasized that any medical practitioner, who signed or made a false entry in the medical register or provided false certificates, would be liable to be fined.[91] On the importance of medical statistics, Dr Mouat stated that it, '…reformulated the past, renders the present fruitful, and prepares the future…the medical information is necessary to control future outbreak or, if possible, to prevent their recurrence by stamping them out…'.[92] It helped to revisit the mistakes and correct them.

The medical registers of the Mauritius estate hospitals provide information about the management of the hospitals according to the Immigration Act or Coolie Law of the colony. These also provide information about the condition of the hospitals in each district, such as—whether the hospitals had acquired the certificate from the medical board or not; how many people, male, female, and children, under indentured contract, were admitted and treated in the hospitals; whether the hospitals provided enough space and beds according to the legal number; whether the supply of medicines and equipment was satisfactory at the hospitals; whether the hospitals followed the provision of providing clean water; whether the hospitals maintained regulations in the Indian languages; what the diet scale of the hospitals was; and whether they were working satisfactorily. This was the schedule of data collection, which was followed by each hospital in each district. However, in answer to these questions there are only two words mentioned—'yes' or 'deficiency'; the reports are also silent on the type of deficiency or the improvement required.[93] Therefore, it is difficult to get information about the types of diseases and their treatment, and the number of patients who suffered from various diseases, apart from the major epidemics.

In contrast to any other overseas country, the situation in Mauritius was different, where the planters had enough power to modify their interests. In Jamaica and Trinidad, it was the responsibility of the government to appoint medical practitioners for the estate hospitals, while the planters in Mauritius exercised their own discretion in employing and paying the medical staff. This provision might have worked as a source of pressure for the medical practitioners and often forced them to work according to the interest of the planters, the doctors were paid by the planters. If they failed to visit estates, their salaries were retained by their employers, in the same way as the wages of the labourers were deducted if they failed to perform their task. Suggestions were thus made for the doctors to be servants of the government, rather than the planters' servants. As always, the planters tried as far as possible to limit government intervention in the administration of health care on the estates. Planters opposed the new regulation which stipulated that if a hospital was not erected within the given time period of three months and within 3 mi. from the camp, any requisition for new labourers would not be accepted by the immigration

PLATE 4.5: Ward of the Moka Hospital—the best of the Government Hospitals in Mauritius

Source: Andrew Balfour, *Report on Medical Matters in Mauritius.*

PLATE 4.6: Part of the Administrative block of New Lepers Asylum,
Pamplemousses district

Source: Andrew Balfour, *Report on Medical Matters in Mauritius.*

department. However, even these measures of the ordinances of 1865
could not bring any betterment to the lives of the Indians. Even the
Ordinance 12 of 1878 did not provide any detailed instruction regarding
the internal management of the hospitals, bath and bedding, kitchen,
sanitary measures, etc.; and the proposed number of beds in the
hospitals was three for the hundred labourers and no treatment facilities
were available for less than thirty labourers.[94] The Labour Law of 1878,
however, reduced this number from thirty to twenty labourers. George
Campbell stated that the legislation of 1867 (Labour Law)—'could only
be suited to the military administration of a conquered people of
desperation and ungovernable character'.

The sugar industry was going through a depression because of
climatic changes and epidemics, such as cholera and malaria. In order
to find a solution to this problem, Governor Barkley came with the
repressive Labour Law of 1868 to bring the Indians back to the estates
as indentured labourers.[95] The ideological ground of this law was that
the planters were still ready to ensure the welfare of Indians on their
estates. In the 1870s, regular medical facilities were extended to the
prisoners and the road labourers as well. The Ordinance no. 11 of 1870
was passed to promote public health in the island of Mauritius.[96] The
General Board of Health as well as the Local Board of Health were
established in Mauritius. The ordinance emphasized on the cleaning of

all public or private roads, drains, sewers, gutters, and watercourses; the purifying and disinfecting of houses, dwellings, premises, yards, and cemeteries; controlling the quarantine station, market areas, butcher shops, and overcrowding of men and animals.[97] At the same time, it aroused the need for the control of the Indian population who were residing outside the estates and thus were spreading, according to them, not only dirt and diseases, but crime as well. A new Medical Enquiry Commission reported that the death rate among free Indians was higher than that among indentured labourers.[98] In spite of all these attempts to improve the conditions of the indentured Indians, the Royal Commission Report of 1875 still proved that their condition had not changed as they were still not paid regularly; ill treatment, violence, and assault were common; no medical facilities was given on time; and commonly received were unjustly blamed for vagrancy, idleness, gang robberies, and filthy habits. Some officials amongst the authority were also of the opinion that there should be a higher medical institute in the colony, and that there should not be separate regulations for the estate and non-estate medical facilities and benefits.

The very first Natal Immigration Law 14 of 1859 defined the medical rights of the indentured labourers in the colony. It said that every owner of the coolies needed to provide proper medical care and medicines to the latter. In case of failure, the owner was liable for an imprisonment not exceeding thirty days and the lieutenant governor was given the right to transfer his coolie to another master.[99] However, this law could not define the establishment and maintenance of the estate hospitals, and could not even enforce the planters to obey it. On the contrary, it stated that 12 shillings per annum had to be deducted for medical services as well as for accommodation from the monthly salary of the indentured. The lack of definition of the medical facilities on estates soon came up when the first group of indentured labourers, after completing their contract and industrial residency, came back to India. These people complained about the irregular payment of wages, ill treatment, abuse and flogging by the planters, and bad or no medical facilities on the estates. They complained that there were more irregularities in the medical sphere than in any other. However, according to law, the masters were bound to provide an estate hospital and a doctor to their labourers. The Coolie Commission of 1872, however, stated that many estates discontinued the estate hospitals because the planters found that Indians were not willing to make use of these institutions.[100] Estates near Durban sent their labourers directly to the

Durban hospital; while many estates had a small building which served as a rudimentary hospital. The Commission, with evidences, showed that Indians were averse to any kind of hospitalization. On this subject Mr Lamport stated—'The coolies are averse to going into hospital, even to the Government Hospital at Durban. There was one at Reunion, but the coolies could not be induced to enter it, and when they were compelled, I had to lock the door to keep them there. They prefer their own huts'.[101]

On the basis of these evidences before the Committee, one member suggested that it was useless to erect hospitals. Initially, many estates deducted one shilling per month from the wages of the labourers for medical expenses. On some estates, doctors were paid one rupee per month per patient and then; only called out whenever necessary; as they were not forced to stay on the estates. On some other estates, the full expenses of sending a sick person to the hospital was paid by the estate. The Commission also questioned the employers' reaction towards the directions of the doctors while treating a patient. Mr Shepstone exposed a serious weakness in this regard, as he stated—'The direction of the medical officers are generally attended to, when the remedies and medicines ordered are simple and inexpensive; but I am afraid that when he recommends or orders rare and expensive medicines, or nutritious and strengthening diet, his directions are not generally attended to by all the employers.'[102]

Thus, evidences show that the employers provided very irregular and disappointing medical treatment to their employees, despite the fact that nearly all reported to the Commission that the services of a doctor—'are available when required'. This criterion of 'requirement' was left to the planters to decide. However, as a result of the discontinuation of indentured labour from India and the Report of the Coolie Commission of 1872, the Natal government revised the Indian Immigration Law no. 2 of 1870.[103] This law required that, under Section 22, an employer with more than twenty labourers had to provide an estate hospital with sufficient medical facilities. Further, the revision added that to keep a check on diseases among the indentured, there was a provision that on every estate or circle (the lowest medical administrative unit), where twenty Indian families were employed by planters, there should be a central hospital for the Indians. The purpose of these hospitals was not only to control or provide immediate treatment to sick Indians, but also to try centralizing the sick.[104] Moreover, the employers were now bound to send a monthly medical report of their estates to the immigration agent. Each employer was also required to retain a qualified, licensed, and registered medical practitioner to attend to the labourers. However, these provisions of health facilities were not provided to the free (non-estate) coolies in the colony. Also, all the unlawfully absent labourers were entitled to lose all claims of wages and allowances, and a fine of 'half penny' for each shilling of their monthly wages, for each day's absence, was charged. Two years later, Law no. 12 of 1872 provided the power to the state to appoint a medical practitioner to attend to the Indian immigrants on various estates. In return, the estate owners had to pay six pence per month to the Natal Treasury for the medical care of immigrants.[105] This amount was further raised to one shilling per month by the Law no. 19 of 1874. The Natal government established the 'Indian Immigrants Trust Board 1872', for better medical treatment of immigrants in the colony and on ships. This trust was responsible for the expenditure on medical benefits, establishment of new hospitals wherever necessary, and the appointment of medical practitioners and surgeons. Every medical officer was required to visit every estate, in which thirty or more Indians were employed, at least once a week; and every other estate, where more than five persons were employed, once a fortnight. Natal, in contrast to Mauritius, thus succeeded in achieving the 'governmentalization' of medical facilities for the indentured labourers. In the Law no. 14 of 1875, it was recommended that in case of the need for the establishment of a small hospital, a levy of one shilling per month could be imposed on the employers; for this purpose. Apart from all these measures, the system of health facilities in the colony, as C.G. Henning stated, can be described as something of a failure. The Wragg Commission, the second official investigation into the conditions and treatment of Indian immigrants in the colony of Natal, revealed the totally unsatisfactory state of affairs in the management of medical care for the sick. An investigation of the Durban depot hospital revealed that the hospital was understaffed as there were shortages of female nurses, and also of wards for men and women, and for infectious or chronically ill patients. The supply of drugs was found to be adequate, but the toilet facilities remained rather primitive.

After the 1890s, when the germ theory started gaining acceptance in medical science, great attention was paid towards the maintenance of these hospitals, and a large amount was spent on the building and architecture of these institutions. Old buildings were distempered in order to disinfect them. A large bathroom was erected in the establishment for the comfort and convenience of the patients. A large new, hospital was established in Durban, which was 110 ft. long and 23 ft. wide, with an 8 ft. verandah on each side. The building was divided into three wards, two for males and one for females; latrines were also erected separately for males and females; and the dead house, attendant's rooms, and quarters for the compounder were put up. This hospital was entirely under the control and management of the medical officer Dr Greene, who resided in the immediate neighbourhood.[106]

However, it would be important to note here that the real picture was very different, as hospitals and other facilities exhausting these were not appropriate when compared to the needs of the Indian population. In this context, the annual report of 1904 would be helpful in throwing light on the real condition of these hospitals. As the medical inspector mentioned, '…the present hospital is insufficient for the requirements of the circle. As the numbers of beds in the hospital is 25, these figures show a dangerous state of overcrowding…in addition to this a number of patients have been visited on the employers' estates and many have also been attended at my house.'[107] This might be a major reason behind the immigrants avoiding going to the hospitals.

In 1904, on the estate of Umhloti Valley (Natal), the medical officer reported that the highest number of deaths among the indentured labourers was from dysentery. The death rate increased at an alarming rate to 91 per 1000, the highest figure when compared to other colonies. The situation went from bad to worse as diseases like dysentery, ankylostomiasis, malaria, and pneumonia; continued to considerably reduce the number of 'healthy males' in the estate. The enquiry committee came to the conclusion that the high rate of death and sickness was due to the unsatisfactory conditions of the estate hospital and the ineffectiveness of the medical officer. The committee demanded that the estate hospital be disbanded, patients be taken to the central hospital, the hospital doctor named Dr Elliot be transferred, and more white supervision on the estate be provided. This also implied that no further recruitment was allowed in the estate until the health conditions improved. This revealed the inefficiency of medical facilities in the estate hospitals.

In Natal, Indians were employed in different sectors of the economy, and not just in the plantations. They were often employed as domestic servants, in railways, in coal mines, etc. The coolies in the railways and coal mines were treated in the coolie railway hospitals and coal mines hospitals respectively. These coolie hospitals were erected on the same footing as the estate hospitals, and abided by the Natal Indentured Laws. The medical benefits mentioned in the indentured laws were, however, not applicable for the domestic servants. The domestic servants were treated by the doctors of the civil hospital. The provision that the master of a servant was obliged to provide medical facilities to the servant whenever required; was made by law.

In the processing of the 'fit body, fit labour', the colonial Natal government took the support of the planters; and thus, the planters were playing the role of arbitrators for the Indian migrants, whose main responsibility was to look after immigrants' medical benefits and health issues. Planters were bound to call a doctor and provide proper treatment if any immigrant fell ill in his estate.[108] It was recommended that every employer keep a clinical thermometer, to measure the temperature of emigrants, for daily use; and if the body temperature of any worker was found to be more than 100 degrees Fahrenheit, then the worker was supposed to be sent to the medical officer.[109] On the plantations, a rule was made that every adult male should get checked weekly. The law also mentioned that if any immigrant failed to fulfil his responsibility regarding his health issues or visit the hospital whenever required, he would have to pay two pounds sterling for each offence in the court.[110]

Contrary to the Mauritius hospital reports, medical reports of Natal estate hospitals provide a lot of information regarding the classification of diseases, the number of patients, and the mortality rate among the indentured, apart from the management of hospitals. The number of deaths among the indentured, caused by different diseases in the colony, is given in Table 4.1. The diseases ranged from the usual ones like: asthma, dysentery, debility, etc. (see Table 4.2); to peculiar ones, such as 'old age' and 'weak intellect'. In the Annual Report of the protector of Indian immigrants in Natal for the year 1902, a total of 11 cases of 'weak intellect' were recorded.[111] The 'old age' and 'weak intellect' were some of those which made labourers less productive for the plantation economy.

The number of patients, shows that the colonial medical regime failed to control the spread of diseases and their causes. In these circumstances, they blamed the Indians for their illnesses; they tried to bring some reforms regarding their sanitation, and also tried to control their food habits and personal hygiene.

The indigenous people were left by the state to look after their health issues by themselves, as they were not economically useful for the

TABLE 4.1: Number of Deaths among Indians and the Diseases Causing them, registered for the Year 1908

Causes of Death	Number	Causes of Death	Number
Measles	21	Old age	16
Influenza	2	Meningitis	13
Whooping cough	18	Diseases of brain and spinal cord	21
Diphtheria	1	Diseases of heart and blood vessels	49
Enteric fever	6	Bronchitis	115
Diarrhoea, dysentery, and enteritis	301	Other diseases of respiratory tract	16
Cerebro-spinal meningitis	3	Pneumonia	256
Anthrax	1	Diseases of stomach	7
Puerperal fever	13	Appendicitis	3
Other septic diseases	6	Peritonitis	14
Tetanus	8	Obstruction of intestine	5
Gonorrhoea	3	Cirrhosis of liver	6
Syphilis	40	Nephritis and Bright's disease	67
Malarial fever	83	Tumours and other affections of female genital organs	1
Tuberculosis of lungs	226	Accidents and diseases of parturition	31
Tuberculosis of other forms	50	Deaths by accidents or negligence	49
Anaemia	7	Burns and scalds	52
Anchylostomiasis	29	Homicide	11
Other intestinal parasites	9	Suicide	32
Cancer	13	Deaths from ill-defined causes	107
Premature birth	25	All other causes	58
Debility and developmental diseases	161	Total	1,955

Source: Annual Report of the Protector of Indian Immigrants in Natal for the year 1908, Commerce and Industry Department (Emigration Branch) Proceedings, July 1909, nos. 12–13, NAI.

TABLE 4.2: Diseases in Indians registered for the Year 1877

Diseases	Numbers	Diseases	Numbers
Adenitis	1	Diarrhoea	14
Asthma	3	Disease of knee joint	2
Bronchitis	6	Dislocation	1
Boils	1	Debility	3
Constipation	1	Fever	53
Cataract	2	Fistula	1
Colic	1	Hernia	2
Contusion	1	Hydrocele	2
Dropsy	4	Incontinence of urine	1
Dysentery	8	Itch	1
Leprosy	9	Malarious cachexia	10
Necrosis of bone	3	Oedema of feet	3
Ophthalmia	4	Piles	1
Paralysis	2	Parturition	1
Skin eruption	2	Rheumatism	9
Splenitis	3	Syphilis	7
Stricture	2	Ulcers	13
Abscess	1	Total	178

Source: Annual Report of the Protector of Immigrants in Mauritius for the year 1877, Revenue, Agriculture and Commerce Department (Emigration Branch) Proceedings, September 1878, nos. 1–2, part A, NAI.

plantation economy. The indigenous population had their own healing practices and healers. Khoisan practices, which included childbirth in women and healing through the use of a range of methods such as poultices, lancing, and incisions, led to the growth of a Creole folk medicine.[112] Until 1889, all private healthcare services were funded by out of pocket payments and were restricted to the White population only.[113] In Natal, initially, all private hospitals were limited to mission hospitals and gave only industry-specific facilities, such as on-site hospitals at large mines. The mission hospitals played an important role in providing health services to the African people in Natal (South Africa). The first two public hospitals were established in 1755: one for the whites and another for the non-Whites.[114] A major epidemic of small pox forced the government to establish public hospitals in the colony for the treatment of the native population. The Public Health Act of 1883 in Natal, and 1894–5 in Mauritius, extended the health facilities to all the inhabitants of the colonies.

4.4 Doctors on Plantations: Mauritius and Natal

…Medical men should be of most efficient and reliable character, subordinates should be zealous and attentive to their duties, and entirely devoted to their performance while the superior should be wholly disengaged from other pursuits, should be free from the interruptions of private practice thoroughly imbued with a conviction of the importance of his high duties—familiar with all modern improvements in the various institutions belonging to his departments—strict in his examination of details—prompt in the disclosure of imperfections, and above all, bold and unflinching in the assumptions of responsibility.[115]

The measures against epidemics and the high rate of sickness and death in the plantation colony raised the expectations from the medical institutions and practitioners. In plantation economy, the government sought doctors who were educated at leading medical schools in Europe and North America. Few highly qualified doctors came until the latter part of the eighteenth century; and those who did come, treated chiefly the white inhabitants in the colonies. During the era of slavery, the slaves either cared for themselves or were treated by apothecaries and surgeons who had been trained by apprenticeship and by hospital instructions; but rarely held a degree.[116] Most of these doctors came from professional, mercantile, and especially planters' families.[117] Richard B. Sheridan argued that in the era of slavery, though white doctors failed to provide basic facilities to the slaves; they made an effort to learn from the folk wisdom of the Blacks, studied their herbal remedies, and searched out indigenous plants that had medicinal properties. Moreover, they became more knowledgeable about how the health of slaves was affected by such problems as malnutrition, fatigue, poor sanitation, and lack of proper clothing and shelter. They urged planters and overseers to provide: the sick and ailing slaves with treatment in hospitals serviced by Black medical attendants; and childcare centres for pregnant women, mothers with children lying-in wards, midwives, and nurses.[118] But in practice, the Black slaves were not benefitted from these measures. Sharla Fett in her pioneer work on the southern slave plantations, shows that the white doctors, during the era of slavery, fulfilled the non-healers' roles as medical experts.[119] She strongly emphasized that during this period, the character of medical treatment was based on the economic values of slaves.[120] In order to prove her point, she cited two cases. In one instance, in 1835, Alfred Eggleston sent an enslaved man, George, to Mettauer, bearing a request for an operation on a 'stricture' (an obstruction of the urinary passage). 'You will please take the case in hand', Eggleston wrote, 'He is a very valuable slave and I feel great solicitude about him'. In another case from 1839, the medical practitioner received a note that bore instructions concerning the treatment of an older slave: '…I have [sent] old Bob to come and see if you can do him any good… If you can without too much expense you will please afford him relief if you can.'[121] She shows that in legal terms, a slave had no independent voice in determining the treatment, no recourse to resist an undesired treatment, and no grounds for seeking restitution for negligence or inappropriate treatment.[122]

Fett further emphasized that, during the slavery period, in some instances, slaveholders intentionally employed medicine as punishment. The context of physical control blurred the line between medicine and plantation discipline, and also treatment and torture. Some enslaved labourers had to choose between the unpleasant effects of medicine and different types of corporal punishment. To cite an example, when Charles Grandy complained of sickness in order to mask the fact that he had not performed his required fieldwork, a suspicious 'boss' ordered him to take a dose of vomit-inducing ipecac. Grandy was left sick for several days, but managed in this difficult way to avoid being whipped. Fett mentions numerous examples in which slave owners forced slaves to drink enormous doses of castor oil and salts, and then incarcerated them under an overturned coffin-like box for the night, effectively burying them in their own waste. Thus, she argues that in the slavery system, medicine became a tool of dominance rather than a measure for restoring health. Apart from that, black bodies were also used as units to conduct various medical experiments, which were not possible and socially not acceptable on the white bodies. White practitioners used to think of the Black female body as being less sensitive to pain than the White female body.[123] The famous experiments included different types of surgery; study of the ability of the women to reproduce, and the effect of anaesthesia on the body; the thickness of the Black body from which the physician peeled off layers of skin to determine how thick the black skin went.

In Europe, until the middle of the nineteenth century, epidemic diseases, rather than endemic illnesses, were the main prompts for government action. Until 1842, in Britain, even after the influential

Chadwick Report of Public Health of 1842, it was not a part of the government policy to manage the healthcare of workers. In Christianity, it was the civic duty of the able people to provide care to the poor, and also give grounds for establishing hospitals for the sick.[124] Initially, the missionaries in the colonies were more concerned with the moral and religious well-being of the labourers rather than with corporeal well-being. They established churches and schools for the Indians. In the course of time, the colonies the higher epidemic zone being forced them to help the white community in imparting the sanitary teachings to the Indians and the native people. In the nineteenth century, medical missionaries offered orthodox medical health care that initially differed little in outcome from that of traditional healers. The purpose and the task of the nurse in missionaries was to—'moralize and save the sick and not simply serve them.'[125] Thus, missionaries played an important role in providing basic health facilities to the natives. Some of them also raised their voices against the indentured practices; but in the long term, missionaries tried to maintain a harmonious situation on the estates by teaching the labourers to follow the belief and behaviour of the white community.

The condition of doctors in the plantations was much better than the doctors on the indentured ships. These voyages always contained danger and risk to life. Therefore, most well-educated and experienced persons, who were looking for a better future and luxurious life, opted for position of medical officers in the colonies. On the other hand, as I have discussed in the previous chapter, most of the surgeons were young and inexperienced. In the colonies, the medical officers also had the opportunity to acquire a great amount of wealth by private practice and by treatment of the planters and their families. Most of the doctors in the colonies also simultaneously held various powerful positions, such as of that of an estate owner, immigrant protector, and even as a magistrate. The planters and the estate doctors had a friendly relation (as an acting magistrate).

The business of medicine in the plantations proved rewarding only for a minority of doctors. In Natal, in the over fourteen medical circles, only seventeen medical officers were employed; in Mauritius, it was seventeen for twenty-five estate hospitals.[126] A successful doctor residing in the estate house was unlikely to pay rent; he was also provided with carriage and horses for free, if there were more than one estates under his charge. Governor Scott (British Guiana) estimated in 1871 that at least two estate doctors were in receipt of over 1000 pounds per annum, while the majority earned less than 500 pounds. Apart from that, these estate doctors also practiced privately. The huge profit from private practice made some of them unwilling to attend estate hospitals, or spare little time for the labourers.

The enquiry reports showed that during times of epidemics, the doctors were least willing to attend to the sick people. At times of cyclones, in Mauritius, it was very difficult for doctors to attend the estate hospitals; because in order to reach some of the estates, the doctors had to cross rivers. Other than that, long distance was a very common cause for the doctors declining to visit the estate hospitals. Therefore, the geographical distance of the location of practice was a major cause for the poor distribution of the health facilities. In order to conquer this difficulty, laws were formulated to train a new class of officers in the hospitals as dispenser stewards. In 1879, about 260 young men received their qualification as dispensers.[127] They could visit camps and provide simple prescriptions to the sick ones in the absence of the doctors. More profit was available for the riskier works; for example, in Mauritius, a doctor received an extra ten pounds per month for attending to the lepers.

In the colony of Mauritius, the beginning of the twentieth century was marked by a higher death rate among the newborn babies and more stillbirths than before. This higher death rate alarmed the officials and forced them to recruit trained female nurses for caring for the newborns. Suggestions were made to train female nurses in the public hospitals of the colony.[128] So, the sugar estate hospitals had the opportunity to acquire the services of properly trained female attendants. In the year 1902, the number of female nurses appointed by the estate hospitals went upto 69, from 43 in 1901, on the recommendation of the Immigration Department.

The circumstances of employment, the tropical climate, the relatively small number of European residents, and perhaps the lack of prestige attached to the colonies, encouraged only a small group of doctors to settle in there. Those who chose this as an opportunity became an expensive affair for the state, as the latter was already expending resources on the building of hospitals, medicines and other facilities. The lack of sources forced the state to look for other options or cheap sources of medical men.

In case of Natal, the Coolie Commission of 1872 saw that since Natal was a small colony, about 120 mi. in length, and had few white residents, it was difficult to get adequate medical staff. The Commission thus suggested for the consideration of government expediency for obtaining the services of qualified 'Native Doctors' from India. It stated—

…We allude to a class of men who have been educated, and have passed the prescribed examination as 'Native Doctors' at some of the Government Medical Colleges in India. Some of these men, it is believed, would be found well-qualified for the charges of coolies on estates. It is probable that the offer of a salary of 60 pounds to 100 pounds per annum would secure the services of men from Madras and Calcutta, who would be found eminently useful not only among their own countrymen…but among Europeans also.[129]

On the other hand, in the colony of Mauritius, the recruitment of Europeans with European degrees was an expensive affair; and so the officials promoted medical education among of the Mauritian natives; in Britain to obtain cheap medical practitioners with European education in England and France. The London School of Tropical Medicine was a chief supplier of medical practitioners to the colonies.

Apart from the geographical and economic limitations, medical provisions and care were also shaped by the overriding influence of the planters. David Aickin rightly stated that: '…the isolation of many estates, combined with the material dependency of doctors and their families upon the goodwill of the estate manager for employment and social contact, undoubtedly undermined medical independence.'[130] Large economic and material resources were at the command of the estate owners and their influence in the political regimes was used to soften the harsher features of life, or conversely, make life intolerable. In Mauritius, doctors were paid and appointed by the estate owners; their wages were liable to be cut in case of the failure to perform their duties. The British Guiana enquiry commission rightly described the status of estate doctors in these words—

…At present their tenure is almost entirely dependent on the will, or rather the caprice, of the managers of estates. Several of the most upright of them have at different times conveyed to me and deplored thus postrom deplored to me their position in this respect; and have shown me that any serious complaint on their part in respect of abuses, which they saw going on under their eyes, would only be followed by the loss of their livelihood, and the installment in their practice of less scrupulous practitioners.[131]

The medical authority of well-educated physicians was bolstered by their social position as white, upper class, and often labour-holding men.

It was inevitable that the medical practitioners would take these social identities with them to their practice. The institution of indentured turned the dyad of patient and physician into a three-way relationship between the patient, physician, and plantation owner. An indentured labourer could not be defined as a white doctor's patient, independent of the equally important relationship of the indentured's holder as the physician's client. This rendered the indentured person's doctor as—'medically incompetent', unable to initiate or prevent treatment without the consent of the masters.

In some cases, the magistrate was responsible for checking whether the estates complied with hospital regulations, and proper medical facilities and ample amount of medicines were given to the patients. However, they also became the victim of their honesty. In reality, the influence of estate owners left very little scope for these officials, such as magistrates or doctors, to exercise their duties. Like doctors, magistrates also resided on or very close to the estates. The close alliance between the forces of the state and plantations can be indicated by the fact that plantation managers were often assigned official roles and posts in some courts. Those who dared to criticize were cast in the group of—'an officious set of people always giving trouble'.[132] During 1865, the stipendiary magistrate of Grand Port made a surprise visit to the hospital at Beaufond and La Rosa estates. He was exasperated to see thirteen Indians practically without clothes lying on gunny bags on the earthen floor. As a result, the estate owners were prosecuted and sentenced to imprisonment, but they soon got their freedom. The magistrate, on the other hand, was transferred to another district, under the pressure of the local planters. In another example, in Natal, the newspaper published, 'An unfortunate case'—

…Jadubanshi, an Indian woman, was charged with refusing to return to her lawful employer, she being an indentured servant. She had been working on an estate at Stanger and in some accident, her baby had been burnt, following which she had come to Durban to make a complaint to the protector and had since refused on every occasion to comply with her indenture. The woman accused her employer and said that her baby was not only burnt, but burnt so severely that he died and her employer deliberately refused to attend to the wounds. The woman's duty in her masters house kept her away from the child from 5 a.m. to 7 p.m. with the exception of two short intervals for breakfast and dinner…after the death of her child, Jadubanshi tells of great hardships, including—the refusal of her employer to give her food for three days, forcing her to grind mealies in a handmill, ill treatment by kicking, and the withholding of wages. The total wages received in the course of a year, she states, was nine shillings. The doctor at the hospital reported the death of the child, but did not consider its condition to be so bad as to warrant special mention. The doctors are employed by the Indian Immigrant Trust Board, which consists of planters and farmers and one can easily imagine that the doctors are not over-anxious to report cases which reflect upon employers…we are very much afraid that many a gruesome tragedy lies hidden because of this.[133]

This case suggested that during any illness, one needed to depend on the doctor's report. If they mentioned that the case was serious and it needed special attention, only then was leave provided to the mother to look after her children or rest from work. But doctors were appointed by the Indian Immigrant Trust Board, which consisted of planters and farmers, who were working in favour of planters and the plantation economy. Doctors in the estates did not just treat the labourers and write prescriptions; they also became the authority to validate the indentured's claims of sickness. In Natal, where the government was able to achieve the centralization of medical practice, it was never separate from the plantocracy. It seemed that the medical men and planters were in an unsaid contract of mutual benefit.

In short, based on the available evidences, it seems that medical provisions for plantation workers were structured primarily by geography, the economics of medical care and the social power wielded by plantation managers rather than by the health needs of the labourers. The estate doctors, and even the government doctors, emerged as a new layer of agents for pursuing the colonial administrative goals in the colony.

All the doctors appointed after independence of the Island were Mauritians, and all the nursing staff came from the Mauritius Nursing Training School. The earlier medical practitioners studied in Britain, and after independence, the majority (other than the nursing staff) were trained in India, and then South Africa and France.[134] In the South African Union, the first faculty of medicines was established at the University of Cape Town in 1920, for training white doctors only; the Black doctors were only trained after the University of Natal Medical School was opened in 1951. Dr Goonam, the Indian lady doctor in Durban, in her autobiography, mentioned that there was not even a high school in Durban in the twenties.[135]

It was only in 1910 that for the first time, two non-white doctors were recruited—one of them was coloured, and the other was a Malay person. Nursing as a profession in South Africa was established for white English-speaking ladies in the last third of the nineteenth century, and was at that time dominated by religious sisterhood. The first Black professional nurse was trained in 1907. It was only after the Second World War when there was a shortage of nurses that the authorities started training Black nurses in large numbers.

Hospital as a Prison House: Resistance of the Indentured

…We are quite willing to establish and maintain hospitals for the use of our Indian labourers, but they refuse to attend there, and the law forbids us to control their attendance against their will, except in cases of contagious and infectious diseases, which fortunately are rare. And even were we to endeavor by such legal means as are in our power to render compulsory the presence of our labourers at the hospital, our neighbors would not in all probability follow the same plan, on the expiration of contracts of service, we should lose all our men, to whom this attendance is extremely repugnant.[136]

There were many instances in which indentured Indians, in times of sickness, refused to go to hospital and, if pressed to do so, invariably made themselves absent either from their dwelling or the estate, and remained absent until they were found by the estate policemen, very often thoroughly exhausted, in a bush or hidden in the cane fields. Others, again remained absent from the roll calls, sometimes for days, simply for fear of being sent to the hospital. Stipendiary Magistrate D.S. Ogilvy, of Flacq district, stated—'consequently I fail to see how employers, in cases such as these, can possibly be held responsible when the blame rests entirely with the Indians themselves.'[137] There was no provision in the law to compel any Indian requiring medical treatment to go to a hospital against his will, even if ordered by the medical officer of the estate or his employer. The result was that both medical officers and employers occasionally had the greatest difficulty in dealing with the sick Indians.[138] The Indians were not against any particular hospital; as J.A. Polkinghorne (Protector of Indian Immigrants in Natal) mentioned; that he did not find any definite object of their refusal, but rather assigned this behaviour to a prejudice in their minds against all hospitals.[139] This prejudice was very common among the Indians till the 1870s. The various epidemics that hit the colony after the 1870s forced Indians to accept the Western medicine for immediate effect. But the lack of medicine and proper health facilities further added to their prejudices against the hospitals. Colonies expensed a large amount of money on the supply of medicines from London. Sometimes, the demand for medicines was so high that it could not be fulfilled by the markets.

In 1865, the Government of Mauritius came up with a law stating that sick Indians should be forced to stay at the hospitals for their treatment, so as to stop them from spreading diseases among other able bodies. The medical regime's oppressions were not only unacceptable to the indentured Indians, but also to the Creoles and ex-apprentices.[140] The compulsory vaccination missions were not popular among the local population of the colony. The government held the planters accountable, and police officers were appointed for the vaccination of Indians. The shortage of attendance of Indians in hospitals made officials opt for a more rigorous regulation and they made the provision that the negligence of hospitals' regulations were liable to be fined.[141] Estate hospitals were small in size and less in number; to top it all, they were always dirty and overcrowded with the serious and accidental cases.[142] Despite laws, however, the Indians could not be forced to oblige to these regulations. Planters could not force their labourers because their neighbouring estate owners were not doing so, and thus they were afraid to lose labourers at the end of their contract due to attrition.

Hospitals during the indentured period generated a negative feeling amongst the labourers, who trusted neither the modern medical methods of treatment nor the intention of the plantation regime. There was a common belief among the Indians that if they ever entered the hospitals, death was inevitable for them.[143] The deteriorated condition of the estate hospitals, lack of medical facilities, too few doctors and attendants, and the high rate of mortality; strengthened the Indians' belief that hospitals were death houses. Even during epidemics of cholera and smallpox, the Indians preferred to remain in their huts, rather than go to the estate hospitals. Dr Davies stated that—'…Indians a most difficult race of men to treat, should you be able to keep them in hospitals during the day, they are sure to stand away at night to their huts and there eat and drink'.[144]

In the plantation economy, estate hospitals had multiple functions, such as to run as a stable and a prison-house. In the absence of any prison in an estate, these so-called hospital buildings were frequently used by the planters as prison-houses for the 'wrong' labourers, who were punished on the grounds of misconduct. This was so common in Mauritius that in 1872, Dr Reid suggested to the Royal Commissioners that the government should send a circular to all the estate owners to stop the practice of using hospital buildings as prisons.[145]

In Natal, most of the estate hospitals were used for administering punishment to prisoners. These prisoners were not allowed to go out and had to use the hospital lavatory for their personal use.[146] A bucket was placed in each room for the prisoners for the very same purpose. The Wragg Commission reported that this was a major cause of the insanitary condition in hospitals. Surgeon Lewer recommended that a hospital was not a good place for locking up drunken and noisy prisoners.

Though laws were passed to regulate estate hospitals on the same footing as civil and military hospitals, and fines were also imposed on the estate owners for the negligence of medical facilities: yet there was not even one proper estate hospital available for the Indians in the Island till 1865. The Government of Mauritius realized that only rules and regulations would not be enough, and the absence of constant and active surveillance would render any legislative reform ineffective in the colony.

The medical officer of Mauritius acknowledged that the admission of Indians to hospitals for treatment was new to their habits and customs. The indentured Indians were not only afraid to lose their caste and religion, but were also afraid of separation from their friends and relatives. Apart from this, the diet rules and discipline within the hospitals were also major issues among the Indians.[147] The main reason for reluctance against the consumption of the hospital food was because of caste and religious considerations. This tendency of Indians, of avoiding hospitals on the grounds of losing their caste, was unbelievable for the medical officers. D.S. Ogilvy observed that the sepoys in India were of higher caste, who did seek medical treatment in the military hospitals, while in Mauritius, most of the Indians were of the lowest castes.[148] From the humanitarian perspective, the strictures of medical practice demanded that patients received the best food suited to their state of health. The stimulating and recuperative properties of food were widely accepted amongst doctors. In the colonies, a sensitivity towards diet for the management of health was considered important. Dietetics also had a long legacy in the Western medical corpus, dating as far back as the Greeks.[149] The Indians refused to follow the diet prescribed by doctors, which they thought impure, according to their own religious points of view. The quality of food was another reason; they preferred better quality of rice and *dhall* cooked in ghee. The labourers from the highland demanded that they should be provided with sesame oil (gingelli) and mustard oil, to cook their meals at the hospitals. The Coolie Commission of Natal mentioned that Indians refused to have hospital food served by a member of another caste, no matter lower or higher than their own. In Mauritius, an indentured reported to Beyts (Protector of immigrants) that he stayed in the hospital only during the day, and he added: '...his food was prepared by his wife and brought to him...he did not sleep in the hospital, come in the morning remained all day...but preferred sleeping in his own house and being taken care of by his wife.'[150]

In Natal, regulations were made for bettering the diet of the sick Indians. Some of the very weak patients were recommended a special diet. The hospital diet for ordinary cases consisted of rice 10 oz., fish ½ oz., and *dhall* ½ oz. as breakfast, dinner, and as tea and supper; hospital reports claimed that the meal was prepared with onions, tamarinds, chilies, curry powder, and garlic, if necessary.[151] Besides this, the special cases were provided with extra articles in their diet, such as mutton, fowl, arrowroot, sago, bread, milk, etc., as and when prescribed by the doctors. In theory at least, it seems that in Natal, the hospitals' food was comparatively better than what was given in the Mauritius estate hospitals and slave hospitals in British West Indies, where the food for a sick slave was, '...often musty, indigestible horse beans, sometimes maze, flour, or rice; sometimes, a dainty, brown biscuit.'[152] However, like expensive medicines, these special diets also incurred extra expenses; therefore, most of the times, the doctor's orders were not exactly carried out by the planters. Very often, complaints were made by inmates about the quality of the hospital food.

Indians preferred to take recourse to 'charlatans' (quacks), rather than go to hospitals for treatment. The biggest reason for the avoidance of hospitals at night was because the Indians did not want to sleep on the hospital beds and mattresses. They preferred the '*charpoy*' (a kind of Indian bed). This demand of *charpoy* was accepted by the medical officers, as Dr Vitry suggested that hospital beds attracted vermin and miasma.[153] Apart from this, the confinement of Indians in the hospitals for treatment, and the strict discipline of the hospital was also a major cause for the avoidance of hospitals. Inside the hospitals, the sick people were only allowed to see their friends thrice in a week. Dr Bolton stated—

...It is already a great difficulty in getting Indians to go to the estate hospitals when these are situated far from the camp. How much greater then will this aversion to hospital treatment be, if the patients have to be sent several miles to the district hospital where they have to submit to discipline, see their friends only three times a week, and not be allowed to go home every night...this end will not be attained by their forcible detention at public hospitals.[154]

The resistance of Indians against the institution of the hospital was so strong that the planters suggested it was better to treat them in their own huts, rather than force them to visit hospitals. Planters forwarded their opinion to the various enquiry commissions, stating that Indians preferred to be treated in their huts, rather than in hospitals. They also argued that the Indians did not even take the medicine prescribed by the estate medical practitioners. On these grounds, they justified their stand that there was no need for estate hospitals.[155] Mr Collard, manager of the Little Umhlanga estate in Natal, stated that: '...after twenty years experience in Mauritius and four years in Natal, I say it is no use to erect hospitals: in fact, they [the coolies] consider it a gaol and confinement'.[156] Raj Boodhoo rightly argued that throughout the indentured period, all efforts were made to force reluctant Indians into submission. This was not the scenario only in Mauritius, but was very common in India as well, where civilians and soldiers refused to be treated in the hospitals. At any time, only those who were attending work received complete rations. The loss of ration and cut in their wages also forced labourers to remain at work, rather than go to the hospitals for treatment. The Indians only visited hospitals when their health deteriorated. A large number of labourers who visited the hospitals did not do so because of any kind of disease; they did so because of 'tiredness'. This shows that there was not enough rest because after six working days, the workers even had to perform 'corvée' on Sundays. For instance, the wife of an indentured labour complained—'...I [Sonnar] am wife of Futtising. I complain that when my husband was in hospital, I had no one to look after my children, and I could not work, and therefore had no rations.'[157]

The treatment of Indian women in hospitals was a knotty issue. Governor A. Phayre (Mauritius) stated that Indian women and children remained in their huts and refused to be treated in the hospitals.[158] In some cases, the women themselves refused to go to any male doctor for any kind of examination. Plantation hospitals were also not safe places for Indian women, as they could be victims of sexual harassment or ill treatment by the doctors. For example, once a doctor gave wine to an indentured woman and made fun of her. The doctor was later held guilty of ill treatment.[159] In another case in 1886, the emigrants made grave allegations against the surgeon superintendent; both of assault and of improper relations with the female emigrants during the voyage, as well as at the quarantine station at Mauritius.

Epidemics such as those of malaria posed a great threat to the indentured women's health and their ability to reproduce. During malaria epidemics, most of the pregnant women had to go for abortions. Many children were stillborn or died soon after their birth. Thus, the health of the women and children (future labourers) became an issue of concern to the officials. Dr Virty reported that in case of the indentured, 'family ties were mixed with cultural constraints'.[160] The Indian males did not allow their women to visit doctors. In one of the cases, a sixteen-year-old pregnant girl was suffering from pain for about twenty-four hours, but she refused to visit the hospital or to allow any doctor to enter her hut to treat her. The father of the girl was irascible and said he would rather cut his throat then let the doctor see his daughter.[161] There were constant complaints by the medical officers regarding the Indian women evading the medical examination. Dr Daruty described the indentured women as the 'uncivilized lot'.[162] There was no law in Mauritius which forced a woman suffering from a contagious venereal disease to be confined in the hospital without her consent.[163] On the other hand, doctors were not allowed to visit the patients in their huts. Women only accepted treatment at the hospitals provided that they were accompanied by their husbands. Consequently, the medical officer reported that women in the hospitals were being attended by their own husbands, in spite of the presence of female nurses in the ward.[164] The reason for the women's reluctance to treatment in the hospitals, as Dr Virty reported was that—

...the private character that had to do with their family obligations...the duties of the wives, the mother or the helpmate will claim as strongly as ever their attention even in sickness; unless indeed they become incapacitated from attending to their labourious and manifold duties. It is only in the extreme case that they consent to be inmates of the hospitals; even when the diseases has made such progress that cure is almost hopeless.[165]

In many hospitals after 1865, there were separate accommodations established for the privacy of the female patients. Female nurses and Indian midwives were also appointed by the government to secure the health of women and children. The regular outbreak of epidemics in the colony and positive changes in the maintenance of the hospitals led the Indians to seek help of the hospitals during sickness. Dr Virty stated that the repugnance would gradually wear off since the hospitals were better than earlier: '...a great change has taken place since the hospitals have become worthy of their name.'[166] In some of the hospitals, Creole women were employed and they were quite efficient in taking care of women and children; but some of the Indian women did not appreciate being treated by them. Recommendation was made by the Chief Medical Officer to the Protector of Immigrants of the island to establish Maternity and Children wards in the colony,[167] which was only fulfilled after the end of indentured recruitment from India. During the year 1881, as the protector reported, 45 per cent women and children died on the estate without receiving any form of healthcare.

In his annual report (1898), the protector mentioned—'the mortality amongst children under ten years of age, is still, I am sorry to say, excessive, and is due in a great measure to the carelessness particularly of free Indian parents [who are] not presenting their children for medical treatment until many of them are almost in the last stage of disease.'[168] The official discourse claimed that Indians adopted 'their own mode of treatment', which invariably ended in the death of the patient, and this was especially so with regards to children.[169] Unfortunately, these reports do not throw light on the mode of treatment of the immigrants, but it goes on to strengthen the point that the immigrants were constantly trying to resist the colonial medical regime and its healing practices, in which the immigrants often had to be kept bound up for treatment.

Among the Indian methods of treatment, the use of herbs and herbal remedies were very popular, as herbs were easy to obtain and this was a known method of treatment in their customs. Doctors and inspectors often complained about the presence of quacks and local healers (mostly Indians) on the estates and villages. Medical inspectors even tried to make some legal arrangements to stop native healers, who illegally drove the trade of medicine in the villages and estates. For example, a reference from Munshi Rahman Khan's *Autobiography of an Indian Indentured Labourer* (Surinam), would be helpful to understand the limited knowledge of colonial doctors about local diseases. While a local Black native could have the required knowledge, and using local herbs and medicines, he would be successful in treating a disease; a qualified European doctor would fail. Rahman Khan also mentioned the unbearable curing methods used in these hospitals, and prayed to God not to send even his enemies to these hospitals. As he mentioned, '…in one night a mere black had accomplished the healing, which had seemed impossible to all the doctors of repute, of high salary and high post, and who could influence the government. The Lord had allowed a Negro, hated by the Europeans, to free me from all my five symptoms by 5 o' clock next morning (*sic*) only diarrhoea still drained me. The witch doctor told me not to worry about it.'[170] The trust and dependence of the sick Indians on the local healers and their treatments can be understood in these words—

...In a non-colonial society, the attitude of a sick man in the presence of a medical practitioner is one of confidence. The patient trusts the doctor; he puts himself in his hands. He yields his body to him. He accepts the fact that pain may be awakened or exacerbated by the physician, for the patient realizes that the intensifying of suffering in the course of examination may pave the way to peace in his body.[171]

Indentured men and women, according to whom the White doctors did more harm than good, responded to the healer-patient relationship with the White doctors with suspicion, and considered it a violation and theft of 'other race' bodies. During the whole indentured period, the relation between the doctor and patient remained that of, 'relations of force'. Nineteenth century white medical discourse adopted a broad array of ideas about the relationship between the spirit, mind, and body expressed in health reform, religiosity, and popular science. At the same time, however, the white planters and the authorities drew a line of essential difference between themselves and the persons they controlled, whom they considered as 'superstitious'.[172] The idea of superstition was applied to distinguish between enlightenment and ignorance, progress and primitivism, reason and irrationality, and medicine and quackery. Moreover, these familiar dichotomies subsumed constructions of race and gender that closely linked coolies, and mostly women, to superstition. The medical regime considered superstition itself as a disease and a racial trait. The idea of superstition thus operated as a racial currency that inflated the value of certain knowledge–holders, while devaluing others. The white planters sought to place themselves on the upper echelons of the hierarchies of scientific and medical knowledge. They looked up to books, medical school instructions, and mentored training as the legitimate path to medical knowledge. The white doctors' claim to medical authority was vested in learned knowledge, class standing, professional training, and male entitlement, in which the experience of the old local women and practices of the 'witch doctor' were not acceptable. While on the other hand, the local healers, in the same manner, pointed to spiritual insights as a legitimate source of their abilities. They approached healing as a collective enterprise. The relational vision of health (in which the patients and the healers shared a relation of trust) placed healing in the context of the broadly conceived 'community' that included living persons, ancestors, spirits, and God.[173] Local health practices redefined the indentured health in terms of a relational vision that emphasized the importance of the community in individual well-being, rather than in terms of soundness or economic value of the indentured bodies. The local-made medicines relied on the strong 'bond of trust' between a healer and a sick person. The sick person had complete trust in the ability of the healer to discern the nature of the disorder, and they also shared a cultural understanding of the illness.

Due to the lack of proper medical care and facilities, some ailing Indians chose the extreme step of ending their life. Records show that one of the major causes for suicide among the Indians was sickness. For example, one of the emigrants on Riviere Noire estate (Mauritius), who was suffering from asthma, committed suicide as he could not work due to his illness. The official record tried to explain the act as having been done, 'with a view to end his sufferings', and that it was a practice not uncommon among Indians.[174] Even the sick and the abandoned Indian women, not finding support, ended their lives by committing suicide. The whole system of medical benefits and facilities was under the control of plantation owners, and in order to have access to these facilities, the labourers had to depend on the owners; they needed to be obedient, hard–working, and of good nature. In the course of drastic epidemics, the plantation owners even tried to negotiate with the labourers in the exchange of medical benefits. The novel, *Gandhiji Bole Theiy* by Abhimanyu Anat depicts how women's sexuality was exploited in the overseas plantations (it was also, at times, used by the indentured to achieve their ends when all else failed). One of the characters of the novel named Daood neglected his master's order by saying, '*jahannum me jaaye malik ka hokum*' (hell to master's order). To teach him a lesson, the master's son came and ordered Daood to send his wife to him. The following dialogue between the husband and wife show a plan to negotiate with the employer, in exchange of sexual gratification, for the benefit of the people of their community.

…Daood (to his wife Jeenat): *Sham ko tumhe Remon sahib ke bete ke yahan jaana hai. Log mar rahen hain bina khana, bina dawai…ise rokane ki koshish to ki ja sakati hai. Ham dono shayad ise kar saken…ek jaati tabah hone se bach jaayegi, ek chhoti si kimat se yahan anaaj pahunch jayega, dawaiyan aa jaayegi…mouka achcha hai. Ek bade uddeshya ke liye thodi der aankhen moond lene se kya anarth ho jaayega? Tum aurat ho Jeenat. Aur aurat ki deh koi roti ka tukada nahin hoti jo kisi ke munh lagane se joothi ho jaaye. Par yaad rahe, apane ko uske hawale karane se pahale souda ho jaana chahiye. Tum pahle use raji kar lena, fir apane ko samarpit karna.*[175]

You have to go to Remon son's place in the evening. People are dying without food and medicine… we can try to stop this. I think we both can do this probably…a race will survive from destruction, a small price will help us to get food, and medicine…it is a good opportunity. What's the harm in closing your eyes for a while for a bigger purpose? You are a woman Jeenat. And a woman's body is not a piece of bread that can no more be of use (*joothi*) by taking a bite. But remember! The deal should be finalized before you give yourself to him. So first make him accept the deal and only then surrender yourself. [Translation mine.]

The biography of Ramgoolam, the Prime Minister of Mauritius, described the condition of hospitals on the island. He described the hospitals as an urban setup, away from the rural areas, to which people had to go after covering long distances. The insufficient supply of medical facilities and inefficient doctors made the situation worse. Language was another barrier between the doctors and the patients. Ramgoolam described an incident when an old woman, who visited the hospital but could not get either the doctor or the hospital staff to help her, was left miserable. He described that when he saw the old woman, he went and asked, 'Can I help you?'; she replied, 'Are you a doctor?'; Ramgoolam said 'no'; the woman replied, 'Then you cannot help me'. He recalled that at that very moment, he decided to become a doctor and help the people in his country.[176]

The rate of death and sickness was higher among the non-estate labourers (free labourers) as compared to the estate labourers. There were some instances when Indian indentured labourers used these hospitals as a way of escaping from the work and also used these institutions as temporary accommodation, as they did not have any other place to stay, live, or eat. A case of an Indian, admitted to the hospital for a bleeding wound in his ankle, can be taken as an example. Whenever it reached a curable stage, he would scratch it repeatedly, till it demanded treatment again. The hospital nurses complained that it was difficult to get rid of this person as he had already spent two months in hospital, and still did not want to leave.[177] In case of Natal, the Coolie Commission of 1872 reported that the habit of Indians feigning sickness to avoid work posed problems for great the employers in the management of labourers. This was known on the estates as 'humbug sickness' and 'shame sickness'.[178] The coolies accepted that many of their numbers did feign illness in order to absent themselves from work to attend their own affairs. The pretended illness also offered an opportunity to the indentured labourers to rest their bodies. For planters, feigning was first and foremost a labour problem, defined by the threat of a deceptive worker. Physicians, in contrast, approached feigning as a difficult challenge to their medical skills and authority. These distinct formulations by planters and physicians led to separate remedies, yet these drew on similar assumptions about the indentured's racial traits. Ultimately, the strategies of both planters and physicians merged, for the enforcement of plantation discipline.

Conclusion

Although labour force and their health issues had a long relationship, right since the slavery period, the economic value of the slaves/labourers forced planters to adopt minimum health measures for them. Sheridan stated that little attention was paid to the health matter of the slaves in Caribbean colonies on the eve of the emancipation of slavery, due to an active and critical approach of the anti-slavery group. These institutions, known as 'sick house', 'hothouse', or 'hospital'—also served largely as prisons. These served the dual purpose of punishing the refractory and keeping patients with sores that were difficult to heal in a recumbent posture.[179] At large, however, the White doctors failed to do any good to the enslaved labourers.

The intervention of Mauritian and Natal governments through various medical legislations, to some extent, slowly opened up the private world of the plantations to official gaze. The regulations to improve provisions in the hospitals on estates provided the bureaucracy with instruments to harmonize indentured trade principles and mass transport of labourers in the colony. The ultimate aim of these medical interventions was the survival and more efficient working of the plantation system. Healthier and more productive immigrants were the means to these ends. The high rate of mortality among the Indian population and the spread of epidemic diseases all over the country widened the gaze of medical profession from the estate to the wider colony. The Mauritian and Natal governments provided Indian labourers with their medical rights, which were publsihed in different Indian languages for the Indians, in order to make them aware of them. However, the planters in Mauritius, who were stronger as a group in contrast to any other country that received indentured labourers, always considered any reform measures related to the labourers as a curtailment of their rights and profits. Though they tried to control and oppose governmental interference regarding the labourers' health issues; but at the same time, the loss of working days due to sickness and fear of Asian epidemic diseases forced them to adopt some of the new health measures. Apart from that, the concept of indentured health fit comfortably with the definitions of 'humane' treatment expressed by White planters interested in preserving their peculiar institutions through reform.

The lack of government control on estate doctors provided the planters with an opportunity for negotiation with the labourers. Medical benefits remained in the hands of the planters, which forced labourers to be obedient and hard-working. On the other hand, labourers recorded their resistance against Western medical treatment and confinement in hospitals, which they believed was against their caste, religion, and cultural norms. Though the Government of Mauritius reformed the medical facilities available to the indentured to some extent: but due to the lack of interest of the planters and avoidance on part of the Indians, it could not achieve its goal till the end of the nineteenth century.

After the 1930s, Mauritius had a comprehensive healthcare service. There were six general government hospitals, three special hospitals for leprosy, tuberculosis, and mental diseases, and twenty-three hospitals on sugar estates with dispensaries attached. All the government hospitals had public dispensaries and outpatient departments. Five mobile government dispensaries travelled across the island. There were forty-three maternal and child-healthcare centres. Mauritius had one mobile public antenatal clinic and two mobile public dental clinics. But even these measures could not cope with the rising population in the colony. The loopholes in the measures became very clear when, in the 1940s, there was an outbreak of malaria as an epidemic for the third time, which caused the death of a large section of the population in Mauritius. After the unification of South Africa, the Public Health Act of 1919 established the first union-wide public health department in the colony. In 1945, several community health centres were set up. These centres were the forerunners of community-based primary healthcare centres, with the health of the population as the prime concern. In spite of all these measures, health facilities in the South African Union remained limited and inadequate during the colonial period. Studies show that even now, in the twenty-first century, South Africa is grappling with health issues, some of which have emerged in fatal forms.

Notes

1. James Patterson Smith, 'Empire and Social Reform: British Liberals and the "Civilizing Mission" in the Sugar Colonies, 1868-1874', *A Quarterly Journal concerned with British Studies*, vol. XXVII, no. 2, 1995, p. 270.
2. Ibid.; Arthur Mills, 'Our Colonial Policy', *The Times*, London, 4 January 1878.
3. Mills, 'Our Colonial Policy'.
4. The condition of the commissariat store where the depot site was allotted and constructed; see Marina Carter, *Servants, Sirdars & Settlers: Indians in Mauritius, 1834-1874*, Delhi: Oxford University Press, 1995, p. 152.
5. *Parliamentary Papers, India*, 1842, vol. XXX, no. 26, Plan of Free Labour Association, pp. 28–9.
6. Carter, *Servants, Sirdars & Settlers*, p. 152.
7. Raj Boodhoo, *Health, Disease and Indian Immigrants in Nineteenth Century Mauritius*, Port Louis: Aapravasi Ghat Trust Fund, 2010, p. 118.
8. Ibid., p. 123.
9. Ibid., p. 121.
10. *The Natal Mercury*, on 6 December 1860, reported that Indians on their arrival were supplied with fish; their barracks had been whitewashed and put in order, and they were provided better accommodations.
11. Revenue and Agriculture Department (Emigration Branch) Proceedings, January 1894, nos. 31–2, part A, NAI.
12. Annual Report of the Protector of Indian Immigrants in Natal for the year 1898, Revenue and Agriculture Department (Emigration Branch) Proceedings, August 1899, nos. 6–7, part A, NAI.
13. French word for a professional nurse.
14. CO 167/376, Special Report of the Chief Medical Officer, 1856, TNA.
15. Hugh Tinker, *A New System of Slavery: The Export of Indian Labour Overseas, 1830-1920*, London: Oxford University Press, 1974, p. 167.
16. Bluff Station in Natal, L/PJ/6/364, India Office Records, British Library, London, UK.
17. Balfour was the Director-in-chief of the Wellcome Bureau of Scientific Research, London.
18. Bluff Station in Natal, L/PJ/6/364, India Office Records, British Library.
19. Notification no. 463A, Mauritius, dated 5 March 1874, Allegation with respect to the quarantine station at Flat Island and Mauritius, Revenue and Agriculture Department, Govt. of Bengal (Emigration Branch) Proceedings, June 1874, nos. 1–2, NAI.
20. Ibid.
21. The Secretary, Annual Report of Indian Immigration Trust Board 1874; cited in Y.S. Meer, *Documents of Indentured Labour: Natal 1851-1917*, Durban: Institute of Black Research, 1980, p. 6.

22. Notification no. 463A, Mauritius, dated 5 March 1874, Allegation with respect to the quarantine station at Flat Island and Mauritius.
23. Ibid.; letter no. 6, from Arthur Payne, Esq. M.D., to the Emigration Agent, Govt. of Mauritius, dated December 1873, Revenue and Agriculture Department (Emigration Branch) Proceedings, June 1874, nos. 1–2, NAI.
24. *The Nautical Magazine*, on November 1896, published an interesting letter from the pen of Sir Sherston Baker, Bart, Editor of the *Law Magazine and Law Review*. The bubonic plague scare was then at its height in Europe. A portion of this interesting letter informs us that on the 7th of August, a short act of Parliament, entitled the Public Health Act, 1896 (59), was passed. This Act repealed the whole of the old Quarantine Act of 1825, which was applied to the United Kingdom, and the many subsequent acts modifying or extending the last-named statute. He also went into figures, and pointed out the expenses, misery, and cruel injustice that quarantine entails, and hoped all lands that were interested in quarantine be guided by modern medical science for their welfare. Quarantine, literally meaning a space of forty days, is exceedingly ancient and doubtless, has its origin in the Jewish ceremonials, in which lepers and unclean people were proscribed for forty days. It should also be remembered that a plague visitation fell upon the Egyptians in the desert in 1471 BC. The Venetians, however, are believed to have been the first to establish what we later came to understand as 'quarantine'; and it is probable that their sanitary regulations against the outbreak of plague were first issued in 1127. All merchants and others coming from the Levant were obliged to remain in the House of St. Lazarus, or the Lazaretto, for forty days before they were admitted into the city of Venice, the Lazaretto there being built on water (it is still standing). It was not until the plague of Marseilles in 1720 that quarantine regulations were thoroughly understood. The old quarantine laws were based on two principles—first, that the epidemic diseases, which at various times had desolated the world, were communicable by contact with persons affected or by contact with things touched by the affected persons. The other principle was that—

> ...The spread of epidemics could be stayed by prevention of this contact. A great modification of opinion had, of late, taken place on this subject; and the majority of medical and scientific men were now convinced that 'contagious diseases' were not always communicable by contact, but rather, might be produced by local and atmospheric causes, and, therefore, such medicines and sanitary measures were not merely drastic quarantine regulations. The College of Physicians of New Orleans, in a report made in 1852, strongly favoured the adoption of sanitary instead of quarantine measures, and have shown the good effects of the former, basing their opinion on the fact that a century ago the yellow fever extended to twelve degrees of latitude further north than it did in the above year, and claiming that its retrogression was to be attributed to sanitary measures and not to quarantine.

It is this same opinion that had been instrumental in the decreasing popularity of the practice of quarantine over consecutive years in the United Kingdom. The rigor with which quarantine was administered in the past, not only abroad but also in England, had sometimes been the product of cruel wrongs. A familiar instance is doubtless known to those travellers who have visited Leghorn. There is on the mole an immense marble statue, representing the Grand Duke's son, who was put to death for breaking quarantine. The story goes thus—

> …A pirate had been committing a series of depredations amongst the boats and other craft belonging to the Duke's dominions, and nobody would attack him. The Duke's son, being braver than the rest, manned a boat and went out to meet that common disturber. After a hard fight the Duke's son overcame and brought away some of the followers of the pirate as prisoners, who of course were put in quarantine, it not being known from whence they came. The son was so elated with his victory that he jumped on shore to tell the news, and thereupon was put to death by his father for breaking quarantine. Remarkable and inhuman, and was rendered doubly so in view of the prostrate condition of the survivors.

See C.W. Brebner, *New Handbook for the Indian Ocean, Arabian Sea and Bay of Bengal: With Miscellaneous Subjects for Sail and Steam, Mauritius Cyclones and Currents, Moon Observations and Sail-making*, Bombay: Times of India Press, 1898, pp. 33–5.

25. Boodhoo, *Health, Disease and Indian Immigrants*, p. 153.
26. Ibid., p. 161.
27. Annual Report of the Protector of Indian Immigrants in Natal for the year 1885, Revenue and Agriculture Department (Emigration Branch) Proceedings, October 1886, nos. 8–9, NAI.
28. Annual Report of the Protector of Indian Immigrants in Natal for the year 1887, Revenue and Agriculture Department (Emigration Branch) Proceedings, September 1888, nos. 16–17, NAI.
29. Annual Report of the Protector of Indian Immigrants in Natal for the year 1892–3, Revenue and Agriculture Department (Emigration Branch) Proceedings, January 1894, nos. 31–2, NAI.
30. Annual Report of the Protector of Indian Immigrants in Natal for the year 1890, Revenue and Agriculture Department (Emigration Branch) Proceedings, November 1891, nos. 15–16, part A, NAI.
31. Annual Report of the Protector of Indian Immigrants in Natal for the year 1898, Revenue and Agriculture Department (Emigration Branch) Proceedings.
32. Meer, *Documents of Indentured Labour*, p. 6.
33. Brebner, *New Handbook for the Indian Ocean*, pp. 33–5.
34. Boodhoo, *Health, Disease and Indian Immigrants*, p. 162.
35. Smith, 'Empire and Social Reform', p. 258.
36. Ibid., p. 259.
37. For further details see Tom Crook, 'Sanitary Inspection and the Public

Sphere in Late Victorian and Edwardian Britain: A Case Study in Liberal Governance', *Social History*, vol. XXXII, no. 4, 2007, pp. 369–93.

38. David Arnold, 'Race, Place and Bodily Difference in Early Nineteenth Century India', *Historical Research*, vol. 77, no. 196, 2004, p. 258.

39. Annual Report of the Protector of Indian Immigrants in Natal for the year 1877, Revenue, Agriculture and Commerce Department (Emigration Branch) Proceedings, October 1878, nos. 24–5, NAI.

40. Ibid.

41. Annual Report of the Protector of Indian Immigrants in Natal for the year 1901, Revenue and Agriculture Department (Emigration Branch) Proceedings, August 1902, nos. 16–18, NAI.

42. Ibid.

43. Shaista Shameen, 'Migration, Labour and Plantation Women in Fiji: A Historical Perspective', in *Women Plantation Workers: International Experiences*, ed. Shobhita Jain and Rhoda Reddock, New York: Oxford University Press, 1998, p. 50.

44. Report of the Protector of Indian Immigrants in Natal for the year 1884, Revenue and Agriculture Department (Emigration Branch) Proceedings, January 1886, nos. 16, NAI.

45. Radhika Chopra, 'Dependent Husbands: Reflections on Marginal Masculinities', in *Navigating Social Exclusion and Inclusion in Contemporary India and Beyond: Structures, Agents, Practices*, ed. Uwe Skoda, Kenneth Bo Nielsen, Marianne Qvortrup Fibiger, London, New York: Anthem Press, 2013, p. 42.

46. Gaiutra Bahadur, *Coolie Woman: The Odyssey of Indenture*, London: Hurst & Company, 2013, pp. 110–11.

47. Major Pitcher and G.A. Grierson Enquiry Report, Revenue and Agriculture Department (Emigration Branch) Proceedings, August 1883, nos. 9–15, NAI.

48. Ibid.

49. 'Reserved Bill for the Consolidation of the Coolie laws of Natal', Home Department (Public Branch) Proceedings, 7 May 1870, nos. 121–2, NAI.

50. Revenue and Agriculture Department (Emigration Branch) Proceedings, July 1903, nos. 30, NAI.

51. Addition to the rule under Natal Mines Act of 1899, Revenue and Agriculture Department (Emigration Branch) Proceedings, August 1903, nos. 5–6, NAI.

52. Anne McClintock, *Imperial Leather: Race, Gender and Sexuality in the Colonial Context*, London: Routledge, 1995, p. 115.

53. Indian Immigration Labour Question, INF-10-226, TNA.

54. Annual Report of the Protector of Indian Immigrants in Mauritius for the year 1902, Revenue and Agriculture Department (Emigration Branch) Proceedings, February 1904, nos. 7–8, NAI.

55. Indian Immigration Labour Question, INF-10-226, TNA.

56. CO 167/263, Mauritius Report of Council, vol. V, 1845, TNA.
57. James C. Scott, *Weapons of the Weak: Everyday Forms of Peasant Resistance*, Yale: Yale University Press, 2008.
58. Prabhu Mohapatra, 'Asian Labour: Culture, Consciousness, Representation', Paper presented at conference on 'Asian Labour: A Debate on Culture, Consciousness and Representations', Manila, 23–5 October, 1997.
59. Working of Section 6, Natal Law 14 of 1875, Revenue and Agriculture Department (Emigration Branch) Proceedings, April 1882, no. 85, NAI. The medical inspector's half-yearly report of 1903 showed that on the Estate Le Vallon, there were 186 new immigrants, that absence among them was prevalent, and that in March 1903 the wages paid amounted to Rs.176, and the deductions amounted to Rs.755, of which Rs.248 was for sickness and Rs.444 for 'absence'. The medical inspector further said that if the coolies were neither paid nor fed, it was no wonder that they died. High death rate on estates in Mauritius among the newly arrived Indian immigrants, Revenue and Agriculture Department (Emigration Branch) Proceedings, September 1904, nos. 8–9, NAI.
60. High death rate on estates in Mauritius among the newly arrived Indian Immigrants, Revenue and Agriculture Department (Emigration Branch) Proceedings.
61. Ibid.
62. Ibid.
63. Article 116 of the Labour Ordinance of 1878, Revenue and Agriculture Department (Emigration Branch) Proceedings, September 1904, nos. 8–9, NAI.
64. High death rate on estates in Mauritius among the newly arrived Indian Immigrants, Revenue and Agriculture Department (Emigration Branch) Proceedings.
65. Ashwin Desai and Goolam Vahed, *Inside Indenture: A South African History, 1860-1914*, Durban: Madiba Publishers, 2007, p. 120.
66. The intending emigrant Indians on their voyages to the overseas colonies received a passenger number on the ships, which became their identity number not only in the colonies, but in official records too. The 'ship list' of indentured labourers are available in various archives and repositories. Each volume of ship list is comprised of tables, with entries inscribed by hand on horizontal lines stretching consecutively across both open pages from left to right. Under different column headings—including registration number, father's name, age, sex, village of origin, caste, and identifying 'body marks'—are the corresponding details of each named individual. In case of Natal, a set of 91 volumes comprises the original register of the 'shipping lists', inventories documenting the arrival of 152,000 Indians to Port Natal between 1860 amd 1911. Of these, 62 volumes document the arrival of vessels from Madras, and 29 are on ships from Calcutta. For further details, see Goolam Vahed and Thembisa Waetjen, 'Passages of Ink:

Decoding the Natal Indentured Records into the Digital Age', *Kronos*, vol. XL, no.1, 2014, pp. 46–7; also available at https://wiser.wits.ac.za/system/files/seminar/VahedWaetjen2013.pdf, accessed 14 November 2014.

67. Meer, *Documents of Indentured Labour*, p. 108.
68. Desai and Vahed, *Inside Indenture*, p. 121.
69. Frequency of the crime of suicide among Indian labourers in Mauritius, Home Department (Public Branch) Proceedings, April 1871, nos. 201–4, NAI.
70. Ibid.
71. Boodhoo, *Health, Disease and Indian Immigrants*, p. 83.
72. Royal Commission Report of 1872, CO 169/15, TNA.
73. CO 167/263, Mauritius Report of Council.
74. CO 167/255, Report of the Committee appointed by the council for the consideration of the minute of His Excellency the Governor, dated 4 July 1844, regarding medical aid and attendance provided for labourers employed in the country districts, TNA.
75. Ibid.
76. In the district of Savanne, there was an average of 1,361 persons for each doctor; in Grand Port, an average of 2,593 labourers were allotted to each doctor; in Riviere du Rempart, the number was 1,780 for each doctor; and in Pamplemousses north and south, 1,059 and 765 respectively for each doctor. CO 167/255, Report of the Committee appointed by the council for the consideration of the minute of His Excellency the Governor.
77. CO 167/255, Report of the Committee appointed by the council for the consideration of the minute of His Excellency the Governor.
78. Carter, *Servants, Sirdars & Settlers*, p. 171.
79. Ordinance no. 40 of 1844. See Saloni Deerpalsingh and Marina Carter, *Selected Documents on Indian Immigration: Mauritius, 1834-1926*, vol. III, Moka: Mahatma Gandhi Institute Press, 1996, pp. 307–9.
80. See Boodhoo, *Health, Disease and Indian Immigrants*, p. 135.
81. W.E. Frere and V.A. Williamson, *Report of the Royal Commissioners appointed to Enquire into the Treatment of Immigrants in Mauritius*, London: William Clowes and Sons, 1875; Cited in Boodhoo, *Health, Disease and Indian Immigrants*, p. 90.
82. Robert Neave, civil and sessions judge from India, was appointed in 1845 to report on the financial losses to the colony caused by the short term of indenture and thus the premature return of indentured Indians to their country. See Deerpalsingh and Carter, *Selected Documents on Indian Immigration*, pp. 218–25.
83. Medical Charity Commission of 1858, cited in Boodhoo, *Health, Disease and Indian Immigrants*, p. 167.
84. Ibid., p. 168.
85. H.T. Rogers, 'Notes on the Epidemic of Malarial Fever which appeared in

Mauritius in 1866-67', in *Transactions of the Epidemiological Society of London*, vol. III, 1874, pp. 200–15, WTL.

86. Deerpalsingh and Carter, *Selected Documents on Indian Immigration*, p. 328.
87. Ibid., Document 4.7.
88. Ibid.
89. Ordinance no. 12 of 1878, CO 169/17, TNA.
90. Deerpalsingh and Carter, *Selected Documents on Indian Immigration*, p. 329, Document 4.7.
91. Ibid.
92. Frederic J. Mouat, 'Medical Statistics, with Especial Reference to Cholera and Syphilis', in *Transactions of the Epidemiological Society of London*, vol. III, 1874, p. 380, WTL.
93. CO 170/119, Half-yearly Report of the Medical Inspector of Estate Hospitals, 1883, TNA.
94. Ordinance no. 12 of 1878, CO 169/17.
95. Evidence given before the Royal Commission of Enquiry regarding the condition and treatment of Indian immigrants, CO 170/97, TNA.
96. CO 170/86, General Board of Health, Mauritius, TNA.
97. CO 167/880/9, Public Health of Mauritius, TNA.
98. CO 167/353, General Board of Health, Mauritius, TNA.
99. The Natal Immigration Law 14 of 1859, CO 180/1, TNA.
100. Report of the Coolie Commission, in the letter from A. Musgrave, Esq. Lieutenant-Governor of Natal, to the Secretary of State, Agriculture, Revenue and Commerce Department (Emigration Branch) Proceedings, February 1873, nos. 16–19, p. 13, NAI.
101. Ibid.
102. Ibid., p. 16.
103. For further detail on the Coolie Commission of 1872, see Chapter 1.
104. Annual Report of the Protector of Indian Immigrants in Natal for the year 1899, Revenue and Agriculture Department (Emigration Branch) Proceedings, January 1901, nos. 10–12, NAI.
105. CO 180/4, Indian Immigration Law no. 12 of 1872, TNA.
106. Revenue and Agriculture Department (Emigration Branch) Proceedings, February 1892, nos. 6–7, NAI.
107. Annual Report of the Protector of Indian Immigrants in Natal for the year 1904, Commerce and Industry Department (Emigration Branch) Proceedings, September 1905, nos. 1–2, part A, NAI.
108. Ibid.
109. Report of John F. Elliot, Indian Medical Officers Verulam district, in the Annual Report of the Protector of Indian Immigrants in Natal for the year 1903, Revenue and Agriculture Department (Emigration Branch) Proceedings, July 1904, nos. 3–4, NAI.

110. Annual Report of the Protector of Indian Immigrants in Natal for the year 1904, Commerce and Industry Department (Emigration Branch) Proceedings, September 1905, nos. 3–4, NAI.
111. Annual Report of the Protector of Indian Immigrants in Natal for the year 1902, Commerce and Industry Department (Emigration Branch) Proceedings, September 1903, nos. 10–12, NAI.
112. Hoosen Coovadia et al., 'The Health and Health System of South Africa: Historical Roots of Current Public Health Challenge', *Health in South Africa*, vol. 374, 2009, p. 819, see https://www.ncbi.nlm.nih.gov/pubmed/19709728, accessed 12 November 2014.
113. Ibid.
114. In 1807, the first health legislation passed in Natal recommended the establishment of a supreme medical committee to oversee all health matters. Ordinance no. 82 of 1830 allowed for the regulation of all health practices in Cape Colony; the other three states—Natal, Transvaal, and Orange Free State—followed the Cape lead.
115. PC 1/2668, Medical Board Proceeding of Mauritius, 9 May 1859, TNA.
116. Richard B. Sheridan, *Doctors and Slave: A Medical and Demographic History of Slavery in the British West Indies, 1680–1834*, USA: Cambridge University Press, 1985, p. 55.
117. Ibid., p. 60.
118. Ibid., p. 70; The conditions of the slave hospitals were bad, being not only destitute of almost every convenience, but filthy to the extreme; the attendants, generally old Negro women, were unfit for active employment. John Luffman, *A Brief Account of the Island of Antigua: Together with the Customs and Manners of its Inhabitants, as well White as Black;.... In Letters to a Friend Written in the Years 1786, 1787, 1788*, London: Printed for and sold by J. Luffman, sold also by Darton and Harvey, 1789, p. 272.
119. Sharla M. Fett, *Working Cures: Healing, Health, and Power on Southern Slave Plantations*, London: The University of North Carolina Press, 2002, p. 29.
120. Ibid., p. 27.
121. Ibid.
122. Ibid., p. 145.
123. Ibid., p. 152.
124. David Aickin, 'From Plantation Medicine to Public Health: The State and Medicine in British Guiana 1838-1914', unpublished PhD thesis, University College London, UK, 2001, p. 75.
125. Coovadia et al., 'Health and Health System of South Africa', p. 30.
126. Natal Immigration Trust Board Report for the year 1901, L/PJ/6/591, India Office Records, British Library.
127. Boodhoo, *Health, Disease and Indian Immigrants*, p. 264.
128. Report of the Estate Hospital for the first half-year of 1902, Revenue and

Agriculture Department (Emigration Branch) Proceedings, August 1903, no. 12, NAI.

129. Coolie Commission of 1872, cited in Meer, *Documents of Indentured Labour*, p. 124.

130. Aickin, 'From Plantation Medicine to Public Health', p. 79.

131. Report of the Commissioners appointed to enquire into the treatment of immigrants in British Guiana, June 1871, CO 111/380, TNA.

132. Aickin, 'From Plantation Medicine to Public Health', p. 80.

133. Extract from *The Indian Opinion*, cited in Commerce and Industry Department (Emigration Branch) Proceedings, July 1912, nos. 43–4, NAI.

134. A.R. Mannick, *Mauritius: The Development of a Plural Society*, Nottingham: Russel Press Ltd., 1979, p. 115.

135. Goonam, *Coolie Doctor: An Autobiography*, India: Orient Longman Limited, 1998, p. 16.

136. D.S. Ogilvy, Stipendiary Magistrate of Flacq district, submitted his Report on Healthcare and Sanitation on the Estates, to the Medical Charity Commission of 1858; cited in Boodhoo, *Health, Disease and Indian Immigrants*, p. 168.

137. Ibid.

138. Annual Report of the Protector of Indian Immigrants in Natal for the year 1899, Revenue and Agriculture Department (Emigration Branch) Proceedings.

139. Annual Report of the Protector of Indian Immigrants in Natal for the year 1885, Revenue and Agriculture Department (Emigration Branch) Proceedings, October 1886, nos. 8–9, NAI.

140. Letter from the Chief Medical Officer to the Colonial Secretary, 29 May 1829, CO 167/212, TNA.

141. Ibid.

142. Medical Charity Report, Stipendiary Magistrate D.S. Ogilvy's report on Flacq district, 1859, CO 167/384, TNA.

143. Extract from the letter of Dr Davies to the Chief Medical Officer, Mauritius, regarding an inspection in Savanne district Ierracine estate camp, 3 November 1845, CO 167/253, TNA.

144. Extract from the letter of Dr Davies to the Chief Medical Officer, Mauritius, CO 167/253.

145. Frere and Williamson, *Report of the Royal Commissioners*, p. 356; cited in Boodhoo, *Health, Disease and Indian Immigrants*, p. 201.

146. Wragg Commission Report of 1885–7, cited in Meer, *Documents of Indentured Labour*, p. 469.

147. Annual Report of the Protector of Indian Immigrants in Natal for the year 1899, Revenue and Agriculture Department (Emigration Branch) Proceedings.

148. Medical Charity Report, Stipendiary Magistrate D.S. Ogilvy's report, CO 167/384.
149. Harold J. Cooks, 'Physical Methods', in *Companion Encyclopedia of the History of Medicine*, vol. II, ed. W.F. Bynum and R. Porter, London and New York: Routledge, 1993, p. 940.
150. Boodhoo, *Health, Disease and Indian Immigrants*, p. 135.
151. Wragg Commission Report of 1885–7, cited in Meer, *Documents of Indentured Labour*, p. 474.
152. Extract from the account of Revd James Ramsay, who had first-hand experience with slavery in St. Kitts, cited in Sheridan, *Doctors and Slave*, p. 272.
153. Annual Report of the Protector of Indian Immigrants in Mauritius for the year 1880, Dr Vitry's report on hospital food, Revenue and Agriculture Department (Emigration Branch) Proceedings, March 1882, nos. 3–4, NAI.
154. A letter from Dr Bolton to the Protector of Indian Immigrants in Mauritius, Revenue and Agriculture Department (Emigration Branch) Proceedings, August 1887, nos. 15–18, NAI.
155. Frere and Williamson, *Report of the Royal Commissioners*, p. 196; cited in Boodhoo, *Health, Disease and Indian Immigrants*, p. 201.
156. Coolie Commission of 1872, cited in Meer, *Documents of Indentured Labour*, p. 124.
157. Meer, *Documents of Indentured Labour*, p. 412.
158. Boodhoo, *Health, Disease and Indian Immigrants*, p. 182.
159. Annual Report of the Protector of Indian Immigrants in Natal for the year 1888–9, Revenue and Agriculture Department (Emigration Branch) Proceedings, December 1890, nos. 1–6, NAI.
160. Annual Report of Dr Vitry, Acting Medical Officer of the Immigration Department for the year 1881. Revenue and Agriculture Department (Emigration Branch) Proceedings, March 1883, nos. 2–4, NAI.
161. Boodhoo, *Health, Disease and Indian Immigrants*, p. 252.
162. Ibid.
163. Letter of the Visiting Medical Officer Janaki, 7 August 1895; cited in Boodhoo, *Health, Disease and Indian Immigrants*, p. 252.
164. Annual Report of Dr Vitry for the year 1881, Revenue and Agriculture Department (Emigration Branch) Proceedings.
165. Ibid.
166. Ibid.
167. Letter from the Chief Medical Officer to the Protector of Indian Immigrants in Mauritius, regarding female hospital attendants, 1884, Revenue and Agriculture Department (Emigration Branch) Proceedings, August 1886, no. 24, NAI.
168. Annual Report of the Protector of Indian Immigrants in Natal for the

year 1898, Revenue and Agriculture Department (Emigration Branch) Proceedings, August 1899, nos. 6–7, NAI.

169. Annual Report of the Protector of Indian Immigrants in Natal for the year 1899, Revenue and Agriculture Department (Emigration Branch) Proceedings, January 1901, nos. 10–12, NAI.

170. Kathinka Sinha-Kerkhoff et al., trs. *Autobiography of an Indian Indentured Labourer: Munshi Rahman Khan, 1874-1972*, Delhi: Shipra Publications, 2005.

171. Frantz Fanon, *A Dying Colonialism*, tr. Haakon Chevalier, New York: Grove Press, 1965, p. 123.

172. Fett, *Working Cures*, p. 44.

173. Ibid., p. 56.

174. Letter from the Chief Medical Officer to the Protector of Immigrants in Mauritius, Regarding female Hospital attendance, Revenue and Agriculture Department (Emigration Branch) Proceedings, August 1886, nos. 24 NAI.

175. Abhimanyu Anat, *Gandhiji Bole Theiy*, Delhi: Rajkamal Prakashan, 2008, pp. 164–7.

176. Seewoosagur Ramgoolam, *Our Struggle: 20th Century Mauritius (Presented by Anand Mulloo)*, New Delhi: Vision Books, 1982.

177. CO 882/2/9, Mauritius correspondence relating to Indian immigrants in Mauritius, TNA.

178. Coolie Commission of 1872, cited in Meer, *Documents of Indentured Labour*, p. 124.

179. Robert W. Fogel, and Stanley L. Engerman, *Time on the Cross: The Economics of American Negro Slavery*, USA: Little Brown and Company, 1974, pp. 120–1. They argued that 'while the quality of slave medical care was poor by modern standards, there is no evidence of exploitation in the medical care typically provided for plantation slaves. The inadequacy of care arose not from intent or lack of effort on the part of masters, but from the primitive nature of medical knowledge and practices in the antebellum era.'

CHAPTER FIVE

Diseases, Sanitation and Discipline
Matters of 'Medical Policing' in the Plantations

'… as regards sanitations, it is next to impossible to make or get most Indians to understand what it is, or to be cleanly in the sense we understood.… A European idea of personal or domestic purity is seldom if ever seen.'

— Report of the Medical Surgeon Avoca Central Estate Hospital, Annual Report of the Protector of Indian Immigrants in Natal for the year 1900

To the European mind, plantation colonies were places of, 'rude chaos', the people, 'child-like', and societies: 'disorderly', 'sick', and 'unclean'. In this engagement with the capitalist plantation system, order was required. Indeed, it was necessary for the Europeans, if they wished to make any impression on the anti-indentured group at home and outside, and among the nationalist leaders in India, to impose their notions of order, discipline, and well-being in the colonies. Indian immigrants, in Mauritius and Natal, were generally considered as 'pests'. They were, by habit, thought to be: 'unclean', 'impure', and 'unhealthy'— and thus were the cause for the outbreak of many epidemic diseases in the colonies.[1] Thus, the plantation regime became a space in which colonial planters could 'educate' the others, and instruct them about the importance of sanitation, health, and cleanliness, among other things. Modern society functioned through laws postulated by the police, and also throng prisons, fines, and social sanctions. According to the Europeans, these modern institutions hardly existed in the Indian, Chinese, and African societies; and even if they were there, they were surely in a degraded form and served purposes vastly different from those required by the modern capitalist society.[2]

From the 1870s on, great measures were taken in the colonies of Mauritius and Natal to improve the sanitary conditions. Measures were also taken to divide the colonies into sanitary zones. Sanitary inspectors were appointed, who were directed to submit annual reports to the magistrate of the respective colony. They were supposed to inquire into the indentured camps, their surroundings, animal sheds, hospitals, dispensaries, river streams, marketplaces, roadsides, butcher houses, and so on. The whole colony was under the direct gaze of these sanitary inspectors. This was not only the case with the colonies. In Britain as well, to keep surveillance across the city—streets, factories and workshops, a group of sanitary inspectors were appointed. In 1900, there were 260 sanitary inspectors, of all descriptions, working in London.[3] The principal duty of all these inspectors was to identify the 'nuisances' and make arrangements for their removal. Environment, social and civil, became the subject of the sanitary inspectors' surveillance. In this context, it can be mentioned here that medical science suggested a causal connection between dirt and disease. Tom Crook stated, 'the necessity of sensory refinement meant that, ideally, inspectors pursued a healthy lifestyle comprising daily exercise, nutritious food, scrupulous personal cleanliness and abstinence from cigarette and alcohol.'[4] Cases were also recorded against stables, builders' yards, boiler makers, and even piano teachers, on account of the noise they created.

This chapter would follow a discussion on the major epidemics in the colonies and to what extent these affected the management of the colonial governments and labour power. It would deal with important questions like those regarding the sanitary measures that were adopted by the government to cope with diseases like malaria, plague, hookworm, and venereal diseases among the indentured as well as the non-indentured labourers. The chapter would also enquire about the conditions of accommodation, rations, and water provisions that were provided to the emigrants, probing, at the same time, into the reasons that made the government extend its health and sanitation policies to the non-indentured labourers of the colonies.

Spread of Epidemics: Malaria and Plague

According to Colonel Nicholas Pike (Consul of the United States of America), '…Fevers once almost unknown in Mauritius are now fast becoming its bane … due to the great increase of the coloured population by immigration from India … India as a country is a source of diseases.'[5] Indians were thus blamed for bringing with them unknown diseases into the heavenly island of Mauritius. Dr C.F. Edwards, the General

Sanitary Inspector of the island, in his speech at the epidemiological society, mentioned that 'the Island of Mauritius formerly had the reputation of being one of the healthiest of the British colonies within the tropics. Its character had sadly changed.'[6] British Medical Officer Dr F.J. Mouat, who came to Mauritius to recuperate in 1851, described the island as a healthy place and tried to localize health resorts in the Indian Ocean where officers from India, affected by the heat and diseases of the Gangetic plains could recover their health. Thus, the colonial discourse provided a biased narration of the outbreak of diseases in the colony. The line of transportation of diseases was very clear—from the sea to the port city, and from the port city to other areas of the island. Slaves were blamed for having brought small pox into Mauritius, while the Indians were blamed for having brought malaria and cholera. The newspapers of Mauritius showed the local feelings about the epidemic diseases, stating that '...the epidemic of cholera could not be engendered by local causes and reappears every year in the colony; therefore, it must have been introduced from India.'[7] Colonial discourses presented the coloured body as a carrier of diseases and not as a victim of colonial rule. Auguste Toussaint, in his account, provided information about the series of epidemics that appeared in the city of Port Louis from the beginning with the French inhabitants. He stated, '...the town was already inhabited by a mixed population, and hygiene was practically unknown; so the slightest infection was likely to spread very quickly.' He wrote that Port Louis suffered heavily from epidemics and cyclones during the French period, but it suffered even rose during the nineteenth century.[8]

There were numerous epidemics that appeared in Mauritius before the malarial fever of 1867, which greatly swelled the death rate in the colony. Some prominent examples are—the epidemics of measles and smallpox in 1837–40; in 1841–5 of small pox and relapsing fever; and the epidemics of cholera in 1854–6 as well as in 1861–3. Leprosy, which came with the slaves in 1770, began to spread to all classes of society, even among some of the prosperous White families.[9] For the first time, the Leper's Enquiry Commission recommended the necessity of the introduction of a Contagious Diseases Act on the island. However, this recommendation was not fulfilled.[10] The Commission mentioned that 114 Indian men and 9 women were affected by the disease; while on the other hand, for the Creole population, this ratio was 73 and 31 respectively. The epidemic of cholera that spread from the Calcutta coolie ship hit the Creole population in the colony harder. It caused the death of 1,623 Creole men and 1,326 Creole women, as compared to

463 Indian men and 80 Indian women. Dr F.J. Mouat measures the effect of the epidemic in these words—'Cholera, in little more than half a century, has probably destroyed more victims and caused more widespread desolation of hearths and homes than all the wars that have been waged from the siege of Jerusalem to the siege of Paris; than all the other plagues …'.[11] Between 1899 and 1906, plague caused about 5,000 deaths on the island.[12]

Dr John Macpherson, in his paper *Epidemiological Trans.*, talked about the transition of 'Asiatic Cholera' from one country to another. He emphasized that these diseases travelled from India to the Arab countries centuries ago, and from there to Persia, Syria, and finally to Africa. He mentioned that 'Asiatic cholera' had attacked a Portuguese settler in Goa in 1629, and it had the same characteristics and symptoms of the disease known as *mordeshi* in India.[13] On the basis of this, he said that Asiatic cholera had its roots in India. Dr Smart again mentioned that in the 1830s, this disease passed from India to Europe; and in the 1870s, it travelled from India to Madagascar; and from there to Mauritius; but it was also possible that the island had been infected on a previous occasion from India, or had grown its own epidemic.[14] Another disease, believed to have come from India, which hit the island, was dengue fever. Besides beriberi; diphtheria, and malnutrition remained as great threats to public health during the entire colonial rule. The malaria epidemic of 1867 proved to be the first fatal epidemic in the island, which forced authorities to adopt sanitation policies for the benefit of public health. Sanitation Inspector Dr Edwards stated that due to this fatal fever and dysentery, the annual mortality rate had steadily increased among the Indian population,—upto 37 and 48 per 1000, in the rural district and the town of Port Louis, respectively.[15]

The outbreak of diseases like malaria, cholera, and plague had a serious impact on Mauritian society and economy. In 1867, the epidemic became a matter of concern not only for the planters and administrators, but also for medical practitioners. In the latter half of the nineteenth century, medical practitioners and scientists tried to search for the causes of malaria and cholera. The London School of Hygiene & Tropical Medicine and the Epidemiological Society of London played an important role in this field of research, particularly from the mid-nineteenth century onwards.

Ronald Ross stated that in 1867 malaria appeared for the first time in Mauritius. Ross calculated that 'one quarter of the inhabitants died during 1867 from all causes and more than one-fifth from fever alone'. The survivors, '…were so prostrated by diseases that the living were scarcely able to bury the dead.'[16] He further stated 'the actual malaria death rate was probably about 90 per mile … those who have witnessed malaria in its worst condition would not doubt these figures.'[17] Dr Henry Rogers, Senior Assistant-Surgeon to the Civil Hospital, stated that the year 1867 will long be remembered in Mauritius as one of the most disastrous in the annals of its history. He stated—'Business suspended, commerce at a standstill, public offices all but empty, railway traffic stopped, anxiety and distress in every household, such were the principal features which to the outer world characterized the presence of the epidemic amongst us.'[18] In May 1867, the government appointed a 'Fever Enquiry Commission' to report upon the causes of the outbreak, and their report was published in 1868. In this report, various hypotheses were presented by the members, in which almost all members and reports blamed the Indian ships, and the Indians and their insanitary conditions for the outbreak of malaria.

The outbreak of the disease raised heated arguments amongst the medical practitioners and researchers in the colony about the causes for its origin. There were two main arguments: one section argued that the disease came with the Indians in their ships; while on the other hand, it was also believed to have had a local origin because of the insanitary living conditions of the Indians there. It was in, as late as the 1890's that the mosquito theorem pointed to the cause of the problem. Ronald Ross proved that the carrier of malaria in Mauritius was 'Pyretophoruscostali', the dangerous African anopheline mosquito, which reached Mauritius before it reached India.

One of the members of this Fever Enquiry Commission, Dr Edwards, stated—'there is little doubt, however, that the disease was of local origin, and results from the bad sanitary condition in which the Indians live.…The prevailing fever, a low form of bilious remittent, was supposed by Mauritians to have been introduced by immigrants from Bombay, and is hence called "Bombay Fever".'[19] On the contrary, Dr A.R. Barraut, (Medical Officer of Health for Port Louis) in his report, stated that—

…I found that the existence of the fever could be traced in the colony as far back as 1838, and that it was chiefly localized among the Indian population, especially in the wretched huts which constitutes the camps of sugar estates. Slow at times in its progress, it broke out on several occasions with remarkable virulence, and caused great mortality. But the belief that it was an exclusively Indian disease was so universal, that though several instances took place among the general population, it attracted but very little attention … by a comparison of the symptoms which were seen in Mauritius, and those which were described as occurring in India, most notable distinctions were found which showed certainly some signs of similarity, but pointed in an especial manner to a difference not only in degree, but also in kind. It was the difficulty which I experienced in finding an appropriate and, at the same time, a legitimate name, for it, that I was so induced to retain its popular appellation of Bombay fever, however unscientific that name could appear.[20]

He stated that in Mauritius, malaria was more easily communicable, as compared to India. Dr Henry Rogers further wondered how this opinion had gained ground that the disease had been imported from India or elsewhere, while there were no newcomers, except one case, who had been found affected with the disease. He argued that the great droughts, the indiscriminate clearance of forestland, the gradually diminishing amount of rainfall, excavation for railways and gas pipelines, and the inundation of 1865, may be some of the causes, among others, for the enumeration of the disease.[21] Dr Edwards blamed government for not occurence sanitary measures as an important measure to prevent the spread of malaria, as he stated—'although repeatedly warned that fever was becoming far more formidable than cholera, they satisfied themselves with passing the most stringent quarantine laws, and turned a deaf ear to the advice and suggestions of those who advocated sanitary measures as the most effectual means of preventing the spread of the disease.'[22] Suggestions were made to adopt measures like reforestation, cleaning of rivers, cleaning of stagnant pools, drainage or filling of marshes, and strict sanitary measures.

In 1881, Dr C. Meldrum issued a detailed report in which he recommended drainage of marshes, re-wooding of mountains and slopes, draining of streams in the interior areas of the island, and strict sanitary rules. He concluded that though the expenditure of the Board of Health had amounted to Rs.1,596,488 during a period of nine years, yet the mortality rate of Port Louis and the rural districts had been on the rise since 1870, and had not been accompanied by any improvement in public health.[23] In 1891–2, Mr O. Chadwick wrote a series of reports on engineering matters, including sanitary works, in Mauritius. He appreciated many of Dr Meldrum's remarks and recommendations; but he objected to too many trees in towns, such as Port Louis, because, as he remarks, 'though forestation is in every respect desirable, a town is not the place for it.'[24] He also recommended underground sewers for Port Louis.

Malarial fever affected the colony once again in 1901–2. The disease ravaged the coastal and lower parts of the island, in spite of the expensive measures taken by the government. In 1901, the government appointed a second Malaria Enquiry Committee. It consisted of Dr Lorans (Chairman), Dr Edwards, Dr Rohan, Dr Clarenc, Dr Bolton, Dr A. Lesur, and M. Daruty de Granpre. The Committee suggested some important measures for the prevention of epidemics in the island. Ronald Ross highlighted the achievements of the Committee in these words—

...Streams...clogged with vegetation were cleaned out, quinine was distributed....Later on M. d'Emmerez de Charmoy was appointed Technical Assistant to the Committee for the purpose of continuing the study of mosquitoes and their haunts, and for disseminating knowledge on the subject among the public....The only defect that can be found in the work of this committee was that it was not generalized, nor continued long enough.[25]

Early in 1906, public alarm was intensified by another outbreak on the high ground—at Phoenix—and soon it spread over the whole island. Ross was appointed by the secretary of the states for the colonies on 9 May 1907, in order to report on the measures taken to prevent the outbreak of malaria in the colony. Ross stayed for three months in Mauritius to collect information and data on the disease. Consequently, he stated in his report, '...possibly the sickness of 1865 was nothing but relapsing fever, and true malaria did not enter until later'.[26]

In his report of 1908, Ross dismissed the entire hypothesis presented by the medical men related to the malaria epidemic of 1867. He suggested that Indians and immigrant ships had been arriving for centuries. Instead, floods and droughts were blamed; but again, they had been occurring for centuries. Disturbance of soil in connection with railways and other works afforded a popular refuge from the difficulty of pinpointing the cause, but it was pointed out that soil had often been disturbed and the largest railway work, constructed in 1864, was not followed by malaria and that laying gas supply pipes in Port Louis in 1864–5 remained equally harmless.

The diseases also caused a serious loss to agriculture, upon which the very existence of the colony depended.[27] Ross described the general picture of the affected areas in these words—

...The wealthiest residents had been practically driven out of the affected regions; the beautiful houses of the planters could be occupied only during two or three months of the cool season, their families could no longer enjoy rural life at the seaside, as they were formerly able to do. Everywhere the villages became more and more deserted. Even the Indian patients sought the upper regions. From five per cent to thirty per cent of the labourers in the malarious plantations was often incapacitated by fever, thus hampering further the resources of the planters, already greatly reduced by the fall in the price of sugar. Houses fell into ruin, or were removed part by part to healthier areas. The population of Port Louis began to diminish. The richer citizens now used it only as a place of business by day, returning to the plateau every evening ... Even the houses were abandoned; and everywhere one saw the ruined basements, overgrown gardens, deserted fountains, and mouldy gateways of the more prosperous past, now surrounded only by the poorest huts of Indians. It is the classical picture of a great endemic epidemic. Plague and cholera visit a country and vanish; but malaria and dysentery remain.[28]

Various preventive measures were adopted to battle malaria, and a sanitary secretary was appointed to spread knowledge and awareness among the public about the disease. Ross showed that during a period of seventy-six years (1831–1906), the death rate was 35.4 per cent in the colony and the average annual death rate per mile of the population was 37.4 per cent.[29] Malaria was responsible for 20 per cent of the deaths in the colony.[30] Bolton, the medical officer of the immigration department, estimated that malaria costs the estates in Mauritius Rs.650,000 a year in loss of labour, and to the labourers themselves, Rs.150,000 in loss of wages, besides similar losses to the general community.[31] The epidemic usually affected the free Indians (whose indentured contract had expired) and the lower classes of the community in the colony the most.[32] Suggestions were made by J.F. Trotter (Protector of Indian Immigrants in Mauritius) that the immigrants should not be allotted, during the first year of their residence in the colony, to estates within the malarial zone, unhealthy plantations, or unhealthy parts of the island. Suggestions were also made by the secretary of state for India to improve the sanitary conditions of the Indian immigrants.

By the 1890s, the mosquito theorem proved to be a solution to the problem of malarial fever. Ross, in his report, stated that the appearance of malaria in a locality depended upon Anophelines mosquitoes, which were capable of carrying the disease, and infecting persons. It was also concluded that the carrier of malaria in Mauritius, the Pyretophoruscostali, might have been introduced a little while before the outbreak. Ross also argued that this carrier had not yet reached India, when it reached Mauritius. Thus, he proved that the whole theory of 'Bombay fever' was false.[33]

Ross suggested that there were three measures which might be employed by public authorities to contain the disease—Anopheline reduction by proper drainage, case reduction by quinine, and isolation or protection from bites of mosquitoes. Ross further suggested that a periodical spleen census and treatment of children in schools and on estates, distribution of quinine, protection of houses from mosquitoes, and the establishment of a suitable organization (with qualified members) for prevention of the epidemic and which brought out an annual malaria report could be helpful to prevent cases on the island.

The primary medicines for the treatment of malaria were quinine and cinchona. In the comatose state which so frequently followed attacks of pernicious intermittent frew: ice to the head, a purgative injection, and a dozen leeches behind the ears when necessary, was the means medical men usually adopted for treatment.[34] The practice of bloodletting or phlebotomy were dominant features of Western medicine in the eighteenth and nineteenth centuries, and the use of medicinal leeches as a mild form of bloodletting achieved immense notoriety in the second quarter of the nineteenth century. The source of leeches in Mauritius was Pondicherry (south India), supplied between February to June, and July to November. There was a great demand for these leeches in Mauritius and the British West Indies, which was apparent from the advertisement in local newspapers. On its journey to the West Indies (1840s–70s), each indentured ship was required by the British government to have on board 100 leeches for each 100 passengers.[35] In European countries, the *Hirudo medicinalis* species of leeches was used for medicinal purpose, but this species was not available in India. Roy T. Sawyer argued that it would have been one of the large, aggressive 'Cattle' leeches *(Hirudinaria manillensis)* which were abundant in certain regions of India.

In 1901, Mauritius was declared as a malarious zone.[36] Ross was of the opinion that, '...a marsh in a malarious country is a nuisance, because it is certainly very dangerous to public health, as known since time immemorial and as recently as proven by the case of the Clairfond marsh in Mauritius.' Therefore, he was in favour of the taking up of legislative and administrative measures to compel planters and owners of the land to remove or discharge the marsh.[37] He stated that—

...There is much talk at present of research and instruction on tropical diseases; but it would seem that, though the cause and the mode of prevention of the most widespread and important of tropical diseases—one that often causes as much sickness as all the other diseases in the tropics put together—have already been discovered and taught, yet that little or no action is to follow the acquisition of that knowledge.[38]

In contrast to Mauritius, which suffered more from diseases like malaria, leprosy, plague, and lunacy: the population of Natal suffered

MAGISTRATE.   •   ASIATIC   •   CORONER

PLATE 5.1: Examining the Unnatural Death of the Asiatic

Source: Medical Report Mauritius, The National Archives of UK.

mainly from small pox, Asiatic cholera, venereal diseases, tuberculosis, leprosy, plague, and some other diseases like those of the foot and mouth, and diseases of the horse, sheep, and cattle—which posed a great threat to the government. In Natal, some of the diseases appeared for the first time in the colonial period. Malnutrition in children, high mortality rate among mothers, lung disorder and mesothelioma in mine workers, along with other sexually transmitted diseases (AIDS/HIV) were common in South Africa.[39] Leprosy appeared during the Dutch rule in the Cape colony and the first victims of this disease were two Europeans, who were involved in the transportation of slaves. In 1849, leprosy appeared in Natal for the first time among the Zulu tribes. It was the epidemic of small pox in Natal that forced the government, for the first time, to pass the Public Health Act of 1883, in order to prevent the epidemic among the inhabitants. It was also for the first time that concern was shown towards the health of the Africans, or the indigenous people of the colony. The Act made notification and inoculation of small pox compulsory.[40] It was further revised under the Public Health Amendment Act of 1897, which separated the curative and preventive care of the disease.

E.H. Cluver (MA, MD, DPH), Secretary of Public Health of the Union, stated that plague appeared for the first time in South Africa in 1899, as a result of the infection introduced from India. During the Anglo-Boer war, a further infection was introduced with forges and other articles imported by the British for military purposes from plague-infected ports in South America and India.[41] In Mauritius, it appeared in 1898.[42] Between 1900 and 1905, there were 1,694 cases reported from different parts of Natal, most of which were from Durban and Ladysmith.[43] Plague emerged as one of the most fatal infectious diseases in Natal. In the initial years of the epidemic, the death rate was reported to be about 50 per cent.

Ernest Hill, in his report on plague in Natal (1902), stated that the first case of plague was discovered in Durban in December 1902. During this period, 221 persons were affected, of whom 162 died; a case mortality of 73 per cent was recorded. After some research, he reached the conclusion that the disease was, in the main, spread by the agency of infected rats and mice. He further stated that—'it has been stated that complete success in the suppression of an outbreak of plague may be anticipated from the application of measures ordinarily adopted for the suppression of outbreaks of epidemic disease, of whatever nature, under rules framed in strict conformity with the principles of modern sanitary science.'[44]

It is interesting to note that rats and mice posed a great threat not only to the British government in Mauritius, but also to the previous Dutch government. Their presence made cultivation impossible, and thus the Dutch settlers were forced to leave the island. The Mauritian medical board of health employed Indian labourers every year to destroy the rats because of sanitary issues. It has been a matter of record in the annual report of the protector of immigrants, informing the number of people that were employed to kill the rats and how many they killed each year in each estate or district.[45] The medical inspector of Mauritius reported that in the district of Flacq, at Bean Champ Estate, two men destroyed about eighty-five rats weekly.[46] In the Estate of Bassin, one man destroyed about twenty rats weekly; in Henrietta, it was about seventy rats weekly by two men; in Trianon, seven men destroyed about fifty rats daily. These numbers reflect that the disease haunted the whole island and steps were taken to kill the rats in order to get rid of the problem. In the Martizburg district in Natal, the town council in 1900 started to pay a small reward for dead rats, in order to keep a check on plague in the district. A few weeks before the appearance of plague in the town, the reward was increased, and on the occurrence of plague, the amount was raised to sixpence a head.[47]

In Natal, the town council was the sanitary authority for the Borough of Durban. Under the Public Health Act, 1901, the town council had, in their respective boroughs, undivided control and responsibility over provisions of public health and sanitation. If the town council failed in any respect to carry out its duties, the government would have made arrangements for the proper execution of the whole or any part of those duties. The appearance of plague in Durban was initially limited to the narrow strip of land called Point. But by the end of the fifth week, it reached the centre of the town. The government paid the entire expenditure incurred for fighting against this disease. The mayor of Durban, the health officer for the colony, the medical officer of health for Borough, and the Port Health officer, were appointed as a committee, with the authority to take measures as might appear necessary.[48] A circular was sent to all medical practitioners detailing the symptoms and diagnostic points of the disease; printed slips were also issued for the guidance of the public, giving simple information as to the manner of spreading of the disease and the dangers to be anticipated, with advice as to how best to obviate the risks.[49] During the epidemic, the governor in council had the power to make new regulations for the speedy interment of the dead or for the destruction or disposal of bodies affected by bubonic plague. Sanitary officers were directed to make provisions for the conduct and direction of the route of funerals. They also guided and controlled the management of cemetery establishments, so that they may not be placed in unsuitable localities.[50] Strict measures were adopted to bury the dead body of the affected patients. The Hindus were allowed to burn their dead on an open pyre, while Mohammedans, who had grave religious prejudices against cremation, were permitted to bury their dead in lead-lined coffins, soldered before the removal.[51] Hill, in his report, was also of the opinion that measures of sanitation should be adopted by the government in order to prevent the spread of diseases.

Hill stated that very few Europeans suffered from the epidemic of plague in Natal, and the Indian and native population became the primary victims of the disease. In Durban, 83 natives were attacked, as against 92 Indians at the same place. He, however, mentioned that there was no ground for saying that Indians were, in general, more prone to diseases, or that the habits of Indians in Natal were conducive to it.[52]

The prosperous Mohammedan merchants proved no more susceptible than the Europeans. It was a question of material prosperity. Indians were attacked in Durban in the ratio of 75 males to 5 females. He further pointed out that the infection was more often contracted at the place of work, than of residence. He concluded the causes of infection in these words:

…The disease attacked with greater severity on persons living in those parts of the town which are maintained least in accord with the principles of Sanitary science … where dwellings are the worst constructed and most dilapidated, where ventilation is most deficient, where overcrowding and filth are greatest, where scavenging is least attended to, there—plague most prevailed among the residents.[53]

As a result of being the primary ones to get effected by the epidemic, the local Indian population became the subject of the inoculation, confinement, segregation, and compulsory hospitalization. During the heyday of plague, Indian coolies' dwellings were often destroyed in order to stop the spread of the epidemic. The Natal Public Health Act (1901) had given rights to the medical officers to remove coolies from the affected areas or houses and prevent them from returning until the danger had passed. They also had the right to destroy the houses of the coolies.[54] The weak social and economic conditions of the coolies made them the soft targets of the disease, which was further aggravated due to the lack of appropriate health administration on the part of the government. In the absence of proper knowledge about the causes of the disease, Indians became labelled as the carrier of epidemics. The reports of enquiry committees on epidemics and their suggestions forced the government to adopt public health policies in the colony in the latter half of the nineteenth century.

The report of the medical inspector and protector of immigrants of the colony ensured that the Indians were enjoying a much better position in Natal as compared to any other country, or even in their own country. Hill stated that the most insanitary areas in the towns of Natal bore no comparison with the normal conditions of an average Indian town. This explains the fact that plague had comparatively so little hold on countries where at least some degree of Western civilization pertained.[55] In his report, Hill admitted that in comparison to the United Kingdom, the general condition of the colony was grossly insanitary.

Sexually transmitted diseases also posed a great threat to the government of both the colonies, but Natal suffered the most. The treatment and regulating measures of venereal diseases (VD) show the connection between medical, moral, and sexual control of the labour class in the colonies. The whole purpose of management and control of VD was actually to increase the labour efficiency of present and future labourers. The annual report of the Protector of Indian Immigrants in Natal for 1903 shows that in this year, a total of 740 cases of diseases were recorded, out of which there were 400 cases of VD, syphilis, and gonorrhoea. More than 50 per cent cases of VD were reported from Natal.[56] A high rate of VD among the indentured made them unfit for labour on the plantations, and thus posed a great threat to the colonial economic policies. This also affected the working of the plantation economy; it devitalized indentured labourer, demasculinized them, and also made them unfit for the purpose. The concerned authorities further stated that it affected not only the existing indentured, but future generations of labourers too. Colonial discourse thus saw VD as a disease that resulted in a 'race eaten up'; a race that was a result of impure sexual intercourse.[57] As the medical officer of Avoca circle of Natal mentioned in his annual report—

…The disease is at the root of nine-tenths of the ailments of all kinds appearing on the sick list of the various estates in the circle. It is sapping the health and strength of the adults, and in many cases the children bear on their bodies evidence of the parents' diseased condition, and in this way not only does the patient suffer, but their helpless offspring too.[58]

Regarding syphilis, Dr Mouat stated—'…for while it does not startle us by violent explosions and great immediate mortality, it is an insidious poison, ever in active, although somewhat secret circulation, and threatens a moral and physical degeneration of the human race, which can and ought to be prevented by every means in our power.'[59]

Thus, Indian sexuality became an issue of colonial 'right' and 'wrong'. Out of the limited Indian indentured immigrants working on the plantation economy, a large number of Indians were suffering from syphilis, gonorrhoea, and other venereal diseases. Indian sexuality was thus debated unabatedly; the colonial government justified that it had a ground to interfere in the private lives of indentured individuals and impose rigid control over their sexual activities, especially of the women. The whole notion of venereal diseases involved a social, moral, and medical reconstruction of: 'sick' and 'healthy', with a focus on the sanitary state of sexual organs of the individuals.[60] In colonial patriarchal society, syphilis and other venereal diseases were portrayed as typical feminine diseases, since women were regarded as their carriers. The transmission line of the diseases was considered to be linear, that is, from female to male. Colonial discourse thus shows that men were the victims of female infection.[61] It was believed that there was no reliable cure for most venereal complaints, and men could not and should not be punished. They saw women as the only site in which they could intervene and the prevention of these diseases was directly associated with control over women. It also provided a tool for the extension of colonized space through the control of the state over female privacy.[62] Sexuality was thus an issue of 'race' and gender differences among the colonizer and the colonized, which provided the colonizer the justification for a supposedly higher moral ground over the indentured labourers. The issues of VD and health were also co-related to the issue of discipline, and so, the state needed to assert and maintain control over the indentured's sexuality in order to sustain its rule.

In the 1890s, a debate took place in senior government circles about the desirability of introducing compulsory genital examination of immigrant labourers; and consequently, in 1892, it was made compulsory. They also made the provision that—'if any Indian, affected with any venereal disease, was not willing to go to the hospital, he may be arrested and taken before the magistrate of the division.'[63] The Indian people resisted against these new laws, which made their body a site of discipline and control. As a protector mentioned in one of his reports, '...Thus women's resistance against the plantation hospital system forced the government to adopt a new policy to control these women and their sexuality.' In these circumstances, they mentioned that the Contagious Diseases Act was of utmost importance to control VD.[64] This was also important as a way to deal with the sexual disorders among the immigrant people, and control them in the name of providing safe sexual intercourse. The role of the Contagious Diseases Act in the plantation economy was thus very clear. It was not about controlling the sexual acts of the immigrants but trying to control VD, and thus providing healthy female partners to the male emigrants. But VD laws failed to control the diseases, as women refused to get examined or go to hospitals, preferring to remain on the estate.[65] In Mauritius, the authorities also tried to control venereal diseases, but they failed to pass the Contagious Disease Act.[66] On the other hand, in order to cure women, the Natal colonial government established a 'Lock Hospital' in 1903, for Indian immigrant women.[67] However, the Indian people were not willing to accept colonial reforms and sanitary programs; they actively expressed their resistance against these reforms. They also tried to hide their medical condition as much as possible, and so there was hardly any reduction in the number of VD cases.[68] In conclusion, it can be said that during the whole indentured era, the government could not control venereal diseases in the colony, which remains a matter of threat to the government of the Republic of South Africa till date.

Ankylostomiasis was another disease which terrified the colonies. It emerged in both the colonies, but Natal suffered more because it spread more in the sub-tropical region. In 1908, a discussion on ankylostomiasis showed that it was especially in the rural area that 50 to 90 per cent of the inhabitants were affected.[69] In Natal, after Asiatic cholera and bubonic plague, ankylostomiasis was the third disease that received a wide space in terms of attention and discussion in official files. Patrick Manson (Medical Adviser to the colonial office) measured the effect of the disease on the human body and found that the most immediate effect of the disease was anaemia. Manson stated—'The anemia may develop in the absence of any complicating condition, but is most prone to show itself when to the ankylostomiasis is superadded such causes of debility as malaria, dysentery, syphilis, tuberculosis, kala azar, pregnancy, insufficient or bad food, and so forth, occurrences common enough in the haunts of the parasites.'[70] Some medical practitioners regard ankylostomiasis, both in the contexts of life and labour capacity of the community, as being in aggregate a more serious disease than even cholera or yellow fever. In Natal, it was discovered by the medical practitioners that the disease was introduced by Indian immigrants in the colony, which soon spread to the local inhabitants. The discussion on tropical medicine in October 1908 shows that a large section of the tribal populations in Zululand, Transvaal, and Natal were affected by this disease. However, it existed in Natal and its surrounding areas because of local causes, and not because of Indian immigrants. The poor working conditions, bad quality of accommodation, insufficient food supplies, and insanitary conditions of the coolie lines were largely responsible for the spread of diseases.

Certain measures were adopted to stop the fresh recruitment of affected people from India.[71] In Natal, the coal mine workers were among the most affected with ankylostomiasis. Broadly, the natives of Transvaal and the Zulu community were the most affected by the disease. The discussion on the tropical diseases among medical practitioners emphasized that the prominent cause of the disease was the sanitation measures in the colony. Manson stated that—

...It is known that the parasite inhabits principally the small intestine; that its eggs pass out with the faeces; that if these are deposited on the ground and exposed to the air in a warm, damp, and shaded spot, the larval worm is quickly hatched out; the larvae, after undergoing several ecdyses, wander about in the damp earth, and may continue to do so, conditions remaining favourable, for at least several months; that if they come in contact with the surface of any part of the human body they penetrate the skin, pass to the lungs, and thence, via the trachea, esophagus and stomach, to the small intestine, where they obtain sexual maturity and produce disease.[72]

New experiments help discover that infection through skin was the usual channel and the skin disease, variously known as 'coolie itch' and 'bunches', was the primary lesion of ankylostomiasis and an indication of the infection. The drugs that were in use for the prevention of ankylostomiasis were thymol, beta-naphthol, and eucalyptus oil in combination with chloroform, castor oil, and *fifix mas*.[73] Manson suggested some measures to prevent the infection, such as by expelling the mature worms, preventing the hatching of the eggs, killing the larvae, and preventing contact of the larvae with the skin. Suggestions were also made to introduce a particular type of latrine to avoid contact with the soil, and a fine was to be imposed on the non-users of toilets. The compulsory use of shoes and tarring of the feet were also suggested as protective measures, but these methods were considered expensive, and most of the native population, their children, and the Indians; were blamed for not being used to these habits. Indians were also prevented from lying down to rest or loaf on the naked earth.

The indentured, however, had an altogether different notion about the causes of diseases as compared to the Western medical theories. According to them, diseases were caused either by evil spirits entering the body or by the wrath of an offended god or goddess. Religion had a powerful impact on the health of an individual, not only in Hinduism and Islam, but also in Christianity. Good health comprised both temporal and spiritual health. Sarla Fett's work on South American slaves shows that the Indian indentured labourers and African slaves shared the same belief about the origin and spread of diseases. Raj Boodhoo, in his work, shows that like in India, *Kalimay* (shrines of Kali representing Shakti or power) were set up on the edges of most sugar estates by the Indians to guard themselves from epidemics and natural calamities like droughts and cyclones. The Indian community even considered the epidemics in the White community or in the colony in general, as a manifestation of the wrath of goddess, as a result of the brutal behaviour of the Whites with the labouring class. As a result of all these epidemics and their consequences, the colonial government was forced to adopt new health and sanitation policies. The threat of the major epidemics forced the government to extend its health policies even to the free labourers and local population of the colony.

Medical Policing: Public Health and Sanitation

> … I hold that in matters affecting the public health, and in consequence, the life, happiness and well-being of the community at large, all legislation should be compulsory; and no one should be permitted, from any selfish motive, to spread abroad pestilence, any more than he should be allowed with impunity to set fire to his own house, without heed of the risk of injury and destruction thereby caused to the dwellings of his neighbours.

The modern sanitary measures were based on the aforementioned idea of 'medical policing' which subjected natives and Indians to strict surveillance. Indians and the native residents were subjected to living in a confined area of the colony, far from the European residences and dwellings. J.S. La Fontaine argued, '…the colonial pattern of the twentieth century set coloured and European urban communities physically apart, separated by sanifaire cordon of uninhabited ground, designed to prevent the spread of disease into the White residential areas.'[74] Free Indians were also the subject of surveillance and were prohibited to walk freely from one place to another. The Indian and native populations were forced to learn the 'civilized' lifestyle of White people, which colonizers thought helped to reduce sicknesses and epidemics in the colony. Ernest Hill, in the context of medical policing in Natal, stated, '…of course, with an Indian or Kaffir population constant supervision is essential, for their ideas of sanitation are not sufficient, in my opinion, to allow them to live in any area where Europeans reside; but while such is the order of things, they will have to conform to the habits of the White men.'[75] As 'Asiatic cholera' attacked most severely the poorest and the weakest, the masses and the Indian camps, it took on a 'class character'. The notion that by staying near the residences of the poor, the wealthy and civilized would also contract cholera and die of it became very popular. The poor, on the other hand, turned feelings of resentment, suspicion, and blame against the wealthy and those in authority.[76] Maynard W. Swanson mentions that the municipality of Durban attempted, in 1870, to establish a location specifically for the Indians, to remove the—'breeding haunts and nursery grounds of disease, misery and discomfort', with which the Indian settlement was believed to have menaced the town. Maynard further points out that in the early 1890s, authorities in Durban tried again to restrict Indian settlements to certain municipal locations in order to achieve, in the words of its Mayor, '…the isolation with better hopes of cure of this our social leprosy'.[77] In short, the metaphoric equation of 'Indians' and 'Kaffirs' with poverty and disease became a steady refrain of 'White' opinion and a preoccupation of the police and health officers in the colony.

In Mauritius, the General Board of Health, composed of one or two medical men, the mayor of Port Louis, the chief medical officer (who was the president of the Board), and half a dozen merchants and planters; was in charge of the medical affairs of the island.[78] Three sanitary officers, a sanitary warden, and two sanitary guardians formed the staff that had charge of the sanitary control of the island. A person with a diploma in sanitary science, public health, state medicine, and hygiene was considered, 'legally qualified' for the practice of medicine as the chief sanitary officer.[79] In Natal, the sanitary inspector, with some constables, and the Emigrant Trust Board were responsible for the medical and sanitary measures being implemented. The colony was divided in two boroughs, Pietermaritzburg and Durban. The health officers of these boroughs were supposed to report to the chief medical officer of the colony.[80] In Mauritius, the department of Medical Public Service comprised two wings—the departments of Medical Charity and Medical Police.[81] The Medical Charity Commission was responsible for providing suggestions on scavenging houses, underground drainage, and construction of the houses for the poor, constructing public baths and washing places, and providing reports on civil hospitals, among others. On the other hand, the duties of the medical police were defined for the preservation of public health in the colony.[82] The resources do not talk about the function of the medical police in the colony. The medical inspector and inspector general of police formed the main authority of the Medical Police department. The responsibility of this department was to stop sick people, such as lunatics, lepers, and other harmful persons, from wandering from one place to another. Furthermore, vagrant Indians, who were blamed for the spread of diseases from one region to another, were also subject to tight surveillance by the medical police. Police service was utilized in times of epidemics to distribute quinine to the affected areas. They also played an important role in the mission of compulsory vaccination in the colony. Police compelled masters to send their Indian servants to the nearest vaccination centre. The purpose of the medical police was not to heal or cure the patients, but to confine and segregate them from the European settlements.

The Government of Mauritius, through Ordinance no. 32 of 1894–5, amended the constitution of the General Board of Health, created a Medical and Health department and formulated the laws related to public health on the Island. The Natal government passed the Public Health Act 4 of 1883. Public health constituted all aspects related to sanitation and health, such as planning of towns and port areas; provisions of drinking water, accommodation, markets, butcher shops; sewerage and drainage; plantation of trees on roadsides; cleaning of rivers and streams; cleanliness of coolie dwellings, public baths, and washing houses; cleaning of cattle sheds and stables, and their proper management.[83] The health officers of the districts and boroughs were responsible for providing weekly reports of the population in their respective areas—number of births and deaths, with causes of death and the number of recorded diseases in area. In the colony of Natal, cattle diseases posed a major threat to the government. Cattle rearing was a chief source of livelihood among the Kaffirs in Natal. Therefore, cows, sheep, goats, and horses were among the first victims of some of the epidemics. They also played an important role in the spread of diseases.

The sanitary inspector and medical police were instructed to confine the lepers and lunatics, who were wandering in the residential areas and public places, to a proper asylum. In the asylum, however, no proper facilities and comforts were available to the inmates. The staff of the hospital shuddered at the thought of touching them due to the fear of infection. In 1875, the lunatic asylums of Mauritius were already overcrowded and it was dangerous to keep inmates there in the hot and humid season.[84] It could have accelerated the spreading of diseases in the colony even further. Therefore, the government tried to get rid of these people by sending them back to India. It was recorded that during 1878, there were on average 681 paupers or lepers seeking admission in the asylum, hospitals, or outdoor relief on a daily basis in the colony.[85] On the subject of confinement of lepers, the protector of Indian immigrants in Mauritius reacted by saying that such measures had been taken but the trouble was that the majority of lepers did not go to the asylum, and preferred to beg from place to place or to sit in public places seeking alms.[86] He further stated that after a point, when they got tired of begging, they applied for the free return passage to their home in

India, and it was only under such circumstances that a leper was ever sent back to his native country. The Government of Mauritius's 'cleaning measures' thus forced the affected Indians to leave the colony. The colonial authority simply turned its eyes away from the needs of these unproductive labour bodies.

Besides the sick bodies, a large proportion of vagrant people were also present in the colonies. In Mauritius, these vagrants posed a great threat to the discipline and sanitary measures for the authority. The government came with various legal measures to tackle these people and labelled them as criminals, believing that they lived on robbery, theft, or begging. Attempts were also made to compel them to the routine of labour. In 1881, there were about 20,000 Indian adult males who were considered vagrants in the colony.[87] The Colonial Registrar General Mr Kyshe, in his report of 1878, suggested that if this class would be allowed to gain an honest livelihood, there would be no need for labour migration from India in the future. He further stated that—

…The population of this already over-populated Island would not thereby increase at such a ratio as to give cause of alarm that, at some future date, probably not far distant, an epidemic, similar to the one which broke out in 1867, when upwards of 40,000 died in one year, will again appear and make sad havoc in our midst.[88]

The suggestion of the registrar general that the prevention of immigration from India was necessary, was declined on the grounds that during 1871–8, there was an increase in the demand of Indian labourers for the sugar industry as compared to their existing population in the colony. The management of vagrants and delinquent Indians remained an issue for checking in both the colonies. The Natal government tried to deal with this by issuing passes to Indians. After 1866, 'coolies' travelling in the colony without a pass was a criminal offence in Natal.

During the mid-nineteenth century, advice literature on plantation management proliferated, and these emphasized on planters' duties, regulation of health, and system of housing; as well as punishments. Through these measures, the planters attempted to extend control and promote plantation productivity, and ultimately maintain the social order of the indentured society. The Indians' weak social and economic position made them prone to various diseases. Apart from that, their working and living conditions also remained poor in quality. On their arrival in the estates, the Indians were provided by their masters with accommodation that was unsuitable for habitation—dark barracks, surrounded by dirt and filth. Initially, no attempts were made by the authority or the government to interfere in the matters of the planters and their management of the labour force. The high morbidity and mortality rates of the Indian population, the reaction of the Indian government, the indentures' own efforts, and most importantly the spread of epidemics in the colony forced the government to interfere in the matters of the coolies. The employers were instructed to provide proper and sufficient rations, clean and pure water, and healthy accommodation to the emigrants. Indians were blamed as vulnerable to disease because of their unhygienic habits. Therefore, they started the sanitation mission for imbibing the ideas of 'cleanliness' and 'civilization' among the labourers. As the immigrant protector of Natal stated, '…if the coolies could be impressed with three main ideas, viz., keep themselves clean, wear clothing in keeping with the climate, drink water either filtered or boiled, I venture to say their ailments would be reduced to a very low percentage.'[89]

The following lines would be useful in providing a glimpse of the multi-purpose accommodations of the coolies—

…The six foot by eight foot CSR room
Is the source of all comfort to us.
In it we keep our tools and hoe,
And also the grinding stone and the hearth.
In it we also kept the firewood.
It is our single and double-storey palace,
In which is made our golden parapet.[90]

A provision was made for the immigrants to make houses from bricks and stones, as the grass huts which they used were not adequate during the winter season, and also caught fire easily. These huts also had no proper provision for ventilation. As reports show, burning and suffocation were a major cause of death among indentured and their children in the colonies.[91] Apart from that, cyclones and hurricanes also played a major role in the destruction of coolie huts in Mauritius. The Avoca district medical officer explained to the protector in his annual report that 'night blindness' was common among Indians. One of the causes for that was the closing of the entrance of the hut when a fire was lit. Damp firewood gave off, '…strong and offensive smoke which filled the place and irritated the eyes very much'. Another cause was the 'bright clear light' and 'reflection on the eyes from the sand' followed by 'utter darkness' on entering the hut.[92]

Single males were forced to share their room with other coolies. Married couples with children were kept together in one room. Therefore, overcrowded dwellings were also a major problem in the coolie camps. Suggestions were made by the immigrant protector that lodging a number of human beings under the same roof added to the causes of disease and fire.[93] In such a situation, the immigrant protector recommended that it would be economical to build two stone walls with a roof placed on it. However, ventilation and air circulation still remained a problem. Sanitary inspectors were instructed to visit the narrow lanes of the coolie camps and make them free from slop and refuse, and were asked to make sure that waste be thrown out of the huts of coolies.[94] Suggestions were also made to raise the walls of the huts to a certain height, so that air could pass through them freely. Dr Edwards described the condition of the Indians' huts in these words—'the camps were all badly constructed, and many were quite unfit for habitation; the huts being small, dark, frequently roofed with iron or tin, ill ventilated, and badly drained'.[95]

The recommended size of the each quarter was 8 ft. by 12 ft. and 10 ft. by 9 ft. for Mauritius and Natal respectively. In both Mauritius and Natal, indentured barracks were constructed back-to-back. In 1903, it was recommended that back-to-back dwellings were contrary to public health regulations. It was only after this, that the measures for making proper dwellings for coolies were accepted in the colonies. These measures, related to the housing of the working class, were started in England during the period of 1800–1850s.[96]

The housing conditions were worse for the free labourers. After completing the contractual period, the indentured had to vacate the coolie house that he was provided with, and look for some other place. Those who were able to save some money could purchase land in the colony and settle there, but most of the people could not save enough money for buying land. Consequently, they were left to roam around the streets of Durban and Port Louis in search of a livelihood. Some of them became day labourers, shopkeepers, servants, and agriculturists, among other things. They were blamed as being the chief carriers of diseases. Dr Edwards in 1867 described their situation in these words—

… it was at this time that hundreds of Indians, whose contracts of services had expired, and finding no employment on sugar estates owing to the financial difficulties of the planters, flocked into the town, or settled themselves in the wretched huts used as dwellings by that part of the population in the suburbs of Port Louis.[97]

Plate 5.2: Coolie Line at the Sugar Estate of Moka

Source: Andrew Balfour, Report on Medical Matters in Mauritius.

These huts (aforementioned) were made up principally of wood from cases that were used to bring merchandise from Europe. The huts were covered with tin, and generally never more than four or five feet in height. Dr Edwards also stated that some enterprising Indians, at times, owned a dozen of these huts, and they reaped considerable profit by lending them to their comrades. The Mauritius Public Health Ordinance recommended that no house would be erected without sufficient provisions for drainage—the size of the drain, its construction material, and level being decided by the Local Health Board of Mauritius. Article 17 of the ordinance decided that in the absence of proper drainage, a penalty of 10 pounds sterling would be levied on the builder, and 5 pounds sterling on the owner of the house.[98] The Natal Public Health Act also provided legal rights to the sanitary inspector to compel people to make provisions for the proper drainage of their premises.

The houses of these free Indians, along with those of the local population, became sites to check by the sanitary inspectors. Employers were made to ensure a healthy environment in the coolie dwellings. Although the aforementioned measures were adopted, there was no visible improvement in terms of sanitation. Consequently, the colonial government came up with more stringent regulations and public health policies. The Natal government passed a 'sanitation law', according to which any Indian who kept his house or premises (included dwellings, hut, and hotels) in such a condition as to be a source of nuisance and injury to health: was liable, on conviction, to a fine or imprisonment.[99] The Natal Public Health Act of 1883 also made the provision that if any person suffering from infectious diseases hired or occupied any house or a part of it, he shall be liable to a penalty of 20 pounds sterling.[100] The Natal Public Health Act of 1894 further increased the amount of this fine from 20 to 50 pounds sterling, or imprisonment with or without hard labour, for a maximum of three months. This act made the provision that—every health officer and sanitary inspector, and any constable or other person; having an order in writing for the purpose signed by a health officer or sanitary inspector, shall have authority to enter any house, building, enclosure, or premises for the purpose of inspection.[101] The Public Health Act of 1894 recommended that every order declaring a disease to be infectious or of epidemic proportion; epidemic shall be published at least four times in the *Natal Government Gazette*, and in each of the four newspapers, and a copy of it should be sent to every registered medical practitioner in the colony.

The hiding of diseases or sick persons became a crime. The inhabitants of the colonies were directed to inform the cause of any untimely death to the sanitary inspector. The Natal Public Health Act pronounced that it was the duty of every medical practitioner, on becoming aware that any patient visited by him was suffering from an infectious or epidemic disease, to send to the district health officer a certificate in the form which may be prescribed—stating the name and residence of the patient, and the disease from which, in the opinion of the medical practitioner, the patient was suffering.[102] On failing to do so, that medical officer would be liable upon conviction by the magistrate to a fine of maximum 100 pounds sterling, and in case of default of payment, to imprisonment with or without hard labour for a maximum of three months.

In Mauritius, the Chinese community was very suspicious about the White's notion of burial and postmortem policies, so they tried to hide their relatives' deaths and sickness and kept it between themselves. The sanitary officers tried to search for some of their loyalists in the Creole population or the Indian community, who could inform the authorities about sicknesses and deaths in the Chinese neighbourhood.[103] The whole country was thus living in fear of epidemics and diseases, and the authorities and overseers tried to avoid direct contact with the coolies.[104]

Initially, planters and the Mauritian authorities did not interfere in the religious ceremonies, and music and dancing occassions among the Indians. There are references to celebrations of Holi and Muharram in

PLATE 5.3: An example of a well-to-do Indian's House in Mauritius

Source: Andrew Balfour, Report on Medical Matters in Mauritius.

these colonies. The planters at times even provided plots of land near the indentured camps or on the riverbanks for setting up shrines. They also contributed financially in the organization of some ceremonies and animal sacrifices.[105] However, during the period of epidemics, public opinion (of the whites) held Indians and their rituals responsible for the spread of diseases in the colonies. The white inhabitants demanded for the prohibition of such acts, which they thought were dangerous for public health. The notions of 'clean' and 'dirty' were associated with these rituals. The celebration of Holi was considered as not only being related to the physical uncleanliness, but also with sexual impurity. During the festival, the intermingling of men and women was considered common in lower classes of Indians. The Tazia festival among Indians also drew enormous crowds. During Muharram celebrations, many Hindus and Muslims built *Tazia* tombs to the martyrs Hassan and Hussain, and carried them on parade. The tombs were then destroyed and thrown into the rivers or the sea.[106] Drinking and smoking (*dakka*) was part of the celebration. Like Holi, this celebratory destruction on Muharram pitted the White community against its practice. In Natal, people filed petitions against the procession in Ladysmith.[107] The White community considered that loud music, beating of drums by naked 'fanatics', and the singing and dancing, was not appropriate for the safety of the colony. Goolam Vahed, in his work on Muharram, quoted Meldrum's observation in these words—

…The pagoda [British colonial name for *Tazia*] was taken to the river, where, after great beating of tom-toms and wild dances, the emblems were immersed, most of the faithful also sprinkling their heads with water. Many children were also baptized by their parents. The top of the pagoda was then covered with white cloth, and the lower part opened. From it were taken basins of what appeared to be boiled rice which was eagerly fought for and devoured. Thus ended the celebration.[108]

The mayor of Durban informed the colonial secretary in 1891 that the festival—'…has become an intolerable nuisance, resulting only in drunkenness and riot'. In 1891, a police officer named Alexander urged the authorities to 'put a stop to this absurd annual Indian Pagoda parading business about our streets … [otherwise] we may expect shortly to have an army of these skull-breaking fanatics taking charge of our Borough.'[109] In 1902, he stated that Muharram was 'nothing more than an excuse for drunkenness, riotous conduct, and vengeful feelings towards those parties they may have a grudge against, particularly the police'. Thus, he tried to regulate the celebration and stopped the procession of *Tazia* in the main street of the colony. These kinds of prohibitions were also regulated in India at religious places, such as Puri and Haridwar. Regulations were also placed on the hajj pilgrimage, which the colonial authority held responsible for spreading diseases and epidemics in India and outside.[110] While in Mauritius and Natal the celebrations of these festivals continued in the countryside, the sanitation officers succeeded in stopping the celebrations in towns and cities near the habitations of white populations.

Thus, through law, police, and terror, the colonial government tried to control and discipline the Indian people. Medical and sanitary science considered that controlling and disciplining the Indian community in the colonies would automatically resolve the problem of public health. The government thus imposed heavy fines on people who neglected the rules of the medical men or sanitary inspectors. The tight surveillance and sanitation rules, however, caused much difficulty to the Indians, who mostly resided in places near waterbodies and forest areas. Governor John Pope-Hennessy referred to the case of one Capoochand, who had been in Mauritius for only nine months and was fined Rs.50 or, twenty days of imprisonment, for breaking a twig from a tree to clean his teeth: and the case of one Rajcoomer and his son, aged ten, both of whom were jailed for the non-payment of fines of Rs.400 each. They accidently broke four pieces of brushwood that were 12 in. long when they were engaged in work on their master's land, adjacent to a forest reserve.[111] The sanitation law and public health act slowly extended to each of the colonies of the British government. The Natal government too had a stringent law regarding sanitation and public health in the colony, but it was the Government of Mauritius that went too far; regarding the fine and punishment for the negligence of public health policy, as could be seen in case of the quarantine law. However, public health conditions underwent little change in spite of such laws and regulations. Most of the Indians were forced to pay fines or remain behind bars because the government failed to provide them with alternative sources of their things of daily use.

The dietary habits of the indentured labourers was another pertinent issue. In both the colonies, the indentured were provided their rations per week in advance. The ration included rice, *dhall*, salted fish, ghee, and salt. For milk, vegetables, and protein, they were dependent on the settlers in the Indian or the local communities, if they could afford it. The diet scales, which were adopted in Indian depots and on emigrant ships, were no more relevant in the colonies. The high rate of sickness among the new arrivals forced the immigrant protectors to recommend a proper diet for the first year of indenture. Women and children received half the ration as compared to the male indentured labourers in Natal. It was also noticed that the provided ration was not sufficient for the able-bodied labourers. Apart from this, the deduction in the recommended amount was also a major issue. In case of Mauritius and Natal, the indentured were recruited in India, wherein they signed a contract in which salted fish was one of the items to eat. But this was provided on very few estates, while other estates tried to substitute it by giving them an additional quantity of *dhall*.[112] Apart from the quantity, the quality of the food was also a major problem and a cause of agitation among the coolies. As an emigrant protector of Natal stated—

… on my recent visit to the Stanger medical circle, the Indians on one estate complained of the quality of the meal issued. A sample was produced, which proved own words, as far as I was able to judge to be altogether unfit for human food. The employer, who was present at the time, had to admit the fact, and immediately ordered a fresh issue.[113]

Rations issued to the indentured were deficit in nitrogenous matter, and they did not receive any fruit.[114] Govinthan (indentured no. 15213) and ten workers employed by Duncan McKenzie of Nottingham, complained to the protector in February 1882, that they had not received rations for three months.[115] Runglal (indentured no. 8558), who worked at Evans of Umgeni, complained in November 1877 that he had only received half rations in the preceding three weeks.[116]

In Natal, during the initial years of the indentured system, employers refused rations to the women and children. The employers then did not see the productive value of women and did not also compel them to work. The Natal planters followed the principle of 'no work-no ration', and as a result, the shortage of rations forced Indian women to (re) assign themselves to different odd jobs, even during the advanced stages of pregnancy or illness. In the 1880s, laws were implemented to support the idea that women should be compelled to work, unless they had a medical certificate to attest otherwise.[117]

It was only in 1900 that the Natal government recommended, at least on paper, that the indentured labourers working in coal mines should be provided with fresh vegetables like potatoes and pumpkins twice in a week, and if the vegetables were not available, then they should get meat (fresh mutton) once in a week.[118] Denise M. Amos, in his thesis, shows that till the beginning of the twentieth century, carbohydrate and protein remained a major part of the working class diet.[119] It was a notion that food containing fat was favourable for manual work. The famous work of E.J. Hobsbawm, *The Standard of Living during the Industrial Revolution: A Debate*, further strengthens this view by showing the variety of food and its consumption by the English working class in the early nineteenth century. His work shows that meat became a part of the regular diet for the working class during the first fifty years of nineteenth century England. Consumption of potatoes increased rapidly, while the consumption of brown bread was replaced by white bread.[120] He also noticed the decline in the consumption of milk and cheese, but not in butter; and that there was little mention of fruits and vegetables in the contemporary dietaries. It was only in 1912 that the discovery of vitamins helped to reduce malnutrition, sickness, and death rate among the working class and their children.[121]

The next concern for sanitation was drinking water and the cleaning of water streams in the colony. Availability of clean drinking water was a major problem in the colony for the coolies. Water for drinking and domestic use was not available near the places of dwelling of the coolies, and no such measure was adopted that would provide them with clean and pure water. Under such circumstances, the coolie population depended on the nearest 'water closet' or river for water for drinking and domestic works, including washing. It was assumed by the White people that Indians were used to this custom and hence, there was no attempt to stop them from using these unclean water sources. After the 1870s, cleaning of rivers and water streams became a part of sanitary measures. The Public Health Ordinance of Mauritius, 1898, considered that the Local Board of Health, was responsible for the cleanliness of rivers and other waterbodies. The ordinance made the provision that polluting the river water or any water closet, which could be injurious to human health, was an offence, and the person responsible was liable to pay 5 shillings per day for the offence.[122] The Natal Public Health Act prohibited the bathing of any being in any river, stream, or waterbody when suffering from a contagious or infectious disease, which was likely to endanger public health.[123] In case of violation of such rules, the person concerned would be guilty of an offence and would be liable to a penalty of maximum 50 pounds sterling. Sanitation rules also prohibited the discharge of dead animals, rubbish, manure, cane trash, any type of filth, and any poisonous, alcoholic, or narcotic substance, into the water of a stream, river, or watercourse, tending to pollute the same.

The first attempt towards improving public health was the making of provisions for pure drinking water for the coolies. The sanitary officers, medical inspectors, and inspector of immigrants were instructed to check the coolie dwellings and provide them with clean drinking water. In Natal, sanitary inspectors were responsible for regulars inspections of the water supplied to the coolies and providing certificates of purity. In Mauritius, the municipality was responsible for the supply of clean water. Immigration laws of the colonies recommended that drinking water should be provided to the indentured near their dwellings. The Natal government considered that it should not be at a distance of more than 600 yds. from the coolie dwellings.[124] Despite these measures, however, the authorities failed to provide pure and clean water to coolies. As the Avoca circle's (Natal) medical officer mentioned, '…One of the stream which flows through a thickly populated district is in an abominable condition and, I hesitate not to say is quite unfit for man or beast to drink in its present state.'[125] The hectic schedule of indentured life and the inconvenience of distance did not allow the labourers to look for alternative sources of water and so, they were forced to use these unclean water sources. In Mauritius, the Ordinance no. 15 of 1883 was framed for the protection of rivers and streams against the filthy discharge from the sugar estates.[126] It formulated that in the matter of defective arrangements for the filthy discharge, the proprietor and estate managers of the estate would be dismissed.

The General Board of Health, in their annual report in 1884, stated that the condition of rivers and streams was the same as earlier—highly polluted and totally unfit for drinking. The sanitary inspector stated—

...It is really to be hoped in the interests of a suffering population, that some stringent measures will shortly be taken by government to prevent such wholesale pollution of the said rivers and streams, which can but prove most dangerous to the health of those who are forced to use such water for drinking purpose, more especially the unfortunate poor, who are unable to provide filters.[127]

The other problem associated with waterbodies in both the colonies was that the Indians were using streams and rivers for their privy purposes. Thus, it became a major problem for the surrounding areas and the White population in the colonies. In 1880, the Government of Mauritius made the provision that employers should provide latrines near the huts of coolies, which was essential for the comfort of immigrants and for effective sanitation.[128] The Natal medical surgeon suggested that a latrine should be made on an estate where at least ten Indian immigrants were employed.[129] Suggestions were also provided about how to keep a check on the free Indian inhabitants, who were free from most of the sanitary control and supervision.[130] The concern here again was the White population's health, as the immigrant protector of Natal noticed that the polluted and filthy water streams could harm the health of the inhabitants of the coastal areas, who were residing in flats there. However, this recommendation for privies started a heated argument in the colonies. Some of the authorities did not support this recommendation; the medical surgeon of Avoca estate stated that, '... the coolie will not keep their premises free from filth and I question very much whether they would make use of latrines if they were provided.'[131]

The general consideration was that the Indians were not used to these 'closets' and therefore, suffered from the lack of personal hygiene and social cleanliness. Thus, the closets near the coolie huts would only increase the filth and dirt in the surrounding areas.

PLATE 5.4: Use of Water Streams by the Indians

Source: Andrew Balfour, Report on Medical Matters in Mauritius.

The sanitary measures and the concern for the health of not only the labourers, but also the White population in particular, forced the government to make compulsory the use of closets by the Indian population by the 1880s. Article 21 of the Public Health Ordinance of Mauritius recommended that no house of greater value than 200 pounds would be built without an adequate privy. In the absence of it, a penalty of 100 pounds was levied. In the case of default of the facility, the local board had the right to direct the owner to leave the place. The penalty for a defective privy was 5 shillings each day.[132] In Mauritius, the latrine service was paid for by the employers.[133] In other parts of the island, especially among the Creole population, the old cesspool was continued till 1918, where no regular services existed. However, in spite of making these regulations, the basic problem remained. Medical men and sanitary inspectors complained that Indians were not utilizing the benefits provided to them by their employers. The Indians avoided these closets because there was no proper cleaning and sanitation measures available; and, overcrowding was also a problem. Dr Andrew Balfour's report on the medical and sanitation issues in Mauritius provides information about the lack of water facilities and closets in sugar estates and even in the estate hospitals.[134]

The colonial government, immigrant protectors, and even the medical officers blamed the Indians for diseases and insanitary conditions in the colonies. Through this, they tried to hide the loopholes of the indentured system and coolie laws, and also the fact that they could not provide proper food, drinking water, and accommodation to the indentured. They argued—'...employers have willingly tried to provide all comfort to their emigrants, but Indians, they are most careless with regard to the matters which lie in their own hands; they make no attempts to adopt their clothing to variations in weather, and are singularly negligent as a rule, in providing any clothing for their infants.'[135]

Indians, and especially the women, were blamed for the higher mortality rate among infants. Certain provisions were made in terms of clothing for the indentured. For example, provisions were made for providing warm clothing during the winter season. In Natal, during winter, both sexes wore old clothes of soldiers. All these measures were adopted to control the high death rate of the immigrant labour force and their children in the plantation economy.

In 1919, E.H. Cluver talked about the concept of good health for each and every individual in the colony:

...The aim of the public health in the first place is to raise the general fitness of the individuals constituting the notion to so high a level as to make them immune from attack by a preventable disease; secondly, its aim is to reduce to a minimum the actual attacking agencies by promoting general sanitation. Our first aim will be attained when we have induced the individual to eat food correct in quantity and quality, to live in an atmosphere with sufficiently high cooling power (*sic*), whose action is not neutralized by incorrect clothing, to have the necessary physical and mental recreation and generally to live in accordance with the findings of the science of physiology. Our aim is to improve the environment in which we live so that the chance of even a susceptible individual becoming infected by disease germs is reduced to a minimum. This will be attained in the first instance by cleanliness, proper disposal of excrement and refuse, so as to eliminate at once the source of much infection and the headquarters of one of its chief transporters, the fly; cleanly habits among human carriers of infection will also largely eliminate their danger to the public.[136]

In Natal, the Public Health Act 36 of 1919, for the first time, established a department of public health in the colony and defined clearly the scope and duties of this department. It also made amendments to the provincial administration and local authorities regarding public health. Although various provisions under the laws were sanctioned for the public health; the situation of the Indian people did not improve. In 1935–6, Dr Goonam (Indian lady doctor in Durban) described the condition of Indian people in these words—'Most of our people were living in slums with bad sanitation, despite the fact that they paid their rents and taxes. In many places there were just sandy tracks instead of roads and no electricity; water supply bore sewage. Unemployment was shockingly high, incidences of crime high and children malnourished.'[137]

As sanitation measures were being taken up, the indentured labour staying in confined areas close to the administrative authorities became the first victims of surveillance. The notion of public health policy heavily depended on the Indian population because of their labour value and slowly extended to the other communities and other parts of the colony. In Port Louis and Durban, the markets, streets, and wharves, and the people and activities associated with them, came under scrutiny towards the end of the nineteenth century. Although these measures seem to have changed the sanitation condition of the cities: these reforms were carried out inconsistently and remained specific to urban areas. The official discourse presented only one side of the picture, wherein they either blamed the Indians for the epidemics in the colony or the French estate owners (who came from peasant stock) for their carelessness in matters of cleanliness.

Disciplining the Labour: Regulating Health

...this class who have been discovered, to believe that their comforts and happiness will result more surely from attention to their duties and obedient to the lawful commands of their masters, than from any temporary advantage that may seem to result to them from posing for a brief time in a court of law as complaints against those to whom their services are due.[138]

In a colonial setting, ideas of racial superiority and modern discipline were closely related. These ideas were upheld and advanced not only by examples and directions but also, when necessary, by curt corrections. The 'raw' indentured labourers were needed to be trained and disciplined, and the most effective and economical way was by physical persuasion.[139] Physical violence, such as whipping and flogging, was also one aspect of plantation discipline, broadly defined. Western notions of order and discipline, of the inter-related system of production and labour that constituted industrial time was believed to be absent in the non-Western societies. The plantation economy was working on the basis of task-oriented management in the field and by time-oriented management in the labourers' social sphere. In the fields, they had to finish the task assigned to them, but they also had to spend a certain amount of time in the fields. The labourers' working hour, arrival time on the estate, and lunch time were managed according to industrial time and clock. E.P. Thompson argued that time management not only helped capitalists to discipline labourers, but also became a means of labour exploitation.[140]

The disobedient and carefree nature of the coolies posed a threat to both planters and medical men. In the planters circle, there was a constant demand, if not an expectation, that employers should have the right to punish workers physically.[141] David Killingray, in his article 'The "Rod of Empire"', argued that humanity and economy, at the same time, dictated that, the use of stick and whip should be regulated. In prison, and in the army, there was a careful ordering of the body and regulated number of lashes, with a medical practitioner in attendance. The same method was adopted to discipline the labourers in the plantation colonies. For each offence, there were a fixed number of lashes decided by the plantation regime in the colonies. Testimonies in magistrate's records and files of the Protector, reveal that violence was woven into the experience of the indentured. Court cases also make this starkly visible. Henry Polak recorded, number of these type cases in 1909. In one of the brutal instances in October 1908, J.L. Armitage was charged with cutting off Manawar's ear lobe with a pocketknife. Armitage's defence was that; '…the government allowed the cutting of sheep ears, and the complainant was no better than a sheep'.[142] In another case, in Natal midland, Ramasamy and Poli were indentured to P.D. Simmons. Although not lawfully married, they lived together and had two little children.

…In February 1909, for some or the other reason, the employer tied the man up to a nail in the wall, and whipped him severely, but as his victim could still wriggle about, he had him tied to the rafters of a room and lashed him with a *sjambok* until he himself was overcome with a fatigue, and the man's back was one mass of raw and quivering flesh.[143]

Poli managed to take Ramasamy and the children to the local magistrate. He listened to their complaints, and ordered them to return to the estate as they did not have a pass. Instead, they walked to Durban and presented themselves to the protector, who promptly arrested them for desertion, and imprisoned them as the law required.[144]

Physical pain was regarded as a salutary means of dealing with offence, the short sharp shock that would punish, discourage, and provide a warning to other offenders.[145] Apart from the legal regulations, flogging was a regular feature in the daily lives of the labourers. Planters and overseers considered that without the whip and stick, it was difficult to force the labourers to fulfill their allotted tasks.[146] The autobiography of the coolie labourers who spent time in the colonies, such as Munshi Rahman Khan and Totaram Sandhya in Surinam and Fiji respectively revealed eyewitness accounts of the brutality of using lashes on the labourers. A woman indicated that the beatings were so routine that they occurred almost by a timetable—'I remember so many cases where immigrants received more than twelve cuts. The back used to swell up, they could not sit down properly and had to be treated at home.'[147] Most of the beatings took place on Fridays or Saturdays, probably with the intention of enabling the victim to recover from the wounds on Sundays. Even women were not spared from physical punishment.

The most brutal form of flogging employed the 'cat-o'-nine-tails'; but certain types of leather whips were also used by the overseers that could equally tear the flesh and inflict long, open wounds. Both the 'cat' and whips were often referred to as 'lash'.[148] In order to reduce the brutality and physical assault on labourers, the Natal government regulated the number of times a labourer could be flogged by the planters or overseers and that too in the presence of medical officers. The planters and overseers used violence to a great extent, to control the indentured labourers. The colonial authority considered that without resorting to physical violence, the small bands of managers would not have been able to supervise large groups of people, who at times were armed with agricultural implements.[149] Thus, physical assault was accepted as a form of punishment and medical officers were made responsible for deciding the number of times a labourer was to be flogged, depending on the capacity of each body. Medical men played an important role in deciding the nature of punishments. Initially, the plantation's brutalities or physical assaults caused a number of deaths and injuries among the labour force. Medical men were appointed to stop the death of the body due to physical assaults, but nothing was done to stop the crime against labourers. Another form of punishment was denial of food for those who were lazy or indifferent about their duties. Consequently, there was widespread malnutrition and illness among the labour force. Planters thus preferred whipping to incarceration because the lash did not generally lead to an extended loss of labour time.[150]

As in England, diseases were often understood in terms of social order, and as a complex interaction between individual behaviour and place.[151] In the colonies, the predisposing causes of disease were cited as the moral degeneration of immigrants (cheap drink leading to chronic levels of drunkenness), and a physical inability to work in the existing climate. This weakness of moral character, as it was understood, led to problems of discipline, which, in turn, provided the unstable conditions necessary for the spread of epidemiological menaces, such as fever.

The colonial governments in Mauritius and Natal, as well as the planters, faced various forms of resistance like suicide, murder, immorality, disobedience towards masters, and sanitary policies by the coolies on almost a daily basis. They saw that liquor, rum, and other intoxicating objects like Indian hemp (known as *gandia* in Mauritius), *dakka* (in Natal) smoking, which is mainly used by Asian people; were the primary causes of crime, social evils, and sickness in the colonies.[152] The Protector Louis Mason mentioned in his report that:

...The Indian hemp nuisance still continues to breed discord between the Indian and his employer. No less than ten men have suffered from hallucination; two men become so violently delirious that the police had to be called upon for protection ... the hemp plant cultivated in this colony acts more powerfully on the nervous system than *ganja* or *gaanja* does in India ... hemp intoxication brings out the proclivities peculiar to an individual, and those who are unfortunately possessed of evil disposition enact deeds of violence, murder and suicide.[153]

The immigrant authority considered Madrasee people as being more addicted to drunkenness, while the people from Calcutta were mostly habitual of opium. The Mauritius immigrant protector mentioned, '... many cases have at various times come before me in which Indians have fatally injured their constitution by over indulgence in the habit of smoking this hemp plant."[154] Medical science considered brandy and rum as beneficial for health. However, Indian hemp or *dakka* caused blindness, mental illness, and sometimes even death. Medical men recognized that Indian hemp was injurious to health and inferior in quality as compared to the countrymade rum.

In the colony, the medical men ascribed that drinking or *ganja*-smoking were well-known causes of mental failure.[155] They had recorded some of the causes for mental illness (see Table 5.1).

On 12 February 1884, the chief medical officer of the Mauritius Beau Bassin government lunatic asylum, in his report, stated—

...In one case the patient had been previously insane and had doubtless suffered from a passing fit of mania; in another, the patient was probably

TABLE 5.1: Number of Patients and the Causes of their Illness

Number of patients	Causes
Five	Hereditary
Eight	Congenital
Seven	*Ganja*
Two	*Ganja* and rum
Six	*Ganja* (more or less doubtful)
Ten	Drink
One	Drink and opium
One	Drink (doubtful)
Four	Grief
Two	Jealousy
Two	Loss of fortune
One	Phthisis and mental diseases
Two	Leprosy
Four	Old age
Two	Hysteria
Two	Puerperal
Six	Epilepsy
Three	Fever
One	Sunstroke
Fifty-seven	Unknown

Source: CO 170/123, Report of the Chief Medical Officer, Government Lunatic Asylum, Beau Bassin, 1884, TNA.

epileptic and a short attack of mania had been induced by drink; in the third case the patient was in advance stage of phthisis, during which disease attacks of mania are not infrequent and he also had trouble connected with his property, which probably determined the attack, the other two cases were due to drink.[156]

The Government of Mauritius, under Ordinance no. 2 of 1846, prohibited the supply and use of Indian *gandia* and cannabis in the colony. In the 1880, the government made a rule that the consumption of cannabis was liable to draw a fine of one thousand rupees. Anyone who was unable to pay the fine was liable to imprisonment.[157] In 1879, the Natal government passed the laws 22 and 23 of 1878: 'Liquor Laws against Coolies in Natal'. With this law, they tried to prohibit Indians

from using liquor. According to this law, the authorities prohibited—
'the smoking, use or possessing by, and the sale, barter of gifts, to any
portion of the hemp plant in the colony.'[158]

In some cases, they allowed and argued that only people of a
civilized character could purchase small quantities of liquor at times,
although there was no particular definition or measured skill for
'civilized character'. Dr Goonam, in her autobiography, stated that—

…My chemist telephoned me one day and said that he had been fined for
supplying me a Winchester of methylated spirit. I was flabbergasted. As
coloured doctors, Indian and African, our supply of methylated spirits was
restricted to two Winchesters per month. The spirit was indispensable in those
days before the invention of disposal syringes, and we nearly always ran short
of it. We had to suffer the ration because Indians and Africans were not
allowed to purchase alcohol, and methylated spirits fell in that category. I had
dropped and broken one Winchester of methylated spirits that month and had
asked my chemist to replace it. The inspector examining his records charged
him for supplying me the spirit illegally! I realised that my chemist would not
help me out in another emergency.[159]

Indians protested against this law and argued that in India, they
could enjoy their freedom. In these circumstances, the Natal government
provided them some relaxation and provided that they could enjoy their
drinks only in the plantation canteens, but they could not take them
outside. This was not only beneficial for them economically, but also
separated them from the other 'civilized' people. Thus, the canteens
became the sites where the authority could keep an eye on the behaviour
of the labourers when they were drunk. The Government of Mauritius,
in the 1860s, imposed heavy duty on the supply of spirits from outside,
and promoted countrymade rum in order to promote the interests of
the sugar industry in the colony.[160] But the planters soon realized, '…
labour was continually absenting themselves from work for the purpose
of going to the nearest canteen, where they remain drinking for the rest
of the day.'[161] Consequently, a rule was made that no wages would be
paid to the indentured labourer who frequented the canteens, hotels, as
liquor shops.[162]

…O, my beloved,
I cannot leave Yagona.
I have left my country, and my caste,
I have left my parents behind also,
But I cannot leave Yagona.

Yagona is the *bhang* [drug] of this island,
Which we drink to pass our nights,
I cannot leave Yagona.[163]

This folksong is one among the multiple expressions that reveal the pain of social and cultural separation of the Indians from their homeland. Thus, these people took to narcotics, *ganja*, and rum as a common means of escape from the drudgery and daily humiliation of life in the colonial plantations. It was a process of adaptation to the new environment in which they were free from their social relations and caste restrictions, and had to adopt new forms of social intercourse, new dress patterns, and dietary habits—that were all a part of this process. The government wanted to modify their behaviour according to the norms of the colonial state; so it tried to impose an idea of 'correct behaviour' and discipline on the indentured. A cannabis smoker was a challenge for the social order, and in case of women, smoking was considered contrary to their feminine nature. James H. Mills argued that by these laws and regulations, they were not only trying to discipline individuals, but the society as a whole.[164] The colonial state presented a negative picture of these *ganja* smokers by relating it to criminality and immorality; therefore, it became synonymous with bad character. The report of the Indian Hemp Drug Commission mentioned that 'drugs do not tend crime and violence'.[165] James Mills argued that the Indian population became marked as a group with social problems in the opinion of colonial authorities through the portrayal of the hemp-user as a dangerous human being.

Apart from these narcotic objects, medical men in the colonies also imposed prohibition on some plant products and local methods of remedy, which they assumed were injurious to the health of the Asiatic indentured, such as raw fruits, wild oranges, berries, opium, and *arrack*. In Flat Island, the Dhangal caste of coolies used a certain kind of grass which they believed to be a curative.[166] Dr Finnimore, the practitioner at the quarantine, found these grasses in the intestines of dead bodies. Consequently, he declared that eating these grasses was one of the causes of cholera. However, it may also be noted that in the second half of the nineteenth century, some of the doctors with Western education used certain plant products such as black pepper, calomel, ginger, and coconut oil, and methods of remedy used by the Indians, in the treatment of their patients.

Conclusion

The widespread outbreak of epidemics in the colonies forced the authorities to adopt several public health policies to prevent the spread of diseases and 'save' the labour force. After the failure of quarantine laws and hospitals in the prevention of the epidemics, colonies were brought under strict sanitation measures. In the late nineteenth century, the health measures were extended to the 'native' people of the colonies as well. Earlier, they were left to use their own traditional healing practices in case of the occurrences of diseases. However, contagious epidemics like 'Asiatic cholera', malaria, plague, and tuberculosis, along with other diseases, forced the government to interfere in the healthcare measures of the local people. During this period, Western medical science proved that freedom from diseases depended not only on proper sanitation, clean water, nutritious food, and fresh air, but also on eliminating disorder, ignorance, and immorality amongst the colony's poor. Drawing together municipal and government policies, as well as individuals, into desirable civic practices became a prime task for the medical practitioners in the colonies. The colonial government reified the medical regime in order to achieve medical, moral, and even sexual control over the poor and the labourers. Sanitation measures in the colony were also regularized through policing, terror, fines, physical punishment, and imprisonment.

Schools, churches, and estate hospitals became centres for the distribution of knowledge to the community of immigrants and natives in the colonies about the importance of sanitation and hygiene. The poor became the target of the public health measures, because the medical regime considered them to be completely unaware about the importance of personal and social hygiene. The Indians were blamed for bringing diseases with them. They were also held liable for insanitation, chaos, and illegitimacy. They were seen as 'carriers' of diseases, rather than as victims of colonial economy. By blaming African slaves or Indian coolies for bringing diseases or epidemics in colonies, the colonial regime ignored the byproducts of the capitalist and industrial setup, which not only created slums and crowded areas, but also introduced many industrial and urban diseases such as tuberculosis, lung diseases, asthma, and so on. They also ignored the sugar mills, coal mines, and several other industries which caused nuisance, insanitation, marshlands, and impurity of water. Moreover, government negligence in matters of native health in the initial phase made them the prime victims of disease.

In both the colonies, the governments failed to prevent the spread of epidemics. It was only after the 1920s that the Government of Mauritius managed to adopt a public health welfare policy and achieved limited success. Again, the unification of the South African Union posed new health challenges for the union government. Colonial subjugation and apartheid dispossession produced a dysfunctional health system in South Africa.

Notes

1. Annual Report of the Protector of Indian Immigrants in Natal for the year 1900, Revenue and Agriculture Department (Emigration Branch) Proceedings, August 1899, nos. 6–7, NAI.
2. David Killingray, 'The "Rod of Empire": The Debate over Corporal Punishment in the British African Colonial Forces, 1888-1946', *The Journal of African History*, vol. XXXV, no. 2, 1994, p. 202.
3. Tom Crook, 'Sanitary Inspection and the Public Sphere in Late Victorian and Edwardian Britain: A Case Study in Liberal Governance', *Social History*, vol. XXXII, no. 4, 2007, p. 373.
4. Ibid., p. 376.
5. Nicholas Pike, *Sub-Tropical Rambles in the Land of the Aphanapteryx: Personal Experiences, Adventures, and Wanderings in and around the Island of Mauritius*, New York: Harper and Brothers, 1873, p. 90. Pike was staying at Port Louis during the malaria epidemics of the mid-1860s.
6. C.F. Edwards, 'On the recent Outbreak of Pernicious Fever in Mauritius', in *Transactions of the Epidemiological Society of London*, vol. III, London: Hardwicke and Bouge, 1874, p. 166; speech of the General Sanitary Inspector of the island at the Epidemiological Society, 2 December 1867.
7. CO 167/376, Cholera Report of Mauritius 1856, TNA.
8. Auguste Toussaint, *Port Louis: A Tropical City*, tr. W.E.F. Ward, London: George Allen Unwin Ltd., 1973, p. 86.
9. Daniel E. Anderson, *The Epidemics of Mauritius: With a Descriptive and Historical Account of the Island*, London: H.K. Lewis & Co. Ltd., 1918, pp. 42, 98.
10. Ibid., p. 100.
11. Frederic J. Mouat, 'Medical Statistics, with especial reference to Cholera and Syphilis', in *Transactions of the Epidemiological Society of London*, vol. III, London: Hardwicke and Bouge, 1874, p. 391, accessed at WTL; read on 11 December 1872.
12. Ronald Ross, *Report on the Prevention of Malaria in Mauritius*, London: Waterlow and Sons Limited, 1908, p. 59. Accessed at LSHTM.
13. Ibid.; Also see W.R.E. Smart, 'On the Distribution of Asiatic Cholera in

Africa', in *Transactions of the Epidemiological Society of London*, vol. III, London: Hardwicke and Bouge, 1874, p. 339, accessed at WTL.

14. Smart, 'On the Distribution of Asiatic Cholera', pp. 354–5.
15. Edwards, 'On the recent Outbreak of Pernicious Fever', 166.
16. Ross, *Report on the Prevention of Malaria*, p. 48.
17. Ibid.
18. H.T. Rogers, 'Notes on the Epidemic of Malarial Fever which appeared in Mauritius in 1866–67', in *Transactions of the Epidemiological Society of London*, vol. III, London: Hardwicke and Bouge, 1874, p. 200; accessed at WTL; Speech by the Senior Assistant-Surgeon to the Civil Hospital, Port Louis, at the Epidemiological Society, 2 December 1867.
19. Edwards, 'On the recent Outbreak of Pernicious Fever', p. 166.
20. A.R. Barraut, 'The Medical Topography of Mauritius, with an account of the Fever which prevailed there in 1867', in *Transactions of the Epidemiological Society of London*, vol. III, London: Hardwicke and Bouge, 1874, p. 192.
21. Rogers, 'Notes on the Epidemic of Malarial Fever', p. 204.
22. Edwards, 'On the recent Outbreak of Pernicious Fever', p. 167.
23. Ross, *Report on the Prevention of Malaria*, p. 54.
24. Ibid.
25. Ibid., pp. 55–6.
26. Ibid., p. 49.
27. Report on the Estate Hospitals for the half-year, December 1902, Revenue and Agriculture Department (Emigration Branch) Proceedings, December 1903, nos. 7–8, NAI.
28. Ross, *Report on the Prevention of Malaria*, p. 55.
29. Ibid., pp. 58–9, 74.
30. Report on the Estate Hospitals for the half-year, December 1902, Revenue and Agriculture Department (Emigration Branch) Proceedings.
31. Ross, *Report on the Prevention of Malaria*, p. 75.
32. Letter from Secretary of State for India, to the Government of India, regarding the epidemic fever which raged in the Island of Mauritius in the year 1867, Home Department (Emigration Branch) Proceedings, June 1870, no. 144, NAI.
33. Ross, *Report on the Prevention of Malaria*, p. 51.
34. Rogers, 'Notes on the Epidemic of Malarial Fever', p. 213.
35. Roy T. Sawyer, 'The Trade in Medicinal Leeches in the Southern Indian Ocean in the Nineteenth Century', *Medical History*, vol. XLIII, 1999, pp. 241–5.
36. Letter from Mr Murray Hammick, C.I.E., I.C.S., Acting Chief Secretary to the Government of Fort Saint George, to the Secretary to the Government of India, regarding the high death rate among the newly arrived Indian immigrants, Revenue and Agriculture Department (Emigration Branch) Proceedings, September 1904, nos. 8–9, NAI.
37. Ross, *Report on the Prevention of Malaria*, p. 121.

38. Ibid.
39. For details see Hoosen Coovadia et al., 'The Health and Health System of South Africa: Historical Roots of Current Public Health Challenge', *Health in South Africa*, vol. 374, 2009, doi: 10.1016/S0140-6736(09)60951-X, pp. 817–34; published online 25 August 2009, see https://www.ncbi.nlm. nih.gov/pubmed/19709728, accessed 12 November 2014.
40. Ibid., p. 819.
41. E.H. Cluver, *Public Health in South Africa*, Johannesburg: Central News Agency, 1939, p. 156. WTL.
42. In India, at the same time, the fatal epidemic of bubonic Plague occurred in the principal port and central commercial city of Bombay; and through the maritime networks, it spread from there to other European colonies. Aditya Sarkar's work on this topic shows the impact of plague on the Bombay working class, especially the Muslim weaver community (as plague suspect), of Midnapura in Bombay. He shows the government's efforts of urban social control during the epidemic. He addresses the crises of labour relations in terms of the unrest provoked by the plague control policy. The labourers' threat of their withdrawal of labour—means of survival of city, forced government and municipal administrative authorities to adopt new policies. For details, see Aditya Sarkar, 'The City, its street and its Workers: The Plague Crisis in Bombay, 1896-98', in *Working lives & Working Militancy: The Politics of Labour in Colonial India*, ed. Ravi Ahuja, Delhi: Tulika Books, 2013, pp. 1–46.
43. Cluver, *Public Health in South Africa*, p. 156. WTL.
44. Ernest Hill, *Report on the Plague in Natal 1902-03*, London: Cassell and Company Limited, 1904, p. 7.
45. Annual Report of the Protector of Indian Immigrants in Mauritius for the year 1886, Revenue and Agriculture Department (Emigration Branch) Proceedings, April 1888, nos. 8–9, NAI.
46. Appendix of the Mauritius half-yearly report of the Medical Inspector for the year 1905, Revenue and Agriculture Department (Emigration Branch) Proceedings, May 1904, nos. 9–10, NAI.
47. Ibid., p. 48.
48. Hill, *Report on the Plague in Natal*, p. 11.
49. Ibid., p. 14.
50. CO 181/49, Public Health Act of Natal, TNA.
51. Hill, *Report on the Plague in Natal*, p. 18.
52. Ibid., p. 28.
53. Ibid., p. 37.
54. CO 181/49, Public Health Act of Natal, TNA.
55. Hill, *Report on the Plague in Natal*, p. 7.
56. Annual Report of the Protector of Indian Immigrants in Natal for the year 1903, Revenue and Agriculture Department (Emigration Branch) Proceedings, December 1903, nos. 3–5, NAI.

57. Annual Report of the Protector of Indian Immigrants in Natal for the year 1883, Revenue and Agriculture Department (Emigration Branch) Proceedings, October 1884, nos. 3–4, NAI.

58. Annual Report of the Protector of Indian Immigrants in Natal for the year 1878, Home, Revenue and Agriculture Department (Emigration Branch) Proceedings, December 1879, no. 41, NAI.

59. Mouat, 'Medical Statistics, with especial reference to Cholera and Syphilis', p. 384.

60. Sabyasachi R. Mishra, 'An Empire "De-Masculinized": The British Colonial State and the Problem of Syphilis in Nineteenth Century India', in *Diseases and Medicine in India: A Historical Overview*, ed. Deepak Kumar, Delhi: Tulika Books, 2001, p. 167; Also see Philippa Levine, *Prostitution, Race and Politics: Policing Venereal Disease in the British Empire*, New York, London: Routledge, 2003, p. 5; Kenneth Ballhatchet, *Race, Sex and Class under the Raj: Imperial Attitudes and Politics and their Critics*, New York: St. Martin's Press, 1980.

61. Douglas M. Peers, 'Soldiers, Surgeons and the Campaigns to Combat Sexually Transmitted Diseases in Colonial India, 1805-1860', *Medical History*, vol. XLII, 1998, p. 146.

62. Mishra, 'An Empire "De-Masculinized"', p. 167; Also see Sarah Hodges, '"Looting" the Lock Hospital in Colonial Madras during the Famine Years of the 1870s', *Social History of Medicine*, vol. XVIII, no. 3, 2005, pp. 379–98.

63. Annual Report of the Protector of Indian Immigrants in Natal for the year 1891, Revenue and Agriculture Department (Emigration Branch) Proceedings, February 1892, nos. 6–7, NAI.

64. Annual Report of the Protector of Indian Immigrants in Natal for the year 1887, Revenue and Agriculture Department (Emigration Branch) Proceedings, September 1888, nos. 16–17. NAI.

65. Annual Report of the Protector of Indian Immigrants in Natal for the year 1885, Revenue and Agriculture Department (Emigration Branch) Proceedings, October 1886, nos. 8–9, NAI.

66. CO 170/130, Report of the Mauritius Medical Inspector for the estate hospital, 1884, TNA.

67. Annual Report of the Protector of Indian Immigrants in Natal for the year 1903, Revenue and Agriculture Department (Emigration Branch) Proceedings, July 1904, nos. 3–4, NAI.

68. Annual Report of the Protector of Indian Immigrants in Natal for the year 1899, Revenue and Agriculture Department (Emigration Branch) Proceedings, January 1901, nos. 10–12, NAI.

69. Patrick Manson et al., 'Discussion on Sanitation in Reference to Ankylostomiasis in the Tropics', *The British Medical Journal*, vol. II, no. 2496, 1908, p. 1348.

70. Ibid.

71. Ibid., see Chapter 2.
72. Manson et al., 'Discussion on Sanitation', p. 1348.
73. For the effect of these medicines on Indians and their reaction see Chapter 2.
74. Mouat, 'Medical Statistics, with especial reference to Cholera and Syphilis', p. 380.
75. J.S. La Fontaine, *City Politics: A Study of Léopoldville, 1962-63*, Cambridge: Cambridge University Press, 1970, p. 19.
76. Hill, *Report on the Plague in Natal*, p. 9.
77. Maynard W. Swanson, 'The Sanitation Syndrome: Bubonic Plague and Urban Native Policy in the Cape Colony, 1900-1909', *The Journal of African History*, vol. XVIII, no. 3, 1977, p. 389.
78. CO 179/230, Plague at Durban, TNA; Swanson, 'The Sanitation Syndrome', p. 390; also see Alison Bashford and Carolyn Strange, 'Isolation and Exclusion in the Modern World: An Introductory Essay', *Isolation Places and Practices of Exclusion*, ed. Carolyn Strange and Alison Bashford, London and New York: Routledge, 2003, pp. 1–20.
79. CO 170/89, General Board of Health, 1873, TNA.
80. CO 169/27, Public Health Ordinance, 1903-04, TNA.
81. CO 181/49, Public Health Act of Natal, TNA.
82. PC 1/2668, General Board of Health, 9 May 1859, Para 9, TNA.
83. Ibid., Para 10.
84. CO 180/49, Public Health Act of Natal, 1883, TNA.
85. Transfer of lunatic coolies from Mauritius to India, Revenue, Agriculture and Commerce Department (Emigration Branch) Proceedings, June 1876, nos. 6–8, NAI.
86. The total population of Indians in Mauritius during 1878 was 242,000. Proposal for diminishing the large number of vagrants amongst the Indian population of Mauritius, Revenue and Agriculture Department (Emigration Branch) Proceedings, March 1881, nos. 60–1, NAI.
87. Letter from J.F. Trotter, Protector of Indian Immigrants in Mauritius, to the Colonial Secretary, Mauritius, Revenue and Agriculture Department (Emigration Branch) Proceedings, February 1892, no. 19, NAI.
88. Proposal for diminishing the large number of vagrants amongst the Indian population of Mauritius, Revenue and Agriculture Department (Emigration Branch) Proceedings; also see Richard B. Allen, 'Vagrancy in Mauritius and the Nineteenth Century Colonial Plantations World', in *Cast Out: Vagrancy and Homelessness in Global and Historical Perspective*, ed. A.L. Beier and Paul Ocobock, Ohio: Center for International Studies, Ohio University, 2008, pp. 140–61.
89. Proposal for diminishing the large number of vagrants amongst the Indian population of Mauritius, Revenue and Agriculture Department (Emigration Branch) Proceedings.

90. Annual Report of the Protector of Indian Immigrants in Natal for the year 1890, Revenue and Agriculture Department (Emigration Branch) Proceedings, November 1891, nos. 15–16, part A, NAI.

91. Brij V. Lal, *Chalo Jahaji: On a Journey through Indenture in Fiji*, Suva, Fiji: Fiji Museum, Prashant Pacific, 2000, p. 115.

92. Revenue and Agriculture Department (Emigration Branch) Proceedings, August 1899, nos. 6–7, NAI. The protector of Indian immigrants in Natal, in his report (1893), stated that—

   ...Thirteen deaths occurred amongst young children from burns. Enquiry into each case was made at the time, and proved, in the majority of cases, purely accidental, and attributable mainly to neglect, or want of care on the part of parents in leaving their children unprotected in their house with a fire burning, into which the children probably crawled, or by some means or other, their clothing became ignited.

   Also see, Revenue and Agriculture Department (Emigration Branch) Proceedings, January 1894, nos. 31–2, NAI.

93. Report of the Medical Surgeon, Avoca Central Estate Hospital; Annual Report of the Protector of Indian Immigrants in Natal for the year 1886, Revenue and Agriculture Department (Emigration Branch) Proceedings, August 1887, nos. 15–20, NAI.

94. Annual Report of the Mauritius Emigrant Protector for the year 1902, Revenue and Agriculture Department (Emigration Branch), November 1903, nos. 19–20, NAI.

95. Annual Report of the Protector of Indian Immigrants in Natal for the year 1884, Revenue and Agriculture Department (Emigration Branch) Proceedings, January 1886, nos. 16, NAI.

96. Edwards, 'On the recent Outbreak of Pernicious Fever', p. 167.

97. Denise M. Amos, 'Working-class Diet and Health in Nottingham, 1850–1939', unpublished PhD thesis, University of Nottingham, UK, 2000.

98. Edwards, 'On the recent Outbreak of Pernicious Fever', p. 167.

99. CO 169/09, Mauritius Public Health Ordinances, Measures to Promote Public Health in Mauritius, TNA.

100. Annual Report of the Protector of Indian Immigrants in Natal for the year 1894, Revenue and Agriculture Department (Emigration Branch) Proceedings, January 1894, nos. 31–2, NAI.

101. CO 181/49, Public Health Act of Natal, TNA. The term 'infectious diseases' included the diseases—bubonic plague, small pox, cholera, diphtheria, membraneous croup, scarlatina or scarlet fever, and leprosy, and fevers like typhus, typhoid, relapsing, etc. The term 'epidemic disease' meant any disease which the health officer of the colony would order to be regarded as being epidemic, until the order was revoked; and such order would state whether it is to be implemented in the whole colony, or to any specified district or districts.

102. CO 181/49, Public Health Act of Natal, TNA.

103. Ibid.

104. Anderson, *Epidemics of Mauritius*, p. 98.

105. Baba Ramchandra stated that,—'Overseers were not even accepting a piece of paper from the coolie hands, a long stick was in use for this purpose and the papers were destroyed soon after authorities had a look on it. The piece of papers used by coolies was burned in order not to spread the disease.' For details see the Private Papers of Baba Ramchandra, NMML.

106. Raj Boodhoo, *Health, Disease and Indian Immigrants in Nineteenth Century Mauritius*, Port Louis: Aapravasi Ghat Trust Fund, 2010, p. 307.

107. John D. Kelly in her work shows that Holi was popular among the lower classes and castes of the Indian society in Fiji, and Diwali, among the urban rich and middle class. She talks about the political and economic aspects of acceptation and transformation of rituals in the colony. For details, see John D. Kelly, 'From Holi to Diwali in Fiji: An Essay on Ritual and History', *Man*, n.s., vol. XXIII, no. 1, 1988, pp. 40–55. Goolam Vahed's work on Muharram celebration in Natal shows that among the immigrant authorities, Muharram was known as 'Coolie Christmas'. The Natal government permitted three days' annual leave during the Muharram festival to the coolies. During the festival, a number of crimes and suicide cases were reported in the local newspaper. For example, a man named Hassan Baccus committed suicide by slitting his throat; a woman named Patchay confirmed that some men had made 'forcible connection' with her. See Goolam Vahed, 'Constructions of Community and Identity among Indians in Colonial Natal, 1860-1910: The Role of the Muharram Festival', *The Journal of African History*, vol. 43, no. 1, 2002, pp. 80–3.

108. Muharram festival in Natal, Revenue and Agriculture Department (Emigration Branch) Proceedings, January 1880, nos. 6–7, NAI.

109. J. Meldrum, 'The Moharrem festival in Natal', cited in Vahed, 'Constructions of Community and Identity', p. 85.

110. See Vahed, 'Constructions of Community and Identity', p. 89.

111. The pilgrimage part of Puri, known as Native Puri was distinct from the 'non-native', described as a sanatorium. 'Native Puri, on the other hand, was considered as a "valley of death", viewed as dirty, a source of contamination, chaotic and "disorderly"'. The haj pilgrims were seen as the most likely carriers of the epidemics. Sourabh Mishra argued that the Ganges delta was the 'natural home of cholera'; and the Indian pilgrims, owing to their 'almost professional filthiness', acted as 'exceptionally dangerous vectors of transmission'. International pressure forced the Indian colonial government to impose the quarantine policy against haj pilgrimage vessels and restriction on the passage of Indian vessels through the Suez Canal. For details, see Sourabh Mishra, *Pilgrimage, Politics, and Pestilence: The Haj from the Indian Subcontinent, 1860-1920*, Delhi:

Oxford University Press, 2011; Mark Harrison, *Public Health in British India: Anglo-Indian Preventive Medicine 1859-1914*, Delhi: Cambridge University Press, 1994, pp. 117–38; Biswamoy Pati, "'Ordering' 'Disorder'" in a Holy City: Colonial Health Intervention in Puri during the Nineteenth Century', in *Health, Medicine and Empire: Perspectives on Colonial India*, ed. Biswamoy Pati and Mark Harrison, Delhi: Orient Longman, 2001, p. 296; Sourabh Mishra, 'Beyond the Bounds of Time? The Haj Pilgrimages from the Indian Subcontinent, 1865-1920', in *The Social History of Health and Medicine in Colonial India*, ed. Biswamoy Pati and Mark Harrison, London and New York: Routledge, 2009, p. 32.

112. Cited in Boodhoo, *Health, Disease and Indian Immigrants*, p. 288.
113. Annual Report of the Mauritius Emigrant Protector for the year 1902, Revenue and Agriculture Department (Emigration Branch) Proceedings.
114. Annual Report of the Protector of Indian Immigrants in Natal for the years 1891–92, Revenue and Agriculture Department (Emigration Branch), January 1883, nos. 1–2, NAI.
115. CO 179/254, Report of Natal medical inspector, January 1880, TNA.
116. Cited in Ashwin Desai and Goolam Vahed, *Inside Indenture: A South African History, 1860-1914*, Durban: Madiba Publishers, 2007, p. 118.
117. Ibid.
118. Annual Report of the Protector of Indian Immigrants in Natal for the year 1899, Revenue and Agriculture Department (Emigration Branch) Proceedings, January 1901, nos. 10–12, NAI. A provision was made by law that no employer shall be allowed to demand work from a pregnant woman after expiration of seven months of pregnancy, or from the mother of a child that is less than three months of age. During this period, the employer shall be bound and obliged to provide such women with food and rations on the minimum scale provided by the original contract of service between the employer and the women. It is, however, remarkable to note that these rules were not applicable on the re-indentured women who opted for not working because of any medical reason. Thus, it can be seen that in 1911, the Natal government took very optimistic steps in order to protect the interests of Indian women and their children, but only for those who would be cheap and reliable labour power for the economy. This provision was made by law only for the indentured women; Also see extract from 'Indian Opinion', Commerce and Industry Department (Emigration Branch) Proceedings, December 1911, no. 3, part B, NAI; H.S.L. Polak also objected to women doing hard manual labour and suggested that 'this system of forced labour' on women should be abolished. See Y.S. Meer, *Documents of Indentured Labour: Natal 1851-1917*, Durban: Institute of Black Research, 1980.
119. Addition to the rules under the Natal Mines Act of 1899, Revenue and Agriculture Department (Emigration Branch) Proceedings, August 1903, nos. 5–6, NAI.

120. Amos, 'Working-class Diet and Health', p. 32.
121. E.J. Hobsbawm and R.M. Hartwell, 'The Standard of Living during the Industrial Revolution: A Discussion', *The Economic History Review*, n.s., vol. XVI, no. 1, 1963, p. 134. Hobsbawm dismissed the earlier assumptions that the industrial revolution raised the standard of living of the factory workers in England. Instead, he argued that industrial revolution had increased slum areas and raised the rate of spread of epidemics in urban areas. He further stated that legislation on sanitary measures can hardly be said to have begun in 1840 and the improvements that were made could not cope up with the rising population of the urban areas.
122. Ibid.
123. CO 169/09, Public Health Ordinance of Mauritius, measures to promote public health in Mauritius, TNA.
124. CO 181/49, Natal Public Health Act 1894, TNA.
125. Addition to the rules under the Natal Mines Act of 1899, Revenue and Agriculture Department (Emigration Branch) Proceedings.
126. Annual Report of the Protector of Indian Immigrants in Natal for the year 1887, Revenue and Agriculture Department (Emigration Branch) Proceedings.
127. CO 170/123, Report of the Sanitary Work of the General Board of Health, TNA.
128. Ibid.
129. Provision of kitchen and closets in the dwellings of Indian immigrants in the colonies, Revenue and Agriculture Department (Emigration Branch) Proceedings, February 1882, nos. 8–9, NAI.
130. Ibid.
131. Annual Report of the Protector of Indian Immigrants in Natal for the year 1887, Revenue and Agriculture Department (Emigration Branch) Proceedings.
132. Ibid.
133. CO 169/09, Measures to promote Public Health in Mauritius, TNA.
134. Anderson, *Epidemics of Mauritius*, p. 91.
135. Andrew Balfour, *Report on Medical Matters in Mauritius, 1921*, Mauritius: Authority of the Governor P.G. Bumstead, 1921, p. 7.
136. Annual Report of the Protector of Indian Immigrants in Natal for the year 1890, Revenue and Agriculture Department (Emigration Branch) Proceedings.
137. Cluver, *Public Health in South Africa*, p. 253.
138. Goonam, *Coolie Doctor: An Autobiography*, Hyderabad: Orient Longman Limited, 1998, p. 100.
139. Annual Report of the Emigrant Protector of Natal for the year 1884, Revenue and Agricultural Department (Emigration Branch) Proceedings.
140. Killingray, 'The "Rod of Empire"', p. 202.
141. E.P. Thompson, 'Time, Work-Discipline, and Industrial Capitalism', *Past*

& Present, vol. XXXVIII, 1967, pp. 56–97. In his article, Thompson stated, 'those who are employed experience a distinction between their employer's time and their "own" time. And the employer must use the time of his labourer, and see it is not wasted: not the task but the value of time when reduced to money is dominant. Time is now currency: it is not passed but spent.'; see p. 61.

142. Killingray, 'The "Rod of Empire"', p. 204.

143. Henry S.L. Polak, *The Indians of South Africa, 1909*, Esplanade: G.A. Natesan & Co., 1909, p. 35, cited in Desai and Vahed, *Inside Indenture*, p. 110.

144. Ibid.

145. CO 179/254, the Indian Coolie Ramasamy, TNA.

146. Killingray, 'The Rod of Empire', p. 203.

147. The use of the 'cat-o'-nine-tails' in military punishment was ended by 1908; thereafter, the whip or cane were the official instruments for flogging. By 1871, the maximum number of lashes was reduced to twenty–five, following the death of a person in the army. In 1880, it was abolished by the Army Act, but remained in practice in the military prison till 1907. Flogging by the cat or lashes was considered brutal, but the whip remained in use in the plantations.

148. A survivor from Fiji; see Gaiutra Bahadur, *Coolie Woman: The Odyssey of Indenture*, London: Hurst & Company, 2013, p. 124.

149. Killingray, 'The Rod of Empire', p. 203.

150. Desai and Vahed, *Inside Indenture*, p. 103.

151. Fogel and Engerman argued that in order to control the slave labour force, whipping was a measure; but the decline of the use of whipping as an instrument of labour discipline outside South America appears to have been influenced by economic consideration. They stated that the planters were using mild whipping as the form of corporal punishment, which was also practiced within families. They pointed to a reference to the whipping of a disobedient wife in Matthew's Bible. Robert W. Fogel and Stanley L. Engerman, *Time on the Cross: The Economics of American Slavery*, vol. I, Boston: Little Brown and Company, 1974, p. 147.

152. Christopher Hamlin, *Public Health and Social Justice in the Age of Chadwick: Britain, 1800-1854*, Cambridge: Cambridge University Press, 1998, p. 19.

153. Liquor Law of Natal, Home, Revenue and Agriculture Department (Emigration Branch) Proceedings, November 1879, nos. 35–6, NAI.

154. Annual Report of the Protector of Indian Immigrants in Natal for the year 1885, Revenue and Agriculture Department (Emigration Branch) Proceedings.

155. CO 167/292, increased duty on spirit in order to prevent the consumption of it in the colony, TNA; Also see, Annual Report of the Protector of Indian Immigrants in Natal for the year 1887, Revenue and Agriculture Department (Emigration Branch) Proceedings.

156. CO 170/123, Report of the Chief Medical Officer, Government Lunatic asylum, Beau Bassin, 1884, TNA.
157. Ibid.
158. Boodhoo, *Health, Disease and Indian Immigrants*, p. 88.
159. Annual Report of the Protector of Indian Immigrants in Natal for the year 1887, Revenue and Agriculture Department (Emigration Branch) Proceedings.
160. Goonam, *Coolie Doctor*, p. 64.
161. CO 167/292, increased duty on spirit in order to prevent the consumption of it in the colony, TNA.
162. Annual Report of the Protector of Indian Immigrants in Natal for the year 1891, Revenue and Agriculture Department (Emigration Branch) Proceedings.
163. Mines Act of Natal for the year 1899, Revenue and Agriculture Department (Emigration Branch) Proceedings.
164. Quoted in Brij V. Lal, 'Approaches to the Study of Indian Indentured Emigration with Special reference to Fiji', cited in Marina Carter and Khal Torabully, *Coolitude: An Anthology of the Indian Labour Diaspora*, London: Anthem Press, 2002, p. 101.
165. James H. Mills, *Madness, Cannabis and Colonialism: The 'Native-Only' Lunatic Asylums of British India, 1857–1900*, Great Britain: Macmillan Press, 2000, p. 7.
166. *Marijuana: Report of the Indian hemp Drugs Commission, 1893-1894*, Silver Spring, MD: Thos. Jefferson Pub. Co., 1969.
167. Boodhoo, *Health, Disease and Indian Immigrants*, p. 310.

Conclusion

Medicine played a pervasive role in the plantation economy. It did not remain simply a medicinal intervention treating the sick in coping with diseases, but became 'an ideological set of opinions and practices'.[1] Medicine, as argued by the historians, was itself a source of power for the colonial state; but in the plantation economy, it played an important role in the legitimization of the indentured trade. The gulf between different categories of 'civilized' and 'uncivilized', the 'European' and the 'other', 'white' and 'black', 'paternalistic' and 'childish'—became further widened by the activities of doctors who measured, counted, documented, and deliberated over the body of immigrant labourers and the 'native' people such as Creoles and Zulus. Medicine worked as a disciplining hand of the state. David Aickin stated 'medicine was nevertheless part and parcel of this wider system of plantation "government" over the labour…was part of an informal system of authority which, aside from helping to enhance the utility and productivity of labour, gave rationale and justification for preserving white dominance.'[2]

This study has tried to delineate the relationship between diseases, medical care, and health provisions given to the indentured labourers in colonial Mauritius and Natal. It has shown that the purpose of, and role played by, medicine in both colonies gradually changed over a long period. In the initial period, till the 1870s, medical provisions were given only to the indentured labourers. After 1870s, the colonial government extended the health-care provisions to the indentured family as well. During the late nineteenth century, the colonial government had taken some initiatives to adopt public health policies. The focus of government's attention was the urban workforce rather than the rural population. Apart from the creation of basic pillars of the system such as law, police, courts, and prisons for governance; the colonial government also established the hospitals, lunatic and leprosy asylums, and other so-called significant paraphernalia for sustenance and survival of the plantation economy. The English model was emulated and town councils, mayors, local boards, officers of health, town clerks, etc., were made on similar lines, in the colonies.

During the initial phase, in Mauritius, the immigration of indentured labourers was managed by the planters themselves. The government was not directly involved in the recruitment processes. The abusive process of recruitment was, however, later severely attacked by the anti-slavery groups. At times it so happened that many of the recruits were physically 'unfit' to travel and work in the plantation economy. These sick and weak labourers were regarded as burdensome. It was believed that they constituted an unmanageable population group, and therefore, posed a threat to the law and order of the colony. The initial attempts at controlling immigrants through vagrancy laws failed. High mortality and sick rates caused absenteeism among the labourers. The recruitment of the 'young', 'healthy', and 'able-bodied'; remained a challenging task in both Mauritius and Natal. The scientific measures and the need for a particular type of body, such as: 'able body', 'sick body', 'reproductive body (pregnant)', and 'mother's body', were taken into consideration. In order to recruit 'able-bodied' labourers, as well as to reduce the high mortality and sick rate on the voyages, the Government of Mauritius passed a number of laws and regulations which were later on adopted by the Natal government. Both the Indian and Mauritian governments took the initiative and passed the Emigration Act of 1842, which regulated the health-related concerns of labourers. Further, in order to curtail the absenteeism among the labourers, planters were forced to provide medical facilities to the labourers. Initially, no estate hospitals were available to treat the indentured on the estates. The sick were kept in prison hospitals, used for both treatment and control of prisoners and labourers. After 1842, altogether three acts and ordinances were passed in Mauritius to further the medical facilities provided to the indentured labourers.

This work has also tried to delineate the concerns related to public health. The anxieties for better accommodation, nutritious food, potable drinking water; as well as medical and lavatory facilities in Calcutta and Madras depots, and then on the ships, in the destination depots, the quarantine stations, and finally on the estates and their hospitals: intertwined with the capitalists' agendas of plantation economy. This can be further unravelled by the very fact that the quality and quantity of nutritious food for the indentured labourers emerged, for the first time, as a debatable issue among the authorities. These concerns reflect how significant the vigour of plantation economy was, so that in order to make it more durable and productive, the government took every precaution to make the body of the labourers healthy and fit.

The Indians were regarded as 'disease carriers' and 'polluting agents'; and it was believed that they had contaminated the Mauritius Island. Therefore, segregation in the quarantine station was seen as something essential by the government. Mauritius adopted a stringent quarantine law, which became an example for the rest of the world. However, the poor condition of and lack of facilities at the quarantine station, further increased the hardships of the newly arrived Indians. The Government of India raised its voice against the ruthless laws of the quarantine station of Mauritius, but it went unheard. However, the imposition of quarantine could not prevent the spread of epidemic diseases like cholera across the island. In Natal, the lack of facilities such as proper food, clean drinking water, medical facilities, and centralization or confinement of the new arrivals at one place added to the morbidity and mortality rates. The strict quarantine laws in Mauritius raised debates among the medical practitioners and authorities. Few officers were in favour of sanitary reform on the island, and they criticized the heavy expenditure on quarantine facilities which were used to put a check on the epidemics and diseases. These criticisms consequently laid the basis of the public health measures that were taken up.

Indians were affected by various diseases such as dysentery, cholera, smallpox, hookworm, syphilis, gonorrhoea, chest infection, and several types of fevers. There were several outbreaks of smallpox during the nineteenth century, and the threat of Asiatic cholera during the late nineteenth century was also a great source of concern. In the colonies, Indians were blamed for their insanitary habits and were regarded as the cause for these epidemics and diseases. In Natal, Indians were characterized as 'pest[s]' and being 'semi-civilized'.[3] The indentured Indians and their behaviour became a subject of study for the colonial authorities. It was concluded that these diseases were spread because the Indians lived in dirty dwellings, had no notion of sanitation, ate improper food, and drank polluted water from open streams. The plantation states did not provide the Indians with proper drinking water facilities and ventilated huts, but blamed them for their conditions.

The invalids, lepers, vagrants, mentally unstable, and the old were often sent back to India because they were regarded as burdensome. The Government of India, despite protests, was unable to convince the Mauritian and Natal authorities to discontinue the policy of sending back people who were 'more dead than alive'. The Indian population in

Natal was steadily rising; and in order to prevent further Indian immigration, the Natal government adopted rigorous recruitment and rejection policies.

Several laws were passed to provide adequate medical facilities to the labourers; but the estate hospitals were always overcrowded. They lacked trained staff and medical facilities to handle the concerns of the plantation labourers. The planters, however, saw these laws as an instrument of curtailment of their power. On the other hand, the Indians considered these hospital treatments and Western medical practices as alien; and their religious and caste prejudices also prohibited them from using the hospital beds and eating the food. The immigrants thus raised their voices against the compulsory confinement of the sick in the hospitals. They were also against the compulsory medical examination of the womenfolk by male doctors.

The Poor Law Commission, established in 1853 in Mauritius, dealt with the health of the paupers. It, however, did not have adequate funds to set up a sufficient number of public hospitals, dispensaries, and poor houses. Such was the condition that throughout the nineteenth century, only one leprosy asylum was set up—the Barkly Asylum at Beau Bassin—and it was soon overcrowded. In both colonies, the governments depended on Catholic religious bodies to set up dispensaries for the local population. Revd Dr Lancelot Parker Booth (1850–1925) established St Aidan's Mission Regional Hospitals in Natal, for 'free Indians'. He perceived that the greatest need lay in medical services for the underprivileged classes. Consequently, in the backyard of the Mission House, he opened a dispensary where he could attend to the medical needs of the thousands of poor subjects of Durban.[4] The purpose of the mission hospitals in the colonies lay less in the physical well-being, but more in the spiritual conversion of the Indian population.

Through medical and sanitation programs, the colonial government also extended its control and supervision over the public and private lives of the labourers as well as the local populations. The Contagious Disease Act and establishment of the lock hospitals for the compulsory genital examination of indentured women in Natal was a direct intervention into the lives of Indians. The governments of Mauritius and Natal tried to control the sale of alcohol and drugs such as *gandia* and *dakka*. The public health measures came with more stringent sanitation rules and regulations in the colonies. Planters were made responsible for providing 'proper' and 'healthy' accommodation to the labourers; the 'natives' of the colony were also directed to keep their premises free from disease and dirt. Planters were made responsible for the upkeep of the surroundings of the labourers' huts and to keep them free from stagnant water. Non compliance of these rules became a punishable offence. The rhetoric of 'public health', 'cleanliness', and 'proper feeding', which emerged from the 1880s, helped in the establishment of Western medicine's supremacy over all other indigenous methods of treatment. The Medical Health Department and the Poor Law Commission were merged together in 1912.

At the beginning of the twentieth century, experts in the field of science and medicine from England, such as Edwin Chadwick, Ronald Ross, Andrew Balfour, and Ernest Hill among others, visited the colonies and helped local administrators and practitioners to devise new sanitation and health plans. Governors like Napier Broome and Pope-Henessy tried to remove the differentiation line between the indenture healthcare and that of the rest of the population in Mauritius. Gradually, the government removed separate medical schemes for Indians, and devised a program of healthcare for the whole population of Mauritius. In Natal, separate health measures continued to be used by the government for the Africans, Indians, and for the Europeans. The need for better health provisions for the European population in the colonies forced the government to implement public health measures. During the earlier part of the twentieth century, Mauritius was setting up new laboratories and research centres. Natal at that time was busy solving the new political problem of the Union of South Africa. In Natal, the resistance of 'natives', the Boer war, the unification of South Africa, political movements by Mahatma Gandhi, and the strike by indentured labourers in 1913–14: proved to be significant political upheavals for the government. The annual public health reports of Natal only collected data about the diseases and deaths of the Europeans and the Indian population in different parts of the colony. The report completely eschewed concerns related to sickness and mortality among the 'natives'. This very important data shows that the native population of the colony was not the part of the public health policy.[5] It was only during the epidemic of 1902, that the high mortality rate among the natives drew the attention of Natal government.

During the late nineteenth and early twentieth century, a great concern for the public health policies in both the colonies emerged. In Natal, the public health department was established. The major work of the public health department was to—record the birth and death rates, causes of death and outbreak of diseases, record the general sanitary conditions in the colony, ensure supply of sufficient and clean water to the people, keep a record on the jail barrack's sanitation, register for vaccination, inspect barracks, markets, cemetery, and butcher houses, plant trees on both sides of the roads, inspect water streams, etc.: in order to avoid nuisance in public places and causal conduct in sanitation measures. The negligence of sanitation rules became a legal crime. During epidemics, the government initiated free distribution of DDT spray and quinine in rural areas. Laboratories were established in Mauritius to check the purity of milk and other food items. In the rural areas, mobile dispensaries were started in order to reach the local population and make them aware about the importance of sanitation. But all these measures proved insufficient in Mauritius, as an epidemic of malaria hit again in the 1940s.

Indians were blamed for bringing diseases to Mauritius and Natal and a great check and balance system, was imposed on the Indian population in these colonies. The colonial government overlooked the links between commercialization, industrialization and epidemics in the colonies. Indians were not carriers of diseases; they were rather actually the victims of these diseases. The process of commercialization made the port city and capital, Port Louis and Durban respectively, vulnerable to the epidemics. There were several reports that recorded the complaints of nuisance created by the sugar mills and distillery waste; that polluted the water streams and helped in further breeding of mosquitoes, which eventually proved to be the main cause of the malaria epidemic.[6] Sanitary inspectors were forced to take legal action against the mill owners and planters for negligence of sanitary measures. Further research may explore the links between commercialization, industrialization and the prominent diseases in the colonies. The history of epidemics and diseases from the period of abolition of indenture in the 1920s till Independence will not only reveal the role of government in curtailing deadly diseases, but also locate how the rhetoric of public health played a significant role in legitimizing the governance of masses.

Notes

1. John M. Eyler, *Sir Arthur Newsholme and State Medicine 1885-1935*, Cambridge: Cambridge University Press, 1997, p. xi.
2. David Aickin, 'From Plantation Medicine to Public Health: The State and Medicine in British Guiana 1838-1914', unpublished PhD thesis, University College London, UK, 2001, p. 260.

3. Annual Report of the Protector of Indian Immigrants in Natal for the year 1881, Revenue and Agriculture Department (Emigration Branch) Proceedings, August 1882, nos. 15–16, NAI.

4. History of St Aidan's Mission Regional Hospital, Health Department, Province of Kwazulu-Natal, 2001, see www.kznhealth.gov.za/Staidans/history.htm, accessed 5 August 2014.

5. Public Health Report of 1902, CO 181/52, Public Record Office, The National Archives of UK, Kew, 1902, p. 2.

6. Ibid., p. 6.

APPENDICES

Appendix A

Plan of the Mauritius Free Labour Association Instituted under the Sanction of Government

1

The object of the occasion is to afford relief to the urgent and imperative demand which now prevails in the colony for agricultural labour, by the encouragement of immigration into Mauritius of the natives of India, Madagascar, Muscat, and other countries, with their families, on a system favorable to the immigrants, and the conditions enumerated in the following circles.

2

All the proceedings of the Association shall be in strict conformity to the existing laws, and to the principles on which the Emancipation Act of parliament is founded.

3

Agents shall be appointed by the Association with the approbation and under control of government, to reside at Calcutta, Madras, or other ports of India at Madagascar, Muscat and all other places where it may be deemed necessary.

4

The agents shall act in concurrence with the local authorities of the places where they reside, and afford them every information they may require.

5

The agents shall receive the applications of emigrants. And assure themselves that they act of their own free will, without any deception or constraint.

6

They shall cause the emigrants to be visited by a medical officer to ascertain that they are not infirm or diseased, and, if practicable, cause them to be vaccinated previous to embarkation.

7

They shall, in all cases, preferably admit the applications of men wishing to emigrate with their wives and children.

8

For emigrants who may require it, the agents shall provide food and lodging, previous to embarkation, during such time as may be necessary.

9

They shall provide a free passage for the emigrants to Mauritius, and give in advance to each individual, on embarkation, a suit of clothing and a blanket.

10

The emigrants shall, in no case, be called upon to enter into any engagement, previous to their arrival in the colony.

11

The agents will see that the rules established by the Act 5th and 6th William IV, Cap. 53, commonly called the Passenger Act, be strictly observed, particularly as regards the number of passengers on board, the shipping of sufficient provisions, of a supply of medicines, medical attendance, and the sea-worthiness of ships.

12

The agents shall inform the emigrants of the conditions on which they are to be employed at Mauritius, and guarantee, to them, as a minimum, in the name of the Association, the following amount of wages, food and clothing with lodging, and medical attendance.

WAGES

For Indians

Men	5 C rupees or 10 shillings per month
Women	4 C rupees or 8 shillings per month
Children of both sexes from 10 to 18 years	4 C rupees or 8 shillings per month.

For Labourers from Madagascar, Muscat and other places

Men	2½ dollars or 10 shillings per month
Women	2 dollars or 8 shillings per month
Children of both sexes from 10 to 18 years	1 to 1½ dollars or 4–6 shillings per month.

RATIONS, DAILY ALLOWANCES

For Indians of both sexes above 10 years of age

Rice	1 lb 10 oz avoirdupois weight
Dholl or Salt Fish	3 oz avoirdupois weight

Ghee   1/2 oz avoirdupois weight
Salt   1/4 oz avoirdupois weight
For those below 10 years, half rations.

For labourers from Madagascar, Muscat and other places, of both sexes above 10 years of age

Rice   1 lb 10 oz avoirdupois weight
Salt meat   10 oz avoirdupois weight
For those below 10 years, half rations.

CLOTHING

All the emigrants will receive annually the articles hereafter enumerated, or an equivalent in money if they prefer it.

Indians
Men and boys above 10 years

2 *dhooties* of 4 yards each per annum.
1 jacket per annum.
1 lascar cap per annum.
1 blanket or *cumlie* per annum.

Women

10 yards of blue or white *Gurrah*
1 blanket or *cumlie*

Girls from 10 to 15 years

6 yards of blue or white *Gurrah*
1 blanket or *cumlie*

Labourers from Madagascar, Muscat and other places
Men and boys above 10 years

2 pairs of cotton trousers per annum.
2 cotton shirts per annum.
1 lascar cap per annum.
1 blanket per annum.

Women

10 yards of blue or white *Gurrah*
1 blanket.

Girls from 10 to 15 years

6 yards of blue or white *Gurrah*
1 blanket.

13

On their arrival at Mauritius, the immigrants shall be provided by the Association with lodging, food, and medical treatment, if required during such reasonable time, as the local government may think proper to determine.

14

The emigrants shall be entirely free to choose their employers at the highest rate of wages, and on the most favourable conditions to be obtained.

15

The emigrants will, like the other labourers of the colony, be under the protection of the colony, be under the protection of the magistrate already appointed for that purpose; they will enjoy the free exercise of their religion, and the children will have the benefit of the free schools.

16

They shall be allowed a free passage to their own country, after five years' services in the colony, and if they choose to return before the expiration of that period, it shall be at their own expense.

17

In order to meet the expense attendant on the immigration of labourers, government has been solicited to impose a special tax not exceeding £14,000 annually; and will be further requested to advance the sums required for that purpose, and to recover the same, by means firstly of the special tax above-mentioned; secondly of payments to be made annually by the employers of immigrants during a period of four years.

18

The inhabitants of the colony, who may be in want of labourers, will be requested to inform the Association of the precise number required by each of them; and the Association will proportion the assistance to be given to emigrants to the applications made for them and to the funds at its disposal.

19

The applicants for the labourers, will be required to bind themselves under a sufficient guarantee, to receive the immigrants into their service on their arrival, if willing to engage with them; at least, the rates of wages, food, and clothing specified above in article 12, as well as lodging and medical attendance, and to make the annual payments mentioned in article 17.

20

The functions of the members of the association are essentially gratuitous and

the members shall not, in that capacity, derive any personal advantage from the measures of the Association.
Port Louis, 4 June 1840.[1]

Note

1. 'Plan of the Mauritius Free Labour Association instituted under the Sanction of government', Home Department (Public Branch) O.C., 12 May 1841, no. 20, NAI.

Appendix B

'Coolies immigrating to Mauritius will receive the following rates of wages:

Coolies who have returned to India from Mauritius and are re-emigrating will receive:

Rupees 580 for the first year, 600 for the second year, 680 for the third year, 700 for the fourth year, 780 for the fifth year. The ordinance further reside that "They will receive in addition rations consisting of rice, maize, or *manice*, *dholl*, salt fish, ghee or oil, and salt. Boys under 12 years of age will receive three-fourths of the amount of rations allowed to adult emigrants. They will also be furnished with dwellings for themselves and for their families and with medical care for the sick."

Females are not required to work unless they choose. If they wish they can find employment and will be engaged for one year at the rate of Rs 3 per month and rations.'

'There are magistrates in the different districts of Mauritius who have been appointed to hear all complaints of labourers and to see that justice is done to them. There is also an officer called the protector whose special duty is to watch over their interests.'

'More than 206,000 coolies from Calcutta, Madras and Bombay are now in Mauritius. Many of them have become proprietors of land and have settled there. Many other have returned to India with a large amount of savings.'

'Coolies coming to the emigrants depot at Madras and enrolling themselves as emigrants without the intervention of recruiters or contractors will receive the following rewards:

For every male emigrant above 17 years of age under fifty, rupees: 580.
For female emigrant above 17 years of age under fifty, rupees: 280.
For emigrants between 12 and 17 years, half the above rates.
For children under 12 years, nothing.'

'Coolies from the *moffussil*, prior to leaving their district, must present themselves before the district magistrate and obtain a pass from him.'

Signature of the Protectors
Signature of Mauritius Emigrant Agent[1]

Note

1. Mauritius Ordinance no. 1 of 1879, Home, Revenue and Agriculture Department (Emigration Branch) Proceedings, January 1880, nos. 24–6, NAI.

Appendix C

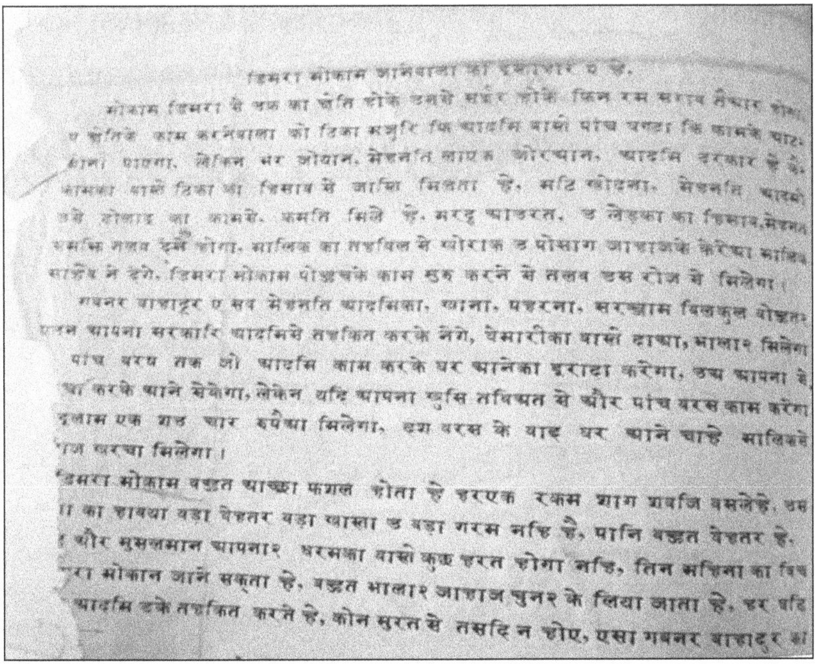

PLATE C.1: Notice to the Intending Migrants for the *Demerara*

Source: CO 167/415, Indian Indentured Labourers in the British and French Colonies.

Appendix D

Medical License for the Voyages under Section 76 of Act II of 1870

_____

is hereby licensed to act in medical charge of 1870, passed by the council of the Lieutenant-Governor of Bengal. The license shall remain in force during the pleasure of the Lieutenant-Governor of Bengal, and may at any time be cancelled in the event of misconduct or inefficiency.[1]

Forms of License and Classification of Vessels

From – A.M. Mackenzie, Esq., Junior Secy to the Govt of Bengal

To – The Protector of Emigrants, Calcutta.

I am directed to inform you that the Lieutenant-Governor has been pleased to decide that licenses to carry emigrants by sea shall not be granted to steam or sailing ships leaving Calcutta, unless they have been classed as A1 at Lloyds', Veritas, or some other recognized European or American underwritten agency, or have been pronounced here, in Calcutta, by at least two competent surveyors or shipping after a full and careful survey, in the manner prescribed by Lloyds' Rules, to be fully equal to vessels classed A1 as above.

Report on the Survey of the A1 class iron/wooden ship _____, registered tonnage _____, owners _____, master _____, chartered for the provisions of the Indian Emigration Act.

1. State of hull, and how ascertained.
2. Thickness and conditions of decks.
3. State of masts, spars, rigging, and sails.
4. State of ground tackle.
5. The number, description, and condition of pumps, fire-engines, and hoses.
6. Instruments, charts, books, signals, &c.
7. Number, description, and condition of boats.
8. Extent and nature of accommodation for emigrants.
9. Position and extent of hospital, galley, and privy accommodation.
10. Means for securing ventilation and light.
11. Power and condition of steam engines, and of condenser, if any.
12. Qualifications of officers and the number of crew.
13. General remarks.

NOTE

1. Medical License under Section 76 of Act II of 1870, Revenue and Agriculture Department, Govt of Bengal (Emigration Branch) Proceedings, September 1870, nos. 5–9, NAI.

Appendix E

Register of Cholera cases

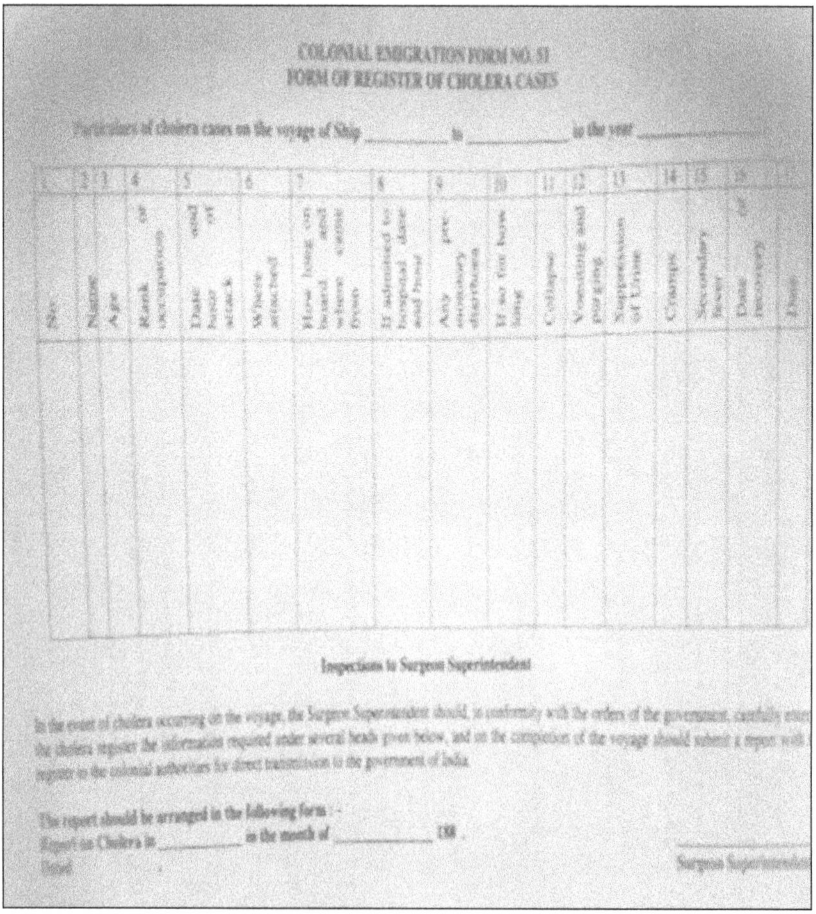

COLONIAL EMIGRATION FORM NO. 51
FORM OF REGISTER OF CHOLERA CASES

Particulars of cholera cases on the voyage of Ship ________ to ________ in the year ________

1	2	3	4	5	6	7	8	9	10	11	12	13	14	15	16	17
No.	Name	Age	Rank or occupation	Date and hour of attack	Where attacked	How long on board and where came from	If admitted to hospital date and hour	Any premonitory diarrhoea	[illegible]	Collapse	Vomiting and purging	Suppression of Urine	Cramps	Secondary fever	Date of recovery	Death

Instructions to Surgeon Superintendent

In the event of cholera occurring on the voyage, the Surgeon Superintendent should, in conformity with the orders of the government, carefully enter [illegible] the cholera register the information required under several heads given below, and on the completion of the voyage should submit a report with [illegible] register to the colonial authorities for direct transmission to the government of India.

The report should be arranged in the following form :-
Report on Cholera in ________ in the month of ________ 188 .
Dated

Surgeon Superintendent

PLATE E.1: Colonial Emigration form for Registering Cholera Cases

Source: CO 167/376, Cholera in Mauritius.

Appendix F

TABLE F.1: Medical Instruments and Appliances for Ship Hospitals and Dispensaries for a Hundred Emigrants

Articles	(a) Proceeding to places west of the Cape or to Fiji via Australia	(b) Proceeding to places east of the Cape or to Fiji via Torres Straits	Remarks
	Number	Number	
Case of instruments containing— tourniquet, artery forceps, dissecting forceps; three amputating knives; three scalpels; one gum-lancet; tooth instruments (viz., upper and lower molar, upper and lower incisor stump forceps and elevator) in separate case; trephine amputating saw; probang; bone forceps; needles; ligature, silk; soft iron wire and horse hair for sutures; a small tracheotomy tube, double; ear syringe, brass (Maw's), with Toynbee and Abernethy's nozzels; and two midwifery forceps, one long and one short; hydrocele trochar and canula.	1 case	1 case	
Case containing two enema syringes, a stomach pump (Maw's), and a syphon.	1 case	1 case	
Pocket dressing case (Maw's), with Symes and Paget's knives and female catheter.	–	Pocket dressing case, single (Maw's)	
Post mortem case (Maw's)	1	1	
Clinical thermometers (one minute or less).	6	6	
Catheters, metallic, 4, Nos. 1, 4, 6, 8, 12.	7 in case	7	
Catheters, gum elastic, 2, No. 8			
Scale and weights (grain dispensing)	1 set	1 set	
Two-ounce measure glass	3	2	
Minim measure glass	2	1	
Pint measure, pewter	1	1	
Four-ounce pewter pots for administering medicines.	6	4	
Infusion pots	2	2	

Articles	(a)	(b)	Remarks
Pestle and mortar (Wedgewood)	1	1	
Glass rod stirrers	2	1	
Tin funnels	2	2	
Glass funnels	1	1	
Spatulas	2	2	
Camel-hair pencils	12 assorted	8	
Blood-porringer (=16 oz.)	1	1	
Pins, in paper, half safety pins, assorted	2 packets	2 packets	
Scissors (best)	1	1	
Knife, pocket	1	1	
Slab for pills, marked	1	1	
Tape	1 bundle	1 bundle	
Common splints	2 sets	1 set	
Long splints	1 set	1 set	
Tow, fine	2 lbs.	1 lb.	
Cotton, wool	3 lbs.	1½ lb.	
Infant's feeding bottles (Allenbury's)	6	6	
Nipples for feeding bottles	1 dozen	1 dozen	
Feeding spoons	6	3	
Test tubes in case	1 nest	1 nest	
Matches, patent safety	1 gross boxes, safety	½ gross boxes, safety	
Pill boxes in nests	2 dozens	1 dozen	
Sponges, surgical, small	½ dozen	¼ dozen	
Litmus paper	2 books	1 book	
Slipper bed-pan (earthenware)	1	1	
Invalid feeding cups	3	2	
Spirit lamps	1	1	
Artery forceps (Spencer Well's)	6	6	
Double channelled uterine catheter	1	1	
Douche case	2	1	
Aseptio hypodermic syringe with platinum needles.	1	1	
Syringe (Higginson's best tropical)	2	1	
Choloroform inhaler (Junker's)	1	1	
Eye dropper	6	3	
Aspirator (Dimlaoy's)	1	1	
Microscope with one 1/12 object glass	1	1	Baker's plantation microscope is suitable

Articles	(a)	(b)	Remarks
Disinfectants.			
Calvert's powder, or Jeyes' sanitary powder, 1/2 each.	500 lbs.	300 lbs.	In 2-lb. packets
Commercial carbolic acid 1/2 and Jeyes' perfeot purifier, or the disinfectant known as " Izal," 1/2.	6 gallons	4 gallons	If desired by Surgeon Superinten- dent phenyle may be substituted for one-fourth the quantity of carbolic acid.
Sulphur, common	30 lbs.	20 lbs.	
Books.			
Squire's Companion to British Pharma- copoeia, latest edition, and *Martindale's Extra Pharmacopceia.*	1 copy	1 copy	

N.B.—*The surgical instruments and appliances which can be so constructed and are so supplied by instrument maker should be the* aseptic *patterns.*

The total quantity of each drug or article required to be supplied shall be regulated according to the above scale in either column (a) or column (b), as the case may be, in proportion to the length of the voyage and to the total number of emigrants to be carried.

CERTIFIED that we have supplied the above medical stores according to prescribed scales for .... emigrants under conveyance to ....; and that special attention has been paid to the provision of drugs that they are fresh and of the best quality.

CERTIFIED that I have carefully checked the quantities supplied with the scale requirements, and have found them correct. Certified also that the packing of the medical stores generally is satisfactory.

DATED

The *Druggists*

DATED

The *Surgeon-Superintendent*

Ship

TABLE F.2: Quantity of Food (as Medical Comforts) to be Shipped for a Hundred Emigrants

Articles	(a) In a ship bound to places west of the Cape and to Fiji via South Australia calculated for a voyage of 20 weeks	(b) In a ship bound to places east of the Cape or to Fiji via Torres Straits calculated for a voyage of 12 weeks	How to be packed	Remarks
	lb.	lb.	In 1-lb and ½-lb tins	
Chicken broth	50	50		
Mutton broth	50	None		
Meat Peptonoid's Carnrick's or other approved	1	½	In 4-oz. tins	Should the Surgeon-Superintendent desire it, Brand's Essence of Beef or Bovril shall be substituted for the whole or a portion of these peptonoids.
Brands Essence of Beef or Bovril	1	½		
Milk, preserved	480	240	Ditto	One-half of the preserved milk shall be of either the "Anglo-Swiss" or the "Nestle's Condensed Swiss" brand, at the option of Surgeon-Superintendent. The other half shall be unsweetened milk, and be of either the "Dhalls," "1st Swiss," or the "Cow's Head" brand, at the option of the Surgeon- Superintendent. Where unsweetened milk, which is not condensed, is shipped, the quantity carried shall be five times the prescribed quantity. The contents of a pound tin mixed with 1/2 a gallon of warm water makes good milk. The article is intended to be used at the Surgeon's discretion for infants, nursing mothers, invalids and others to whom the issue may be considered expedient.
Food for Infants (Nestle's Allenbury's or Mellin's also Plasmon)	25+	12+	In bottles or tins	For 100 infants. The quantity should he reduced proportionally if the number of infants to be carried is less than 100. Allenbury's Milk Food (Nos. 1 and 3) is preferable.

Sago	80	40	In tins	
Arrowroot	80	40	-Do-	
Soojee	50	25	-Do-	
Flour (fine)	30	None	In barrels	
Sugar	600	300	In bags	
Tea	5	None	In tins	
Bael fruit (candied)	30	15	-Do-	
Lime juice	40 gallons	15 gallons	In bottles	If not the whole, at least two-thirds shall be non-alcoholic.
Brandy	8 gallons	3 gallons	In bottles	At Surgeon's request, port or any other approved wine may be substituted in such quantity as may be equivalent to the money value of not more than one-third of the total quantity of brandy to be shipped according to scale. The port wine should be of good quality.

The total quantity of each drug or article required to be supplied shall be regulated according to the above scale in either column (a) or column (b), as the case may be, in proportion to the length of voyage and to the total number of emigrants to be carried.

* Vide Government of India Notification No. 514, dated 7th March 1893, published in the *Gazette of India* dated 11th March 1893.
Vide Government of India Notification No. 3872–16-6, dated 31st October 1901, published in the *Gazette of India* dated 2nd November 1901.
Vide Government of India Notification No. 1310-30-4, dated 4th June 1902, published in the *Gazette of India* dated 7th June 1902.
Vide Government of India Notification No. 804-57-4, dated 28th July 1904, published in the *Gazette of India* dated 30th July 1904.

TABLE F.3: Quantities of Medicines and Medical Supplies for more than a Hundred Emigrants

Number of emigrants	Quantity
Above 150 but under 250	Half more than the quantity prescribed, according to scale for 100 emigrants.
Above 250 but under 350	Twice more than the quantity prescribed according to scale for 100 emigrants.
Above 350 but under 450	Thrice more than the quantity prescribed according to scale for 100 emigrants.
Above 450 but under 550	Four times more than the quantity prescribed according to scale for 100 emigrants.
Above 550 but under 650	Five times more than the quantity prescribed according to scale for 100 emigrants.
Above 650 but under 750	Six times more than the quantity prescribed according to scale for 100 emigrants.
Above 750 but under 850	Seven times more than the quantity prescribed according to scale for 100 emigrants.
Above 850 but under 950	Eight times more than the quantity prescribed according to scale for 100 emigrants.

The total quantity of each drug or article required to be supplied shall be regulated according to the above scale in either column (a) or column (b), as the case may be, in proportion to the length of voyage and to the total number of emigrants to be carried.

Notes
1. All volatile medicines and acids shall be put up in strong stoppered bottles, and the acids shall be carefully packed in a small case with sands.
2. Chloroform, and the syrup of the iodide of iron, shall be in blue glass bottles, or covered from light by dark paper.
3. All the drugs, etc., shall be properly labelled and the quantities clearly marked on each article.
4. Poisons shall be specially distinguished.
5. Whenever more than 16 ozs. of an article are required, it shall be supplied in at least two vessels, one for use, and the other for store.

Source: Revision of the Scale of Medical Stores required to be put on board Emigrant Vessels by the Colonial Emigration Rules, Commerce and Industry Department (Emigration Branch) Proceedings, December 1907, nos. 8–13, NAI.

Appendix G

Appointment of Ship Surgeon

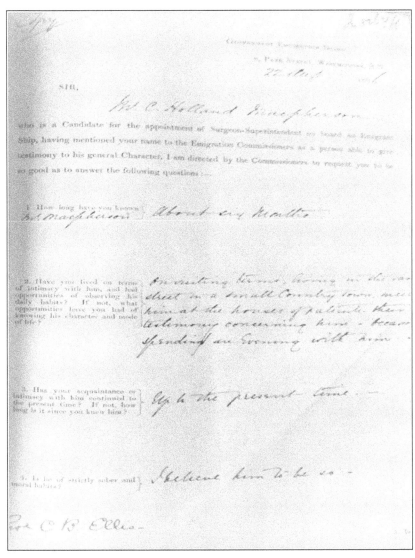

PLATE G.1: Application form for the Appointment of the Ship Surgeon on Emigrant Ships, page 1.

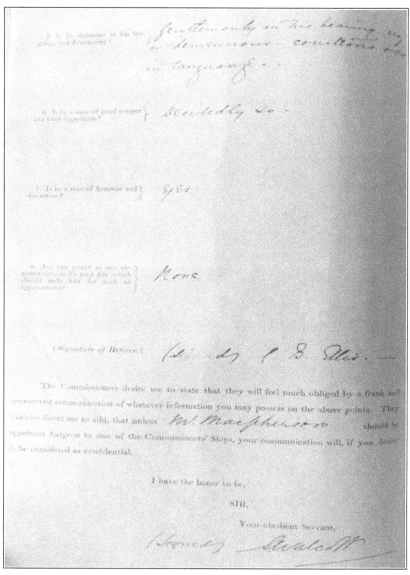

PLATE G.2: Application form for the Appointment of the Ship Surgeon on Emigrant Ships, page 2.

Source: CO 167/495, Appointments of Surgeons.

Appendix H

The Diary of H. Hitchcock, Surgeon-Superintendent of the *Umvoti*, left Madras on 26 October 1882, reached Natal on 1 December 1882

25th October 1882: The coolies in the depot were mustered this morning at 5:30 and ready for inspection of the Medical Inspector and Protector of Emigrants. The emigrants were inspected and marched down the beach and treated under the Pier, from whence they were embarked on board the baroque *Umovati* where they were received and made comfortable 'tween decks'. There were 173 men (including twenty boatmen for the Port of Natal), forty-five women and thirteen children.

26th: 5:30 p.m. Came on board and found many of the emigrants seasick. No. 207 Latchmanam attempted to throw himself overboard; he was handcuffed by the captain and kept on the 'poop' for a few hours. The man has evidently indulged himself with some narcotics. He was boisterous and excitable. Sailed from Madras Harbour at 7:00 p.m. with fair wind.

28th: Strong SW winds from 2:00 a.m. Seasickness on the increase. At noon, was abreast of cyclone. Heavy rains and squalls at 5:00 p.m.

29th: Emigrants improving. Owing to the inclemency of the weather this morning dry provisions were issued. In the evening cooked food given.

31st: 8:30 a.m. Rain and squalls. Mutton and potatoes for breakfast. The sheep weighed only twenty-five pounds after being dressed. The emigrants were dissatisfied. The captain promised to them two sheep every alternate week and one in the intermediate week.

1st November 1882: Calm night, heavy rains this morning. Sky overcast. Emigrants doing well…[some] sirdars, topazes, and cooks were dis-rated since embarkation as they were found useless and other substituted.

5th: Nos. 71, 201, and 205 stole ship's onions and potatoes. To be deprived of one meal and to do a week's extra duty.

6th: Two sheep were given last evening for the emigrants which weighed fifty pounds after being dressed. Calm night. Heavy rain. Nos. 26 and 27 admitted with mumps. No. 91 Anushan has been very troublesome since embarkation, finding fault with his meals, regarding quantity and quality. He has the option of taking his allowances of ghee which he considered insufficient. Threatens to make his compliant in Natal.

7th: No. 91 Anushan's turn this day to holystone 'tween decks; refused to do it, pretending to be ill. He was taken down by the captain and set to work. Another case of mumps this morning, no. 122. Rain in the afternoon. Emigrants ordered 'tween decks'.

8th: Captain Reeves objects to the women cleaning rice to free it of gravel 'tween decks, and instead on its being done on the seaward side of the deck, where the wash tubes are placed for bathing and near to the hospital and sailors' house. I told the Captain it would be very inconvenient for the women at work, as they are likely to be interfered with by the crew, and the (male) emigrants and the uncertainty of the weather, but Captain Reeves will not listen. At 3:30 p.m. the weather was threatening and a heavy fall of rain soon followed. The rice, which was partly cleaned, had to be gathered up. One of the crew, Wagner, was in a fair case of mumps under treatment. I directed the compounder to serve out the rice 'tween decks'. This also the captain objected to. The women and children, with the rest, had all to sit in the wet 'poop' and deck, and take their meals.

9th: All those vaccinated on the 2nd instant have failed. I have this morning vaccinated the captain, a gentleman passenger, and an apprentice, and an apprenticed lad, and vaccinated the ship's carpenter. I have to state that the weather was rather threatening at about noon, when the women should have commenced sifting rice for their afternoon and tomorrow's meals, and the consequence was that the rice could not be cleaned and thereby the coolies had to partake of their meals with gravel and sand in their cooked rice. Further, I must state from the quantity of husks in the rice I have my apprehension of bowels complaints showing itself amongst the emigrants. As it is I have had some cases of dysentery and diarrhoea attributable to the rice not being sifted hitherto. I may mention that the captain volunteered yesterday that he would look after the rice being sifted, and that he requested me and my assistant not to 'bother' ourselves about it, but he had taken no action whatever to have it done.

12th: While the compounder was serving out the morning issue of water, one of the boatmen named Govindan asked the compounder to serve out their rice. The compounder told him that he was busy serving out the water and when done, he would be attended to. Govindan would not keep quiet and asked again in a most impertinent and insolent manner to serve out the rice. The compounder took no notice of him, and then the boatman began to make use of very indecent language. The compounder turned around, said that he will not serve out their rice first but would serve them last. All the boatmen then in a body refused to wait and the compounder brought the matter to my notice. This was not the first occasion that they have kept giving trouble. They are a most impudent, insolent and unbearable lot. They were sent up to the deck. In spite of all orders given by me and the captain they seem to take no notice of it. Three of the ringleaders were brought before the captain, and they were asked the cause of their behaviour. They stated that they felt hungry, and in consequence of their rice the day previous being with gravel and sand, they had to throw it overboard and eat nothing. The captain told them that women were put to clean the rice daily, to sift out the stones and what more they wanted! They were warned that if they for the future don't behave better, they will be punished. The women were at work again sifting the rice, and no less than seven women changed, and only cleaned one bag…this was caused, as stated by them, that the wind on the 'seaside' of the hospital on the deck was too strong for them to sift the rice, and asked permission from the compounder to have it sifted 'tween decks'. This was refused by the captain.

14th: The emigrants refused taking their supply of tobacco, some threw it overboard, being bad and unfit for use. The third officer states that there is no better tobacco to be had on board. Two sheep were given for the use of coolies.

20th: No. 40 Karuppayi taken ill with labour pains. Not confined as yet.

21st: No. 40 Karuppayi was instrumentally delivered of a stillborn child at 3:00 p.m. Mr. Le Febour was instructed to throw the baby overboard at night when the emigrants were asleep.

23rd: No cooking could be carried on this morning owing to the inclemency of the weather. Dry provisions to be issued to the emigrants.

24th: The woman who was instrumentally delivered is progressing favourably.

26th: There was a boxing match this morning 'tween deck' an emigrant coolie and a boatman, the former got the worst of it.

27th: 'Mumps' continues amongst the emigrants, all the cases are terminating.

1st December 1882: Arrived a port and anchored at 6:00 a.m. Shortly after was towed-in by the steam tug 'kovdoo' and the emigrants disembarked.

Source: Cited in Ashwin Desai and Goolam Vahed, *Inside Indenture: A South African Story, 1860-1914*, Durban: Madiba Publishers, 2007, pp. 34–6.

Appendix I

The Diary of Dr John McIntyre during the voyage of the *Umovoti*, departed from Madras on 25 August 1888.

25th August: 235 Indians embarked. So far as I could tell, none was affected with venereal disease. I think the men are unusually well fitted for emigrants to Natal. I consider them, as a body, superior to any I have seen. We sailed at about one o'clock this morning. Some emigrants are sick so little rice could be eaten at breakfast. They will have dry food for supper.

26th: Breakfast of dry food was issued and cooked rice and *dholl* will be given for supper. Tin vessels were issued yesterday. Today the badges of the sirdar cooks and topazes will be issued. Tomorrow I shall issue the clothing.

27th: Comparatively cool morning, cloudy but dry. The blankets have been issued. Three blankets and six bundles of clothes over. I think a mistake to have so few spare blankets. There are four beds in hospitals and I think two blankets to each bed would be a modest estimate if the beds were occupied. It is only prudent to provide for such and, by no means unlikely contingency. Why are mattresses provided if blankets are unnecessary? Supper: rice, *dholl*, and potatoes.

28th: Owing to the crowding of men around the neighbourhood of the hospital, and as the available space on the poop was taken up, I requested Captain Reeves to remove the sail under repair to make room for the Indians. This he refused to do, claiming the space on the poop as his right and he required it to navigate the vessel. In an hour, however, he removed the sail, his chairs, and the awning; his wife and himself went below to dine. He is evidently much offended but I cannot help it. I have understood the emigrants as entitled to as much space as they may require. I also understand habitual sail repairing on the poop is forbidden. The tobacco and soap were issued at noon.

29th: So far, the people have been as docile as well-bred children.

30th: Been a very stormy night and this morning continues to blow hard, with a heavy sea, so that no cooking can be done. I had written a note before going on deck, asking the captain to put the awning over the poop, and quarter decks to protect the Indians from the sun, which I considered dangerous the past two days. Last night an Indian woman (single) assaulted several other women below, and threatened to strike the *aya* and the chief male sirdar too; this morning I enquired into the matter and warned the woman not to repeat the offence. At the inspection there was one case of dysentery, two of earache. Supper: rice, *dholl*, and fish.

31st: It's been quite a gale with torrents of rain and a heavy sea all night; this morning, the wind abated slightly; but it still rains so that breakfast must be given below … I inspected all the males and found two with venereal disease of recent date and mild types, two new cases of mumps and a few cases of diarrhoea … 3:00 p.m.: all on deck.

1st September: About 2:00 p.m. it was black on the northern horizon and a squall was expected. About 3:00 p.m. I was below and heard the captain call for his coat. Shortly after hearing a conversation I went on deck to send the people below. The captain and men were busy taking down the awning. I was looking on when the captain came to me in a rage and said it was my fault that awning were never put up in these latitudes, that he had no sleep for three nights and all because of me. Ever since Tuesday last he has been as sulky as if he was at a funeral and is constantly finding fault with the Indians for some or other imaginary indiscretion.

3rd: The soap, tobacco and oil are to be issued as per the rules once per week. Captain Reeves says tomorrow is the proper day, and has only yielded to give soap after a long senseless argument, insisting that from Tuesday to next Tuesday inclusively is only a week and not eight days. Supper: rice and *dholl*.

4th: Captain Reeves, till the end of the voyage, took every opportunity of showing his disregard and defiance of the rules. In the last entry in the diary I have given the inside surface of the ship's hospital and I would suggest that a hospital of suitable dimensions and properly fitted for the purpose be erected, before the *Umvoti* is permitted to carry Indians again. The fire places are also dangerous and the railway around the bulwark's ought to be higher and covered with netting to prevent young and old falling overboard. There are some other objectionable points in Captain Reeves' conduct and in respect of the ship's fittings, but I think I have said enough to show I consider him unfit to carry coolies.

Source: Cited in Ashwin Desai and Goolam Vahed, *Inside Indenture: A South African Story, 1860-1914*, Durban: Madiba Publishers, 2007, pp. 37–9.

Appendix J

PLATE J.1: Indian Women and Children Present themselves for Medical
Treatment, Mauritius

Source: INF-10-228, Mauritius Hospitals.

Appendix K

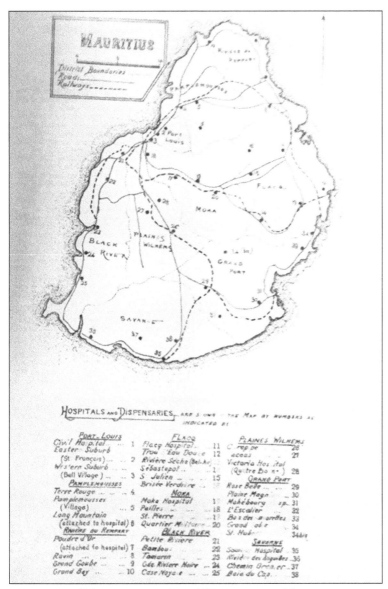

PLATE K.1: Hospitals and Dispensaries in Mauritius

Source: CO 167/868/13, Annual Report of the Protector of Indian Immigrants in Mauritius for the year 1928.

Bibliography

PRIMARY SOURCES

PUBLISHED OFFICIAL REPORTS

Annual Report of Protector of Emigrants, Calcutta, Shimla: Government of India, 1857–1920.

Annual Report of Protector of Emigrants, Madras, Shimla: Government of India, 1860–1920.

Annual Report of the Indian Immigration Trust Board of Natal, Shimla: Government of India, 1874–1910.

Annual Report of the Protector of Immigrants, Colony of Mauritius, Shimla: Government of India, 1860–1920.

Annual Report of the Protector of Immigrants, Colony of Natal, Shimla: Government of India, 1860–1920.

Balfour, Andrew, *Report on Medical and Sanitary Matters in Mauritius, 1921*, Mauritius: Authority of the Governor P.G. Bumstead, 1921.

Chadwick, Edwin, *Report on the Sanitary Condition of the Labouring Population of Great Britain*, London: W. Clowes and Sons for H.M. Stationery off., 1843, see https://babel.hathitrust.org/cgi/pt, accessed on 26 July 2014.

Frere, W.E. and V.A. Williamson, *Report of the Royal Commissioners appointed to Enquire into the Treatment of Immigrants in Mauritius*, London: William Clowes and Sons, 1875.

Geoghegan, J., *Coolie Emigration from India*, Calcutta: Government of India, 1874.

Grierson, George A., *Report on Colonial Emigration from the Bengal Presidency*, Calcutta: Government of India, 1883.

Hill, Ernest, *Report on Plague in Natal 1902-03*, London: Cassel and Company Limited, 1904.

Marijuana: Report of the Indian Hemp Drugs Commission, 1893-1894, Silver Spring, MD: Thos. Jefferson Pub. Co., 1969.

Mouat, Frederic. J., *Rough Notes of a Trip to Reunion, the Mauritius and Ceylon:*

with Remarks on their Eligibility as Sanitaria for Indian Invalids, Calcutta: Thacker, Spink and Co., 1852.

Ross, Ronald, *Report on the Prevention of Malaria in Mauritius,* London: Waterlow and Sons Limited, 1908.

UNESCO, *The African Slave Trade from the Fifteenth to the Nineteenth Century: Reports and Papers of the Meeting of Experts Organized by UNESCO at Port-au-Prince, Haiti, 31 January to 4 February 1978*, vol. 2, The General History of Africa Studies and Documents, Paris: United Nations Educational, Scientific and Cultural Organization, 1979.

UNPUBLISHED OFFICIAL SOURCES

National Archives of India

Home Department (Public Branch) Proceedings, Government of India, 1857–1871.

Revenue, Agriculture and Commerce Department (Emigration Branch) Proceedings, Government of India, 1871–1879.

Home Revenue and Agriculture Department (Emigration Branch) Proceedings, Government of India, 1879–1881.

Revenue and Agriculture Department (Emigration Branch) Proceedings, Government of India, 1881–1905.

Commerce and Industry Department (Emigration Branch) Proceedings, Government of India, 1905–1920.

Public Records Office, Kew

The Immigration Department Records for Mauritius, 1913–1920, CO 571.

Report of the Medical Officers on Immigrant Voyages, n.d., CO 384/ 110.

Records from Mauritius

Original Correspondence of Mauritius, 1778–1951, CO 167.

Entry Books, 1810–1872, CO 168.

Mauritius Acts and Ordinance, CO 169.

Mauritius Sessional Papers, CO 170.

Mauritius Register of Correspondence, CO 356.

Records from Natal

Natal Register of Correspondence, 1849–1910, CO 357.

Natal Register of Correspondence, CO 358.

Natal Entry Books, 1852–1872, CO 405.

Natal Original Correspondence, 1846–1910, CO 179.

Acts, Ordinance and Proclamation for the Colony of Natal, CO 180.

Sessional Papers of Natal, CO 181.

Natal Blue Books of Statistics, CO 182.

War and Colonial Department and Colonial Office: Natal Miscellanea, CO 183.

Indian Office Records: London

Commerce and Industry Department (Emigration Branch) Proceedings, 1905–20.

Confidential Commerce and Industry (Emigration Branch) Proceedings, 1915–22.

Education, Health and Lands Department (Emigration Branch) Proceedings, 1923–31.

Home, Revenue and Agriculture Department (Emigration Branch) Proceedings, 1879–81.

India: Public Proceedings, 1834–7.

Revenue, Agriculture and Commerce Department (Emigration Branch) Proceedings, 1871–79.

Revenue and Agriculture Department (Emigration Branch) Proceedings, 1881–1905.

Revenue and Agriculture Department (Emigration Branch) Proceedings, 1921–23.

PRIVATE PAPERS

Baba Ramchandra Papers, File 2A, Notebook 2, NMML, Delhi.

HOUSE OF COMMONS PAPERS, PARLIAMENTARY PAPERS

A letter from the Secretary to the Government of India to the Committee appointed to inquire respecting the exportation of hill coolies, dated the 1st day of August 1838, on the report made by that Committee, 1841, session 1.

Convention between Her Majesty the Queen of the United Kingdom of Great Britain and Ireland and South African Republic, February 1884 (Cmd. 3914).

Copies of all orders in Council, or colonial ordinances for the better regulation and enforcement of the relative duties of masters and employers, and articled servants, tradesmen and labourers, in the colonies of British Guiana and Mauritius, 1837–8 (vol. 180).

Copies of correspondence addressed to the Secretary of State for the colonial department, relative to the introduction of the Indian labourers into Mauritius; and of the report of the Commissioners of inquiry into the present condition of those already located in that colony, 1840 (vol. 331).

Copies of correspondence relative to the Emigration of Indian labourers into Mauritius, 1844 (vol. 356).

Copies of despatches from Sir William Nicolay on the subject of free labour in Mauritius, 1840 (vol. 58).

Correspondence relating to the emigration of labourers to the West Indies and Mauritius, from the west coast of Africa, the East Indies, and China, 1844 (530).

Correspondence relating to the Indian Relief Act, 1914 (in Continuation of Cmd. 7265 of 1914), South Africa; Indian Relief Act, October 1914 (Cmd. 7644).

Correspondence relating to the introduction of Indian labourers into Mauritius, 1842 (vol. 26).

Correspondence relating to the Royal Commission of Enquiry into the condition of the Indian immigrants in Mauritius, 1875 (Cmd. 1188).

Dispatch from the Governor of Mauritius, enclosing the report of the Committee appointed to inquire into the state of the Indian immigrants, and the effect of the existing regulations in regard to their engagements, 1845 (vol. 641).

East India (indentured labour), report to the Government of India on the conditions of Indian immigrants in four British colonies and Surinam, by Mr James McNeill, Indian Civil Service, and Mr Chimman Lal, part I, Trinidad and British Guiana, 1914–16 (Cmd. 7744, 7745).

Papers related to the grievances of Her Majesty's Indian subjects in the South African Republic, September 1895 (Cmd. 7911).

Papers related to the laws and regulations in force in colonies under responsible government respecting the admission of immigrants (Colonies: Immigration), July 1904 (Cmd. 2105).

Regulations made and orders issued by the Government of Bengal for the protection of coolies (labourers), proceeding to and from the Mauritius, or any other place, 1843 (vol. 148).

Report of the Commissioners appointed to enquire into the treatment of immigrants in British Guiana, 1871 (Cmd. 393), (Cmd. 393-I), (Cmd. 393-II).

Report of the Indian Inquiry Commission: South Africa: Indian Inquiry (Strike in Natal), April 1914 (Cmd. 7265).

Report of the Royal Commissioners appointed to enquire into the treatment of immigrants in Mauritius, 1875 (Cmd. 1115).

Newspapers, Journals, and Correspondence:

Natal Government House, correspondence relating to Indian questions, 1897–1910, NMML.

Natal Mercury, Durban, 1891–1915, NMML.

South African Medical Journal, 1860–1920, IML.

SECONDARY SOURCES

ARTICLES

Arnold, David, 'Medical Priorities and Practice in Nineteenth-Century British India', *South Asia Research*, vol. 5, no. 2, 1985, pp. 167–83.

Arnold, David, 'Race, Place and Bodily Difference in Early Nineteenth Century India', *Historical Research*, vol. 77, no. 196, 2004, pp. 254–73.

Atterbury, Paul, 'Steam & Speed: Industry, Power & Social Change in 19th-Century Britain', *The Victorian Vision*, see http://www.vam.ac.uk/content/articles/s/industry-power-and-social-change, accessed 19 November 2014.

Bose, Neilesh, review of *The Black Hole of Empire: History of a Global Practice of Power by Partha Chatterjee, Reviews in History*, review no. 1307; see http://www.history.ac.uk/reviews/review/1307, accessed 19 November, 2014.

Brain, J.B. and P. Brain, 'The Health of Indentured Indian Migrants to Natal 1860-1911', *South African Medical Journal*, vol. 62, no. 20, 1982, pp. 739–42.

Chakrabati, Pratik, '"Signs of the Times": Medicine and Nationhood in British India', *Osiris*, vol. 22, 2009, pp. 188–211. http://www.ncbi.nlm.nih.gov/pmc/articles/PMC2858439, accessed 14 October 2014.

Coovadia, Hoosen et al., 'The Health and Health System of South Africa: Historical Roots of Current Public Health Challenge', *Health in South Africa*, vol. 374, 2009, pp. 817–34, see https://www.ncbi.nlm.nih.gov/pubmed/19709728, accessed 12 November 2014.

Crook, Tom, 'Sanitary Inspection and the Public Sphere in Late Victorian and Edwardian Britain: A Case Study in Liberal Governance', *Social History*, vol. 32, no. 4, 2007, pp. 369–93.

Curtin, Philip D., '"The White Man's Grave": Image and Reality, 1780-1850', *Journal of British Studies*, vol. 1, no. 1, 1961, pp. 94–110.

———, 'Epidemiology and the Slave Trade', *Political Science Quarterly*, vol. 83, no. 2, 1968, pp. 190–216.

Ernst, Waltraud, 'The Indianization of Colonial Medicine: The Case of Psychiatry in Early-Twentieth-Century British India', *NTM International Journal of History & Ethics of Natural Sciences, Technology & Medicine*, vol. 20, no. 2, 2012, pp. 61–89. See www.ncbi.nlm.nih.gov/pubmed/22555368, accessed 24 July 2014.

Freund, Bill, 'Indian Women and the Changing Character of the Working Class Indian Household in Natal 1860-1990', *Journal of Southern African Studies*, vol. 17, no. 3, 1991, pp. 414–29.

Ghosh, Amitav, 'Of Fanas and Forecastles: The Indian Ocean and Some lost Languages of the Age of Sail', *Economic and Political Weekly*, vol. 43, no. 25, 2008, pp. 56–62.

Gillion, K.L., 'The Sources of Indian Emigration to Fiji', *Population Studies*, vol. 10, no. 2, 1956, pp. 139–57.

Guha, Sumit, 'Nutrition, Sanitation, Hygiene, and the Likelihood of Deaths: The British Army in India c. 1870-1920', *Population Studies*, vol. 47, no. 3, 1993, pp. 385–401.

Harries, Patrick, 'Plantations, Passes and Proletarians: Labour and the Colonial

State in Nineteenth Century Natal', *Journal of Southern African Studies*, vol. 13, no. 3, 1987, pp. 372–99.

Harrison, Mark, 'Public Health and Medicine in British India: An Assessment of the British Contribution', based on a paper delivered to the Liverpool Medical Society on 5 March 1988; see http://www.evolve360.co.uk/Data/10/Docs/10/10Harrison.pdf, accessed 22 July 2014.

Hobsbawm, E.J. and R.M. Hartwell, 'The Standard of Living during the Industrial Revolution: A Discussion', *The Economic History Review*, n.s., vol. 16, no. 1, 1963, pp. 119–34.

Hodges, Sarah, '"Looting" the Lock Hospital in Colonial Madras during the Famine Years of the 1870s', *Social History of Medicine*, vol. 18, no. 3, 2005, pp. 379–98.

Huttenback, Robert A., 'Indians in South Africa, 1860-1914: The British Imperial Philosophy on Trial', *The English Historical Review*, vol. 81, no. 319, 1966, pp. 273–91.

———, 'Some Fruits of Victorian Imperialism: Gandhi and the Indian Question in Natal, 1893-99', *Victorian Studies*, vol. 11, no. 2, 1967, pp. 153–80.

Jain, Ravindra K., 'Freedom Denied? Indian Women and Indentureship', *Economic and Political Weekly*, vol. 21, no. 7, 1986, pp. 316–21.

Jeffery, Roger, 'Recognizing India's Doctors: The Institutionalization of Medical Dependency, 1918-39', *Modern Asian Studies*, vol. 13, no. 2, 1979, pp. 301–26.

Kelly, John D., 'From Holi to Diwali in Fiji: An Essay on Ritual and History', *Man*, n.s., vol. 23, no. 1, 1988, pp. 40–55.

Killingray, David, 'The "Rod of Empire": The Debate Over Corporal Punishment in the British African Colonial Forces, 1888-1946', *Journal of African History*, vol. 35, no. 2, 1994, pp. 201–16.

Lal, Brij V., 'Veil of Dishonour: Sexual Jealousy on Fiji Plantation', *Journal of Pacific History*, vol. 20, no. 3, 1985, pp. 135–55.

Lewis, Colin A., 'The South African Sugar Industry', *The Geographical Journal*, vol. 156, no.1, 1990, pp. 70–8.

Madhwi, 'Recruiting Indentured Labour for Overseas Colonies, circa 1834–1910', *Social Scientist*, vol. 43, no. 9–10, 2015, pp. 53–68, see www.jstor.org/stable/24642373, accessed 20 February 2019.

Mahmud, Tayyab, 'Colonialism and Modern Constructions of Race: A Preliminary Inquiry', *University of Miami Law Review*, vol. 53, no. 4, 1999, pp. 1219–46. See http://digitalcommons.law.seattleu.edu/faculty/501, accessed 21 December 2014.

Manson, Patrick et al., 'Discussion on Sanitation in Reference to Ankylostomiasis in the Tropics', *The British Medical Journal*, vol. 2, no. 2496, 1908, pp. 1347–54.

Mohapatra, Prabhu P., '"Restoring the Family": Wife Murders and the Making of a Sexual Contract for Indian Immigration Labour in the British

Caribbean Colonies, 1860-1920', *Studies in History*, vol. 11, no. 2, 1995, pp. 227–60.

———, 'Eurocentrism, Forced Labour, and Global Migration: A Critical Assessment', *International Review of Social History*, vol. 52, no. 1, 2007, pp. 110–15.

———, 'Antimonies of Contract: Genealogies of Labour Relation in 19th Century India', paper presented at the 7th International Conference on Labour History, 27–9 March 2008, Noida.

Peers, Douglas M., 'Soldiers, Surgeons and the Campaigns to Combat Sexually Transmitted Diseases in Colonial India, 1805-1860', *Medical History*, vol. 42, no. 2, 1998, pp. 137–60.

Radhakrishna, Meena, 'Of Apes and Ancestors: Evolutionary Science and Colonial Ethnography', *Indian Historical Review*, vol. 33, no. 1, 2006, pp. 1–23.

Reddock, Rhoda E., 'Freedom Denied: Indian Women and Indentureship in Trinidad and Tobago, 1845-1917', *Economic and Political Weekly*, vol. 20, no. 43, 1985, pp. WS79–WS87.

Reddy, M., 'Structural Adjustment Policies: Agricultural Growth and Rural Poverty', *Journal of South Pacific Agriculture*, vol. 5, no. 1, 1998, pp. 61–8.

Richardson, Peter, 'The Natal Sugar Industry 1849-1905: An Interpretative Essay', *The Journal of African History*, vol. 23, no. 4, 1982, pp. 515–27.

Sawyer, Roy T., 'The Trade in Medicinal Leeches in the Southern Indian Ocean in the Nineteenth Century', *Medical History*, vol. 43, 1999, pp. 241–5.

Sen, Samita, 'Unsettling the Household: Act VI (of 1901) and the Regulation of Women Migrants in Colonial Bengal', *International Review of Social History*, vol. 41, 1996, pp. 135–46.

Shlomowitz, Ralph and John McDonald, 'Babies at Risk on Immigrant Voyages to Australia in the Nineteenth Century', *The Economic History Review*, n.s., vol. 44, no. 1, 1991, pp. 86–101.

———, 'Mortality of Indian Labour on Ocean Voyages 1843-1917', *Studies in History*, vol. 6, no.1, 1990, pp. 35–65.

Smith, James Patterson, 'Empire and Social Reform: British Liberals and the "Civilizing Mission" in the Sugar Colonies, 1868-1874', *Albion: A Quarterly Journal concerned with British Studies*, vol. 27, no. 2, 1995, pp. 253–77.

Swanson, Maynard W., 'The Sanitation Syndrome: Bubonic Plague and Urban Native Policy in the Cape Colony 1900-1909', *Journal of African History*, vol. 18, no. 3, 1977, pp. 387–410.

Tayal, Maureen, 'Indian Indentured Labour in Natal, 1890-1911', *The Indian Economic and Social History Review*, vol. 14, no. 4, 1980, pp. 519–29.

Thompson, E.P., 'Time, Work-Discipline, and Industrial Capitalism', *Past & Present*, vol. 38, 1967, pp. 56–97.

Vahed, Goolam, 'Construction of Community and Identity among Indians in

Colonial Natal, 1860-1910: The Role of the Muharram Festival', *The Journal of African History*, vol. 43, no. 1, 2002, pp. 77–93.

Vahed, Goolam and Thembisa Waetjen, 'Passages of Ink: Decoding the Natal Indentured Records into the Digital Age', *Kronos*, vol. 40, no. 1, 2014, pp. 45–73. Available on https://wiser.wits.ac.za/system/files/seminar/VahedWaetjen2013.pdf, accessed 15 December 2018.

Vatuk, Ved Prakash, 'Protest Songs of East Indians in British Guiana', *The Journal of American Folklore*, vol. 77, no. 305, 1964, pp. 220–35.

CHAPTERS IN BOOKS

Abramova, S.U., 'Ideological, Doctrinal, Philosophical, Religious and Political Aspects of the African Slave Trade', in *The African Slave Trade from the Fifteenth to the Nineteenth Century: Reports and Papers of the Meeting of Experts Organized by UNESCO at Port-au-Prince, Haiti, 31 January to 4 February 1978*, vol. 2, The General History of Africa Studies and Documents, Paris: United Nations Educational, Scientific and Cultural Organization, 1979, pp. 16–30.

Allen, Richard B., 'Vagrancy in Mauritius and the Nineteenth Century Colonial Plantations World', in *Cast Out: Vagrancy and Homelessness in Global and Historical Perspective*, ed. A.L. Beier and Paul Ocobock, Ohio: Ohio University, 2008, pp. 140–61.

Arnold, David, 'Vagrant India: Famine, Poverty and Welfare under Colonial Rule', in *Cast Out: Vagrancy and Homelessness in Global and Historical Perspective*, ed. A.L. Beier and Paul Ocobock, Ohio: Ohio University Press, 2008, pp. 117–39.

Barraut, A.R., 'The Medical Topography of Mauritius, with an account of the Fever which prevailed there in 1867', in *Transactions of the Epidemiological Society of London*, vol. III, London: Hardwicke and Bouge, 1874, pp. 183–99.

Bashford, Alison and Carolyn Strange, 'Isolation and Exclusion in the Modern World: An Introductory Essay', *Isolation Places and Practices of Exclusion*, London and New York: Routledge, 2003, pp. 1–19.

Beall, Jo., 'Women under Indentured Labour in Colonial Natal, 1860-1911', in *Women and Gender in Southern Africa to 1945*, ed. Cheryl Walker, Cape Town: David Philip/London James Curry, 1990, pp. 146–67.

Chandra, Jayawardena, 'Farm, Household and Family in Fiji Indian Rural Society', in *Overseas Indians: A study in Adaptation*, ed. George Kurian and Ram P. Srivastava,, New Delhi: Vikas Publishing House, 1983, pp. 141–79.

Chopra, Radhika, 'Dependent Husbands: Reflections on Marginal Masculinities', in *Navigating Social Exclusion and Inclusion in Contemporary India and Beyond: Structures, Agents, Practices, ed.* Uwe Skoda et al., London, New York: Anthem Press, 2013, pp. 41–54.

Cooks, Harold J., 'Physical Methods', in *Companion Encyclopedia of the History of Medicine*, vol. II, ed. W.F. Bynum and Roy Porter, London and New York: Routledge, 1993, pp. 1275–1300.

Edwards, C.F., 'On the recent Outbreak of Pernicious Fever in Mauritius', in *Transactions of the Epidemiological Society of London*, vol. III, London: Hardwicke and Bouge, 1874, pp. 166–71.

Emmer, P.C., 'The Great Escape: The Migration of Female Indentured Servants from British India to Surinam, 1873-1916', in *Abolition and its Aftermath: The Historical Context, 1870-1916*, ed. D. Richardson, London: Frank Cass, 1985, pp. 245–66.

———, ed., 'The Meek Hindu: The Recruitment of Indian Indentured Labourers for Service Overseas, 1870-1916', *Colonialism and Migration: Indentured Labour Before and After Slavery*, Dordrecht/Boston/Lancaster: Martinus Nijhoff Publishers, 1986, pp. 187–207.

Gerbeau, Hubert, 'Engages and Coolies on Reunion Island Slavery's Masks and Freedom's Constraints', tr. Bernard Delfendahl, in *Colonialism and Migration: Indentured Labour Before and After Slavery*, ed. P.C. Emmer, Dordrecht/Boston/Lancaster: Martinus Nijhoff Publishers, 1986, pp. 209–36.

Lal, Brij V., 'Labouring Men and Nothing More: Some Problems of Indian Indenture in Fiji', in *Indentured Labour in the British Empire*, ed. Kay Saunders, London and Canberra: Croom Helm, 1984, pp. 126–54.

Metcalf, Thomas R., 'Indian Migration to South Africa', in *Studies in Migration: Internal and International Migration in India*, ed. M.S.A. Rao, New Delhi: Manohar Publication, 1986, pp. 345–62.

Mishra, Sabyasachi R., 'An Empire "De-Masculinized": The British Colonial State and the Problem of Syphilis in Nineteenth Century India', in *Diseases and Medicine in India: A Historical Overview*, ed. Deepak Kumar, New Delhi: Tulika Books, 2001, pp. 166–79.

Mishra, Sourav, 'Beyond the Bounds of Time? The Haj Pilgrimages from the Indian Subcontinent, 1865-1920', in *The Social History of Health and Medicine in Colonial India*, ed. Biswamoy Pati and Mark Harrison, London and New York: Routledge, 2009, pp. 31–44.

Mouat, Frederic J., 'Medical Statistics, with Especial Reference to Cholera and Syphilis', in *Transactions of the Epidemiological Society of London*, vol. III, London: Hardwicke and Bouge, 1874, pp. 376–97.

Nevadomsky, Joseph, 'Changes Over Time and Space in the East Indian Family in Rural Trinidad', in *Overseas Indians: A Study in Adaptation*, ed. George Thomas Kurian and Ram P. Srivastava, New Delhi: Vikas Publishing House, 1983, pp. 180–213.

Pati, Biswamoy, '"Ordering" "Disorder" in a Holy City: Colonial Health Intervention in Puri during the Nineteenth Century', in *Health, Medicine and Empire: Perspectives on Colonial India*, eds. Biswamoy Pati and Mark Harrison, Delhi: Orient Longman, 2001, pp. 270–98.

Persaud, Anil, 'Transformed Over Seas: "Medical Comforts" Aboard Nineteenth Century Emigrant Ships', in *Labour Matters: Towards Global Histories Studies*, ed. Marcel van der Linden and Prabhu Mohapatra, New Delhi: Tulika Books, 2009, pp. 22–56.

Rogers, H.T., 'Notes on the Epidemic of Malarial Fever which appeared in Mauritius in 1866-67', in *Transactions of the Epidemiological Society of London*, vol. III, London: Hardwicke and Bouge, 1874, pp. 200–15.

Sarkar, Aditya, 'The City, its Streets and its Workers: The Plague Crisis in Bombay, 1896-98', in *Working Lives and Worker Militancy: The Politics of Labour in Colonial India*, ed. Ravi Ahuja, Delhi: Tulika Books, 2013, pp. 1–46.

Shameen, Shaista, 'Migration, Labour and Plantation Women in Fiji: A Historical Perspective', in *Women Plantation Workers: International Experiences*, eds. Shobhita Jain and Rhoda Reddock, New York: Oxford University Press, 1998, pp. 49–65.

Smart, W.R.E., 'On the Distribution of Asiatic Cholera in Africa', in *Transactions of the Epidemiological Society of London*, vol. III, London: Hardwicke and Bouge, 1874, pp. 336–55.

Books

Adas, Michael, *Machines as the Measure of Men: Science, Technology, and Ideologies of Western Dominance*, Ithaca and London: Cornell University Press, 1989.

Allen, Richard B., *Slaves Freedmen and Indentured Labour in Colonial Mauritius*, Cambridge: Cambridge University Press, 1999.

Anat, Abhimanyu, *Gandhiji Bole Theiy,* Delhi: Rajkamal Prakashan, 2008.

Anderson, Clare, *Convicts in the Indian Ocean: Transportation from South Asia to Mauritius, 1815–53*, Great Britain: Macmillan Press, 2000.

———, *Subaltern Lives: Biographies of Colonialism in the Indian Ocean World, 1790-1920*, Critical Perspectives on Empire, New Delhi: Cambridge University Press, 2012.

Anderson, Daniel E., *The Epidemics of Mauritius: With a Descriptive and Historical Account of the Island*, London: H.K. Lewis & Co. Ltd., 1918.

Arnold, David, *Colonizing the Body: State Medicine and Epidemic Disease in Nineteenth-Century India*, California: University of California Press, 1993.

———, ed., *Imperial Medicine and Indigenous Societies*, Delhi: Oxford University Press, 1989.

Backhouse, James, *A Narrative of a Visit to the Mauritius and South Africa*, London: Hamilton, Adams, 1844.

Bahadur, Gaiutra, *Coolie Woman: The Odyssey of Indenture*, London: Hurst & Company, 2013.

Ballhatchet, Kenneth, *Race, Sex and Class under the Raj: Imperial Attitudes and Politics and their Critics*, New York: St. Martin's Press, 1980.

Bhana, Surendra, *Indentured Indian Emigrants to Natal, 1860-1902: A Study based on Ships' Lists*, New Delhi: Promilla & Co., 1991.

Boodhoo, Raj, *Health, Disease and Indian Immigrants in Nineteenth Century Mauritius*, Port Louis: Aapravasi Ghat Trust Fund, 2010.

Bowman, Larry W., *Mauritius: Democracy and Development in the Indian Ocean*, London: Westview Press, 1991.

Brain, J.B., *Christian Indians in Natal, 1860-1911: An Historical and Statistical Study*, Cape Town: Oxford University Press, 1983.

Brebner, C.W., *The New Handbook for the Indian Ocean, Arabian Sea and Bay of Bengal: With Miscellaneous Subjects for Sail and Steam, Mauritius Cyclones and Currents, Moon Observations and Sail-making*, Bombay: Times of India Press, 1898.

Carter, Marina, *Servants, Sirdars and Settlers: Indians in Mauritius, 1834-1874*, Delhi: Oxford University Press, 1995.

———, *Voices from Indenture: Experience of Indian Migrants in the British Empire*, New York: Leicester University Press, 1996.

Carter, Marina and Khal Torabully, *Coolitude: An Anthology of the Indian Labour Diaspora*, London: Anthem Press, 2002.

Chatterjee, Partha, *The Black Hole of Empire: History of a Global Practice of Power*, Princeton: Princeton University Press, 2012.

Chevalier, Haakon, tr., *A Dying Colonialism*, New York: Grove Press, 1965.

Christopher, Emma, *Slave Ship Sailors and their Captive Cargoes, 1730-1807*, New York: Cambridge University Press, 2006.

Cluver, E.H., *Public Health in South Africa*, Johannesburg: Central News Agency, 1939.

Cohn, Bernard S., *Colonialism and its forms of Knowledge: The British in India*, Princeton: Princeton University Press, 1996.

Crawford, D.G., *A History of Indian Medical Service 1600-1913*, vols. I and II, London: W. Thacker & Co., 1914.

Cumpston, I.M., *Indians Overseas in British Territories, 1834-1854*, London: Oxford University Press, 1953.

Curtin, Philip D., *Death by Migration: Europe's Encounter with the Tropical World in the Nineteenth Century*, New York: Cambridge University Press, 1989.

Deerpalsingh, Saloni and Marina Carter, *Selected Documents on Indian Immigrants: Mauritius, 1834-1926*, vols. II and III, Moka: Mahatma Gandhi Institute Press, 1994–6.

Desai, Ashwin and Goolam Vahed, *Inside Indenture: A South African Story, 1860-1914*, Durban: Madiba Publishers, 2007.

Emmer, P.C., ed., *Colonialism and Migration: Indentured Labour Before and After Slavery*, Dordrecht/Boston/Lancaster: Martinus Nijhoff Publishers, 1986.

Eyler, John M., *Sir Arthur Newsholme and State Medicine, 1885-1935*, Cambridge: Cambridge University Press, 1997.

Fanon, Frantz, *L'An Cinq, de la Révolution Algérienne*, Paris: François Maspero, 1959.

Fett, Sharla M., *Working Cures: Healing Health and Power on Southern Slave Plantations*, London: The University of North Carolina Press, 2002.

Fogel, Robert W. and Stanley L. Engerman, *Time on the Cross: The Economics of American Negro Slavery*, Boston: Little Brown and Company, 1974.

Foucault, Michel, 'The Politics of Health in the Eighteenth Century', in *Essential Works of Foucault, 1954–84, Vol. 3: Power*, ed. Michel Foucault, James D. Faubion, tr. Robert Hurley et al., New York: The New Press, 1994.

Gandhi, Mohandas Karamchand, *The Collected Works of Mahatama Gandhi 1906-1913*, Delhi: The Publications Division, Ministry of Information and Broadcasting Government of India, 1958–82.

———, *Dakshin Africa ke Satygrah ka Itihas*, New Delhi: Sasta Sahitya Mandal, 1959.

Gay, Peter, *Education of the Senses*, vol. 1 of *The Bourgeoisie Experience: Victoria to Freud*, New York: Oxford University Press, 1984.

Ghosh, Amitav, *Sea of Poppies*, Delhi: Viking, 2008.

Gillion, K.L., *The Fiji Indians: Challenge to European Dominance, 1920-1946*, Canberra: Australian National University Press, 1977.

Goonam, *Coolie Doctor: An Autobiography*, Hyderabad: Orient Longman Limited, 1998.

Hamlin, Christopher, *Public Health and Social Justice in the Age of Chadwick: Britain, 1800-1854*, Cambridge: Cambridge University Press, 1998.

Hangloo, Rattan Lal, ed., *Indian Diaspora in the Caribbean: History, Culture and Identity*, New Delhi: Primus Book, 2012.

Harrison, Mark, *Public Health in British India: Anglo-Indian Preventive Medicine, 1859-1914*, New Delhi: Cambridge University Press, 1994.

Headrick, D.R., *Tools of Empire: Technology and European Imperialism in the Nineteenth Century*, New York: Oxford University Press, 1981.

———, *The Tentacles of Progress: Technology Transfer in the Age of Imperialism, 1850-1940*, New York: Oxford University Press, 1988.

Henning, C.G., *The Indentured Indian in Natal, 1860-1917*, New Delhi: Promilla & Co., 1993.

Hewa, Soma, *Colonialism, Tropical Disease and Imperial Medicine: Rockefeller Philanthropy in Sri Lanka*, Lanham, Maryland: University Press of America, 1995.

Hobsbawm, Eric, *The Age of Revolution: 1789-1848*, England: Clays Ltd., 2008.

Jain, Shobhita and Rhoda E. Reddock, eds., *Women Plantation Workers: International Experiences*, New York: Oxford University Press, 1998.

Kelly, John D., *A Politics of Virtue: Hinduism, Sexuality, and Countercolonial*

Discourse in Fiji, Chicago and London: The University of Chicago Press, 1991.

Kirby, Percival R., ed., *Andrew Smith and Natal: Documents Relating to the Early History of that Province*, Cape Town: The Van Riebeeck Society, 1955.

Kishor, Giriraj, *Girmitiya Gandhi*, ed. Nirmala Jain, New Delhi: Vani Prakashan, 2001.

Kondapi, C., *Indian Overseas, 1838-1949*, New Delhi: Indian Council of World Affairs, 1951.

Kumar, Anil, *Medicine and the Raj: British Medical Policy, 1835-1911*, New Delhi: Sage, 1998.

Kumar, Deepak, ed., *Science and Empire: Essays in Indian Context, 1700-1947*, New Delhi: Oxford University Press, 1991.

———, ed., *Disease and Medicine in India: A Historical Overview*, Delhi: Tulika Books, 2001.

Kumar, Deepak and Raj Shekhar Basu, eds., *Medical Encounters in British India*, New Delhi: Oxford University Press, 2013.

Kuper, Hilda, *Indian People in Natal*, Durban: Natal University Press, 1960.

La Fontaine, J.S., *City Politics: A Study of Léopoldville, 1962-63.* Cambridge: Cambridge University Press, 1970.

La Guerre, John Gaffar, ed., *Calcutta to Caroni: The East Indians of Trinidad*, Caribbean: Orient Longman Limited, 1974.

Lal, Brij V., *Chalo Jahaji: On a Journey through Indenture in Fiji*, Suva: A Prashant Pacific Book, 2000.

Levine, Philippa, *Prostitution, Race and Politics: Policing, Venereal Disease in the British Empire*, New York, London: Routledge, 2003.

Luffman, John, *A Brief Account of the Island of Antigua: Together with the Customs and Manners of its Inhabitants, as well White as Black;…. In Letters to a Friend Written in the Years 1786, 1787, 1788*, London: Printed for and sold by J. Luffman, sold also by Darton and Harvey, 1789.

Mangru, Basdeo, *Benevolent Neutrality: Indian Government Policy and Labour Migration to British Guiana, 1854-1884*, London: Hansib Publishing Limited, 1987.

Mannick, A.R., *Mauritius: The Development of a Plural Society*, Nottingham: Russel Press Ltd., 1979.

Marquard, Leopold, *The Story of South Africa*, London: Faber and Faber Limited, 1955.

McClintock, Anne, *Imperial Leather Race, Gender, and Sexuality in the Colonial Contest*, New York, London: Routledge, 1995.

Meer, Y.S., *Documents of Indentured Labour: Natal 1851-1917*, Durban: Institute of Black Research, 1980.

Metcalf, Thomas R., *Ideology of the Raj*, vol. III, part 4 of *The New Cambridge History of India*, New Delhi: Cambridge University Press, 1998.

———, *Forging the Raj: Essays on British India in the Heyday of Empire,* India: Oxford University Press, 2005.

Metz, Helen Chapin, ed., *Indian Ocean: Five Island Countries*, Washington: Federal Research Division; Library of Congress, 1995.

Mills, James H., *Madness, Cannabis and Colonialism: The 'Native Only' Lunatic Asylums of British India, 1857-1900*, Great Britain: Macmillan, 2000.

———, *Cannabis Britannica: Empire, Trade, and Prohibition, 1800-1928*, Oxford: Oxford University Press, 2003.

Mishra, Amit Kumar, *Mauritius*, New Delhi: National Book Trust, 2008.

Mishra, Sourav, *Pilgrimage, Politics, and Pestilence: The Haj from the Indian Subcontinent, 1860-1920*, Delhi: Oxford University Press, 2011.

Mittal, Jitendra Kumar, *Mauritius*, Delhi: Rajpal & Sons, 1972.

Mookherji, S.B., *The Indenture System in Mauritius, 1837-1915*, Calcutta: Firma K.L. Mukhopadhyay, 1962.

Northrup, David, *Indentured Labour in the Age of Imperialism, 1834-1922*, Cambridge: Cambridge University Press, 1995.

Packard, Randall M., *White Plague Black Labour: Tuberculosis and the Political Economy of Health and Disease in South Africa*, California: University of California Press, 1989.

Palmer, Mabel, *The History of the Indians in Natal*, Cape Town: Oxford University Press, 1957.

Pati, Biswamoy and Mark Harrison, eds., *Health, Medicine and Empire: Perspectives on Colonial India*, Delhi: Orient Longman Limited, 2001.

———, eds., *The Social History of Health and Medicine in Colonial India*, UK: Routledge, 2009.

Pike, Nicholas, *Sub-Tropical Rambles in the Land of the Aphanapteryx: Personal Experiences, Adventures, and Wanderings in and around the Island of Mauritius*, New York: Harper and Brothers, 1873.

Polak, Henry S.L., *The Indians of South Africa, 1909*, Esplanade: G.A. Natesan & Co., 1909.

Porter, Dorothy, *Health, Civilization and the State: A History of Public Health from Ancient to Modern Times*, London and New York: Routledge, 1999.

Prasad, Dharmendra, *Hind Mahasagar ka Moti: Mauritius*, New Delhi: Pustakayan, 1993.

Ramsharan, Prahlad, *Mauritius ka Itihas*, Delhi: Rajpal & Sons, 1979.

Ramgoolam, Seewoosagar, *Our Struggle: 20th Century Mauritius (Presented by Anand Mulloo)*, New Delhi: Vision Books, 1982.

Robinson, John, *Notes on Natal: An Old Colonist's Book for New Settlers*, Durban: Robisnon & Vause, 1872.

Saha, Panchanan, *Emigration of Indian Labour, 1834-1900*, New Delhi: People's Publishing House, 1970.

Sanadhya, Totaram, *Fiji Dwip Mein Mere Ikkis Varsh* (My Twenty-One Years in the Fiji Islands), originally published in Agra: Rajput Anglo-Oriental Press, 1914; 4th edn, Delhi: Pandit Banarasidas Chaturvedi, 1973; Also, Totaram Sanadhya, 'Mere Fiji Dwip me Ikkis Varsh and the Second Abolition', lecture at University of Maryland, Baltimore, 4 April 2012;

see www.youtube.com/watch?v=fMDS6iM8oWE, also available on http://www.hindisamay.com/vividh/fizi-dveep-me-mere-21-varsh.html, accessed 24 December 2014.

Said, Edward W., *Orientalism: Western Conceptions of the Orient*, India: Penguin Books, 2001.

Saunders, Kay, *Indentured Labour in the British Empire, 1840-1920*, London: Croom Helm, 1984.

Sehrawat, Samiksha, *Colonial Medical Care in North India: Gender, State, and Society, c.1840-1920*, New Delhi: Oxford University Press, 2013.

Sheridan, Richard B., *Doctors and Slaves: A Medical and Demographic History of Slavery in British West Indies, 1680-1834*, USA: Cambridge University Press, 1985.

Singh, Ranbir, *Mauritius: The Key to the Indian Ocean*, Delhi: Arnold-Heinemann, 1980.

Sinha-Kerkhoff, Kathinka et al., trs., *Autobiography of an Indian Indentured Labourer: Munshi Rahman Khan, 1874-1972*, Delhi: Shipra Publications, 2005.

Thomas, Hugh, *The Slave Trade: The History of the Atlantic Slave Trade, 1440-1870*, London: Papermac, 1998.

Thomson, David, *Europe since Napoleon*, Delhi: Surjeet Publications, 2007.

Tinker, Hugh, *A New System of Slavery: The Export of Indian Labour Overseas, 1830-1920*, London: Oxford University Press, 1974.

Toussaint, Auguste, *Port Louis: A Tropical City*, tr. W.E.F. Ward, London: George Allen Unwin Ltd., 1973.

———, *History of Mauritius*, tr. W.E.F. Ward, London: Macmillan, 1977.

Vivek, P.S., *From Indentured Labour to Liberated Nation: Public Policy and Small Planters in Mauritius*, Bangalore: Focus Press Publication, 2007.

Wolstenhole, G.E.W. and Maeve O'Connor, eds., *Immigration: Medical and Social Aspects*, London: J. & A. Churchill Ltd., 1966.

UNPUBLISHED WORKS

Aickin, David, 'From Plantation Medicine to Public Health: The State and Medicine in British Guiana 1838-1914', unpublished PhD thesis, University College of London, UK, 2001.

Amos, Denise M., 'Working-class Diet and Health in Nottingham, 1850-1939', unpublished PhD thesis, University of Nottingham, UK, 2000.

Gillion, K.L., 'A History of Indian Immigration and Settlement in Fiji', unpublished PhD diss., Australian National University, Australia, 1958.

Mohapatra, Prabhu, 'Asian Labour: Culture, Consciousness, Representation', paper presented at Conference on 'Asian Labour: A Debate on Culture, Consciousness and Representations', Manila, 23–5 October, 1997.

Nicole, Robert E., 'Disturbing History: Aspects of Resistance in Early Colonial Fiji, 1874–1914', unpublished PhD thesis, History Department, University of Canterbury, New Zealand, 2006.

Index

Lightning Source UK Ltd.
Milton Keynes UK
UKHW011929200223
417092UK00031B/745/J

9 789390 232697